Scandinavian politics today

PARADOX:
- social capital despite incentive
- universalism creates social capital
  - procedural justice

need-based decreases social capital
↳ incentive to lie

sustainability → **Social capital**

Contact (tolerance ↑↑)
Conflict (tolerance ↓) ↑ own
Constrict (↓↓) PUTNAM

counteracted by integration policy
- identity (improved social cap.
          labour market int

+ dem. change

Kumlin & Rothstein

Security

After

Andrén (77) → post WWII security options
- isolated neutrality
- pan-nordic alliance → Swedish foreign sec. (1948)
- joining a superpower

Neoliberal institutions

Soviet view on SUE:
'council of Europe... an auxilery implement to NATO' Allison '85

3pt def.
→ long lasting social divisions
  «objectifiably» identifiable groups
→ common way of life
→ organisationally institutionalized.

Social Cleavage

Lipset & Rokkan

Dalton, Flanagan, Beck
- realignment
  - sector employment
  - gender
  - globalization
  - value based

- owners v. workers
- church v. state
- (colony v. empire)
- *centre v. periphery
- *land v. industry

MANCHESTER
1824
Manchester University Press

Politics Today

Series editor: Bill Jones

Scandinavian politics today

Second edition

David Arter

Manchester University Press

Manchester and New York

distributed in the United States exclusively by Palgrave Macmillan

First edition published 1999 by Manchester University Press

This edition published 2008 by Manchester University Press
Oxford Road, Manchester M13 9NR, UK
and Room 400, 175 Fifth Avenue, New York, NY 10010, USA

Distributed in the United States exclusively by
Palgrave Macmillan, 175 Fifth Avenue, New York,
NY 10010, USA

Distributed in Canada exclusively by
UBC Press, University of British Columbia, 2029 West Mall,
Vancouver, BC, Canada V6T 1Z2

British Library Cataloguing-in-Publication Data
A catalogue record for this book is available from the British Library

Library of Congress Cataloging-in-Publication Data applied for

ISBN   978 0 7190 7853 8   *paperback*

This edition first published 2008

17 16 15 14 13 12   10 9 8 7 6 5 4 3

Typeset by R. J. Footring Ltd, Derby
Printed in Great Britain
by Bell & Bain Ltd, Glasgow

Contents

Part VI: The strategic security environment

Tables

Preface

When Bill Jones approached me to revise *Scandinavian Politics Today* for a second edition, my hope (very quickly dashed!) was that 'cosmetic surgery' might suffice, simply dotting the 'i's here and crossing the 't's there, so to speak. In the event, this second edition represents a complete rewrite – major surgery, if you will – and only chapter 2, 'Nation-building and state-building', has survived relatively unscathed. This is because if a week is a long time in politics, *à la* Harold Wilson, the eight-year period since *Scandinavian Politics Today* first came out is a veritable eternity in the life of a textbook, particularly when so much has changed. For example, when Finland adopted a new constitution in 2000, which, in significantly reducing the formal powers of the head of state, meant it could no longer be described as a case of 'semi-presidential government', it was obvious that chapter 11 would need substantial revision. Equally, the analysis of the strength of Scandinavian social democracy would need some recasting given that in 2000 there were Social Democratic/Labour prime ministers in all the Nordic states except Iceland, whereas seven years later this was true only in Norway. Indeed, in both Denmark and Finland the Social Democrats are no longer the largest party and, at the November 2007 general election, the Danish party polled its worst result since 1906. Account would also have to be taken in the 'international relations' chapters (part VI) of the implications for the special US–Icelandic relationship of the departure of American forces from the military base at Keflavík in 2006, the Danes' and Swedes' rejection of the euro in referenda in 2000 and 2003, respectively, and the radical transformation of the security environment of northern Europe subsequent to the Baltic states' membership of both the North Atlantic Treaty Organisation and the European Union. Then there were the international ramifications for Denmark of the Muhammad cartoon episode in 2006 and the possible damage caused to the Finns' reputation abroad following the Jokela school massacre in November 2007. The statistic that appeared widely in the global media coverage of the event hardly painted a glowing picture of Finnish society – the Finns have the highest incidence of murders in western Europe. In short, the text would require more than simply a 'makeover': it would need rethinking in its entirety and this would also allow for the incorporation of the fresh approaches and new empirical findings of the Nordic political science literature over recent years.

However, the basic aim of the second edition remains the same as that of the first edition: namely, to describe and analyse the contemporary politics of the five nation states of Denmark, Finland, Iceland, Norway and Sweden and the three Home Rule territories of Greenland, Faeroes and Åland that together make up the Nordic region or *Norden*. The book does not attempt a fully comprehensive description of political practice and there are, for example, no chapters on local government, the legal system or even that celebrated Scandinavian institution the ombudsman, although these are, of course, mentioned in passing. Nor is any attempt made to undertake a country-specific 'Cook's tour' of the Nordic region, with, say, four chapters on Sweden, the largest and best-known of the Scandinavian states, two on Denmark, Norway and Finland, one on Iceland and one for all three Home Rule territories. Rather, the approach is systematic-ally thematic and comparative, drawing on the current themes in the political science literature. If this approach is ambitious, it is designed to produce a book with 'value added' over the more run-of-the-mill textbook treatment and one which will be of interest not only to students of Scandinavia but also to those wishing to see Scandinavian politics and policy-making in a wider compara-tive perspective. The terms 'Nordic' and 'Scandinavian', incidentally, are used interchangeably in the hope that purists will not take undue offence.

Some time ago, Kenny MacAskill, the minister of justice in the Scottish National Party government in Edinburgh, mentioned that he had read the first edition of this book and found it 'most informative'. He added that the only part that he had found hard going was the history of the language conflict in Norway! This brought to mind my old English teacher who, when we were studying *Paradise Lost*, spoke of the monosyllabic grandeur of Miltonic verse, citing as an illustration the celebrated lines 'Long is the way/And hard, that out of hell leads up to light'. It is to be hoped that readers of this second edition will not experience symptoms of 'long is the way and hard' syndrome, but rather that the book sheds some considerable 'light' on the politics and govern-ment of the Scandinavian states as they negotiate the globalised world of the new millennium.

D.A.
Kinneff, Aberdeenshire

Abbreviations

BEAR	Barents Euro-Arctic Regional Council
CBSS	Council of Baltic Sea States
CFSP	common foreign and security policy
CPSU	Communist Party of the Soviet Union
CSCE	Conference on Security and Co-operation in Europe
DEVA	Demokraattinen vaihtoehto (Democratic Alternative)
DKP	Danmarks kommunistiska parti (Danish Communist Party)
EC	European Community
ECSC	European Coal and Steel Community
EEA	European Economic Area
EEC	European Economic Community
EFTA	European Economic Area
EMU	Economic and Monetary Union
EU	European Union
FCMA	(Treaty of) Friendship, Co-operation and Mutual Assistance
GDP	gross domestic product
IKL	Isänmaallinen kansanliike (Patriotic People's Movement) (Finland)
KGB	Komitet Gosudarstvdnnoi Bezopasnosti (Committee of State Security)
NATO	North Atlantic Treaty Organisation
NCM	Nordic Council of Ministers
NKP	Norges kommunistiska parti (Norwegian Communist Party)
OECD	Organisation for Economic Co-operation and Development
PPG	parliamentary party group
SALT	Strategic Arms Limitation Talks
Sfp	Svenska folkpartiet (Swedish People's Party)
SKDL	Suomen kansan demokraattinen liitto (Finnish People's Democratic League)
SKP	Suomen kommunistinen puolue (Finnish Communist Party)
SKP	Sveriges kommunistiska parti (Swedish Communist Party)

TPSL   Työväen ja pienviljelijäin sosialidemokraattinen liitto (Social
        Democratic Opposition) (Finland)
UN   United Nations
UNNRA   United Nations Relief and Rehabilitation Administration
VAT   value-added tax
WFTA   West European Free Trade Area

Part I

Scandinavia past and present

1

The eight quills of the swan

Nordic council
- *Denmark*   - *Faeroes*
- *Finland*   - *Greenland*
- *Iceland*   - *Åland*
- *Norway*
- *Sweden*

An eagle sometimes flies low but a hen never reaches any great heights.

(Virolainen 1969: 469)

So read the postscript of a letter which, citing from Lenin, was sent by an indignant communist in Helsinki to the Finnish prime minister Johannes Virolainen. It was in response to a circular which the premier believed would market the government's performance to voters in the capital city in the long run-up to the 1966 general election. We are left in no doubt about who the hen is, or, indeed, about the prime minister's ability to see the humorous side of things! This chapter, however, is not about eagles, still less hens; rather, it focuses on a particular swan – the eight-quilled swan of Nordic co-operation depicted in the logo of the Nordic Council and representing the five nation states of Denmark, Finland, Iceland, Norway and Sweden, and the three Home Rule territories of the Faeroes, Greenland and Åland. It offers a broad introduction to the (changing) geo-politics of the Nordic region and views co-operation and, more frequently in an historical light, conflict between the member states in a longitudinal perspective. There were times when relations between the Nordic countries fell very much into the 'ugly duckling' category and the prospect of sustained solidarity of purpose in Norden seemed remote.

History divides the Nordic region in two: the *former imperial states* and the twentieth-century *successor states.* Denmark and Sweden fall into the former category. Denmark was undoubtedly the driving force in the region from the late fourteenth century to the early sixteenth. Thus the Danish and Norwegian monarchies were united in 1380 (Denmark acquired Iceland in the process) and Norway was incorporated into Denmark in 1536. Moreover, Denmark dominated the Kalmar Union of the three Scandinavian kingdoms of Denmark–Norway and Sweden between 1397 and 1523. Norway remained part of Denmark until 1814, when, as a by-product of the Napoleonic Wars, it passed to Sweden, although Iceland was linked with the Danish crown until

1944. After Denmark's heyday, Sweden emerged as the leading light in the region. Indeed, at its prime in the seventeenth century, Sweden was a great power, controlling a multi-ethnic empire in the Baltic. It incorporated areas inhabited by Swedes, Danes, Norwegians, Finns, Lapps, Ingrians, Estonians, Latvians and Germans. Of the successor states, Norway was the first to gain independence from Sweden (to which it had been conjoined in a personal union) following a referendum in 1905. Finland, part of Sweden until 1809 and a Grand Duchy of the czarist Russian empire thereafter, unilaterally declared its independence on 6 December 1917 in the aftermath of the Bolshevik revolution in St Petersburg. Finally, Iceland gained limited self-government in 1874, autonomy in 1904 and independence in a personal union with Denmark in 1918. It became the last of the Nordic states to achieve full independence, following a referendum in 1944.

Some quarter of a century ago Basil Chubb wrote *The Government and Politics of Ireland* (Chubb 1982) as part of a planned series on small European democracies which was never completed. The five nation states that comprise Norden would have been prime candidates for inclusion. True, there has been a tendency to view the Nordic region as 'much of a muchness' – a homogeneous whole 'up there', so to speak, which can be treated as one. The Nordic states in short have occasionally suffered from the lack of differentiation inherent in the classic London cabbie's query: 'What's the weather been like abroad?' Equally, when viewed from both an historical and a contemporary standpoint – that is, through the windows of both the past and the early years of the new millennium – it is clear that the Nordic states have been linked by geography, history and common linguistic bonds and that out of this admixture there has emerged at least a degree of common identity and sense of belonging to the north.

A brief overview of the Nordic region today

In 1980 the Finnish director Risto Jarva produced a delightful allegorical film called *The Year of the Hare* (*Jäniksen vuosi*) in which he charts the friendship which develops when a businessman, returning home by car, accidentally injures a hare and follows it into the forest, where he nurses it back to health. When he finally returns to Helsinki, having opted out of the rat-race and lived rough with the hare, his bills are still awaiting him and his wife is less than pleased. Only the hare remains loyal when he is committed to a debtor's prison! Mention of hares or more particularly rabbits readily brings to mind Giovanni Sartori's axiomatic assertion in relation to comparative analysis that it is impossible to compare stones and rabbits: we must compare broadly like with like, not least so as to classify different sub-types of the species. What, then, are the *prima facie* similarities and differences between the Nordic states in the first decade of the new millennium?

An obvious and integral feature has to do with the 'politics of scale', since, with the possible exception of Sweden, all the Nordic states may be considered small democracies. Iceland, which in 2007 had a population of 309,699, could, as Gunnar Helgi Kristinsson (1996) has noted, be regarded either as the smallest of the European small states or a relatively large *micro-state*. In fact, in so far as micro-states not only have very small populations but – as in the case of Andorra, Monaco and San Marino – are also 'heavily dependent on neighbouring states for diplomatic support' (Archer and Nugent 2002: 5) and do not have an independent foreign policy, Iceland is best regarded as the smallest of the European small states. It is the only Nordic state never to have applied for membership of the European Community (EC)/European Union (EU) and, distinctively in the region, has a special relationship with the United States through its 1951 Defence Agreement (Thorhallsson 2004). *[handwritten margin note: Iceland 1951 Defence Agree-]*

Altogether, the population of Norden today is just under 25 million (table 1.1). Each boasting well over 5 million inhabitants, Denmark and Finland have populations about the same size as that of Scotland, whilst Norway's is somewhat smaller. With the exception of Denmark, moreover, the Nordic states are relatively sparsely populated. Iceland (3.0 inhabitants per square kilometre), Norway (14.5) and Finland (15.6) are the three countries with the lowest population densities in Europe and there is considerable regional variation within all three. For example, over two-fifths of the total Icelandic population lives in Reykjavík and two-thirds in the capital and its hinterland constituency of Reykjanes. On accession to the EU in 1995, large areas of northern Finland and northern Sweden received special (so-called Objective Six) support from the structural funds, created specifically to accommodate the Nordic newcomers and available in those districts with under eight inhabitants per square kilometre. Even in Denmark, which in 2007 had 126.4 inhabitants per square kilometre, the comparative population density was well under the EU average of 179.2 and that of small states such as Belgium (343.6 in 2003) and the Netherlands (481.9 in 2004).

Table 1.1 *The population size and density of the Nordic states in 2007*

Country	Total population	Inhabitants per km^2
Denmark	5,447,084	126.4
Finland	5,276,955	15.6
Iceland	309,699	3.0
Norway	4,681,100	14.5
Sweden	9,122,269	22.2
Total	*24,837,107*	*EU average 179.2[a]*

[a] Calculated as an average of the twenty-five EU member states in 2004.
Source: Statistical Yearbooks of the Nordic countries and Eurostat.

Table 1.2 *Total civilian employment in the Nordic states by major economic sectors in 2005 (%)*

Sector	Denmark	Finland	Iceland	Norway	Sweden
Agriculture	3.7	5.1	7.6	3.6	2.3
Industry	21.9	26.0	22.6	19.8	22.8
Services	74.4	68.9	69.6	76.6	74.9

Source: United Nations Economic Commission for Europe, *Trends in Europe and North America 2005.*

The smallness of the Nordic democracies, it has been suggested, has permitted the personalisation of relations between the relatively small elite class of politicians and administrators, which in turn has conduced towards pragmatic solutions and compromise politics. Indeed, several writers have characterised the Nordic states as a distinctive sub-type of liberal democracy – 'consensual democracies'. Others have spoken of a 'Nordic model' of government, whilst Sweden in particular has been much admired as the archetype of an advanced welfare state. Similarities in the nature of politics and government in the Nordic states will, of course, be central to the ensuing chapters of this book.

All the Nordic states have been affected by 'economies of scale' in the obvious sense that the small size of the domestic market has dictated a strong export orientation and its concomitant, a deep commitment to free trade. In structural terms, the Nordic countries have reached roughly comparable stages of economic development. To put it another way, the Nordic states are typical post-industrial, information-based, service-dominant economies. The proportion engaged in the primary sector has dwindled to under 3 per cent in Sweden and under 10 per cent in Iceland; manufacturing industry employs between one-fifth and just over one-quarter of the labour force across the Nordic region, whilst services average 72.9 per cent (table 1.2).

As small states, linked by geography, a shared history and common linguistic bonds, the Nordic countries readily lend themselves to comparative analysis. Boasting striking structural and behavioural similarities in, among other things, their party systems, electoral choices and patterns of interest group representation, and influencing each other's developments by means of diffusional impulses – the post-Second World War expansion of the institution of the ombudsman is a notable case in point – the political agenda in the Nordic states often mirrors issues and challenges facing all the member states of the region to varying degrees. There is, moreover, widespread informal inter-governmental consultation in preparing responses to these challenges, as well as formal co-operation at the regional level. Yet the many common denominators should not obscure clear lines of differentiation and demarcation. In short, the Nordic states exhibit important lines of intra-regional variation. They may all be rabbits or stones *à la* Sartori, but there are distinguishing features.

In the field of domestic politics, there are obvious institutional differences within the Nordic region, most notably the fact that Denmark, Norway and Sweden boast constitutional monarchies whereas Finland and Iceland have directly elected presidents. Constitutional provisions, of course, do not always indicate much about the actual distribution of power; convention is important and so, too, is the influence of political parties. None the less, the existence of dual executives in two of the states of the region suggests the need to explore the historical backdrop of the constitution-building process, as well as the extent to which the balance of power within the executive arm has changed.

In the foreign and security policy area, there has been a clear bifurcation within the Nordic region since the Second World War. Denmark, Norway and Iceland were founder members of the North Atlantic Treaty Organisation (NATO), which was formed as the Cold War took hold in 1949. Iceland, in fact, has neither an army of its own nor a secret service. Sweden, in contrast, has championed a position of neutrality since 1814 and Finland, too, aspired to be neutral (principally as a means of maintaining its post-war independence from the Soviet Union) and currently describes its policy as one of military non-alignment. The essential security policy configuration that emerged in the late 1940s came to be known as the 'Nordic balance' and reflected the differing needs and interests of a bloc of states that occupied a frontier position between capitalism and communism.

Equally, there have been different responses among the states of the region to the increased pace of European integration. Whilst Denmark since 1973 and Finland and Sweden since 1995 have been full EU members, the Norwegian people have twice (in 1972 and 1994) voted against accession, despite agreements supported by the overwhelming majority of the political elite. The result has been that Norway and indeed Iceland have contented themselves with membership of the European Economic Area (EEA), which came into force in 1994 and which grants access to the EU single market, although excluding sensitive areas such as agricultural, environmental and regional policy. Finnish and Swedish membership has given the EU a Nordic dimension, as well as a common border with Russia.

Finally, in the geo-economic context, all the Nordic economies have been export-led and they have been affected by, and adapted in varying degrees to, the process of globalisation. The Finnish mobile-phone giant Nokia – with a world market share in 2007 of around 36 per cent – is perhaps a limiting case in this respect. Nokia employs over 68,000 people in 120 countries and has production factories in China, India, Germany and, most recently, Romania, in addition to the town of Salo in Finland. Its contribution to the Finnish economy is enormous. Thus, Nokia's share of total exports (excluding those of its partners) is about one-quarter and the value of its net sales amounts to approximately the same as the annual Finnish budget. Similarly, only four of IKEA's production factories are in Sweden – accounting for less than one-fifth of total production – the majority being in eastern Europe.

The Nordic states: the 'other European community'?

Pointing to a common Nordic identity and the complex web of relations between the member states and Home Rule territories in the region, Turner and Nordquist (1982) referred in the early 1980s to 'the other European community'. Various forms of regional co-operation have evolved, particularly during the twentieth century, when the Nordic states comprised a frontier bloc between fascism and communism between the two World Wars and the pluralist democracies and (Soviet) people's democracies during the Cold War. Notable, for instance, was the Norden Association (Foreningen NORDEN), which was founded in 1919 and today has over 70,000 members and about 550 local branches across the region. It capitalised on the co-operation between Denmark, Norway and Sweden during the First World War and quickly extended its network of commercial associations, interest groups and individual citizens to Iceland (1922) and Finland (1924). It has traditionally emphasised educational and cultural contacts, whilst among its recent projects has been 'Hello Norden', a telephone and Internet service, launched by the Swedish branch of the Norden Association in 2001, which offers advice to Nordic citizens who have 'got stuck' in the bureaucracy or need clarification of the regulations when relocating to another Nordic country.

The most notable cross-national achievement, however, has been the Nordic Council (Nordiska Råd), set up on a Danish initiative in 1952 as a forum for inter-parliamentary co-operation. The official symbol of Nordic co-operation is the swan, its eight quills representing the constituent parts of the region – the nation states of Denmark, Finland, Iceland, Norway, Sweden and the three Home Rule territories of Greenland, the Faeroes and Åland. The last-mentioned trio will be examined in more detailed in the next chapter, on nation-building and state-building in Norden, but warrant the briefest note *en passant*.

Greenland (Kalaallit Nunaat in the native Inuit language) covers an area of 2 million km^2, although only about 342,000 km^2 are free from a permanent ice cap. It had a population in 2005 of 56,969 persons, 90 per cent of them Inuit-speaking Eskimos. *Inuit* means 'people'. Greenland obtained autonomy within the Danish kingdom in 1979 and three years later voted in a referendum to leave the EC. When it left the EC, Greenland negotiated 'Overseas and Countries Association' status, which permits favourable access to European fishing markets, whilst a fishing agreement is renegotiated every five years. Its capital is Nuuk and the official language is Kalaallisut, or West Greenlandic.

The Faeroes (Føroyar) comprise seventeen inhabited islands covering an area of 1,400 km^2 with a population in 2003 of 47,700. In 1948 the Faeroes accepted Home Rule status as a self-governing community within the Danish state. Faeroese is the official language and the capital is Torshaven.

Åland (Ahvenanmaa in Finnish) comprises fifty inhabited islands covering a land area of 1,481 km^2 and had a population in 2006 of 26,766, 40 per cent of them living in the only town, Mariehamn. Since a League of Nations

Table 1.3 *The composition of the Nordic Council in 2007*

Country/Home Rule territory	Assembly	Delegates
Denmark	Folketing	16
Faeroes	Lagting	2
Greenland	Landsting	2
Finland	Eduskunta	18
Åland	Landsting	2
Iceland	Alþingi	7
Norway	Storting	20
Sweden	Riksdag	20
Total		87

ruling in 1921, Åland has been an autonomous and demilitarised province of the Finnish Republic. The official language is Swedish.

The Nordic Council comprises eighty-seven members nominated by the five national parliaments and the executive bodies of the three autonomous territories (table 1.3). In the Scandinavian languages *ting* means 'assembly', and the Nordic voters thus have 'tings' on their mind when they go to the polls in general elections.

Each member of the Nordic Council has a deputy, and the Council holds an annual session, usually in November. The role of the Nordic Council will be considered more fully in chapter 13, but one of its earliest achievements was the creation in 1952 of a passport union, which meant thereafter that trips between Nordic countries did not require a passport. A common labour market treaty in 1954 also enabled people to move freely within the region in search of work without the need for permits, and so on – a development several decades ahead of the achievement of the free movement of labour in the EU. Nordic co-operation was further consolidated in 1971 with the creation of the Nordic Council of Ministers. Each country has a minister of Nordic co-operation. It is important to emphasise that, much like the European Parliament, the Nordic Council is a consultative and advisory body, although, unlike the European Parliament, it is not directly elected. It issues recommendations and statements of opinion, which may be addressed to the Nordic Council of Ministers or one or more of the national governments. The Nordic Council parleys in the manner of a national parliament and has assumed an increasingly parliamentary character. It boasts four cross-national party groups – Social Democrats, Conservatives, Centre and Left Socialists/Greens – and five standing committees – Culture, Education and Training; Welfare; Citizens' and Consumer Rights; Environment and Natural Resources; and Business and Industry. Since a party group must have at least five members and representatives from at least three Nordic countries, there are also several non-aligned members. But although the Nordic Council has the basic parliamentary infrastructure of standing committees and party groups, it is not a legislature in the sense of having legislative powers.

Language and culture

In a longer-term perspective, the Nordic countries share linguistic links and a common, intertwining history. The region has six Scandinavian languages – Icelandic, Faeroese, Norwegian (in two forms – see chapter 2), Danish and Swedish – and three non-Indo-European languages – Finnish, Sáme (Lappish) and Kalaallisut (West Greenlandic). The Scandinavian languages are most clearly related to the other Germanic languages, including English, German, Dutch (including Flemish) and Frisian. These are all descended from proto-Germanic – a dialect of Indo-European – and they have influenced one another (Haugen 1976: 27). Einar Haugen notes, for example, the obvious similarities between the Old Icelandic *hús*, the German *Haus*, the Dutch *huis* and the English *house* (Haugen 1982: 7). Indeed, today, a typical Swede, Jonas Johansson – Johansson was the most common surname in 2007 – can, with a certain amount of effort, communicate with Danes and Norwegians when he speaks Swedish and they use their own languages. Icelandic and Faeroese are, however, quite another matter. Icelandic is distinctive in having faithfully retained the structure and lexicon of Old Scandinavian and, curiously, it is the only Scandinavian language which still lacks an indefinite article (Haugen 1976: 33). The semi-Icelandic spelling might suggest that Faeroese is an Icelandic dialect, whereas its form is somewhere between Icelandic and West Norwegian dialects, with enough distance from both to make it unintelligible to speakers of those languages, unless it is spoken very slowly (Haugen 1976: 34).

In any event, as mentioned, Swedes, Norwegians and Danes can, with goodwill, understand each other's languages, something the Nordic Council assumed in its journal *Nordisk Kontakt*, which covered topical events in the region in the various national tongues (there was a Finnish-language summary but no Icelandic). During the Viking age, Norse (Old Scandinavian) was for a time a 'world language', spoken not only all over Scandinavia but in the courts of the Scandinavian rulers in England, Scotland, Ireland, France and Russia. Even today the Old Norse derivation of words is plain. For example, *haar*, the cold sea mist familiar along the east coast of Scotland, derives from the Old Norse *hárr* and is a close relative of *gråhår*, that is, 'grey hair' or 'hoary' in modern Norwegian. On the subject of the Scandinavian languages, Swedish is a second national language in Finland, spoken as the native tongue by a minority of about 5 per cent of the population, and learned with widely varying degrees of enthusiasm and competence by the rest of the population. Finland is not only the sole bilingual state in the Nordic region, but one of only four EU states to have two official Community languages as official national languages (the others are Belgium, Ireland and Malta).

Table 1.4 *The Sámi parliaments in Norden*

Country	Year founded	Sámi population	Number of members of parliament	Number of registered voters	Turnout in last election (%)
Finland	1996	6,000	21	5,155 (2003)	55.2
Norway	1989	40,000	39	12,538 (2005)	71.2
Sweden	1993	17,000–20,000	31	7,180 (2005)	66.0

Sources: www.samediggi.fi; www.sametinget.se; www.sametinget.no.

Of the three languages in the Nordic region that are not Indo-European, Finnish and Sámi belong to the same language family. Like the Finns (discussed shortly), the origins of the Sámi (Lapps) is shrouded in uncertainty, although it is widely assumed that the earliest ancestors of the present Sámi belonged to the Komsa people, who occupied the territory around the Arctic Ocean after the last Ice Age, probably around 7000 BC. Sámi is a Finno-Ugric language, though not mutually intelligible with Finnish, which is spoken across northern Norway, Sweden and Finland and the Kola peninsula in north-west Russia. There are in fact ten Sámi languages, although an estimated 75–90 per cent of Sámi speakers use North Sámi, most of them living in Norway. Today, in the order of 30,000–50,000 *speak* Sámi – many of the older generation are illiterate – and they form a majority in four Norwegian communes and one in Finland. A common orthography for the Sámi languages was adopted in 1978.

The cultural autonomy of the Sámi as an indigenous people is guaranteed in the Finnish and Norwegian constitutions and in recent years Sámi parliaments have safeguarded the interests of the population (table 1.4). (Although, in Finland and Norway, the Sámi parliaments fall within the authority of government departments, they are not part of the state administration.) In March 2000, moreover, a cross-national Sámi Parliamentary Council was established, of twenty-one members, with equal representation for the Finnish, Norwegian and Swedish Sámis and observer status for the Russian Sámis. The Council's action plan for 2006–7 prioritised Sámi research, youth questions and Sámi language provision. At present, the Sámi College (Sámi Allaskuvla) in Kautokeino, in northern Norway, founded in the late 1980s, is the only university in the Nordic countries where most of the instruction is given in Sámi, although the Sámi language and culture can be studied in three Finnish universities and in Oulu there is a professor, lecturer and senior researcher in Sámi.

Finnish, now an official EU language, is the 'odd one out' (see table 1.5) among the national languages of Norden in not being Scandinavian. Logically structured compound nouns – *rautatiekirjakaupassa*, for example, means 'in the

Table 1.5 *Finnish as the 'odd one out'*

English	Swedish	Finnish	German	French	Italian	Spanish
sun	sol	aurinko	Sonne	soleil	sole	sol
Sweden	Sverige	Ruotsi	Schweden	Suede	Svezia	Suecia
mother	mamma	äiti	Mutter	mère	madre	madre
midnight	midnatt	keskiyö	Mitternacht	minuit	mezzanotte	medianoche
photograph	fotografi	valokuva	Photographie	photo	fotographia	fotographia
centre	centrum	keskusta	Zentrum	centre	centro	centro

bookshop at the railway station' – have given it a reputation as a difficult language, which it probably does not deserve. Conversely, many of the Finns who emigrated to Sweden in the early 1970s (following the wholesale amalgamation of small farms in the central northern part of the country) and many Finnish politicians over the years have failed to master Swedish. When in 2003 the new Finnish prime minister, Matti Vanhanen, paid his first official visit to Sweden, his Swedish was so sketchy that he was obliged to converse with his Swedish counterpart in English! As to the third non-Scandinavian language, there are in fact three main Greenlandic dialects – West Greenlandic (Kalaallisut) being the most widely spoken – and they are clearly related to Inuktitut, an Inuit language spoken in Canada, particularly in the Home Rule territory of Nunavut.

The historical roots of Nordic co-operation – and conflict

Language links reflect an intertwined past. Indeed, it might well be argued that until the sixteenth century Swedish or Danish history was virtually indistinguishable from Scandinavian history as a whole. In briefly tracing some of the main lines of Scandinavian development, it needs to be emphasised that, whilst there are early historical precedents for twenty-first-century regional co-operation, the story is essentially one of rivalry. To attempt a thematic history of Norden in a few paragraphs would be folly if it did not provide such an important backdrop to modern developments. The brush strokes, however, will necessarily be broad.

Despite a growing body of research by bio-anthropologists, philologists and archaeologists, knowledge of the settlement of the north remains sketchy. It does appear, however, that Scandinavia was populated by continental Europeans at the end of the Ice Age. Norwegian archaeologists have suggested that between 10000 and 9000 BC the first pioneering sea-fishing communities migrated from the North Sea continent between England and Denmark and settled along the western coastal strip of Norway as far north as Finnmark and the Rybachy peninsula. It is possible that Scandinavia was then covered, much like Greenland today, by an ice cap except for its western coastal strip. These first settlers appear to have gradually advanced inland towards northern Sweden and possibly reached the northernmost tip of Finnish Lapland. Around 6000 BC a second wave of migrants from Germany and Denmark pushed northwards via Sweden, eventually reaching northern Lapland. Interestingly, grave findings have indicated that late Palaeolithic (early Stone Age) settlers in central Europe and their Mesolithic (middle Stone Age – around 8000 BC) descendants in the Scandinavian peninsula were Europoids, who had comparatively large teeth. In contrast, as Christian Carpelan (1997) has noted, the ancient skulls of the Uralic peoples who settled in north-eastern Europe (including Finland) reveal they had relatively small teeth.

The impact of the so-called New Stone Age about 2500 BC was particularly marked in Denmark. The revolutionary introduction of agriculture, possibly as a result of immigration from the south, led to the domestication of sheep, goats and pigs, whilst flint-working achieved high levels of excellence and artistry, and flint axes and knives, as well as Danish amber, were exported to the Mediterranean region. Immigrants also brought to Denmark the skills of working with bronze. Shipbuilding, moreover, developed from simple canoes to seafaring craft requiring up to thirty oarsmen and this facilitated trade with the Baltic area. It seems safe to conclude that from about AD 500 the Nordic tribes began to be clearly distinguishable from the Germanic tribes. With its islands, and the woods and marshes of southern Jutland, Denmark was a relatively self-contained area in which two tribes came to dominate – the Jutlanders in the west and the Danes in the east. The two tribes merged into a nation about AD 700, and by 800 the Nordic language was well developed.

If the Nordic tribes migrated northwards from western Europe, the origins of the Finns are far from clear, although it seems they derived from the distant east. Academic opinion remains divided on many essentials concerning where they came from. The philologist R. E. Burnham (1956) argues that they emanated from the Finno-Ugrian community, which about 2000 BC was probably based in the region north of the Caucasus and comprised mostly fishermen and hunters. The historian Eino Jutikkala (1989) undertakes an interesting review of the various theories of the origins of the Finns but fails materially to add to Burnham's submission. The latter proceeds to argue that around 1000 BC the West Finns and Volga Finns moved north – in all likelihood as far as the middle Volga – and some time thereafter the West Finns left the Volga Finns and migrated north-west towards the Baltic. That they reached the southern shores of the Baltic, Burnham insists, is confirmed by the large number of Lithuanian loan words in the Finnish language. They include *karva* (hair), *hammas* (tooth), *taivas* (sky), *silta* (bridge) and *villa* (wool). The word for mother, *äiti* – surely one of the ugliest words in Finnish – is also a Lithuanian loan word. By the advent of the Christian era, the West Finns had split into separate groups. The Estonians stayed put, but the immigration of Finns into Finland began in the first century AD and continued for several centuries. By AD 500, however, there were only three small settlements in Finland: the Hämäläiset spread into the interior; the Suomalaiset remained in the south-west; and the Karjalaiset were concentrated in the area around Lake Laatokka (Ladoga). (The latter was acquired by the Soviet Union in 1939–44.)

The settlement of Norden was followed by the Viking era, AD 700–1000, which, following in the wake of the disintegration of Charlemagne's empire and the emergence of weak and competing states, was a period of Scandinavian expansionism. The reasons for the rise of the Vikings remain contested and the overpopulation theory is now rather discredited. What is not in dispute is that the Vikings were pagan Scandinavian warriors – 'pirates' or 'sea robbers' who emerged from the north, in T. K. Derry's (1979) words – who pillaged much of England, Normandy and the Baltic coast and the nascent monarchies and gradually replaced them with regional tribal communities. The Vikings even reached Italy and the Black Sea. John Marsden has noted that whilst the etymology of the Old Norse *vikingr* has never been fully resolved, the masculine noun *vikingr* translates as a 'sea raider' and the associated feminine noun *viking* as 'a raid from the sea' (Marsden 1993: 7). Krístjan Eldjárn has argued that the noun *vikingr* derived from the verb *vikja*, meaning 'going away' or 'leaving home', and that, accordingly, the viking was a man 'who left his northern homeland in the company of a warband in search of whatever might be sought across the sea' (see Marsden 1993: 17). Another possibility is that the word derived from the Old Norse *vik*, meaning 'bay', since the Vikings usually operated from inlets or bays. The word *vik* is still used in modern Scandinavian, and Reykjavík in Icelandic, for example, means 'smoky bay' (Magnússon 1977: 8).

In any event, the Vikings' targets varied. Simplifying somewhat, the Norwegian Vikings set their sights on Scotland and the areas northwards, the Danish Vikings set theirs on England and France, whilst the Swedish Vikings looked east, to Russia. Indeed, during the Viking period many Swedes took part in the colonisation of Russia, and in the process Swedish chieftains came to control considerable areas in Finland. The Swedish word *rus* originally meant 'rower' and the Swedish Vikings who founded the Russian empire also gave it its name, Russia, or in Scandinavian Ryssland.

When the first Norwegian Vikings settled in Iceland at the end of the ninth century there were already a number of Irish monks and hermits on the island. As early as AD 795, in fact, there is an account of a few Irish hermits staying in Iceland between the months of February and August. When the Vikings arrived 100 years later this devout band of Christians could not endure their rowdiness, and the hermits fled, probably to Greenland. However, the Vikings plundered Irish slaves *en route* to Iceland, and this would explain the latter's mixed Nordic–Celtic tradition. According to Jon R. Hjalmarsson (cited in Ervamaa 1996), Iceland is divided into an eastern Scandinavian and a western Atlantic mentality, and in Iceland there has been intermittent discussion of whether the nation is more Irish or Norwegian. Certainly some of the outstanding heroes of the sagas, such as Kormák, Njál and Kjartan, have Celtic names. In any event, the Age of Settlement in Iceland (874–930) took place during the Viking era, when powerful farmers from Norway refused to pay taxes to King Harald Finehair, who was in the process of uniting Norway and its territories. It ended in 930, with the foundation of the Alþingi and the beginning of an independent Icelandic commonwealth of tiny chieftaincies. The Alþingi or parliament was held for a week or two in the second half of June – in the open air – on the 'assembly plain' of Thingvellir. Attendance was open to everyone, but the proceedings were dominated by the thirty-nine *goðar*, or chieftains (local bigwigs), who, in turn, represented the free farmers (*bændr*). (Farm labourers and women did not have full political rights.) It was a remarkable system of representative democracy, in which each chieftain was obliged to explain his vote in the Alþingi on every issue. Indeed, unlike the petty kingdoms in Norway and Ireland, which often fought to defend or extend their borders, the power of the *goðar* was not based on the resources of an exploitable realm (Byock 1993: 113). In the words of Birgit and Peter Sawyer, they were 'lords of men, not territory' (Sawyer and Sawyer 1993: 86) or, in the strikingly modern terminology of Jesse Byock, 'they were leaders of interest groups that were continually jockeying with one another for status' (Byock 1993: 124). Ultimately, following growing conflict and rivalry between a diminishing number of ever more powerful *goðar*, the commonwealth began to disintegrate and in 1264 Iceland submitted to the rule of the Norwegian king. The commonwealth, incidentally, was also the period when the most distinguished literary work was produced.

The Norwegian Vikings also took Shetland and Orkney from the Picts, whilst during the first decades of the ninth century expeditions originating mainly in western Norway descended on the Hebrides and the Scottish mainland. The Hebrides were quickly overrun and subsequently linked with the Isle of Man in a Norse kingdom. Orkney and Shetland remained under Norwegian jurisdiction until 1468 (from 1380, with the union of the two crowns, Danish–Norwegian jurisdiction). They were governed by a *foud* or local governor, who collected the king's fines and taxes. On occasions the king himself would descend to impose a greater measure of obedience. In 1090 the Norwegian monarch, Magnus Barelegs – so called because he abandoned Viking trousers for a kilt – sent a task force across the North Sea to remind the people of Orkney and Shetland who was lord (Magnusson 1990: 6). Whilst Shetland is poorly served by northern writers, Orkney had a saga – in Icelandic *saga* means simply 'something said' – composed on its earls and their contemporaries, covering its history up to about 1200. That the Norwegian Vikings extended down into the northern part of the Scottish mainland is evident in the fact that Norse names feature prominently in Caithness toponymy. All the place names ending in '-gill', '-wick' and '-toft' indicate Nordic origins and the Scandinavian settlers in east Caithness referred to the Scottish mainland to the south as 'Sudland' and it has remained Sutherland (Logan 1991: 42).

About AD 800 the Danish Vikings began their campaigns against England and when in 886 the king of Wessex, Alfred the Great (871–99), was forced to concede his territories north of a line from London to Chester, an independent Viking kingdom of Danelaw was set up and thousands of Danes settled there permanently. Alfred stemmed the Viking tide and the influx of Danish peasants, but Sweyn Forkbeard (985–1014) subsequently reduced all the English provinces, compelled London to surrender and forced the English king to flee to France. Sweyn's death led the English king to venture back, but in 1015 his son Knud (Canute) captured the entire country and was crowned king of England. Soon afterwards he also became king of Denmark (after the death of his brother) and soon after that acquired the southern part of Norway. His empire disintegrated after the loss of his second son, Hardeknud, in 1042, and the Viking period ended when the Norwegian king Harald Hardrada was defeated by the Saxon Harold Godwinson at Stamford Bridge in 1066.

Christianity, which came to Denmark from northern France and had spread to the rest of Scandinavia by the end of the twelfth century, may be regarded as a major import of the later Viking era. It meant the Nordic kingdoms were simultaneously incorporated into the western cultural community. To put it another way, the Vikings who went on their way as pagans took a variety of new ideas and techniques with them and were far from impervious to Christian influences.

King Harald Bluetooth (935–85), who was successful in binding the several Danish kingdoms into one domain under his rule, was the first Danish monarch to become a Christian. However, the church did not become fully established until the reign of Sweyn Estridson (1047–74) – an archbishopric was established in Lund in 1103 – and, accordingly, Christianity and paganism co-existed for a considerable period. The same was true in Iceland, where the commonwealth was nominally Christian, but although the pagan deities were dead, the ancient spirit of pride and feud flourished to the end. In short, the process of converting the Icelanders was slow.

The same was undoubtedly true in Norway. Indeed, following some progress of Christianity into the eastern districts, where the Danish influence was strongest, there was a revival of paganism under Earl Haakon, who in the last quarter of the tenth century based his rule on the staunchly heathen Trøndelag region of central Norway. With its interests directed towards the east, Sweden remained a heathen country even longer, and no Swedish king was converted until 1008. Even then the advent of Olof Skotkonung marked the beginning of a century of religious conflict. However, in AD 1154 King Eric IX of Sweden led the first crusades into Finland and thus began its systematic conquest. Place names show that Swedes had been moving along the coast from the Åland islands for at least a century before. But Finland became part of the Swedish kingdom in the early Middle Ages and the Swedish acquisition of the areas populated by the Suomalaiset in the south-west was followed by the immigration of Swedish colonists who settled in the coastal areas. As a result, the Swedish–Finnish language boundary remained fairly constant until the second half of the nineteenth century, when the Swedish districts began to shrink as a result of increased Finnish migration to the coastal areas. It is important to emphasise that the conquered areas were not, however, treated as colonies, but soon acquired equal status with other parts of the Swedish kingdom. Hence, in 1362, representatives from Finland participated in the election of the Swedish king. From then, too, Finns continued regularly to take part in meetings of the estates of the realm. The great law code of 1734 was in some ways the culmination of this process.

The activities of the Vikings and early Christians pre-dated the advent of a distinctive period of early co-operation between the Scandinavian kingdoms in the form of the Kalmar Union. This 'Golden Age' has become a (justifiable) part of the mythology of contemporary Nordic co-operation. Nor was its inception unimpressive. At a solemn ceremony at Kalmar in Sweden, close to the then border with Denmark, on Trinity Sunday in June 1397, sixty-seven bishops, prelates, nobles and other bigwigs signed a parchment in which they recognised the union of the three Scandinavian kingdoms under Queen Margaret of Denmark and Norway and her grand-nephew, Eric of Pomerania. The Kalmar Union constituted the second largest aggregation of European territories under a single sovereign and formed part of a general trend towards the creation of larger political units, as for example in the emergence of Poland–Lithuania, the Burgundy dominions and the expansion of the principality of Moscow. The Kalmar Union was Danish-dominated – its central administration was based in Copenhagen – and was directed against the Hanseatic League. When, after Margaret's death, Eric imposed higher taxes, the popularity of the Union fell and in 1434 Swedish hostility to Danish rule led to a peasant uprising. It was joined by the nobility and prompted the convocation of the first Riksdag (Swedish parliament) in 1435.

Vilhelm Moberg (1971: 65) notes how at this time Swedish political songs, supposedly the creation of the populace but in reality commissioned by the authorities, invariably presented the Danes as an inherently bad lot and sought to instil the myth of the diabolical Dane. A Gotland song from 1449, which is one long orgy of hatred of the Danes, ran to twenty-eight verses, each ending with the stern warning 'Swedish men, be watchful still!' Further evidence of Danish–Swedish suspicion and rivalry during the Kalmar period can be gleaned in the aftermath of the marriage in 1468 between James III of Scotland and Margaret of Denmark. The marriage treaty amounted to a full diplomatic and military alliance, and thereafter the Swedes regarded the Scots (as allies of the Danes) with considerable misgiving. In 1473, as David Ditchburn (1990: 80) has noted, the Swedish Council of State wrote to the Danzig authorities concerning the arrest of two Danzig ships in the vicinity of Alvsborg Castle. One had been released, but the other remained under arrest because it was suspected that Scots, 'that is enemies of Sweden', were aboard.

Looking back, the Kalmar Union was a glorious admixture of fact, fiction and fraction. It functioned at best intermittently for over a century, disguised deep-seated regional rivalries and collapsed altogether with the advent of

Christian II (1513–23), a contemporary of Henry VIII in England, who sought to impose a Renaissance-style monarchy by, *inter alia*, reforming the central administration, introducing new legal codes (based on the Dutch model) and instituting a single official language. All this was less than well received by the nobles who were the king's rivals for power. A bloodbath in Stockholm in 1520 brought the Swedish bigwigs to heel, but in December 1522 a rebellion was launched by eighteen nobles from Jutland, in northern Denmark, four of whom were bishops. Copenhagen and Malmö remained loyal to Christian II, but when the estates of Jutland paid homage to Frederick, Christian's uncle, who had enlisted the support of the Hanseatic League, the king's nerve failed and in April 1523 he beat a hasty retreat to the Netherlands. Two months later Gustav Vasa, who had also allied himself with the Hanseatic League, was elected king of Sweden. The Kalmar Union was dead; in 1527 Gustav Vasa was crowned Gustav I of Sweden; and he proclaimed the Reformation and the legal basis of a unified state.

If the final collapse of the Kalmar Union mirrored the divisions between the Nordic lands, the simultaneous impact of the Reformation united them spiritually under the banner of Lutheranism. The Reformation in Scandinavia was total, and this is important when we come to analyse the historic cleavages that moulded the nascent party systems in the region. Space precludes any discussion of the progress of the Reformation in Norden except to note the contribution of the same Christian II whose reformism prompted the disintegration of the Kalmar Union. In fact, Christian's ecclesiastical revisionism pre-dated the protest of Martin Luther in Germany and when a young Danish student and former monk, Hans Tavsen, returned from Wittenberg and began preaching Lutheran doctrines, he was befriended and protected by Christian II's successor, Frederick I (1523–33). His son, Christian III, convened a meeting of the national assembly, the Rigsdag, in Copenhagen in 1536, which voted to abolish the old church organisation and eliminate the political and religious powers of the Catholic clergy. Christian III forced bishops from office, sequestered ecclesiastical property and set in train the organisation of the new Lutheran church as the state church, with the monarch as its head. It was during the Reformation that Finnish became a written language, thanks largely to the efforts of Mikael Agricola, whose translation of the New Testament appeared in 1548.

Conflict rather than co-operation has been the dominant motif of this historical sketch of Norden through the ages, and the continuing struggle for domination in the Baltic led in the seventeenth century to the emergence of Sweden as a great power. Successive wars with Russia resulted in the annexation of Estonia in 1595, the south-east coast of the Gulf of Finland in 1617 and Livonia in 1621. These areas were not incorporated into the Swedish kingdom but administered separately as conquered provinces. In 1630 King Gustav Adolf II took Sweden into the Thirty Years' War on the continent and, although he was killed in action, Sweden acquired various north German territories under the Peace of Westphalia in 1648. Incidentally, during Gustav

Adolf's reign, possibly as many as 30,000 Scottish officers enlisted and contributed to establishing the Swedish 'great power' ascendancy to east and south. For them, in Robert Monro's words, Gustav Adolf was 'The Captain of Kings and King of Captains, Gustav the invincible, the most valiant captain of the World' (Åberg 1990: 96). True, the majority of officers fell in battle or died of sickness in the camps, whilst some returned to Scotland. However, many Scottish officers settled in Sweden and they and their sons introduced new families into the houses of the nobility: Douglas, Hamilton, Ramsay, Sinclair, Forbes and Duvall, to name but a few.

Denmark refused to give up its status as 'cock of the north' without a fight, and war with Sweden recurred at almost regular intervals. The Danes were the undoubted losers. At the Treaty of Bromsebro in 1645 the Swedes acquired Jämtland, Halland, Harjedalen and Gotland, and at Roskilde in 1658 the provinces of Skåne, Blekinge and Bohuslän. To this day the Skåne dialect reflects its Danish past, whilst the region cherishes an identity separate from the rest of Sweden. For years a Skåne Party has been active in local elections. There has been a strong tendency, moreover, for the people of Skåne to look southwards to Copenhagen and more recently to Brussels, and it was no coincidence that Skåne was one of the strongest pro-EU regions in the Swedish accession referendum in November 1994. A road and rail bridge across the sound now links Skåne and Copenhagen and regional representatives in the Swedish Riksdag have even called for Danish to be taught in Skåne schools.

If Sweden became a great power in the seventeenth century, it was reduced to a shrunken remnant of its former glory in the eighteenth. As Russia and the north German states gained in strength, Sweden's hegemony in the Baltic began to disintegrate. By 1720 the north German territories had been ceded to Hanover and Prussia. Then, crucially, in the Great Northern War of 1700–21, the armies of King Karl XII were well beaten in Russia, and Russia absorbed the Baltic countries and parts of south-east Finland. This defeat had important domestic consequences, since the death of Karl XII led to a new constitution and the so-called Era of Liberty, half a century in which parliament was largely predominant and two proto-parties emerged in the Riksdag. The so-called Hats opposed Russia and strove to win back the lost Baltic territories; the Caps, in contrast, pursued a conciliatory line towards Russia. When conflict between Russia and Sweden continued, in the so-called Hats' Russian War (1741–43), the Scottish general James Keith headed a Russian force which in 1741 successfully captured Lappeenranta in eastern Finland from the Swedes and he was accordingly honoured by the Russians with the title of governor general of Finland (Hall 2007). The arms of the Keith family are in the top right quarter of the University of Aberdeen's coat of arms and he appears to be the only student of the university to have ruled any of the Scandinavian countries (however briefly!) (Nihtinen 1998).

By the beginning of the nineteenth century, the two imperial states in Scandinavia, Denmark and Sweden, had lost all vestiges of great-power status and had become largely reactive players on the European stage. Certainly the lesson of the Napoleonic Wars was that no single Nordic country was able to influence the actions of the new powers in the Baltic. Sweden was unable to prevent Alexander I's deal with Napoleon which led to a treaty joining Finland with Russia in 1809. Before the turmoil was over, however, the turncoat Napoleonic marshal Jean-Baptiste Bernadotte became Swedish king and was rewarded for his 'conversion' at the Congress of Vienna in 1815, when the great powers confirmed the transfer of Norway from Denmark to Sweden. No matter that the previous year the Norwegians had elected their own king and drafted a constitution, the Eidsvoll constitution, which, still in force today, is the oldest surviving form of government in Europe. Denmark was allowed to hold on to Iceland, Greenland and the Faeroes. In short, from the early nineteenth century to the early twentieth, the political map of Scandinavia comprised the former imperial powers of Denmark and Sweden and the three 'colonies' of Iceland, Finland and Norway. The impact of nationalism was to lead to demands for greater independence, which was achieved in widely varying circumstances in Norway in 1905, Finland in 1917 and Iceland in 1944 (see chapter 2).

As to Nordic co-operation in the nineteenth and twentieth centuries, Sweden did nothing to help the Danes in their losing war with Austria and Prussia for Slesvig-Holstein in 1864, although Swedish relations with Norway were mostly amicable and Norway was conceded without a fight in 1905. A tiff between Sweden and Finland over the Åland islands was resolved only by a League of Nations resolution in 1921, but Nordic co-operation intensified significantly during this inter-war period. Even in autumn 1939 the Scandinavian kings and Finnish president met in Stockholm to express their support for Finland, which was being confronted with Soviet aggression (Salmon 1997). It intensified further in the early Cold War years, when Norden comprised a bloc of states on the frontier between capitalism and communism.

Nordic co-operation early in the new millennium: a dying swan?

The accelerated process of integration in western Europe and the contemporaneous disintegration of the Soviet empire in eastern Europe beginning in 1989 not only significantly altered the geo-political position of the Nordic states but, somewhat paradoxically too, challenged the existing institutions of Nordic co-operation. Three main points will suffice at this stage, since a more detailed discussion will follow in chapter 13.

First, the collapse of the Soviet Union, the recovery of Estonian, Latvian and Lithuanian independence and the emergence of the Russian Federation marked the demise of the ideological rift that had divided the Baltic region during the Cold War years, with the result that Nordic co-operation has to a degree been superseded, or at least challenged, by the wider concept of Baltic co-operation. The three Baltic republics have formed a Baltic Council, modelled on the Nordic Council. The Council of Baltic Sea States embraces all the states along the shores of the Baltic (north and south), including Russia, and the EU has representation on various organs of regional co-operation, among them the Barents Euro-Arctic Regional Council (BEAR), set up in 1993. For their part, the Nordic states are members of the Arctic Council, which was set up on a Canadian initiative in September 1996 and places emphasis on cross-national environmental protection in circumpolar regions (Nuttall 1997).

Second, Finnish and Swedish accession to the EU in 1995, complementing Danish membership from 1973, gave the EU a Nordic dimension, whilst also highlighting intra-regional divisions over the 'European project' at both elite and mass levels. Norway and Iceland are not full EU members and now enthuse about Nordic co-operation, not least (although it is not of course stated in such terms) to 'keep in touch' with developments in Brussels through the Nordic members of the Union. Equally, there have been obvious differences between the Nordic members over strategic developments within the EU. Finland became a founder member of the Economic and Monetary Union (EMU) in 1999, whereas Denmark in 2000 and Sweden in 2003 have rejected EMU membership following popular referenda. For the Nordic EU members, moreover, there is the resource problem of staffing the organs of Nordic co-operation as well as those of the EU.

Third, whilst all the Nordic states have access to the EU's single market (in the cases of Norway and Iceland through the EEA) the region includes, in the shape of the Faeroes and Greenland, a genuine geo-economic periphery, which has generated centrifugal strains. Greenland, as mentioned, left the EC following a referendum in 1982 and four years later a West Nordic Council was formed with its secretariat in Reykjavík. History has shown that the economic (as well as political) interests of the Nordic states and Home Rule territories have differed over the years and this remains true to this day.

A final point is in order. Whilst this introductory chapter has emphasised the comparability of the Nordic countries as small states, the notion of a small state has been relatively little debated – at least in the international relations literature – and it may well be a case, in Barry Buzan's terms (cited in Joenniemi 1997), of a concept with 'little flavour and not much kick'! In other words, although small states are frequently alluded to in international relations discourse, their structural conditions – that is, how to define and operationalise them – remain inexact. Of course, cynics might suggest that small states are simply those that have no one to intimidate and hence place great value on shared sovereignty. Certainly the distinction between small and large states appears real enough within international organisations and is reflected in the institutional balance in the EU for example. Equally, network theory – which emphasises the way influence can be exerted through backstage contacts – suggests the small–large dichotomy can easily be exaggerated.

Pertti Joenniemi (1997) has even referred to 'smart states' and smartness is clearly not a function of size. Which, if any, of the Nordic states fall into the smart state category will be left to the judgement of the reader.

Summary

1.   The Nordic region, or Norden, comprises five nation states and three Home Rule territories, with a combined population of just under 25 million persons, and the nation states in particular readily lend themselves to comparative analysis.

2.   They are small pluralist democracies ranging from the smallest of the European small states (Iceland) to one of the largest of the European small states (Sweden). The small size of the political class, some argue, has encouraged personalised elite relations and a pragmatic, compromise-dominated style of policy-making.

3.   Partly because of the co-operative nature of inter-elite relations, but also by dint of the absence of cross-cutting socio-political cleavages based on language, religion and so on, the Nordic states have been said to comprise a distinct sub-type of liberal democracy and to form a bloc of 'consensual democracies'.

4.   The Nordic states include the three most sparsely populated countries in Europe (Iceland, Norway and Finland), and significant EU subsidies – from the structural funds, INTERREG programme, etc. – have been of paramount importance in maintaining a demographic infrastructure in peripheral areas.

5.   They are today typical post-industrial, information-based, service-dominant economies, which, by dint of small domestic markets, are necessarily export-oriented. Flagship brands such as Nokia and IKEA betoken a significant measure of success in competing in the global marketplace

6.   The Nordic states have a shared history, common linguistic bonds and a common state Lutheran religion. Of the six Scandinavian languages, Danish, Norwegian and Swedish are mutually intelligible, whilst Swedish is an official national language in Finland.

7.   The roots of Nordic co-operation are often traced deep into a common historical past. In reality, the Kalmar Union (1397–1523) was an intriguing admixture of fact, fiction and fraction.

8.   Whilst the grassroots Norden Association originated after the First World War, the institutionalisation of Nordic regional co-operation – with the foundation of the Nordic Council in 1952 – was broadly contemporaneous with incipient economic integration in western Europe and the emergence of the Franco-German inspired European Coal and Steel Community, although its purview was narrower and there was no pooling of economic resources.

9.   In recent years Nordic co-operation has been challenged by the broader concept of Baltic co-operation and the exponential process of European

integration. For the non-EU Nordic states of Iceland and Norway, regional co-operation has assumed added importance as a forum for agenda-setting and informational exchange, whereas for Denmark, Finland and Sweden there are resource constraints on maintaining a bureaucracy at both Nordic and EU levels.

10. Although the small states that form the Nordic region readily lend themselves to comparative analysis, there is a danger of overstating the common denominators and underestimating their differences. They may not be as different as stones and rabbits, but a variety of institutional configurations and political practices will emerge in the course of this book.

References

Åberg, Alf (1990) 'Scottish soldiers in the Swedish armies in the sixteenth and seventeenth centuries', in Grant G. Simpson (ed.), *Scotland and Scandinavia, 800–1800*, John Donald: Edinburgh, pp. 90–9.

Archer, Clive and Nigel Nugent (2002) 'Introduction: small states and the European Union', *Current Politics and Economics of Europe*, 11 (1), pp. 1–10.

Burnham, R. E. (1956) *Who Are the Finns? A Study in Pre-history*, Faber & Faber: London.

Byock, Jesse L. (1993) *Medieval Iceland*, Hisarlik Press: Enfield.

Carpelan, Christian (1997) *Where Do the Finns Come From?*, Finfo 12/97, Ministry of Foreign Affairs: Helsinki.

Chubb, Basil (1982) *The Government and Politics of Ireland*, second edition, Longman: London.

Derry, T. K. (1979) *A History of Scandinavia*, Allen & Unwin: London.

Ditchburn, David (1990) 'A note on Scandinavian trade with Scotland in the later Middle Ages', in Grant G. Simpson (ed.), *Scotland and Scandinavia, 800–1800*, John Donald: Edinburgh, pp. 73–89.

Ervamaa, Tomi (1996) 'Etäinen Islanti varjelee visusti koskemattomuuttaan', *Helsingin Sanomat*, 28 June.

Hall, Allan (2007) 'So why is James Keith Scotland's unknown soldier?', *Scotsman*, 30 October.

Haugen, Einar (1976) *The Scandinavian Languages*, Faber & Faber: London.

Haugen, Einar (1982) *Scandinavian Language Structures. A Comparative Historical Survey*, Max Niemeyer Verlag: Tübingen.

Joenniemi, Pertti (1997) 'A critique of the concept of small states', paper presented at the nineteenth annual conference of the National Committee for the Study of International Affairs (in association with the Finnish Institute in London) on 'Small States and European Security', Dublin, 20–22 November.

Jutikkala, Eino (1989) 'The colonisation of Finland and the roots of the Finnish people', in Max Engman and David Kirby (eds), *Finland. People, Nation, State*, Hurst: London, pp. 16–37.

Kristinsson, Gunnar Helgi (1996) 'Iceland and the European Union', in Lee Miles (ed.), *The European Union and the Nordic Countries*, Routledge: London, pp. 150–65.

Logan, F. Donald (1991) *The Vikings in History*, HarperCollins: London.

Magnusson, Magnus (1990) 'The Viking road', in Grant G. Simpson (ed.), *Scotland and Scandinavia 800–1800*, John Donald: Edinburgh, pp. 1–12.

Magnússon, Sigurdur A. (1977) *Northern Sphinx. Iceland and the Icelanders from the Settlement to the Present*, Hurst: London.

Marsden, John (1993) *The Fury of the Northmen*, BCA: London.

Moberg, Vilhelm (1971) *Min Svenske Historia II. Från Engelbrekt till och med Dacke*, Nordstedt & Söners: Stockholm.

Nihtinen, Atina (1998) 'Turulla ja Skotlannilla vuosisataiset siteet', *Turun Sanomat*, 21 January.

Nuttall, Mark (1997) 'The Arctic Council: can co-operation be sustained?', *Polar Record*, 33 (185), pp. 99–100.

Salmon, Patrick (1997) *Scandinavia and the Great Powers, 1890–1940*, Cambridge University Press: Cambridge.

Sawyer, Peter and Birgit Sawyer (1993) *Medieval Scandinavia*, University of Minnesota Press: Minneapolis, MN.

Thorhallsson, Baldur (ed.) (2004) *Iceland and European Integration*, Routledge: London.

Turner, B. and G. Nordquist (1982) *The Other European Community. Integration and Co-operation in Nordic Europe*, Weidenfeld & Nicolson: London.

Virolainen, Johannes (1969) *Pääministerinä suomessa*, Kirjayhtymä: Helsinki.

2

Nation-building and state-building, 1809–1944

She did not love her country, only her plot and shack,
A few yards of the stream, and the lava, rough and black.
(Guðmundur Friðjónsson, 'The widow by the stream', cited in Karlsson 1995: 36)

The aim of this chapter is to provide a brief but necessary historical background to the emergence of the present arrangement of five nation states and three Home Rule territories in the Nordic region. It proposes to do so in a comparative and thematic fashion, organising the material around the twin concepts of nation-building – the development of a sense of national identity – and state-building – the process of achieving independence, that is, sovereign control of affairs. How did the five-plus-three equation come about and why not two-plus-six, that is, two imperial states and six peripheral ones, as in the aftermath of the Napoleonic Wars or, indeed, eight nation states? Since the burden of our early discussion will be on the process of nation-building rather than the detailed sequence of events leading up to the achievement of sovereignty, three background points are in order.

1 Nineteenth-century nationalism, in the spirit of Hegel and Herder, argued that the boundaries of the state should be contiguous with those of the nation and that the nation and state should constitute an organic whole. Primacy was given to language as the heart of the nation and the nineteenth-century nationalists also contended that a nation had the right to self-determination.
2 Nation-building does not always precede state-building: it can be the other way round. Ukraine and Belarus are modern examples of 'nationless states', that is, states that emerged (in 1991) without a significant sense of national identity. However, whereas in newly independent Ukraine there was a vigorous programme of Ukrainianisation, President Alexander Lukashenko in Belarus seemed intent on reunion with Russia and destroying the symbols of nationality (Arter 1996: 30–43).

3 Recent history teaches us that the creation and recognition of new states
   has had less to do with the intrinsic merits of the nationalist claims than
   with considerations of *realpolitik*, political expediency and big-power perceptions. Illustrations of this last point range from the role of the United States
   in recognising Thomas Masaryk's Czechoslovakia in 1919 to the recognition by the European Union (EU), and particularly Germany, of Bosnia and
   Croatia in 1991, and to US and subsequently British recognition of Kosovo
   as a 'sovereign and independent state' in February 2008. Effective marketing
   will, of course, affect the external view, witness in addition to Masaryk's successful mobilisation of pro-Slavic sentiment in the United States the impact
   of the legal writings of Leo Mechelin in promoting the notion of a Finnish
   state in the second half of the nineteenth century (Jussila 1989: 90–2).

Before reviewing the impact of nineteenth-century nationalism in Norden
on a country-by-country basis, it may be helpful to summarise the overall picture.

1 Nationalism affected the whole region, including the imperial 'centres' – as
   is evident, for example, in the activities of the Gothic Society in Sweden – but
   it had its greatest force in the Nordic 'peripheries' or colonies. As mentioned
   in chapter 1, from 1815 onwards Norway was in a personal union with
   Sweden; Finland was a Grand Duchy of the Romanov czarist empire; and
   Iceland was under Danish absolutism.
2 The 'national question' was socially divisive and gave rise to the first
   embryonic political parties. In Finland, the Finnish Party emerged in the
   1870s and the Swedish Party in the 1880s. By 1900 the Finnish Party had
   split into a liberal wing, the so-called Young Finns (*nuorsuomalaiset*), and
   a conservative wing, the Old Finns (*vanhasuomalaiset*), much as there was
   a split between the Young Czechs and Old Czechs in the Bohemian provinces of the Austro-Hungarian empire at the beginning of the twentieth
   century (Garver 1978: 60–87). In Norway in the 1880s, Venstre (literally
   the 'Left') emerged to represent the Norwegian nation (ordinary people)
   and its language, Landsmål, against Høyre (literally the 'Right'), based on
   the Sweden-oriented officials controlling the 'proto-state', that is, the rudimentary structures of government in Kristiania (Oslo). In Iceland, the most
   culturally homogeneous of the Nordic colonies, with no regional dialects,
   the Independence Party, founded in 1929, succeeded a Home Rule Party,
   formed in 1907, to press for full sovereignty from Denmark.
3 The left–right split on the 'national question' reflected and reinforced cultural antagonisms between the countryside on the one hand and the towns
   and particularly the capital cities on the other. To the rural dweller, not
   only was the lifestyle of the towns foreign, but the towns and especially the
   capitals seemed to harbour agents of a foreign state. The officials in Norway
   were often educated in Copenhagen and were (formally at least) in the

employ of the Swedish crown. Similarly, the civil servants in Helsinki were Swedish- not Finnish-speaking and worked for the Russian czar.

Turning to a brief overview of nation-building and state-building in the Nordic region, an obvious distinction can be drawn between those 'stateless nations' which went on to achieve statehood (Finland, Norway and Iceland) and the territories that have not achieved independence (the Faeroes, Greenland and Åland). Table 2.1 presents a brief chronology of events in Norden up to 1922, when Åland achieved autonomy.

Finland: nationalism under czarism

The basic structures of the Finnish state considerably pre-dated independence. Self-government or Grand Duchy status was granted by Alexander I following the Russian annexation in 1809 and extended by Alexander II (1856–81). The statue of Alexander II in Senate Square in Helsinki between the university and the Council of State (cabinet) building is a reminder to this day that Finland, in contrast to the Congress Kingdom of Poland (the Russian partition), enjoyed enhanced autonomy under this particular ruler of Russia. Indeed, the quadricameral Assembly of Estates (Nobles, Merchants, Clergy and Peasants) met regularly after 1863, which was also the year in which Alexander II issued a decree requiring officials and the courts to accept documents in Finnish. Within two decades all officials were to use Finnish in their written communications with speakers of that language. In 1865 Finland gained its own currency and national bank and in 1877–78 a small Finnish army (of 5,000–6,000 men) was created. Incidentally, the emergence of Finnish as an official language by the 1880s meant that, on ceremonial occasions at least, the Grand Duchy was a multilingual country. In 1885 the Assembly of Estates was opened by the czar in Russian and his speech was translated into Finnish and Swedish by senator (minister) Molander. The field marshal as presiding officer responded for the House of Nobles in French, the Speaker of the House of Merchants responded in Swedish and the Speakers of the Houses of Clergy and Peasants in Finnish (Klinge 1996).

Apart from an interlude of authoritarian management from St Petersburg at the end of the nineteenth century, referred to by Finnish historians as 'the era of Russification' – during which, *inter alia*, the czar sought for the Russians in Finland the rights the Finns enjoyed in Russia – Finland enjoyed a unique and prosperous position as a Grand Duchy of the Russian empire. At the beginning of the twentieth century, as Timo Vihavainen (1997) has observed, only about 6,000 people or 0.2 per cent of the population of 3 million in the Grand Duchy were Russians, despite the fact that Finland was not far from the Russian capital. Moreover, whilst Finnish citizens had wide-ranging rights in Russia, to work in offices and to conduct business, for example, the Russians

Table 2.1 *Nation-building and state-building in Norden, 1809–1922:*
a chronology of events

Year	Events
1809	Finland becomes a Grand Duchy of the Russian empire and Alexander I announces at a meeting of the Estates in Borgå (Porvoo) that he has 'elevated Finland to be counted among the nations'
1814	*14 January*. Treaty of Kiel. Norway is ceded by Denmark to the King of Sweden to constitute a kingdom (in a 'personal union') with Sweden Danish prince Christian Frederick is elected as Norwegian regent. The Norwegian Storting subsequently accepts the union as inevitable and Christian Frederick leaves for Denmark in October 1814
1815	*Summer*. Formal Act of Union is passed by the first regular Norwegian Storting and enacted in identical form by the Swedish Riksdag
1831	Czar Nicholas I approves the founding of the Finnish Literature Society
1835	Elias Lönnrot's Finnish folk epic *Kalevala* is published
1845	Re-establishment of the Icelandic Alþingi (abolished in 1800) as a consultative assembly following the efforts of Jón Sigurðsson, an Icelandic nationalist and philologist living in Copenhagen
1848	Following revolutionary activity across Europe, the Danish king abolishes absolute monarchy and a constitution is introduced, although there is no mention of Iceland, which is never represented in the Danish Folketing
1856	Following the Crimean War, the Åland islands are demilitarised on a Swedish initiative by the Treaty of Paris
1863	Regular meetings of the Finnish Estates and the Finnish nationalist J. V. Snellman becomes a senator (minister)
1865	Finland gets its own currency
1869	Start of annual sessions of the Norwegian Storting
1871	Denmark establishes the post of governor general in Iceland
1872	Oscar II succeeds his brother Karl XV as king of Sweden–Norway
1874	Icelandic Alþingi gains legislative powers and Iceland its own constitution (modelled on the Danish constitution of 1848)

Table continues opposite

had no such rights in Finland. Finland did not contribute to the Russian state budget and its share of defence expenditure was very modest. Moreover, although Finland was not represented in the Russian Duma (parliament), it was offered the possibility and, in any event, Finland had its own citizenship, finance, administration and army.

Indeed, according to Osmo Jussila (1989: 88), 'Finland was already a state' when it gained full sovereignty in December 1917, by which he meant that it was an 'internally independent state'. Jussila notes that a Council of Government was set up in Åbo (Turku) in autumn 1809 – it was redesignated the

1878	Finnish conscript army is formed
1884	Johan Sverdrup's Landsmål-based Venstre, following election wins in 1879 and 1882, demands to govern Norway. After heightened tension the Swedish king, Oscar II, reluctantly concedes the principle of ministerial responsibility in Norway
1898	The Storting votes to remove the union symbol from the flag of the Norwegian merchant marine
1899	Nicholas II's February Manifesto ushers in a period of Russification in Finland
1902	Finnish achieves equal status with Swedish as an official language
1904	Iceland gains Home Rule, with an Icelandic minister in Reykjavík
	16 June. Eugen Schauman shoots dead the Russian governor general in Finland, Nikolai Bobrikov, before turning the gun on himself
1905	Peaceful dissolution of the union of Norway and Sweden. In a referendum the Norwegians vote four to one in favour of King Haakon VII. Czar Nicholas II's October Manifesto clears the way for radical electoral and parliamentary reform in Finland
1906	The Finnish Union is founded and over 100,000 people Finnicise their surnames in one year
1907	Foundation of the Icelandic Home Rule Party (the forerunner of the Independence Party, founded in 1929)
1912	Hannes Kolehmainen wins a track gold for Finland at the Olympic Games
1917	*6 December*. Finland declares itself independent following the collapse of czarism and the Bolshevik revolution in Russia
1918	The establishment of an Icelandic state in a personal union with Denmark
	8 January. Lenin recognises Finnish independence
	16 May. White victory ends Finnish civil war
1921	*June*. The League of Nations rules that Finland should have sovereignty over the Åland islands
1922	*9 June*. The Åland Landsting convenes for the first time on what is to become Autonomy Day

Senate in 1816 – and Finland possessed in the nineteenth century an adminis-trative apparatus with independent tax-raising powers (i.e. it was a 'finance state'), along with a developed legal system. Paavo Haavikko (1991: 90) has also noted that the nineteenth-century Finnish state – the term 'Grand Duchy' was not willingly used – obtained loans from Europe and called its rail network the 'State Railways', whilst the Finnish military unit was known as the Finnish Guard. Certainly the existence of a proto-state during the nine-teenth century was reflected in the character of the nationalist movement, which was distinctively hybrid in form. As Risto Alapuro has observed in *State and Revolution in Finland*:

In Finland there evolved the kind of nationalism that mixed features of the form of nationalism customary in Western Europe – nationalism as a 'civic religion', i.e.

support for the existing state – with the form of nationalism customary in Eastern
Europe, which aimed at liberation from the multinational empires and from a
ruling class which spoke another language. (Cited in Engman 1995a: 182)

Thus Finnish nationalists like Z. Yrjö-Koskinen sought to conquer the Swedish-
speaking bureaucracy, and hence the machinery of the proto-state, by creating
a new upper class which in language and outlook would be at one with the
people.

Finnish nationalism in turn fuelled Swedish nationalism within Finland,
or in Eric Hobsbawm's (1990) term 'counter-nationalism', towards the end
of the nineteenth century. The Swedish nationalist movement, in short, was a
direct response to the Finnish-speaking one. The Swedish-speaking population
was (and remains) territorially disparate, comprising the fishing population along the southern coastline and in the south-western archipelago, the
farmers of the north-west (Ostrobothnia) and the upper classes in the towns
and capital city. Earlier they had not felt a sense of affinity or identity on the
basis of language. However, counter-nationalist mobilisation was anchored
in the concept of the 'Finland Swede', *Finlandssvensk*, a term which served
effectively to unite the minority-language speakers (Engman 1995a: 191–8).
The national question, therefore, split the population along language lines and
a Swedish People's Party (Svenska folkpartiet, Sfp) emerged with the achievement of mass democracy in 1906.

Decisive in Finland's significant politico-economic development in the
nineteenth century was the fact that the Grand Duchy was allowed to evolve
undisturbed for long periods. There was a lively debate about the main issues of
the day in both the Estates (particularly the House of Peasants) and the press
(serving both language communities), whilst customs autonomy and access
to the Russian market (especially St Petersburg) brought economic progress.
Finnish soldiers were educated and trained in the Russian army and Finnish
researchers travelled extensively in Russia. Max Engman has noted that there
were as many Finns in St Petersburg in the nineteenth century as the combined
total in all the largest Finnish towns (Engman 1995b: 140). All that changed
drastically at the start of the new century. Then Russification bound together
both nationalisms in a common resistance to the reductionist course pursued
by the czar against the Finnish proto-state. The aim of the Russification policies
embarked on by Nicholas II and the imperial authorities in St Petersburg was
in large part to achieve greater efficiency and security by imposing uniformity
on and greater central control over the peripheral regions.

There was, incidentally, a parallel in the Germanisation programme in
Slesvig, which Denmark had ceded after the war with Austria–Prussia in
1864. Between 1898 and 1901 Ernst von Köller, the president of Slesvig, with
the full backing of the German emperor, Wilhelm II, expelled Danish citizens
deemed to be politically active in the province. However, the Danish minority drew together, and clubs and networks were set up to direct educational,

cultural and political activities. Interestingly, Prussian officialdom met with equally tenacious resistance from the much larger Polish population in the eastern provinces (Posen) (Kirby 1995: 171–2).

In Finland the period of Russification was heralded by Nicholas II's February Manifesto in 1899, which subordinated Finnish laws to imperial Russian laws. The following year, 1900, saw a decree ordering the gradual introduction of Russian as the main language of the state, whereas, before, Russian had been largely confined to channels of communication between Finland and St Petersburg (Polvinen 1995: 172–8). In 1901, moreover, there was a decree disbanding most of the Finnish army. The proposed conscription of Finns into the imperial Russian forces gave the Finnish opposition an ideal cause around which to unite. Even so, during 1903 there was a wave of expulsions from Finland: they included the politicians Leo Mechelin and Victor Magnus von Born and the lawyer Carl Mannerheim, elder brother of Gustav, who was to be the White commander-in-chief during the Finnish civil war of 1918 and leader of the Finnish army in the Winter War with the Soviet Union in 1939–40 and the Continuation War between 1941 and 1944 (Jägerskiöld 1986: 12).

There were many twists and turns in the story, but it culminated on 16 June 1904, when Nikolai Bobrikov, the Russian governor general in Finland, was dramatically assassinated whilst appearing before the crowd on a balcony of the Council of State building in Helsinki. The perpetrator of the deed, Eugen Schauman, an upper-class Finn, then shot himself. In his book *Five Shots in the Senate* (*Viisi laukausta senaatissa*) Schauman's biographer, Seppo Zetterberg (1986), revealed other than purely nationalist motives behind the assassination. None the less, in the unlikely place of a wall in a hairdresser's shop in central Helsinki, Zetterberg subsequently discovered a copy of a note which Schauman had in his pocket at the time of the fateful deed. It was an appeal to the czar to moderate the Russification programme. The note was held by Russian soldiers and the czar never received it. At the time, Russia was embroiled in a losing war with Japan, a by-product of which was the czar's October Manifesto of 1905, with its commitment to constitutional reform. It facilitated radical political restructuring in Finland, with the introduction of a unicameral assembly (the Eduskunta), replacing the quadricameral Estates, and a universal franchise, including previously excluded groups such as tenant farmers, agricultural labourers and factory workers.

With this restructuring, Finland also became the first country in Europe to give women the vote and the first in the world to permit them to stand as candidates in general elections. Nineteen female members of parliament were returned in 1907, compared with 181 men. One of them, Hilma Räsänen, from the rural district of Viipuri, close to the Russian border, representing the Agrarian Party, introduced Bills which would have banned the sale of cigarettes to persons under sixteen years and opened up agricultural schools to women. She quickly became disillusioned with party politics, however, did not stand in the 1908 general election and opposed the creation of a women's section within the Agrarian Party (on the grounds that there was no need for a special men's section). It was 1941 before the Agrarian Party created a Women's Organisation (Pohls 1997: 248–9).

The superimposition of mass democracy on a predominantly rural society spawned two new parliamentary parties: the Social Democrats, which, with the support of the rural proletariat, became at a stroke the largest party of its kind in Europe; and the Agrarians, based on the family-sized farms in the north-west (Ostrobothnia) and south-east (Karelia), which became the 'hinge group' of governing coalitions following independence (Arter 1978). In practice, however, the extent of the political modernisation achieved in 1906–7 flattered to deceive, since Nicholas II, precisely as in Russia, found flimsy pretexts for repeated dissolutions of the Eduskunta. This period of sham democracy ended with the collapse of czarism in Russia in 1917.

Summing up, nation-building in nineteenth-century Finland concentrated on the promotion of the Finnish language – in offices, schools, newspapers and official correspondence – a task facilitated by the non-obstructive stance of the Russian imperial power for the bulk of the second half of the century. Ironically, most of the early Finnish nationalist leaders had Swedish as their first language – in part they wanted to protect their position as the administrative class – and it was their endeavours that triggered a counter-nationalist Swedish backlash. Russification at the beginning of the twentieth century contributed to conjoining the 'two nationalisms' (although the point should not be exaggerated) and there is no doubt that Finns, whatever their first language, celebrated the victory of Hannes Kolehmainen at the 1912 Olympics. Abroad, Finland was already seen as a separate country. A rudimentary state had existed before the impact of cultural nationalism in the 1830s. There was a basic constitutional framework, a domestic Senate (government) with tax-raising powers and Alexander I convened a meeting of the Estates in Borgå (Porvoo) in 1809. Until halted by Russification, state-building proceeded rapidly from the 1860s with the introduction, *inter alia*, of a Finnish army and currency. At the same time, Mechelin's writings promoted the notion of a Finnish state abroad. Yet it needs to be emphasised that, although nationalism was in many ways a potent force, Finnish independence (i.e. the completion of the state-building process) owed far more to events in St Petersburg and in particular to the Bolshevik revolution in November 1917. The Finns simply seized an unforeseen opportunity and unilaterally declared themselves independent on 6 December 1917. At the beginning of the year they had no more envisaged complete independence than had the Estonians and other Baltic provinces of Russia, which took similar advantage of the crisis.

The March revolution in St Petersburg, which marked the demise of czarism, had significantly altered matters. Finland gained freedom of association and the right to strike, with the result that there developed a high level of civic mobilisation, within both the party organisations and the trade union movement. A public meeting in Suomussalmi church on 7 April 1917, attended by about 2,000 persons, mostly loggers and smallholders, supporting the Social Democrats and Agrarians respectively, went so far as to demand independence. As Reijo Heikkinen (1997) has commented, the peripheral location of Suomussalmi, far from the capital city, Helsinki, or the Russian capital, St Petersburg, doubtless nurtured the illusion of a weak central authority and the possibility of effective popular pressure. Yet when the Agrarian J. A. Heikkinen and clergyman F. Nordlund, who were authorised to convey the demand for independence to the 'Helsinki gentlemen', presented it to the Speaker of the Eduskunta, the Social Democrat Kullervo Manner, he is reputed to have replied, 'The idea is good, but its realisation rests with Hindenberg and God'! This was a reference to the fact that sections of the Finnish elite believed, or at least hoped, that a German victory in the First World War would facilitate the liberation of Finland from Russia.

In the event, the bourgeois Senate's declaration of independence on 6 December 1917 was opposed by the Social Democrats in the Eduskunta, whilst, mirroring developments in Russia, there followed a civil war and an ideological struggle for the soul of the newly independent Finnish state. Indeed, although Lenin recognised Finnish independence on 8 January 1918, he clearly hoped (and believed) that a socialist-controlled Finland would subsequently seek union with Bolshevik Russia. These early weeks of the new year were tense times and Gustav Mannerheim, a Swedish-speaking Finn, who had attained high rank in the imperial Russian army (see above), travelled to Vaasa in north-west Finland – where the Senate had relocated and the White headquarters would be based – on 18 January 1918 with a passport in the name of Gustaf Malmberg, a commercial traveller. This was because the train journey was dangerous, with Red Guards and Russian soldiers (who had not returned home) guarding communications (Jägerskiöld 1986: 49). Similarly, P. E. Svinhufvud, the chairman of the Senate (prime minister), escaped from the Red stronghold of Helsinki and with several colleagues seized an icebreaker, which took them to Tallinn in Estonia. They finally reached Vaasa on the Finnish coast on 24 March, by way of Germany. It was in fact German *Jäger* infantrymen who liberated Helsinki from the Reds and the political right then planned to install a German prince, Carl-Friedrich of Hesse, on the Finnish throne. In order to patch up relations with the British and French, Mannerheim was asked to go to London and Paris to try to make contact with the governments of the western powers. On 10 November 1918 he landed at Aberdeen, although, ironically, the next day the armistice between the belligerents was announced, ending the World War after more than four years of fighting (Jägerskiöld 1986: 69). It also ended the monarchists' plans and in 1919 the Eduskunta adoped a republican constitution.

Though the Finnish civil war ended in a White victory on 16 May 1918, the divisions and bitterness it generated pervaded the entire inter-war period (Upton 1980). It was not until 1938 that the Social Democrats attended the Independence Day parade. The Finnish civil war divided people in the same

village, even the same family. Moreover, although casualties were high on
both sides, more people lost their lives in prisons and in the executions that
followed than in the war itself. Significantly, 'civil war' is only one of four
terms used in Finnish to describe the conflict of spring 1918 – White sympa-
thisers invariably use the term 'freedom struggle' (*vapaussota*) – and when an
exhibition was opened in Lappeenranta at the beginning of 1997, so great
was the organiser's concern to come up with a neutral characterisation that
it was simply called 'War in Southern Karelia' ('Vuoden 1918 sotaa Etelä-
Karjalassa', *Karjala*, 23 January 1997). Even now there is a feeling that not
all the wounds have healed.

Nation and state in nineteenth-century Norway

Before the impact of cultural nationalism in the 1830s and 1840s and the
politicisation of the issue of the union with Sweden in the 1880s and 1890s,
Norway, like Finland, had the trappings of a proto-state. Indeed, the period
between 1814 and 1884 has been characterised by Jens Seip (1963) as the
'regime of officials', seventy years of centralised, bureaucratic rule inherited
from the era of Danish absolutism. Importantly, however, this domestic executive did not operate in isolation. A Norwegian constitution had been drafted by
the 'Eidsvoll men' during the 1814–15 interregnum and granted voting rights
which, for the time, were extremely liberal. Moreover, in contrast to practice
elsewhere in the Nordic region, the Eidsvoll constitution provided not for the
typical diet of estates but for a modern unicameral assembly, the Storting.
True, the Norwegian state-builders provided parliamentary checks and balances against a tyranny of the numerically preponderant peasants – 'the estate
of the most foolish' (*narragtigste ting*), as they were disparagingly referred to in
educated legal circles (Kaartvedt 1964: 174). This was achieved by requiring
the Storting to divide into two internal chambers when considering certain
laws, the lawyers in the smaller 'division', or Lagting, giving a final detailed
reading to measures emanating from the larger division, the Odelsting. This
'qualified unicameralism' or 'modified unicameralism' survived until 2007,
when a United Storting voted unanimously to abolish the Lagting after the
2009 general election. Indeed, the Lagting never functioned as a specialist
body of lawyers, and the extent to which it became party politicised seriously
undermined its capacity to check government legislation. Annual meetings of
the Storting took place from 1869.

Importantly, the transfer of Norway from Denmark to Sweden by the Treaty
of Kiel in January 1814 – the formal Act of Union was passed by the first
regular Storting in summer 1815 and enacted in identical form by the Swedish
Riksdag – by no means negated the work of the Eidsvoll men, although the
election of a Norwegian king, the Danish prince Christian Frederick, of course,
proved abortive. Only really the 'federative function' – that is, the direction

of foreign policy – was vested in the Swedish crown and for long periods the union with Sweden was regarded with indifference by ordinary Norwegians. Indeed, during the period of harmonious relations between the two countries in the middle of the nineteenth century, Norwegian public opinion may well have regarded the Swedish connection as an asset in relation to the possibility of Russian encroachment into northern Norway (Derry 1979: 234–5). Certainly, when in 1814 the Storting president (Speaker), W. F. K. Christie, led a deputation from Norway he addressed the Swedish king, Carl XIII, as his 'elected and acknowledged sovereign' and then declared to the assembly of Swedish dignitaries: 'You offer us the hand of a brother; we grasp it with an honest handshake and we shall never withdraw our hand' (Derry 1973: 16).

If, as in Finland, the new imperial link was for the most part unproblematic, the advent of cultural nationalism in Norway prompted a desire to dissolve the cultural residue of the previous imperial connection by divorcing the national language from Danish. The literary pre-eminence of Danish in Norway both before and after the break with Denmark needs emphasis. Danish was the written language in Norway until the middle of the nineteenth century: there was no printing press in Norway until the 1780s; no university until 1811 (Norwegian officials studied at the University of Copenhagen); and writers, too, moved to Denmark. The provincial capital, Christiania, named after the Danish king, was given a Norwegian K only in the 1890s and became Oslo only as late as 1928 (although a part of the capital with that name had always existed). However, in the 1830s and 1840s the force of cultural nationalism threw up three literary figures – Henrik Wergerland, Peter Christen Asbjørnsen and Jørgen Moe – who collected folk stories related to them by ordinary folk in a variety of Norwegian dialects. What they wrote was, in practice, Danish with 'Norwegianisms', the idea being to search for the *Volkgeist*, the true spirit of the nation. However, in a separate initiative, so to speak, Ivar Aasen in 1836 announced a plan for 'an independent and national language' based on a synthesis of rural dialects, chiefly from western Norway and ostensibly closest to Old Norse, and this construct was named Landsmål. In the late 1850s, a second able exponent of Landsmål was the journalist and poet Aasmund Olavsson Vinje, who employed it for his new periodical, *Dølen*, or *Dalesman* (Derry 1979: 235). By the late 1860s, after Knud Knudsen had systematised Riksmål, a Norwegianisation of the standard language of the educated elite, a situation of effective bilinguality obtained in Norway. Riksmål was Danish in orthography and structure, but east Norwegian in pronunciation and vocabulary. The two 'languages' had contrasting constituencies: Landsmål dominated in the countryside, whereas Riksmål prevailed among the educated urban classes. Both were literary languages, the population speaking dialects closer to one or the other. The two, however, sought to develop a Norwegian identity – a national identity – by contrasting means: Landsmål (later Nynorsk) involved a radical 'bottom up' approach of deriving legitimacy from the grass roots; Riksmål worked, so to speak, more gradually, from the top down.

Oscar II succeeded his brother Karl XV as King of Sweden–Norway in 1872, whilst the advent of annual sessions of the Storting three years earlier – in line with practice in the new bicameral Swedish Riksdag – led to the politicisation of the language question. For the nationalist Johan Sverdrup, in other words, annual sessions provided the means with which to achieve his goal of accountable parliamentary government in Norway (Jensen 1963: 118–31). In the 1880s Sverdrup formed Venstre, a Landsmål-based alliance between urban radicals and the large population of nationalist-minded farmers, which sought to bring the government (i.e. the Norwegian ministry) under the control of the Storting by requiring its members to take part in parliamentary debates (as in Sweden). Venstre was predicated on diffuse cultural and political opposition not only to the language but also to the very morality of the Establishment classes, and the language issue was integrally bound up with teetotalism and low-church revivalism. By the time Sverdrup formed Venstre, following victories in the 1879 and 1882 elections, Oscar II had vetoed the so-called Inclusion Bill three times (the Bill obliged the bureaucrats in the Norwegian ministry to participate in parliamentary debates). There were in fact rumours that the Swedish king was contemplating mobilising the army for a *coup d'état* against the parliamentary majority, and Venstre for its part organised a network of riflemen's associations to act as a popular militia against the regime of officials. Historians have even spoken of the risk of civil war. Ultimately, however, in 1884, the impeachment of the Høyre ministry led to a Venstre cabinet and obliged Oscar to concede the principle of ministerial responsibility. The Storting mural depicting the events of 2 August 1884 extols the introduction of parliamentarianism as the most significant development in Norway since the Eidsvoll constitution in 1814. Sverdrup is characterised as a brilliant debater and outstanding statesman and is referred to as 'the Gladstone of Norway' (Fuglum 1978).

Sverdrup also facilitated local ballots on the language to be used in schools; at the time, two-thirds of schools used Landsmål – mainly in western and southern Norway – but that represented only about 35 per cent of the population. When viewed in historical perspective, as Stein Rokkan (1966) observed, Landsmål formed an intrinsic element in a counter-culture embracing three mutually reinforcing cleavages – language, religion and teetotalism. We shall return to this in connection with our later discussion of the origins and development of the Nordic party systems (in part II of the book).

The attainment of responsible government – ministers accountable to parliament – in 1884 was a fundamental achievement of the nation-building process in Norway and also advanced the cause of state-building. The achievement of full independence followed peacefully in little more than two decades. The sequence of events began in December 1898, when the Norwegian parliament voted to remove the union symbol from the flag of the Norwegian merchant marine, something which Oscar II was obliged to sanction, since the Bill had gone through the Storting the requisite three times.

At the beginning of the twentieth century the principal divide in Swedish politics was between the Liberals and Social Democrats on the one hand, demanding universal voting rights, and various shades of Conservatives, on the other. The Conservatives sought a stronger defence system and opposed concessions to the Norwegians, some even favouring sending in troops. In the event, the Swedish coalition government headed by Christian Lundeberg, the Conservative leader of the First (Upper) Chamber of the Riksdag, which also contained the Liberal heavyweight Karl Staaff, reached agreement with the Norwegians at Karlstad, midway between Stockholm and Oslo, that the union would be dissolved. Any conflicts would be referred to the International Court of Justice at The Hague. The British *Daily Mail* sent out its war correspondent, Edgar Wallace, just in case, but the military preparations undertaken by both sides ceased (Ehrenmark 1975: 32). Indeed, in November 1914 the three kings of Denmark, Norway and Sweden met in Malmö to demonstrate the unity between the three countries.

Several factors combined to facilitate Norwegian independence in 1905. First, there was no significant body in Sweden willing to fight to maintain the union. Next, the belligerent forces of 'Great Swedish nationalism' in the 1890s failed to coalesce. Finally, there were leading figures on the Swedish right – for example Rudolf Kjellén and Harald Hjärne – who publicly doubted the wisdom of continuing the union. At the time there was much concern in nationalist circles in Sweden about the exodus of emigrants to the New World and the influx of Jewish pedlars, Russian saw sharpeners, Galician farm workers and Finnish lumberjacks. During the 1880s alone, about 325,000 Swedes emigrated to the United States. Interestingly, the Norwegians in the 1905 referendum demonstrated that constitutional monarchy was still regarded as the natural form of government, voting four to one in favour of having a king (Haakon VII) rather than a republic. Haakon VII was recruited from the Danish court (Greve 1983: 1). As Prince Carl of Denmark he was the thirty-three-year-old son of the Danish crown prince and princess, and his maternal grandfather was Carl XV of Sweden and Norway.

It might be added as a postscript that Norway remains officially bilingual and citizens have the right to send and receive official communications in their own language, though the language question had lost much of its political saliency by the 1950s. Today approximately 12 per cent of the Norwegian population has Nynorsk as its mother tongue and this is the official language in 114 communes (compared with 160 in which it is Bokmål/Riksmål and 158 which are linguistically neutral). The 'language question' can none the less still arouse strong feelings. The Oslo correspondent of *Helsingin Sanomat* has related how in the 1980s her father-in-law, a chemist in Fredrikstad, sent out a new employee to buy a book of stamps. When the messenger returned with stamps marked *Noreg*, the Nynorsk for 'Norway', the chemist was so incensed the employee was dispatched back to get stamps with *Norge*, the Bokmål version of 'Norway', on them. Moreover, in summer 2007 old animosities were aroused when Erling Mae, the leader of the Conservatives (Høyre) controlling the Oslo city council, proposed the abolition of compulsory Nynorsk in the city's schools. In the capital city area, Nynorsk may be loosely compared to 'compulsory Swedish' in Finnish schools, in that the majority of pupils do not understand why they should study it when they will probably never use it. Whilst Nynorsk proponents dismissed the Conservatives' proposal as election propaganda in the run-up to the autumn 2007 local government election, the language question has clearly retained some capacity to mobilise voters, especially in the Bokmål-dominated capital city.

Iceland: nationalism off the beaten track

When compared with the other Nordic 'colonies' or peripheries, the conditions for the rise of nationalism in nineteenth-century Iceland seemed less than propitious. The rise of nationalism in the 1830s and subsequent demands for political independence were based on a population of barely 60,000, which was overwhelmingly rural, being based on farming and fishing. Accordingly, even more than in the cases of Finland and Norway, Iceland did nothing to underwrite Ernest Gellner's (1983) hypothesis that nationalism is connected with the process of industrialisation and the concomitant development of a national bourgeoisie. It was not until the beginning of the twentieth century that the mechanisation of fishing took place.

Iceland was geographically distant from the European cultural mainstream and also, unlike Finland and Norway, physically removed from the imperial power, Denmark. In that respect it had much in common with the Faeroes and Greenland, along with Orkney, Shetland and the Hebrides. The contrast with the Northern and Western (Scottish) Isles, however, was striking, since in the latter the languages in use by the seventeenth and eighteenth centuries reflected the historical influence of the former imperial power (Denmark–Norway), the proximity of Scotland and, to an extent, earlier trade links with the defunct Hanseatic League. Certainly in the thirteenth century the Icelanders would have needed no interpreters in the Hebrides, since, whilst Gaelic was the dominant language, the leaders of society at least must have spoken fluent Norse (Smith 1990: 25–7). None of the Hebridean chiefs and kings who visited Norway is said to have had language difficulties. Most Shetlanders, moreover, still spoke a Norse dialect in 1700, but they could speak Scots just as readily and for 200 years the vocabulary of administration and religion in the islands had been Scots. Indeed, in the sixteenth and seventeenth centuries Shetland's relations with Scandinavia became increasingly tenuous after the impignoration of royal rights in the islands to Scotland in 1469 and its relationship with Scotland, formerly non-existent, grew correspondingly closer. In contrast to these developments, dialectical differences were insignificant in Iceland and, unlike the Shetlanders, who shifted from their Norse dialect, Norn, to Scots (English) during the eighteenth century, Icelandic was never seriously challenged by the imperial tongue, Danish. Hence there was no need for an elite-generated national language to be created and/or codified, and nor did a language conflict emerge in Iceland as in the cases of Finnish versus Swedish and Landsmål versus Riksmål in Norway.

Yet, largely inspired by Jón Sigurðsson, a philologist who lived all his adult life in Copenhagen – where he maintained contact with the generations of students who would become the future elites in Iceland – Iceland did not escape the influence of cultural nationalism (Karlsson 2000: 208). A group of intellectuals became interested in the country's popular culture, language and history, and Sigurðsson became the most prominent leader of the Icelandic independence movement about 1830. Sigurðsson wrote about two-thirds of the thirty volumes of the nationalist publication *Ný félagsrit*, which invoked the *Volkgeist* of Iceland's ancient heritage and a tradition of democracy and equality dating back to the commonwealth, and, after the abolition of royal absolutism in Iceland in 1848, sought to make a case for political autonomy in Iceland. Sigurðsson became a symbol of national identity and, as one representative of the Alþingi (resurrected by royal decree in 1843) put it: 'I have almost become tired of telling one person after another about you, including such details as how large your hands or feet are' (Karlsson 2000: 207). His nationalist publications circulated widely across the country and their extensive readership reflected in no small measure the high levels of literacy in Iceland during the nineteenth century. Significantly, unlike Germanisation in northern Slesvig and Russification in Finland at the turn of the twentieth century, nearly two centuries of Danish absolutism had not involved a sustained programme of Danicisation. In particular, there was a native class of officials – possibly numbering about twenty-five persons in the mid-nineteenth century – who were mainly well educated landowners, and the only real opposition to the independence movement came from the six 'royal members' of the Alþingi (appointed from the civil service), whose loyalties lay with the Danish crown. The Alþingi, it will be recalled, was restored in 1845 (Magnússon 1977: 131).

In mobilising the population around the nationalist cause, the 'myth of a Golden Age', in Anthony D. Smith's (1986) phrase, could be exploited. As noted in chapter 1, Iceland had been a free and independent commonwealth between 930 and 1264, when the epic sagas had been written. However, Gunnar Karlsson has emphasised indigenous social structural factors in explaining the emergence of nationalism in Iceland and especially the higher degree of social and geographical mobility among the Icelandic farming population than elsewhere in Scandinavia. Put another way, there was a relatively low level of differentiation within the agrarian structure, which made it possible to move from being a servant to become a tenant farmer, then an independent farmer and finally a large landowner. Karlsson (1995: 59) concludes:

It was easier and more natural for an Icelander to identify with his or her people than it was for most Europeans in the first half of the nineteenth century because the Icelander had so little else to identify with – no estate or class, no district or region.

Summing up, an embryonic administrative infrastructure, and certainly a native class of officials, mostly large farmers – though hardly a proto-state – existed in Iceland even before the impact of cultural nationalism in the 1830s. True, there was a limited attempt to centralise (Danicise) the Icelandic administration in 1871, when the Danish authorities established the office of governor general. But, as Gunnar Helgi Kristinsson has noted, the governors were torn between loyalty to the mother state (Denmark) and the need to accommodate the domestic power holders (mainly in parliament), as the national assembly, the Alþingi, acquired legislative powers in 1874. The governor's position was thus, as Iceland's last governor put it in 1904, 'that of a louse between two fingernails' (Kristinsson 1996: 446). In any event, the achievement of Home Rule in 1904 largely wiped the slate clean. A parliamentary form of government, with a ministry-based system of administration, followed in the wake of the victory of Danish parliamentarism in 1901, whilst at a stroke the Icelandic ministry in Copenhagen, the governorship in Reykjavík and the regional administration offices (*amt*) were abolished. In sum, in contrast to Finland and Norway, when the executive power finally passed into Icelandic hands, the bureaucracy was generally weak and unable to withstand the onslaught of patronage politics, which, beginning in the Home Rule era, burgeoned at the time of the Great Depression and the organisational development of the political parties in the 1930s (Kristinsson 1996). The achievement of Icelandic independence following a referendum in 1944 left a second outpost of the Danish empire, the Faeroe islands, themselves inspired by the Home Rule status accorded to Iceland in 1904, as a case in Hans Jacob Debes's (1995) submission of a 'stateless nation'.

The Faeroes and Greenland: stateless nations?

The pre-conditions for ethnic identification in the Faeroes were similar to those in Iceland. The Faeroes forms a distinct territory comprising seventeen inhabited islands and covering an area of 1,400 km^2 whose population shares a common spoken language and cultural awareness. As in Iceland, moreover, there was a small indigenous class of officials. Yet whilst a national consciousness grew from the mid-nineteenth century, Home Rule was not achieved until 1948. True, in 1901 Jóannes Patursson was elected Faeroese member of the Danish Folketing and proceeded to pursue a Home Rule programme predicated on a pragmatic and historical approach. Moreover, for decades there was a dispute over the status of the Faeroese language in schools, and in 1938 teachers gained the right to choose between Faeroese and Danish. Even so, until the 1970s Danish remained the exclusive language of the final (matriculation) examinations. Indeed, it was the advent of the Second World War that proved the catalyst for regional autonomy. During the war the Faeroes, under 'friendly' British occupation, governed themselves on the basis of a 'provisional constitution' passed by the islands' Lagting in May 1940. After the war it was not politically possible to return to the pre-war status of *amt* or administrative district, under the Danish crown. On 14 September 1946 a majority of the Faeroese voted for independence and secession from Denmark in a national plebiscite, eight decades after the first signs of Faeroese nationalism. But no Faeroese state was established: instead, in 1948 a majority in the Faeroese assembly approved legislation granting the islands Home Rule status as 'a self-governing community within the Danish state'. As Hans Jacob Debes (1995: 82) notes dolefully: 'The Greenlanders in the course of only about fifteen years of political struggle won as much political influence [via their Home Rule Act of 1979] as the Faeroese had gained over about half a century'.

Recently, to be sure, old separatist sentiments have been reinforced by a new 'Out of Denmark' movement, which has appealed in particular to the younger generation. Initially it mobilised support primarily by means of a petition claiming, *inter alia*, that the bank crisis of the early 1990s had been a Danish plot to acquire the natural resources of the Faeroes. In the mid-twentieth century the economy was essentially based on wool, as reflected in the axiom *føroysk ull – føroysk gull* – 'Faeroese wool, Faeroese gold'. Wool exports – the Faeroes competed mainly with Iceland – were subsequently complemented by the rise of the fishing industry and in particular exports of dried cod. At the beginning of the 1990s the (largely unexplained) disappearance of cod from the traditional fishing grounds, however, plunged the economy into crisis, unemployment reached 30 per cent, emigration to Denmark and the United Kingdom soared and the banks went bankrupt. The return of the cod facilitated economic recovery, whilst soundings indicating the prospect of massive off-shore reserves of oil and gas further fuelled demands for full independence from Denmark. However, a planned referendum on the issue was shelved in 2001 after Denmark insisted it would halt aid within four years if voters favoured the independence proposals. In 2007 the Danish grant amounted to 774 million Danish crowns (some £70 million), or nearly 7 per cent of the Faeroese gross domestic product, and Danish grants have contributed, among other things, to funding two underwater tunnels which, together with several bridges, connect six of the islands. The Social Democrat Joannes Eidesgaard continued as prime minister after elections on the islands in January 2008, heading a coalition which included the Independence Party and the Centre Party, both of which favour independence. However, the failure (thus far) to discover large commercially exploitable oil reserves has undercut demands for independence.

Unlike Iceland, Gellner's modernisation theory could be applied to Greenland, at least indirectly, in so far as the radical transformation of the post-war

Greenlandic economy threw up a relatively young Danish-speaking Inuit elite, which, demonstrating heightened political awareness, sought to nurture a distinct Inuit ethnic identity as a means of making the case for Home Rule. As Mark Nuttall (1994) has noted, whilst the Danish colonial attitude towards Greenland had once been 'isolationist and paternal', being designed to protect the Inuit hunting culture, this changed dramatically after the Second World War. In 1953 colonial status was abolished and Greenland became an integral part of the Danish kingdom. Substantial infrastructural investment from Copenhagen transformed Greenlandic society from one based primarily on small-scale subsistence hunting and fishing to a modern export-oriented economy. The growing divergence between the economic interests of Greenland and Denmark underpinned the increasing demand for Home Rule, however. In 1964 the first political party, the nationalist Inuit party, was formed. Greenlanders voted against joining the European Economic Community (EEC) in 1973 and were incensed by Danish concessions to multinational companies to explore for oil in the fishing grounds off the west coast of Greenland in 1974 (Sørensen 1995).

The Greenlandic elite did not have to create a national language. Danish policy had been designed to protect the indigenous language and a printing house established in the capital, Nuuk, during the 1850s was important for the development of Greenlandic as a written language. The monthly newspaper *Atuagagdliutit*, first published in 1861, performed a role similar to the Landsmål-based contemporary *Dølen* in Norway in providing an organ for the expression of Inuit culture. None the less, the case for a Greenlandic identity in the 1960s and 1970s was based on only one of the three Inuit language groups and in practice imposed it on the others. Kalaallisut, or West Greenlandic, which became the official language after Home Rule, was elevated above the languages of the Inughuit population of the far north around Thule and the Iit on the east coast. This programme of linguistic standardisation based on the use of West Greenlandic in the media and schools (Danish has been effectively reduced to use only in news summaries) was resented as a form of internal imperialism by the older generation of East Greenlanders, who would make their point by communicating with the West Greenlanders in Danish rather than West Greenlandic. In short, unlike the Icelandic and Faeroese cases, the co-existence of three distinct linguistic groupings in Greenland (plus Danish) made claims to a single ethnic identity largely wishful thinking – a case, in Benedikt Andersen's celebrated phrase, of 'imagined community'. If, as Nuttall (1994) contends, such ethno-political symbolism as the Greenlandic flag and national anthem has served to strengthen a Greenlandic national identity since Home Rule, Home Rule itself owed much less to the intrinsic merits of the nationalist case than to pressure on the Danes, particularly from the left-wing Siumut (Forward) Party. With the discovery of zinc deposits in the north and the likelihood of vast oil resources (Greenland is no longer on the economic periphery) Siumut is now pressing the case for full Greenlandic independence

(Fægteborg 1995). Moreover, the establishment in the 1990s of the University of Greenland will doubtless serve as an important training ground for the nationalist elite of the future. In the November 2005 election Siumut won ten of the thirty-one seats in the Greenlandic regional assembly and formed a coalition with the pro-independence left-wing Inuit Brotherhood (seven seats) and the centre-right Atassut (six). At present, Denmark allocates an annual block grant of 3 billion Danish crowns to Greenland, which is equivalent to about half its budget.

Åland: autonomous region rather than stateless nation

Unlike Siumut in Greenland, the case for full independence is not argued by any of the political parties in Åland, despite the fact that the islands, an autonomous province of Finland, have been governed by an Autonomy Act since 1922, have boasted the symbols of territorial solidarity in the shape of their own flag since 1954, their own postage stamps since 1984 and have as an overriding policy objective the strengthening of a sense of regional identity. Historic separatism, moreover, favoured joining Åland with Sweden rather than the achievement of full sovereignty. The Swedish-speaking Åland islands have long-standing links with Sweden. In 1239 Birger Jarl of Sweden went on a crusade to Finland and Åland became subject to the Swedish crown. Indeed, the Åland islands belonged to the kingdom of Sweden until the latter was forced to relinquish both Finland and Åland to Russia in 1809 (Dreijer 1982). Åland then became part of the Grand Duchy of Finland. When the Russian empire began to disintegrate, a secret meeting was held at the Åland Folk High School in Finnström in August 1917, at which representatives of all the Åland districts resolved to work for reunion with Sweden. This aim was communicated to the king and government of Sweden and was backed by a mass petition underwritten by an overwhelming majority of the resident adult population. The newly independent Finnish republic, however, opposed Åland separatism and instead the Eduskunta passed an Autonomy Act in 1920, which at that stage the Ålanders were unwilling to accept. Ultimately, the whole matter was referred to the League of Nations, which, in June 1921, ruled that Finland should have sovereignty of the Åland islands. The Åland assembly convened for the first time on 9 June 1922, which became Åland's Autonomy Day (Johansson 1982).

Nowadays Åland is an autonomous, demilitarised, neutral and monolingual Swedish-speaking province of Finland. The regional assembly (Landsting) and regional executive (Landskapstyrelse) have legislative powers in the fields of education and culture, health, the promotion of industry, internal communications, local administration and the police force. There is a deeply entrenched concept of regional citizenship on the islands, bestowed either by birth or by a five-year period of continuous residence, and citizens of Åland are exempt from military service. Only Finnish citizens, however, can acquire Åland citizenship. Unlike the Faeroes and Greenland, since 1995 Åland has been a self-governing region within the EU. The so-called 'Åland protocol' enshrined exceptions to EU law in respect of regional citizenship, which, it is accepted, remains a prerequisite for owning and holding real estate in Åland and conducting business there. Moreover, unlike practice elsewhere in the EU, only Åland citizens have the right to participate in local elections.

Drawing together the threads of our brief review of nation-building in the Nordic 'colonies' in the nineteenth century and beyond, it is evident, as discussed in chapter 1, that the region boasts a wide diversity of spoken languages. In the hands of educated elites, vernacular languages (often following a process of systematisation and formalisation) provided the principal element in an attempt to construct a national, ethnic or regional identity and in turn to deploy it as a means of legitimising political claims – claims to independence or a significant measure of independence (i.e. Home Rule). Often the 'national identity' was more fiction than fact and people identified mainly with their local area, as is graphically exemplified by our opening quotation. Identity-building often involved, too, the imposition of one dialectical form on the rest and so, in prompting a counter-nationalist backlash, could prove socially divisive. Nationalist claims were pursued by proto-parties or movements – from the Finnish Suomalainen puolue to Siumut – and the early party system in the 'colonies' was both precipitated and organised around the 'national question'. Ultimately, however, the success of nationalist claims was contingent on exogenous factors and changes in the circumstances of the imperial power – the revolution in Russia, along with the aftermath of the First and Second World Wars.

Summary

1.   The aim of the present chapter has been to provide a thematic background to the present five-plus-three arrangement – that is, five nation states and three Home Rule territories – in the Nordic region, using the twin concepts of nation-building, that is, the development of a sense of national identity, and state-building, that is, the process of achieving independence. By definition, the last-mentioned process is incomplete in the Home Rule territories, although there are elements on the North Atlantic periphery, in Greenland and the Faeroes, that seek full sovereignty.

2.   The post-Napoleonic equation was 'two-plus-six', that is, two imperial and six peripheral states. Three territorial changes were by-products of the Napoleonic Wars: Norway was transferred from Denmark and conjoined in a personal union with the Swedish crown; Sweden lost Finland, which in 1809

became a Grand Duchy of the Russian empire; and as a consolation for losing Norway, Denmark, which backed the wrong horse in the Napoleonic Wars, retained Iceland, Greenland and the Faeroes.

3.   Norway and Finland were relatively independent and the process of state-building was already quite well advanced following the territorial changes associated with the Napoleonic Wars. True, in both cases the federative function (foreign policy direction) and the supreme executive power rested with the imperial authority (the Swedish crown and the Russian czar). But, otherwise, the two 'colonies' of Norway and Finland could be regarded as Home Rule territories with constitutions, national assemblies, legal systems and autonomous tax-raising powers. In Norway the 1814–15 interregnum triggered significant institutional modernisation, with the Eidsvoll constitution prescribing a uni-cameral assembly and liberal franchise arrangements. In Finland the extent of state-building was reflected, as Alapuro (1988) highlights, in the hybrid character of the Finnish nationalist movement, which combined a west European element – support for the existing state and administrative apparatus – and an east European element – the search for liberation from a ruling class which spoke another language. In Iceland, in contrast, whilst there was a very small native class of officials, that is, a provincial administration comprising mainly larger farmers, it was not possible to speak of a proto-state.

4.   The Nordic region was affected by cultural nationalism from the 1830s onwards and this emphasised the primacy of language as the heart and soul of the nation. An elite of writers and poets began to focus on the language spoken by ordinary people. At the time, there was no literary language of the people – no written Norwegian or Finnish – but a diversity of spoken regional dialects. The nationalist elites set out by degrees to create one. Indeed, the significance of Elias Lönnrot in the Kalevala in Finland in 1835 and contemporaries such as P. C. Asbjørnsen in Norway was that they wrote up collections of folk stories related by ordinary people in a variety of dialects and thus began the systematisation and standardisation of a national language.

5.   The language of the *literati*, the educated classes and those officials running the colonial administration – the Establishment – was the language of the previous imperial connection, that is, Danish in Norway and Swedish in Finland, and by the second half of the nineteenth century the former imperial tongue, albeit in the case of Riksmål heavily 'Norwegianised', and the systematised national language vied for position. The language conflict was politicised with the advent of regular parliamentary sessions in Finland from 1863 and Norway from 1869.

6.   Accordingly, in the two mainland Nordic 'colonies' of Norway and Finland, the first proto-parties emerged around the 'national question', that is, the language question, in the 1870s and 1880s. The left, directly to translate the Norwegian party Venstre, promoted the political claims of those speaking the national language, Landsmål and Finnish, whilst the right, to translate the Norwegian Høyre, defended the language of, and had clear connections with,

the previous imperial linkage (Riksmål and Swedish) and worked to protect the political pre-eminence bound up with it. In the Norwegian case, the struggle was for control of domestic government. In the Finnish case, Finnish nationalism fuelled Swedish counter-nationalism.

7.   Importantly, therefore, unlike Denmark and Sweden, the embryonic party systems in Norway, Finland and indeed Iceland emerged around an issue of 'high politics' – the national question – rather than economic issues relating to the protection of industry and agriculture, free trade, and so on. It was 1916, more than a decade after the achievement of Home Rule, before two class parties, the farmer-based Progressive Party and the blue-collar Social Democrats, emerged in Iceland. However, the nineteenth-century (non-socialist) left proved inherently unstable and the nationalist parties of the 1870s and 1880s had developed liberal splinter groups (e.g. the Young Finns) by the turn of the twentieth century, that is, before the completion of the state-building process. In Finland in 1906 the superimposition of mass democracy on the national question prompted the counter-nationalist Swedish Party (now working to defend the constitutional rights of the Grand Duchy) to mobilise the newly enfranchised minority-language speakers in a disparate alliance, which, as the Swedish People's Party (Svenska folkpartiet), has become a permanent feature of the Finnish party landscape. Apart from it and Venstre, which in 2005 had ten members elected to the 169-seat Storting (with 4.4 per cent of the national vote), the only other historic nationalist party left in the region is the Icelandic Independence Party. This was the successor to a Home Rule Party founded in 1907, and in the 2007–11 parliamentary session it was the leading party, with twenty-five of the sixty-three seats in the Alþingi.

8.   The impact of cultural nationalism in the Nordic 'colonies' was significant. The period saw the creation and standardisation of a national language and its promotion through basic elementary schooling, newspapers and in official communications. In a significant sense, the proto-state was 'nationalised', with the adoption of national currencies, flags and so on, and the creation of standing armies. In Norway the government was placed under national control in 1884, in the sense that it passed into the hands of a party representing the popular majority. (Admittedly there were still key elements of the nation, including all women, tenants, industrial and agricultural workers, who did not yet have the vote.) Clearly, this 'nationalisation' process in Norway and Finland was considerably facilitated by the fact that both countries were left alone for long periods. Equally clearly, Russification at the beginning of the twentieth century threatened to reverse the gains of the previous century. If Russification mobilised Finns around the national question and the czar's October Manifesto in 1905 (following Russia's defeat by Japan) facilitated the 'nationalisation' of electoral politics in Finland, with the introduction of universal suffrage, it was ultimately the collapse of czarism and the Bolshevik revolution in St Petersburg which created the conditions for Finnish independence.

9. Twentieth-century history teaches that the creation and recognition of new states has had less to do with the intrinsic merits of nationalist claims than with propitious external circumstances, political expediency and great-power perceptions. Marketing the new 'product' has also been important, and in this context the writings of the jurist Leo Mechelin were invaluable in promoting the case for Finnish independence from the mid-nineteenth century onwards. The nationalist J. V. Snellman, the architect of the Finnish currency, whose bronze statue (with the damage to its base from Soviet bombs in 1939 still evident) stands outside the Bank of Finland, was another at that time to be concerned with the image of Finland abroad (Snellman 1996).

References

Alapuro, Risto (1988) *State and Revolution in Finland*, University of California Press: Berkeley, CA.

Arter, David (1978) *Bumpkin Against Bigwig. The Emergence of a Green Movement in Finnish Politics*, Tampere University: Tampere.

Arter, David (1996) *Parties and Democracy in the Post-Soviet Republics*, Dartmouth: Aldershot.

Debes, Hans Jacob (1995) 'The formation of a nation: the Faroe Islands', in Sven Tägil (ed.), *Ethnicity and Nation Building in the Nordic World*, Hurst: London, pp. 63–84.

Derry, T. K. (1973) *A History of Modern Norway, 1814–1972*, Clarendon Press: Oxford.

Derry, T. K. (1979) *A History of Scandinavia*, Allen & Unwin: London.

Dreijer, Matts (1982) 'Ålandsrörelsens uppkomst, utveckling och mål', in Lars Ingmar Johansson (ed.), *Åland i Utveckling*, Ålands landsting: Mariehamn, pp. 9–31.

Ehrenmark, Torsten (1975) *Ingenting att skratta åt*, Askild & Kärnekull: Avesta.

Engman, Max (1995a) 'Finns and Swedes in Finland', in Sven Tägil (ed.), *Ethnicity and Nation Building in the Nordic World*, Hurst: London, pp. 179–216.

Engman, Max (1995b) *Petersburgska vägar*, Schuldts: Loviisa.

Fægteborg, Mads (1995) 'Det grønlandske hjemmestyre', in *Självstyre*, special issue of *Nordisk Kontakt*, 10, pp. 25–37.

Fuglum, Per (1978) 'Norge i stöpeskjeen, 1884–1920', in Knut Mykland (ed.), *Norges Historie 12*, Cappelens: Oslo.

Garver, Bruce M. (1978) *The Young Czech Party 1874–1901, and the Emergence of a Multi-party System*, Yale University Press: New Haven, CT.

Gellner, Ernest (1983) *Nations and Nationalism*, Oxford University Press: Oxford.

Greve, Triv (1983) *Haakon VII of Norway. Founder of a New Monarchy*, Hurst: London.

Haavikko, Paavo (1991) 'State and identity', in *Books from Finland 2*, Helsinki University Library: Helsinki, pp. 89–92.

Heikkinen, Reijo (1997) 'Korpikansa isänmaan asialla', *Helsingin Sanomat*, 21 April.

Hobsbawm, E. J. (1990) *Nations and Nationalism Since 1780. Programme, Myth and Reality*, Cambridge University Press: Cambridge.

Jägerskiöld, Stig (1986) *Mannerheim. Marshal of Finland*, Hurst: London.

Jensen, Magnus (1963) *Norges Historie: Unionstiden 1814–1905*, Universitetsforlaget: Oslo-Bergen.

Johansson, Lars Ingmar (ed.) (1982) *Åland i Utveckling*, Ålands landsting: Mariehamn.

Jussila, Osmo (1989) 'Finland from province to state', in Max Engman and David Kirby (eds), *Finland. People, Nation, State*, Hurst: London, pp. 85–101.

Kaartvedt, Alf (1964) 'Fra Riksforsamlingen til 1869', in *Det Norske Storting gjennom 150 år*, vol. 1, Gyldendahl Norsk Forlag: Oslo, pp. 49–513.

Karlsson, Gunnar (1995) 'The emergence of nationalism in Iceland', in Sven Tägil (ed.), *Ethnicity and Nation Building in the Nordic World*, Hurst: London, pp. 33–62.

Karlsson, Gunnar (2000) *The History of Iceland*, University of Minnesota Press: Minneapolis, MN.

Kirby, David (1995) *The Baltic World, 1772–1993. Europe's Northern Periphery in an Age of Change*, Longman: London.

Klinge, Matti (1996) *Finlands historia*, vol. 3, *Kejsartiden*, Schildts: Helsinki.

Kristinsson, Gunnar Helgi (1996) 'Parties, states and patronage', *West European Politics*, 19 (3), pp. 433–57.

Magnússon, Sigurdur A. (1977) *Northern Sphinx*, Hurst: London.

Nuttall, Mark (1994) 'Greenland: emergence of an Inuit homeland', in Minority Rights Group (ed.), *Polar Peoples. Self-determination and Development*, Minority Rights Publications: London, pp. 1–21.

Pohls, Maritta (1997) 'Eveliina Ala-Kulju ja Hilma Räsänen – kaksi maalaisnaista eduskunnassa', in *Yksi Kamari – Kaksi Sukupuolta. Suomen eduskunnan ensimmäiset naiset*, Eduskunnan kirjasto: Helsinki, pp. 242–61.

Polvinen, Tuomo (1995) *Imperial Borderland. Bobrikov and the Attempted Russification of Finland, 1898–1904*, Hurst: London.

Rokkan, Stein (1966) 'Numerical democracy and corporate pluralism', in Robert Dahl (ed.), *Political Opposition in Western Democracies*, Yale University Press: New Haven, CT, pp. 70–115.

Seip, J. A. (1963) *Fra embedsmannsstat til ettpartistat*, Universitetsforlaget: Oslo.

Smith, Anthony D. (1986) *The Ethnic Origins of Nations*, Oxford University Press: Oxford.

Smith, Brian (1990) 'Shetland, Scandinavia, Scotland, 1800–1700: the changing nature of contact', in Grant G. Simpson (ed.), *Scotland and Scandinavia, 800–1800*, John Donald: Edinburgh, pp. 25–37.

Snellman, J. V. (1996) *Samlade arbeten*, vol. VIII, Edita: Helsinki.

Sørensen, Axel Kjær (1995) 'Greenland: from colony to Home Rule', in Seven Tägil (ed.), *Ethnicity and Nation Building in the Nordic World*, Hurst: London, pp. 85–105.

Upton, Anthony F. (1980) *The Finnish Revolution, 1917–18*, University of Minnesota Press: Minneapolis, MN.

Vihavainen, Timo (1997) '"Tsarismin kausi' ja ruotsalainen vaihtoehto – eurointegraation peruutuspeilistä katsoen', *Helsingin Sanomat*, 4 May.

Zetterberg, Seppo (1986) *Viisi laukausta senaatissa*, Otava: Helsinki.

Part II

Parties in developmental perspective

3

The emergence of the Scandinavian party system(s)

The Swedish party system has been the simplest in any of the democracies. In no other country has the basic left–right scale accounted for so much of the party structure and electoral behaviour.

(Hans Bergström, 1991: 8)

On 24–27 April 1997 at the Radisson SAS Hotel in Bergen, a conference was organised to mark the thirtieth anniversary of the publication of Seymour Lipset and Stein Rokkan's pioneering volume *Party Systems and Voter Alignments*. In their seminal introduction to the book, Lipset and Rokkan (1967) analyse in a developmental perspective the nature and evolution of the cleavage structure underpinning the emergence by about 1930 of the basic West European party systems. This third chapter opens with a brief presentation of the Lipset and Rokkan framework and proceeds to ask: how relevant is their model of the building of party systems in Europe to the Scandinavian experience? How useful is it to an understanding of the structuring of the modern party families and the configuration of the party systems that had evolved in the Nordic region by the end of the 1920s?

Several authors, notably Sten Berglund and Ulf Lindström (1978), have referred to the crystallisation after the historic period of party-building from the 1880s to the 1920s of a basic five-party Scandinavian party system model. The second part of this chapter presents the basic features of this model, with Sweden as the prototype. The principal question is: what are the basic characteristics of the five-party Scandinavian model and how well does Sweden fit the ideal type? The final section of the discussion explores whether there were significant deviations from the model that should be taken into account. It is argued that Finland and Norway diverge(d) from the five-party Scandinavian model, in that not all the parties have been easy to locate on a simple left–right continuum in the manner described in our opening citation from Hans Bergström. The ethno-regionalist Swedish People's Party in the former country and the confessional Christian People's Party in the latter reflect the existence of long-standing political cleavages based on language and religion.

Lipset and Rokkan on party-building: the four formative revolutions

Lipset and Rokkan viewed the main conflict lines moulding the party systems of Western Europe as the increment of four historic revolutions, which will be presented briefly in chronological order. First, there was the *religious revolution* and in particular the legacy of the Reformation in the sixteenth century. In those areas where the impact of the Reformation was partial, a church–state cleavage gave rise at the party-building phase to parties of both Catholic and Protestant denominations. The *de facto* division of the newly unified Germany after 1871 into a Protestant, Prussian-dominated north – which controlled the state and under Bismarck engaged in a *Kulturkampf* against Catholics – and Catholic 'Third Germany' – that is, Bavaria and the 'deep south' – is a case in point (Smith 1982: 13–14). Denominational divisions were also at the heart of the cleavage structure of Dutch party politics, which Arend Lijphart (1975) characterises as *Verzuiling* ('pillarisation'). However, in those countries where the impact of the Reformation was total – England, for example – or where the Reformation had no impact at all – the Catholic states such as France and Italy – religious parties did not usually emerge during the initial party-building phase.

Next, there was the *national revolution*. The impact of nineteenth-century nationalism in the European 'colonies' created a dominant (imperial) versus subject (colonial) culture cleavage and led to parties championing the nation against the foreign-controlled state. They emerged as far afield as Ireland in the 1870s and parts of the Austro-Hungarian empire following the 1867 partition. Thus, in the Bohemian provinces, both an Old Czech and a liberal Young Czech party had emerged by the beginning of the twentieth century (Garver 1978) and, as noted in chapter 2, in the Nordic 'colonies' of Norway, Finland and Iceland the first parties organised around the national question. In Norway the (non-socialist) left was a cultural nationalist party promoting, *inter alia*, the language of ordinary people (the nation), Landsmål, against the Danish-impregnated Riksmål, spoken by the educated Establishment in Oslo. In Finland, the Finnish Party (and subsequent liberal splinter Young Finns) opposed the political and economic power exercised by the elite speaking the minority Swedish language.

Then there was the *industrial revolution* and the commercialisation of both agricultural and industrial production. (Given Lipset and Rokkan's focus on the primary sector, the term 'industrial revolution' is perhaps somewhat misleading.) In any event, conflict was generated between agriculturalists and industrialists over issues such as free trade and protection (Urwin 1980: 96–7). Imports of cheap grain from the Americas, Ukraine and Romania into western Europe in the 1870s prompted demands for agricultural protection and in the Danish case led to a wholesale shift to dairy production. In France the Méline tariff of 1892 proved a retrogressive measure and petrified agriculture for over half a century; in Germany the Bund der Landwirte (a farmers' pressure group) campaigned with only limited success for measures of agricultural protection in the last quarter of the nineteenth century; and in Britain a proposal in 1906 from the Staffordshire Chamber of Commerce to found an interest-specific farmers' party proved stillborn (Arter 1978). In areas where agriculture was not really commercialised, a rural–urban cleavage spawned peasant parties. These were prevalent in central and eastern Europe between the wars and led to the organisation of several Green Internationals in Prague from the 1930s onwards.

Finally, there was the *proletarian revolution*. The emergence of a numerically significant industrial working class created a conflict involving workers versus owners and produced the conditions for the emergence of social democratic labour parties based in varying measure on Marxist ideology. The timing of the emergence of social democratic labour parties varied – in Britain, the most 'proletarianised' country in western Europe, the Labour Representation Committee (LRC) was not created until 1900, later than the social democratic parties in the relatively rural Scandinavia; their power strategies varied – in Germany, for example, from the revolutionary Spartacists to the Kautskyite centrists and Bernsteinian gradualists; and most had as their immediate object the completion of mass democracy and worked together with one of the 'internally created parties' (in Duverger's 1964 term), the Liberals in particular, to achieve it. The attainment of universal suffrage, particularly when coupled with the introduction of proportional representation, in turn facilitated the breakthrough of the social democrats as mass-based parliamentary parties.

The effect of a fifth revolution, not singled out by Lipset and Rokkan, the Bolshevik revolution in St Petersburg in November 1917, was to split the socialist left into social democratic and communist camps and create an anti-system radical left in European politics. In Hungary under Belá Kun and in Bavaria under Kurt Eisner, short-lived communist-style regimes were set up, whilst in bourgeois circles across western Europe the insidious 'red peril' – creeping communism – was viewed with real consternation. Membership of the Comintern was a pre-condition for acquiring the designation 'communist party' and in the aftermath of the First World War the social democratic labour parties agonised over their future direction. In some cases, notably in France, a majority defected and joined the Comintern, leaving Léon Blum, the leader of the French section of the Workers' International, to guard *la vieille maison*.

A brief application of Lipset and Rokkan's model in the Nordic context

How important were Lipset and Rokkan's historic revolutions for the moulding of the Nordic party systems? Taking them briefly in turn, the impact of the religious revolution, that is, the Reformation, was total in Scandinavia and the church–state cleavage was not a salient factor in the process of party-building before 1930. True, various strains of low-church revivalism – groups like the Laestadians in northern Finland and Sweden, the Haugians in Norway and the Grundtvigians in Denmark – created a picture of considerable pietistic pluralism within the confines of the Evangelical Lutheran Church in the last quarter of the nineteenth century and religious differences within the revivalist camp were to a degree party politicised (Madeley 1977). But the main point is that numerically significant religious parties did not form part of the basic Scandinavian party system model as it had emerged by 1930. A miniscule and non-socialist Christian Workers' Party which contested elections in Finland between 1907 and 1919 – winning at best 2.8 per cent of the poll in 1909 – in no sense vitiates this statement.

The national revolution had been completed by the achievement of independence in Norway in 1905 and Finland in 1917, with the result that those nineteenth-century parties that had formed around the national question either regrouped with new names – Conservatives, Liberals and so on – or sought in a variety of ways to modernise their appeal. This was by no means easy. In Norway the Right (Høyre) had represented the continuities with the Danish culture of the educated classes and had defended the Swedish king and his officials in the constitutional struggle of the 1880s. Shortly after the First World War came a distinct change in orientation. Yet, as Rokkan (1967: 395) observed, 'in contrast to the British Conservative Party, the Right in Norway, as in the other Scandinavian countries, was not able to bring about an alliance of urban and rural elites and to create the basis for a broad national movement'. The one nationalist party to survive the achievement of full independence (in 1944) and prosper as a broad catch-all party of the centre-right has been the Icelandic Independence Party.

The cleavage generated by the industrial revolution, that is, the conflict between the agrarian and urban industrial interests, was crucial in shaping the nascent Nordic party systems, and the twin impact of mass democracy and proportional representation in the first two decades of the twentieth century gave rise to Agrarian Parties in Finland (1906), Norway (1915) and Sweden (1921) and to farming-oriented parties in Denmark – where Venstre (sometimes translated as Agrarian Liberals) gained over half the vote in rural Jutland in 1920 – and Iceland – where the Progressive Party, formed in 1916, established itself as the leading non-socialist party between the wars in the small-farming areas in the north and east of the country, in which the co-operative movement was firmly rooted (Kristjánsson 1978: 17–18). Gunnar Helgi Kristinsson in fact has noted that it was formed as a farmer's party (Kristinsson 2001: 133). Though the mechanisation of the forest industry and the subsequent export of timber products betokened the penetration of capitalism into the countryside by the 1870s, the Scandinavian Agrarians were predominantly parties of family-size rather than large commercial farmers, although reconciling the needs of the two did strain cohesion, especially in the

Swedish and Norwegian parties. The Finnish party, in contrast, was closer to the type of peasant party found across central and eastern Europe.

The proletarian revolution did not, as in Britain and elsewhere in western Europe, create a dense industrial working class living and working in large factory towns and cities. True, in Denmark nearly two-thirds, and in Norway and Sweden almost three-fifths, of the economically active population were employed in the non-primary sectors by 1920, and in the Swedish case this figure had almost doubled since 1890. But the industrialisation process was none the less dispersed across the national territory, and was often centred in small, remote and isolated rural localities, and rural society had by no means been displaced by the time of the achievement of universal suffrage. The Scandinavian social democratic labour parties, in other words, could not simply rely on an industrial proletariat for electoral dominance, but were obliged to appeal to a disparate rural proletariat comprising loggers, crofters, agricultural labourers and fishermen. Denmark represented something of an exception, since the high level of farm ownership, coupled with the higher town-based population than elsewhere in the region, meant that social democracy emerged as far more of an urban phenomenon than in the other Scandinavian states (Elder *et al.* 1982: 37). Its electoral support also mirrored the relatively earlier impact of industrialisation in Denmark, since the Social Democratic Party drew upon a labour movement which developed in the context of small, independent unions rather than the larger-scale production in Norway and Sweden.

The communist revolution split the social democratic labour movement, although only in Norway, where the Labour Party was captured by Martin Tranmæl, did a majority split away in the fashion of French developments to join the Comintern. In 1921 a right-wing group left the Labour Party to found the Norwegian Social Democrats and two years thereafter, despite the best efforts of the Soviet Bolshevik Nikolai Bukharin on behalf of the Comintern, the Labour Party itself broke with Moscow, leaving the pro-Soviet minority to found the Norwegian Communist Party (Ersson 2005: 54–5). The latter gained 6 per cent of the vote at the 1924 general election but, following the Social Democratic Party merger with the Labour Party in 1927, the radical left in Norway steadily declined. It assumed sizeable proportions before 1930 (when, incidentally, it was proscribed) only in Finland, where, using the agency of the Socialist Workers' Party, the radical left polled 14.8 per cent in 1922.

In sum, it can be seen that, in addition to the communist revolution, three of the four historic revolutions described by Lipset and Rokkan as underpinning the emergence of the western European party systems had a significant impact in Scandinavia: the national revolution, the industrial revolution and the proletarian revolution. The impact of these three was greatest in the 'colonies', whilst in the metropolitan states of Denmark and Sweden only the two last-mentioned had a real effect on the shaping of the modern party systems.

Sweden as the prototype of the five-party
'Scandinavian party system' model

In Sweden the historic period of party-building from the 1880s to the late 1920s realised a basic two-plus-three configuration and a party system predicated on five '-isms': communism, social democracy, agrarianism, liberalism and conservatism. Restated, there was a bifurcated parliamentary left – a powerful Social Democratic Party flanked by a relatively weak but stable radical left – and a fragmented non-socialist camp comprising essentially town-based Liberal and Conservative parties and, as elsewhere in Scandinavia, a farm-based Agrarian Party. In 1932, for example, the left – the Social Democrats 41.7 per cent and Communists 8.3 per cent – totalled a combined 50.0 per cent of the poll and the non-socialists – Conservatives 23.5 per cent, Liberals 11.7 per cent and Agrarians 14.1 per cent – a combined 49.3 per cent.

When viewed in a comparative perspective, the Swedish party system has been characterised by two striking features. First, there has been its *unidimensionality*. Sweden has approximated most closely the five-party Scandinavian party system model described by Sten Berglund and Ulf Lindström (1978: 18), in which 'parties fall along one dimension (left–right) defined in economic terms'. Hans Bergström (1991: 8) has even insisted that the Swedish party system has been 'the simplest in any of the democracies', in that in no other country has the basic left–right scale accounted for so much electoral behaviour.

A second notable trait has been its *resilience*. Indeed, the Swedish party system became one of the most 'frozen' in Lipset and Rokkan's terms. From the advent of universal suffrage in 1921 until the 1988 general election, the same five parties were represented in the Riksdag. The composition of the Riksdag following the 1985 general election is set out in table 3.1. The combined left gained 51.2 per cent and the three non-socialist parties 46.8 per cent of the poll. Although the parties remain essentially the same, two changes of name need to be noted: the Communists became Left Communists in 1967, whilst, seeking to add an urban string to their bow, the Agrarians adopted the designation Centre Party in 1957. The Norwegian and Finnish parties followed suit in 1959 and 1965, respectively. In 1985 the Christian Democrats, to be sure, achieved parliamentary status when, following an electoral alliance (the legality of which was strongly contested by the Social Democrats) with the Centre Party, their leader, Alf Svensson, was returned to the Riksdag on a Centre slate for Jönköping (Arter 1986: 78–82). It was not until 1988, however, that a new party gained Riksdag representation under its own steam, so to speak, the Greens then clearing the 4 per cent electoral barrier imposed as part of constitutional reform in 1967–69.

Of the two main features of the Swedish party system, it is its resilience that warrants particular emphasis. Thus, whilst electoral instability increased markedly in the 1970s and voters swung sharply between the parties, especially the non-socialist parties, the historic party system manifested a high volatility

Table 3.1 *Party support at the 1985 Swedish general election*

Party	Percentage of vote	Riksdag seats
Non-socialists		
Conservatives[a]	23.6	86
Centre[b]	17.4	56
Liberals	5.8	21
Socialists		
Social Democrats	45.6	166
Left Communists	5.6	20
Others[c]	1.7	0
Total	*100.0*	*349*

[a] Strictly, the Moderate Unity Party (Moderata samlingspartiet).
[b] The Christian Democrat leader, Alf Svensson, was elected on a Centre list in the Jönköping constituency.
[c] Greens.
Source: Arter (1986: 79).

containment threshold. Electoral shifts, in short, were accommodated within the established party system and there was not the fragmentation of existing parties and/or creation of entirely new ones that occurred in Denmark and Norway at the 'earthquake elections' of 1973 (see chapters 5 and 6). For well over six decades, five parties and five parties only monopolised parliamentary representation. In the absence of cross-cutting cleavages and electorally significant parties based on religion or language, the unidimensionality of the Swedish party system, that is, the location of the five traditional parties along a single left–right dimension defined in economic terms, also stands out. Both the Liberals and the Agrarians have conventionally been regarded as centre-based parties in the sense of promoting the interests of small and medium-size entrepreneurs – the Agrarians in the countryside and the Liberals predominantly in the towns. None of the Swedish parties has lent itself to such simple definition as the Agrarian (Centre) Party, which was quintessentially a class party – a party of the farmers, by the farmers, for the farmers.

The stability of the basic contours of the Swedish party system until the late 1980s did not, of course, mean that the individual parties did not change and adapt or that the dynamics of inter-party competition remained constant. Perhaps the most striking feature of the five-party system during its 'frozen period' was that, whilst the relative electoral fortunes of the three non-socialist parties varied, the electoral and governmental supremacy of the Social Democrats prompted Giovanni Sartori (1976) to describe Sweden as 'one-party dominant'.

Among the non-socialist parties, the Liberals, who had split over the question of prohibition – unlike in Norway and Finland, voters at a consultative referendum in 1922 came out against such a draconian step – reunited twelve years later as the People's Party (Folkpartiet). The rider 'Sweden's Liberal Party' was not added until the 1980s. In 1948, having adopted a programme of 'social liberalism', emphasising their acceptance of the Social Democrats' welfare programme, the Liberals dislodged the Conservatives (before 1969 known as the Right Party) as the largest non-socialist grouping in the second Riksdag chamber and held that position (except for a brief interlude between 1958 and 1960) throughout the chairmanship of Bertil Ohlin, until 1966.

Against the backdrop of economic recession, the Agrarians entered into a red–green legislative alliance with the governing Social Democrats in 1933, which provided protection for the farmers in return for higher taxation to fund a social security programme for the working class. Three formal (executive) coalitions with the Social Democrats followed, in 1936, 1939 and 1951, the last, however, proving to be electorally disastrous. In 1956 the Agrarian vote plummeted to an unprecedented low of 9.4 per cent and the following year the party resigned from the coalition and proceeded to adopt the title Centre Party. The change of name was designed to attract the urban middle class, whilst the new programme in 1959 advocated a policy 'that promoted local self-government, decentralised construction of homes and industry and a rich provincial and local cultural life' (Hancock 1972: 122). The Agrarian/Centre Party was dominated throughout the period 1949–71 by its chairman, Gunnar Hedlund – by the mid-1960s he even spoke of the possibility of a merger of the Centre and Liberal parties – and in 1970, with the first election to the new unicameral Riksdag, the Centre became the largest non-socialist party, with 19.9 per cent of the vote (Hadenius 2003: 133).

The nineteenth-century Swedish Right (Höger) did not modernise its name until 1969, when it became the Moderate Unity Party (Moderata samlingspartiet, here more loosely translated as the Conservative Party). Initially opposed to the Social Democrats' welfare programme, ostensibly on cost grounds, the Conservatives modified their stance in the late 1940s. In large part, electoral necessity was the mother of this *volte-face*, since in 1948 the Conservatives lost their status as Sweden's largest non-socialist party. Internal division during Gunnar Hecksher's chairmanship (1961–65), when a younger progressive faction clashed with the 'old guard' over the formation of a united non-socialist electoral front (which Hecksher favoured), led to the creation of a programme committee under the new chairman, Yngve Holmberg, and ultimately to a new programme in 1969. This restated the party's commitment to private ownership and the market economy but also asserted the case for social action to deal with issues of concern, including the preservation of the ecological balance. Two electoral setbacks, in the 1966 local government election and the 1968 general election, however, led to Holmberg's replacement by Gösta Bohman in autumn 1970 (Albinsson 1986: 81–103).

The historic fragmentation of the non-socialist forces in Sweden contributed in some measure, of course, to sustaining the Social Democrats in office and by the mid-1960s increasingly overt recognition of the need for non-socialist co-operation – that is, a united front – began to influence the dynamics of party competition. Put another way, in their concern to end the long-term Social Democratic hegemony, the three opposition parties acknowledged with varying degrees of enthusiasm the need to present a cohesive non-socialist alternative. However, deep-seated suspicions and rivalries, and the perceived need to maintain distinct electoral profiles, complicated the task. During the winter 1965–66 Riksdag session, the non-socialist parties announced a moratorium on intra-bloc conflict – the so-called *Borgfred* – and in June 1966 the Liberals and Centre published a joint programme entitled Middle Co-operation (Hancock 1972: 136–8). But these two parties were conspicuously more industrious in seeking non-socialist co-operation than the Right/Conservatives (which, especially under Hecksher, were deeply divided on the issue), although the Right's adoption of a new name and programme in 1969 reduced to a degree the ideological distance separating the three non-socialist parties.

Despite the tripartite structure of the non-socialist forces, the Social Democrats did not become the dominant electoral and governing party in Sweden until after the completion of the historic phase of party-building and the 'freezing' of the European party systems, which Lipset and Rokkan date at around 1930. However, the Social Democrats quickly distanced themselves from the orthodox Marxism of their original programme and pursued a policy of ideological pragmatism. This, coupled with the party's willingness to co-operate with the non-socialist parties, its commitment to economic growth as the basis of social welfare and its emphasis on the national symbolism of the 'people's home' (*folkhemmet*), enabled the Social Democrats to expand beyond their core working-class constituency to achieve a broad-based appeal (Misgeld *et al.* 1992). The Social Democrats never fell below one-third of the vote in general elections after 1922 and at the final election to the Riksdag's second (lower) chamber in 1968 – the so-called 'Erlander election' because the Social Democratic prime minister had made it clear beforehand that this would be his last as party leader (Esaiasson 1990: 252) – the party gained an absolute plurality of the poll (see table 3.2). In 1932 the Social Democrats assumed the reins of government and (except for three months in 1936) held them continuously until 1976. Moreover, the moderation and continuity embodied in three long-serving chairmen, Hjalmar Branting (1907–25), Per Albin Hansson (1926–46) and Tage Erlander (1946–69), did much to make the party acceptable to a broad cross-section of voters.

The smallest of the five historic Riksdag parties, the Communists, achieved their best inter-war vote at the 1932 general election, when, in the depths of economic recession, they polled 8.3 per cent. This rose to 10.3 per cent in 1944 but fell back to 6.3 per cent four years later and did not exceed 5 per

Table 3.2 *Elections to the Swedish Riksdag's Second Chamber, 1944–68 (%)*

Year	Conservatives[a]	Agrarian/ Centre	Liberals	Social Democrats	Communists
1944	15.9	13.6	12.9	46.6	10.3
1948	12.3	12.4	22.8	46.1	6.3
1952	14.4	10.7	24.4	46.1	4.3
1956	17.1	9.4	23.8	44.6	5.0
1960	16.5	13.6[b]	17.5	47.8	4.5
1964	13.7	13.4	17.1	47.3	5.2
1968	12.9	15.7	14.3	50.1	3.0[c]

[a] Strictly speaking, the Right (Höger) until 1969 and Moderate Unity Party thereafter.
[b] The Agrarian Party changed its name to Centre Party in 1957.
[c] The Communists became Left Party Communists in 1967.
In 1964, local electoral alliances of two or more of the main non-socialist parties gained 1.8 per cent of the national poll and 2.6 per cent in 1968. But at no point between 1944 and 1968 did support for other parties exceed 2.0 per cent of the national vote.
Source: Sydow (1989: 326–7).

cent in any general election between 1948 and the shift to unicameralism in 1970. The party's traditional support derived principally from urban industrial workers, together with timber and mining workers in the peripheral north (Norrbotten). During the Cold War the Communist leadership had a marked nationalist orientation, supporting the Soviet Union in its foreign policy statements but promoting a 'popular front' strategy of co-operation with the Social Democrats in domestic affairs. At crucial junctures the Communists provided minority Social Democratic governments with tactical support, although for their part the Social Democrats eschewed Communist overtures for formal electoral and/or political co-operation (Widfeldt 1997: 92). In the 1960s, under the influence of 'new left' thinking, and led by a new chairman, Carl Hermansson, who was elected in 1964, the Swedish Communists sought to chart an ideological course similar to the Socialist People's Party in Denmark, emphasising their independence from Moscow. A new programme was adopted in summer 1967 which propagated a decentralised model of socialism in which public ownership of major companies and credit institutions would be dispersed among the state, provincial assemblies, local communes and producer and consumer co-operatives (Hadenius 2003: 133). The party picked up support in the mid-1960s, but dropped sharply to 3.0 per cent in 1968, following the Soviet invasion of Czechoslovakia.

Figure 3.1 presents a genealogy of the Swedish party system from the late nineteenth century to the shift to unicameralism in 1970.

Figure 3.1 *The genealogy of the Swedish five-party system from the late nine-teenth century to 1970.*

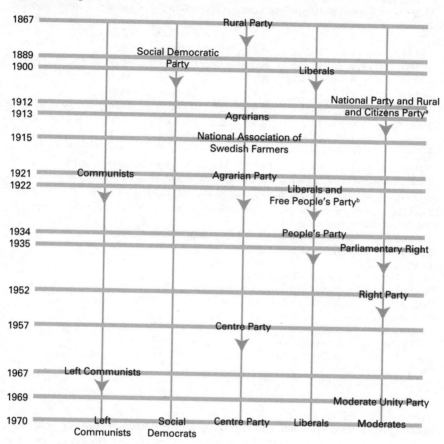

[a]The National Party (Nationella partiet) was based in the upper house and the Rural and Citizens Party (Lantmanna- och borgarepartiet) in the lower house (Second Chamber) of the Riksdag.
[b]In 1922 the Liberals split into an urban group headed by Eliel Löfgren and a majority prohibitionist grouping, the Free People's Party, under Carl Gustaf Ekman.

Deviations from the Swedish prototype in the Nordic region

Minor deviation in Denmark

Outside Sweden, there have been historic variations on the five-party model. Thus, by 1905, the four 'old parties' that have dominated Danish politics had emerged. As in Sweden, these included three non-socialist parties: the nineteenth-century Right became the Conservatives in 1915; an agrarian

Table 3.3 *Elections to the Danish Folketing, 1945–68 (%)*

Year	Cons	SocDems	SocLibs	Libs	SlesvigP	Comms	SocPP	Others
1945	18.2	32.8	8.2	23.4	0.0	12.5	–	5.0[a]
1947	12.4	40.0	6.9	27.6	0.4	6.8	–	5.7[b]
1950	17.8	39.6	8.2	21.3	0.3	4.6	–	8.2[c]
1953*	17.3	40.4	8.6	22.1	0.4	4.8	–	6.4[d]
1953**	16.8	41.3	7.8	23.1	0.4	4.3	–	6.2[e]
1957	16.6	39.4	7.8	25.1	0.4	3.1	–	7.6[f]
1960	17.9	42.1	5.8	21.1	0.4	1.1	6.1	5.5[g]
1964	20.1	41.9	5.3	20.8	0.4	1.2	5.8	3.8[h]
1966	18.7	38.3	7.3	19.3	0.0	0.8	10.9	4.8[i]
1968	20.4	34.1	15.0	18.6	0.2	1.0	6.1	4.5[j]

Cons = Conservative People's Party; SocDems = Social Democrats; SocLibs = Social Liberals (Radikale Venstre); Libs = Liberals (Venstre); SlesvigP = Slesvig Party; Comms = Communists; SocPP = Socialist People's Party.
[a] Justice Party (Danmarks Retsforbundet) 1.9%, Danish Union 1.2%.
[b] Justice Party 4.5%, Danish Union 1.2%.
[c] Justice Party 8.2%.
[d] Justice Party 5.6%, Danish Union 0.8%.
[e] Justice Party 3.5%, Independents (De Unafhængige, 2.7%.
[f] Justice Party 5.3%, Independents 2.3%.
[g] Justice Party 2.2%, Independents 3.3%.
[h] Justice Party 1.3%, Independents 2.5%.
[i] Justice Party 0.7%, Independents 1.6%, Liberal Centre 2.5%.
[j] Justice Party 0.7%, Independents 0.5%, Liberal Centre 1.3%, Left Socialists 2.0%.
*April, ** November.
Source: Berglund and Lindström (1978: 82).

liberal party, Venstre, took the name of the nineteenth-century left; and, distinctively, a splinter social liberal party, the Radicals (Radikale Venstre), emerged in 1905. As elsewhere in the Nordic region, except Iceland, the Social Democrats became electorally dominant, achieving the status of leading party in 1924 and maintaining it until 2001. However, the Danish Communist Party lacked the continuity of parliamentary representation of the Swedish radical left. It was not represented in the Folketing until 1932, when, during the recession, it won two seats. In 1945 it achieved its best result – 12.5 per cent (see table 3.3) and eighteen parliamentary seats – and gained two cabinet portfolios. However, after 1960 the leading radical leftist party was the Socialist People's Party, formed as a breakaway group in 1959 by the Communist leader Aksel Larsen (Logue 1982). It gained 6.1 per cent in its first general election, in 1960, drawing votes from the towns and the capital, Copenhagen, in particular (Borre and Stehouer 1970: 51–2).

How deviant is the Danish case in relation to the Scandinavian (Swedish) five-party model? According to Berglund and Lindström (1978: 18), 'the presence of more [or less] than five parties constitutes a deviation from the model, but that is to a lesser degree as long as the parties compete on the same left–right dimension'. In other words, if unidimensionality is the criterion, Denmark represents a relatively minor deviation. True, before the Second World War, and from 1953 to 1960, the Slesvig Party, representing the German minority in southern Jutland, elected one member of the Folketing. However, two significant deviations elsewhere in Scandinavia, one at the initial party-building phase – the Swedish People's Party in Finland – and the other after the 'frozen period' – the Christian People's Party in Norway – warrant emphasis in that they reflect non-'functional' (i.e. non-economic) cleavages. In the Finnish case, it was an ethno-cultural cleavage between Finns and Finland Swedes; in Norway it was the product of confessional high church–low church conflict.

Significant deviations in Finland, Norway and Iceland

The first significant deviation saw the emergence at the time of the introduction of mass democracy in 1906 of an ethno-regionalist party in Finland in the form of the Swedish People's Party (Svenska folkpartiet, Sfp), representing the Swedish-speaking minority. Jan-Magnus Jansson (1993: 85) describes the Sfp simply as a language party, adding that 'it has formed an integral part of the Finnish party system and has no counterpart in the other Nordic countries'. Indeed, although the Swedish-speaking minority, the so-called 'Finland Swedes', has been concentrated in two regions – along the west coast and on the islands, on the one hand, and in the capital city area, on the other – Tapio Raunio has noted that the Sfp is 'a rather exceptional regionalist party' in that today 'its policy objectives do not include separatist or autonomous goals' (Raunio 2006: 123). It simply works to protect and promote the interests of the national language minority.

The political cohesion of the language minority has been high. Early in the twenty-first century, about 70 per cent of Finland Swedes vote for the Sfp and, in 2003, 93 per cent of the Sfp's supporters had Swedish as their mother tongue (Paloheimo and Sundberg 2005: 181). However, the Sfp's support has declined broadly in line with the size of the national language minority. In 1900, Finland Swedes constituted 12.9 per cent of the total population – see table 3.4 – and at the first Eduskunta election, in 1907, the Sfp polled 12.6 per cent, to become the fourth largest party. At the centenary of mass democracy in Finland, in 2007, when the proportion of Finland Swedes had dropped to a little over 5 per cent of the total population, the Sfp polled 4.6 per cent. This was precisely the same figure as in 2003, when there were fifteen Swedish-speaking Finns among the 200 Eduskunta members. In 1936, in contrast, the number had been twenty-eight (Bengtsson and Grönlund 2005). Table 3.5 sets out the results of elections to the Eduskunta between the end of the two wars with the Soviet Union and the 1970 election, which marked the rise of right-wing populism in the region. Yet although as an electoral force

Table 3.4 *The Finland Swede population as a percentage of the total Finnish population, 1880–2003*

Year	Number	Percentage of population
1880	294,900	14.3
1890	322,600	13.6
1900	349,700	12.9
1910	339,000	11.6
1920	341,000	11.0
1930	342,900	10.1
1940	354,000	9.6
1950	348,300	8.6
1960	330,500	7.4
1970	303,400	6.6
1980	300,500	6.3
1990	296,700	5.9
2003	285,327	5.5

Source: Finlandssvensk Rapport 20, *Finlandssvenskarna 1990. En Statistisk Översikt* (Svenska Finlands Folketing: Hangö, 1992).

the Sfp has become a minor party, surpassed in support by the Greens, it has been a major governmental player for much of its existence. The Sfp has been a member of forty-five of the sixty-three 'political cabinets' (i.e. excluding the 'caretaker governments' of officials and experts) since independence – only the Agrarian/Centre Party has participated in more – and its governing potential has increased since the Second World War with the declining importance of the language issue. The Sfp has been a member of every cabinet between 1979 and 2007 and it is in fact the only party to have been continuously in government over that period.

The Sfp participated actively in the state-building process between 1917 and 1919, being a member of the bourgeois Senate (cabinet) which declared Finnish independence on 6 December 1917. Its followers were largely engaged on the White side in the ensuing civil war and, although failing thereafter to secure the constitutional monarchy favoured by its majority, the Sfp was instrumental in building checks and balances into the republican constitution enacted in 1919. In much the manner of developments in the new Czechoslovak Republic, where German-language minority parties participated in central government by 1926, the Sfp regularly co-operated in cabinet with Finnish-speaking parties, the first being the Rafael Erich's National Coalition Party, in 1920–21.

The original Swedish Party, which dated back to the 1890s and dominated two of the houses in the quadricameral Diet of Estates, the Nobility and the Merchants, was a counter-nationalist force. It was based on an educated urban

Table 3.5 *Elections to the Finnish Eduskunta, 1945–66 (%)*

Year	Cons	Libs	Sfp	Agrarian/ Centre	SocDems	FPDL	Others
1945	15.0	5.2	7.9	21.3	25.1	23.5	2.0
1948	17.1	3.9	7.7	24.2	26.3	20.0	0.8
1951	14.6	5.7	7.6	23.2	26.5	21.6	0.8
1954	12.8	7.9	7.0	24.1	26.2	21.6	0.4
1958	15.3	5.9	6.7	23.1	23.2	23.2	2.6[a]
1962	15.0	6.3	6.4	23.0	19.5	22.0	7.8
1966	13.8	6.5	6.0	21.2	27.2	21.2	4.1

Cons = Conservatives (Strictly, National Coalition, Kansallinen kokoomus); Libs = Liberal People's Party (1945–51 National Progressive Party, 1951–66 Finnish People's Party); Sfp = Swedish People's Party; the Agrarians took the name Centre Party in 1965; SocDems = Social Democrats; FPDL = Finnish People's Democratic League (Suomen kansan demokraattinen liitto).
[a]In 1958 the Social Democratic Opposition polled 1.7 per cent and this became the Social Democratic League (Työväen ja pienviljelijäin sosialidemokraattinen liitto), which polled 4.4 per cent in 1962.
Source: Törnudd (1968: 159–65).

elite which sought to create a Finnish–Swedish identity among the disparate minority population as a means of responding to Finnish nationalism. As Max Engman (1995: 191) has remarked, before the end of the nineteenth century 'the upper class, the residents of towns and the agrarian population had had very little to do with each other, and had not felt any sense of affinity on the basis of language'. He adds that it was not until the beginning of the twentieth century that the term 'Finland Swede' was coined. However, when the Sfp was founded, in 1906, it constituted a modern mass catch-all party which embraced all the elements of the Swedish-speaking population.

The Sfp's emergence was facilitated by the development in the 1880s of a Swedish-speaking primary school network and the subsequent foundation of Danish-style folk high schools (*folkhögskolor*) – there were eleven in Swedish-speaking Finland in 1907 – which provided a measure of adult education (Sundberg 1985: 44). Together they created an infrastructure for the growth of a popular Finland Swede movement, whilst also vesting the teachers with an important role in building a sense of ethnic consciousness. The spread of Swedish-speaking youth clubs – there were 165, with a total membership of 8,000 in 1908 – consolidated developments and prefaced the high political mobilisation of the Finland Swede population. Ultimately, however, the vast social chasm between the town-based elites and the Swedish-speaking countryside was bridged by the advent of mass democracy. The urban 'classes' were obliged to forge an electoral link with the rural 'masses'. In consequence, the Sfp's creation was followed by a period of intense organisational activity and it is probably reflective of the nascent sense of ethnic community that by, autumn 1908, about 50,000 people – 45 per cent of the Sfp's vote in 1907 – were party members (Sundberg 1985: 46).

During the first years of national independence, the Sfp was suspected of harbouring separatist elements (i.e. of having Åland's disease'), or at least of containing persons who favoured the establishment of self-governing Swedish regions. It was faced with aggressive threats from the so-called 'real Finns' (*aitosuomalaisuusliike*) to Fennocise such Swedish-speaking fortresses as Helsinki University, the country's only state university. The aim of the 'real Finns' was to abandon bilingualism and reduce Swedish to a regional minority language. Though they recruited a following mainly from university students, the Agrarian Party supported much of the cause of the 'real Finns' as, later, did the radical rightist Patriotic People's Movement (Isänmaallinen kansan-liike, IKL) and to a lesser extent the other non-socialist parties. The Social Democrats adhered rigidly to bilingualism and regarded the language question, in the words of their leader, Väinö Tanner, as a 'sixth-rate issue'. That meant growing collaboration between the Sfp and Social Democrats to prevent extensive changes to the language legislation. All in all, concern to defend the second national language against the assault on it from the 'real Finns' meant that the Sfp was widely seen between the wars as occupying a reactionary position well to the right of the political spectrum. In contrast, the Sfp sees itself today as a non-socialist party located close to the political centre and has even attracted a small proportion of its support from so-called bilinguals – Finland Swedes with Finnish-speaking partners. Indeed, the Sfp's historic standing as a language party has been challenged and to a degree compromised by the need to respond to the quickened pace of ethnic assimilation by attracting bilingual and Finnish-speaking electors (Sundberg 1984: 91–108).

Summing up, throughout its existence the Sfp has been a party of cultural defence, protecting and promoting the culture of the language minority across the national territory. It has not been a regionalist party in the radical (and strictly anti-systemic) sense of advocating regional separatism. Nor has it pushed for the regional devolution of power within the existing framework of the state, although there were devolutionists during the years immediately after independence. It has not been a regionalist party either in the sense that its primary logic has been the promotion of particular regional economic interests. If it may be considered a regional party by default – rather than by design – in that its support base has had very clearly defined regional contours, it none the less needs emphasis that language has dictated partisanship and not geography or class (Arter 1994).

Viewed from an electoral perspective, all the nascent Nordic party systems exhibited pronounced regional contours; in that these ecological variations reflected socio-economic factors in particular areas – the level of industrial-isation and/or urbanisation, the nature of farm-holding arrangements, the structure of the workforce, and so on – they were not necessarily incompatible with a left–right class placement of the political parties. 'Region', in short, is not to be viewed as an independent variable, although, as we have seen, socio-economic conditions provided parties with 'natural environments'. In Norway, however, like Finland, the nascent party system reflected multidimensional cleavages in so far as economic conflict lines were insufficient to explain the nature and structure of the emergent party system. Rather, socio-cultural antagonisms created the basis for a centre–periphery dimension. Thus, on the basis of Rokkan's original analysis, Derek Urwin (1997) identifies three elements in an historic counter-culture in south-west Norway:

1 a language conflict between speakers of rural Nynorsk (formerly Landsmål) and the language of the urban centre(s), Bokmål (Riksmål);
2 fundamentalist evangelical opposition to the control and direction of the Lutheran state church;
3 moral opposition in the form of a vigorous anti-alcohol movement.

The Christian People's Party (Kristelig Folkepartiet), founded in Hordaland in the south-west in 1933, has embraced all three components of the Norwegian counter-culture. In 1965, for example, 41 per cent of the party's voters were Nynorsk speakers, 63 per cent belonged to a religious (revivalist) organisation and 84 per cent were actively teetotal (Listhaug 1997: 85). The party is clearly not easy to locate on an orthodox left–right continuum.

Initially, the Christian People's Party was regionally based; it did not contest elections nationally until 1945 (see table 3.6). True, a Christian party had been discussed in Norway as early as 1919 – at a time when the small non-socialist Christian Workers' Party was contesting its last general election in Finland – but its creation in 1933 reflected growing dissatisfaction with the

Table 3.6 *Elections to the Norwegian Storting, 1945–69 (%)*

Year	Labour	Con-servatives[a]	Liberals	Agrarian/ Centre	Christian People's	Com-munists	Others
1945	41.0	17.0	13.8	8.1	7.9	11.9	0.3
1949	45.7	17.8	13.5	7.9	8.5	5.8	0.8
1953	46.7	18.8	10.0	9.0	10.5	5.1	0.0
1957	48.3	18.9	9.6	9.3	10.2	3.4	0.3
1961	46.8	20.0	7.2	9.3	9.6	2.9	4.2
1965	43.1	21.1	10.2	9.9	8.1	1.4	6.2
1969	46.5	19.6	9.4	10.5	9.4	1.0	3.6

[a]The Conservatives are literally the 'Right' (Høyre).
The Socialist People's Party gained 2.4 per cent in 1961, 6.0 per cent in 1965 and 3.5 per cent in 1969.
Source: Furre (1993: 503–4).

Liberal Party, the secular elements within it and, in particular, the way the party had reneged on its strict prohibitionist stance by presiding over the re-opening of liquor outlets – some 300 in Bergen – despite the 'local option' which followed the repeal of 1926. The organisational impetus behind the Christian People's Party's decision to put up a national slate of candidates in 1945 came from the affiliation of the Oxford Group, a revivalist body concentrated in the 1930s among the upper middle class in Oslo, which provided two of the Christian People's Party's most notable leaders, Erling Wikborg and Olav Bryn. However, the character of the party changed little over the years and, as John T. S. Madeley (1977) has observed, in the context of the confessional parties of the period, it represented a rather distinctive type: a non-denominational party directing itself at individual Christians. The Christian People's Party has seen itself as a centre party – closer to the left in social policy matters but on the non-socialist side in protecting the basic inviolability of private property. We shall return to it in chapter 6, in connection with the subsequent emergence of Christian parties in Denmark, Finland and Sweden.

Iceland deviated most from the five-party Scandinavian party system model. Completed before the achievement of full independence in 1944, the historic party-building phase witnessed the emergence of a basic quadripartite structure (table 3.7). On the centre right there were two parties: the Progressive Party was a farmers' party in all but name, whereas, unlike in the other Nordic countries, conservatism and liberalism merged in 1927 in the form of a broad-based Independence Party. There was a comparable

Table 3.7 *Elections to the Icelandic Alþingi, 1942–67 (%)*

Year	Social Democrats	Progressive Party	Independence Party	United Socialist Party	Others
1942	14.2	26.6	38.5	18.5	2.2
1946	17.8	23.1	39.5	19.5	0.1
1949	16.5	24.5	39.5	19.5	0.0
1953	15.6	21.9	37.1	16.0	9.3[a]
1956	18.3	15.6	42.4	19.2	4.5[b]
June 1959	12.5	27.2	42.5	15.2	2.5[c]
October 1959	15.2	25.7	39.7	16.0	3.4[d]
1963	14.2	28.2	41.4	16.0	0.0
1967	15.7	28.1	37.5	13.9	4.8[e]

[a] National Preservation Party 6.0 per cent, Republican Party 3.3 per cent.
[b] National Preservation Party 4.5 per cent.
[c] National Preservation Party 2.5 per cent.
[d] National Preservation Society 3.4 per cent.
[e] Independent Democratic Party 1.1 per cent, Union of Liberals and Leftists 3.7 per cent.
Source: Kristinsson (1991).

bifurcation on the centre left, although the radical left (United Socialist Party) was generally stronger than the Social Democratic Party, which was weak by Scandinavian standards. The conjoining of liberalism and conservatism under the nationalist umbrella will be discussed in chapter 4, as will the electoral strength of the radical left in Iceland.

Summary

1. In Sweden the historic phase of party-building produced a basic two-plus-three configuration and a party system based on five 'isms': communism, social democracy, agrarianism, liberalism and conservatism. By 1930 there was a bifurcated parliamentary left – a powerful Social Democratic Party, flanked by a relatively weak but stable radical left – and a fragmented non-socialist bloc consisting of essentially town-based Liberal and Conservative parties and a farmer-based Agrarian Party.

2. Two distinctive features of the Swedish party system were noted: its unidimensionality and its resilience. Structured around only two of Lipset and Rokkan's formative revolutions – the industrial revolution and the proletarian revolution, that is, conflict between industrialists and agriculturalists and between workers and owners – the Swedish party system 'froze' and the same five parties were represented in the Riksdag from the first democratic election, based on universal and equal voting rights, in 1921, to the advent of the Greens, in 1988.

3. If Sweden, with its five parties ranged on a simple left–right continuum, may be regarded as the exemplar of a 'Scandinavian party system model', Denmark until 1973 represented only a minor departure from it. This is because, as Berglund and Lindström assert, the deviation is not significant as long as the parties still compete on a left–right scale. The split in the old nineteenth-century Left, which in 1905 resulted in two Liberal groupings, the Radicals and Agrarian Liberals, cannot in truth be understood simply in economic terms. But until the 'earthquake election' in 1973 there was a stable party system in which the parties protected and promoted essentially class interests.

4. Elsewhere in Scandinavia, the left–right scale did not provide a comprehensive basis for understanding the structuring of the nascent party systems. The impact of the national revolution in moulding the nineteenth-century proto-parties in Norway and Finland (and later in Iceland) was noted, as too was the role of counter-nationalism in mobilising the minority Swedish-speakers in Finland. In Iceland the successful resolution of the national question – that is, the achievement of full independence – was the primary rationale of the Independence Party, which attracted support across the socio-economic spectrum (see table 3.7). In Norway a centre–periphery dimension was identified and importance was attached to the existence of a counter-culture in the south-west of the country (based on language, religion and teetotalism) for

understanding the structure of the non-socialist bloc and the development of a Christian People's Party in particular. In sum, the multidimensionality of the emergent party systems of Norway, Finland and Iceland suggests the need to refer to Scandinavian party systems in the plural and not to a single Scandinavian party system.

References

Albinsson, Per (1986) *Skiftningar i Blått*, Kommunfakta Förlag: Lund.

Arter, David (1978) *Bumpkin Against Bigwig. The Emergence of a Green Movement in Finnish Politics*, Tampere University: Tampere.

Arter, David (1986) 'The Swedish general election of 1985: increased political influence for the Left-Communists', *Journal of Communist Studies* 2 (1), pp. 78–82.

Arter, David (1994) 'The Swedish People's Party: a regionalist party by default?', European Consortium of Political Research Paper, Madrid, 17–22 April.

Bengtsson, Åsa and Kimmo Grönlund (eds) (2005) *Den finlandssvenska väljaren*, Vasa: Åbo Akademi, Institutet för finlandssvensk samhällsforskning.

Berglund, Sten and Ulf Lindström (1978) *The Scandinavian Party System(s)*, Studentlitteratur: Lund.

Bergström, Hans (1991) 'Sweden's politics and party system at the crossroads', *West European Politics*, 14 (1), pp. 8–30.

Borre, Ole and Jan Stehouer (1970) *Fire Folketingsvalg, 1960–68*, Akademisk Boghandel: Århus.

Duverger, Maurice (1964) *Political Parties. Their Organisation and Activity in the Modern State*, Methuen: London.

Elder, Neil, Alastair H. Thomas and David Arter (1982) *The Consensual Democracies?*, Martin Robertson: Oxford.

Engman, Max (1995) 'Finns and Swedes in Finland', in Sven Tägil (ed.), *Ethnicity and Nation Building in the Nordic World*, Hurst: London, pp. 63–84.

Ersson, Svante (2005) 'Den yttre vänstern i Norge oche Sverige', in Marie Demker and Lars Svåsand (eds), *Partiernas århundrade*, Santérusforlag: Stockholm, pp. 51–77.

Esaiasson, Peter (1990) *Svenska Valkampanjer 1866–1988*, Allmänna Förlaget: Stockholm.

Furre, Berge (1993) *Norsk historie, 1905–1990*, Det Norske Samlaget: Oslo.

Garver, Bruce M. (1978) *The Young Czech Party, 1874–1901, and the Emergence of a Multi-party System*, Yale University Press: New Haven, CT.

Hadenius, Stig (2003) *Modern svenska politisk historia. Konflikt och samförstånd*, sixth edition, Hjalmarson and Högberg: Stockholm.

Hancock, M. Donald (1972) *Sweden. The Politics of Postindustrial Change*, Dryden Press: Hinsdale, IL.

Jansson, Jan-Magnus (1993) *Hajaannuksesta yhteistoimintaan*, Gaudeamus: Tampere.

Kristinsson, Gunnar Helgi (1991) *Farmers' Parties: A Study in Electoral Adaptation*, Félagsvísindastofnun Háskóla Íslands: Reykjavík

Kristinsson, Gunnar Helgi (2001) 'The Icelandic Progressive Party: trawling for the town vote?', in David Arter (ed.), *From Farmyard to City Square? The Electoral Adaptation of the Nordic Agrarian Parties*, Ashgate: Aldershot, pp. 132–61.

Kristjánsson, Svanur (1978) *The Independence Party. Origins, Organization, Ideology and Electoral Bases*, University of Iceland: Reykjavík.

Lijphart, A. (1975) *The Politics of Accommodation*, second edition, University of California Press: Berkeley, CA.

Lipset, S. M. and S. Rokkan (eds) (1967) *Party Systems and Voter Alignments*, Free Press: New York.

Listhaug, Ola (1997) 'The decline of class voting', in Kaare Strom and Lars Svåsand (eds), *Challenges to Political Parties*, University of Michigan Press: Ann Arbor, MI, pp. 77–90.

Logue, John (1982) *Socialism and Abundance. Radical Socialism in the Danish Welfare State*, University of Minnesota Press: Minneapolis, MN.

Madeley, John T. S. (1977) 'Scandinavian Christian Democracy: throwback or portent?', *European Journal of Political Research*, 5, pp. 267–86.

Misgeld, Klaus, Molin Karl and Klas Åmark (eds) (1992) *Creating Social Democracy: A Century of the Social Democratic Labour Party in Sweden*, Pennsylvania University Press: Philadelphia, PA.

Paloheimo, Heikki and Jan Sundberg (2005) 'Puoluevalinnan perusteet', in Heikki Paloheimo (ed.), *Vaalit ja demokratia Suomessa*, WSOY: Helsinki, pp. 169–201.

Raunio, Tapio (2006) 'The Svenska Folkpartiet: the gradual decline of a language party', in Lieven de Winter, Marga Gómez-Reino and Peter Lynch (eds), *Autonomist Parties in Europe: Identity Politics and the Revival of the Territorial Cleavage*, ICPS: Barcelona, pp. 123–39.

Rokkan, S. (1967) 'Geography, religion and social class: cross-cutting cleavages in Norwegian politics', in S. M. Lipset and S. Rokkan (eds), *Party Systems and Voter Alignments*, Free Press: New York, pp. 367–444.

Sartori, Giovanni (1976) *Parties and Party Systems*, Cambridge University Press: Cambridge.

Smith, Gordon (1982) *Democracy in Western Germany*, second edition, Heinemann: London.

Sundberg, Jan (1984) 'Ethnic maintenance in an integrated mass democracy', *West European Politics*, 7 (3), pp. 91–108.

Sundberg, Jan (1985) *Svenskhetens dilemma i Finland. Finlandssvenskarnas samling och splittring under 1900-talet*, Finska Vetenskaps-Societeten: Helsingfors.

Sydow, Björn von (1989) *Vägen till enkammarriksdagen*, Tidens Förlag: Stockholm.

Törnudd, Klaus (1968) *The Electoral System of Finland*, Hugh Evelyn: London.

Urwin, Derek W. (1980) *From Ploughshare to Ballotbox*, Universitetsforlaget: Oslo.

Urwin, Derek W. (1997) 'The Norwegian party system from the 1880s to the 1990s', in Kaare Ström and Lars Svåsand (eds), *Challenges to Political Parties. The Case of Norway*, University of Michigan Press: Ann Arbor, MI, pp. 33–59.

Widfeldt, Anders (1997) *Linking Parties with People? Party Membership in Sweden*, Göteborg University: Göteborg.

4

The historic strengths of
the five main types of party

Social structural conditions have been favourable for Swedish social democracy.
Paradoxically, its rise to power in the 1930s and 1940s was based not so much
on the working class as on the rural classes.

(Esping-Andersen 1990: 38)

Chapter 3's description of the two-plus-three Scandinavian party system
model using Sweden as our case study, and its note on the historic deviations
in Finland, Norway and Iceland, tell us relatively little about the dynamics of
the party system in the region up to 1970 or in particular about the relative
electoral strengths of the party families. Accordingly, this chapter seeks to
identify and explain the varying strengths of the main party types at the polls.
Four prominent features are emphasised:

1 the electoral supremacy of social democracy in Denmark, Norway and most
   notably Sweden;
2 the strength and resilience of agrarianism in Finland;
3 the strength of the radical left in Finland and Iceland;
4 the merger of liberalism and conservatism as a catch-all centre-right in
   Iceland.

The electoral supremacy of social democracy in Denmark,
Norway and most notably Sweden

The electoral supremacy of the Social Democratic/Labour parties in Denmark,
Norway and Sweden, together with the strong position of the Finnish Social
Democratic Party, can be seen from table 4.1. In the general elections between
1920 and 2007, the Finnish party averaged 27.4 per cent of the vote, the
Danish Social Democrats 36.3 per cent, the Norwegian Labour Party 37.6
per cent and the Swedish Social Democrats 42.6 per cent. The Swedish party

Table 4.1 *The average percentage poll of the mainland Nordic Social Democratic/Labour parties, 1920–2007*

Country	1920–2007	1920–39	1940–71	1972–2007
Denmark	36.3	37.6	39.3	32.1
Finland	27.4	33.1	24.7	24.5
Norway	37.6	31.8	45.5	35.4
Sweden	42.6	38.7	47.6	41.6
Iceland	16.8	–	14.6	19.4

has been continuously the largest party since 1917 and the Norwegian party since 1927. The Danish Social Democratic Party was the largest party between 1924 and 2001 – in the last three Folketing elections it has been surpassed by the Liberals (Venstre) – whilst since Finnish independence in 1917 the Social Democrats have topped the poll on all but four occasions. In contrast, the Icelandic party averaged only 14.6 per cent in elections between 1942 and 1971 and 19.4 per cent thereafter. However, the reorganisation of the Icelandic left in the late 1990s brought the Social Democratic Alliance up to nearly one-third of the vote.

The heyday of Finnish social democracy was in the decade before independence, when the party averaged two-fifths of the vote. In 1916 it polled 47.3 per cent and claimed an absolute majority of 103 of the 200 parliamentary seats – the only time a single Finnish party has ever done so. In an overwhelmingly agrarian society, one of the Social Democrats' main election themes was the 'crofting question' (*torpparikysymys*) and, whilst there was much ambivalence about the creation of a class of independent smallholders, and indeed some internal opposition to it, the 100,000 campaign leaflets the parliamentary group distributed in support of 'land for the landless' clearly contributed to the support the Social Democrats gained from the rural poor, particularly in southern and central Finland (Iivari 2007: 22, 46).

The 'golden age' of Danish social democracy was in the 1930s. Contesting the 1935 election using the slogan 'Stauning [the party chairman] or chaos', the Danish party achieved its best-ever result, 46.1 per cent. In 1934 Thorvald Stauning was instrumental in modernising and moderating the Social Democrats' programme with a new document entitled 'Denmark for the People', which sought to make the party a 'people's party'. In contrast to Sweden and Norway, where the surge of social democracy coincided with a period of economic growth and increasing affluence, the Danish Social Democrats achieved their best result when seeking, in close co-operation with the Social Liberals (Radikale Venstre) and Liberals, to manage Denmark out of the slump.

The peak years of Norwegian social democracy were between 1945 and 1969, when the Labour Party's average support of 45.4 per cent was only 1.5 percentage points below that of its more celebrated Swedish counterpart. In the 1950s the Norwegian party's average poll was in fact *higher* than that of its Swedish counterpart (Esping-Andersen 1985: 327–9). This was the era of what has been described as 'the social democratic order' (Heidar 2001: 4) or, in Jens Arup Seip's words, the 'Labour Party State' (Bergh 1977: 16), and in 1957 the Labour Party polled a record 48.3 per cent. There was a broad inter-party consensus around the pragmatic 'welfare capitalism' strategy of the ruling Labour Party.

Uniquely among the Nordic Social Democratic parties, the Swedish Social Democrats have on two occasions – in 1940 and 1968 – won an absolute majority of the vote. As in Norway, the best years of Swedish social democracy comprised the quarter of a century after the Second World War, when the party averaged 46.9 per cent of the vote. In the final election before the shift to unicameralism, and the last under Tage Erlander's leadership, in 1968 the Swedish party gained 50.1 per cent of the vote for the Second Chamber. Its winning margin of 34.4 percentage points over the second-placed Centre Party is the greatest winning margin achieved by any political party in the Nordic region and the turnout reached an all-time record of 89.3 per cent.

A systematically comparative analysis of the historic electoral strength of social democracy in Scandinavia would need to focus, among other things, on: the impact of universal suffrage and proportional representation, as well as social structural factors; and the Social Democratic parties' mass membership, readiness to forge cross-class alliances, broad-based mobilisation strategies and eschewal of dogmatism.

1. The impact of universal suffrage and proportional representation

The most dramatic effect of the simultaneous introduction of mass democracy and proportional representation was in Finland, in 1907, where the Social Democratic Party, created in 1899, became at a stroke the largest of its kind in Europe, with 37 per cent of the vote and 40 per cent of the Eduskunta seats. Facilitated by Nicholas II's October Manifesto in 1905, Finland shifted from an antiquated unicameral Diet of Estates to a unicameral 200-seat Eduskunta. Under the old 'estates' system, 70 per cent of the population was denied the vote; in 1907 all persons aged over twenty-four years were enfranchised and also had the right to stand as candidates. At that time, 98 per cent of Finns aged over ten years could read, but only 39 per cent of those over fifteen could write. Hence at elections voters simply drew a red line under the candidate of their choice. *Red Line* (*Punainen viiva*) is the title of a novel by Ilmari Kianto, first published in 1909, in which the writer portrays the way social democracy became the new religion – the 'spiritual epidemic' of the very poor inhabitants of the outlying countryside of central northern Finland, around Suomussalmi. They are pictured doggedly skiing to the polling station – the first democratic election was held on 15–16 March 1907 – and drawing their red lines with such fervour that 'wood splinters flew out from under their fingernails'. In the main they backed the socialist 'agitators', who had seemed to promise them 'free medicine from the chemists' shops'. Indeed, the new 'proletarian' party promised at least to 'halve famine and evil' (Karonen 1997)! All in all, as David Kirby (1995: 237) has noted, the striking success of the Finnish Social Democratic Party in 1907 'owed little to Marxist ideology or declared policies, but rather its ability to strike a resonant chord amongst people living in wretched conditions in which vibrant visions of a radical and total trans-formation were far more attractive than cautious promises offered by remote gentlemen in smart town clothes'.

In contrast to Finland, the parliamentary breakthrough of social democracy elsewhere in mainland Scandinavia spanned the period 1884–1908 and ante-dated the completion of mass democracy. Indeed, in Denmark, Norway and Sweden, the rise of social democracy could reasonably be considered as both cause and effect of the completion of universal suffrage. The Danish Social Democrats, founded in 1871, gained Folketing representation for the first time in 1884, when they won two seats, and by 1898 the figure had risen to twelve. In Norway, the Labour Party broke into the Storting in 1903 and in Sweden the Social Democratic Workers' Party, founded in 1889, first gained representa-tion in the Riksdag's Second Chamber in 1908, when it managed 14.8 per cent of the vote. In all three cases, the introduction of proportional representation after the First World War facilitated and accelerated the establishment of the Scandinavian Social Democrats as leading parliamentary parties.

2. Social structural factors

Social structural conditions at the time of the creation of mass electorates meant that social democracy in Scandinavia drew heavily on the countryside as well as the towns. This was because, although witnessing growing indus-trialisation, the Nordic region still comprised predominantly rural societies. On the eve of the First World War, levels of urbanisation remained relatively low – they were highest in Denmark, where, in 1910, 40 per cent of the popu-lation lived in towns – and industry was dispersed throughout the countryside. Moreover, even after the Second World War, Sten Sparre Nilson observed that a clear dividing line between industrial workers and farmers was often difficult to draw, since many workers owned a plot of land and many farmers held part-time jobs, for example as loggers, in the winter. He concludes that 'a great many people in the rural districts regard themselves as being both farmers and workers, a fact which has certainly facilitated the spread of Social Democratic influence in the countryside' (Nilson 1958: 114).

3. The mass membership character of Scandinavian social democracy

The rise of Scandinavian social democracy was integrally bound up with the high levels of associationalism in the region. There was a high member–voter ratio, close links to the trade union movement and a network of clubs, co-operative shops and newspapers reinforcing a sub-culture of labour solidarity. Comparative data are not readily available, but on the basis of Edvard Thermanius's figures, membership of the Swedish Social Democratic Workers' Party in 1932 stood at 296,507 and its vote 1,040,673 (Thermanius 1933: 192, 194). This would give a member–voter ratio of approximately 1–3.

4. The Social Democrats' readiness to forge cross-class alliances

The electoral rise of Scandinavian social democracy was facilitated by the co-operation it entered into with the non-socialist parties to achieve universal suffrage, whilst its electoral expansion – as well as consolidation as a ruling party – in the 1930s was facilitated by renewed co-operation with the non-socialists, particularly the Agrarians, with a view to managing the economies out of recession. In Sweden, for example, the leaders of the Social Democratic Workers' Party, Hjalmar Branting, and of the Liberal Coalition Party, Karl Staaff, worked closely in the struggle for democracy and parliamentary government (Birgersson *et al.* 1981: 48–64). Equally, faced with spiralling unemployment and a credit crisis, the Danish Social Democrats in 1933 struck a cross-party deal – the so-called *Kanslergadeforliget* – with the Radicals and Liberals, in which the latter secured increased aid for agriculture and provisions to maintain farm prices, whilst the Social Democrats gained protection against cuts in workers' wages and the promise of support for social reforms (Miller 1991: 101).

5. The Social Democrats' broad-based mobilisation strategies

In contrast to Britain, the historic strength of Scandinavian social democracy was based on its ability to mobilise and appeal to the rural proletariat of agricultural workers, small tenants, fishermen and lumberjacks, together with the employees of industrial concerns situated in isolated rural areas. In other words, it targeted both the industrial and agricultural working class and not simply urban factory workers. Based on iron-ore mining, hydro-electric power and timber, the industrialisation process was dominated from the outset by large industrial concerns dispersed across the national territory in small and remote rural localities, which were ideally suited to absorb excess (displaced) agrarian labour. Working-class mobilisation was also assisted, as Esping-Andersen (1990: 38) has observed in the Swedish context, by the absence of a British-style 'aristocracy of labour' – that is, the existence of a strong skilled worker and craft tradition. The Swedish blue-collar working class, in short, was comparatively undifferentiated. Moreover, by the end of the 1920s, the Social Democrats in Denmark, Norway and Sweden were presenting themselves as moderate revisionists – people's parties, not class parties, building a national home (society) in which all the people could be happily accommodated, so to speak.

6. The Social Democrats' eschewal of ideological dogmatism in favour of the pursuit of practical reform policies

The Social Democrats institutionalised their power base, both in the country and in government, by means of reformist policies designed to promote welfare capitalism – that is, an advanced welfare state sustained by the wealth generated by the private sector. As Esping-Andersen (1990: 57) concludes in respect of Sweden, the Social Democratic Workers' Party 'managed to build a welfare state that pleased the workers and the middle classes'. The question of social democracy and the welfare state will be taken up again in chapter 8.

The strength and resilience of agrarianism in Finland

It was not so much the emergence of farm-specific parties in the Nordic region that was distinctive – as mentioned in chapter 3, peasant parties arose across central and eastern Europe in the period before and after the First World War – as the fact that they persisted until the late 1950s in Sweden and Norway and to 1965 in Finland. In Finland, moreover, when the Agrarian Party (Maalaisliitto) followed its Swedish and Norwegian sister parties and changed its name to Centre Party (Keskustapuolue), it was both the largest single party, with 23.0 per cent of the vote, and the leading party of government, and had been the 'hinge group' in coalition-building since the first years of independence (Arter 1979).

All three Scandinavian Agrarian (with a capital A) parties were early twentieth-century creations, facilitated by the introduction of universal suffrage and proportional representation – the Finnish party was formed in 1906, the Norwegian one in 1915 and the Swedish one in 1921 – although the Swedish party had a forerunner in the shape of the Rural Party (Lantmannapartiet). Thus, as in Denmark, the embryonic Swedish party system formed around essentially economic issues – taxation, tariffs and so on – rather than the national question, as in Finland and Norway, and until the mid-1880s the dominant group in the Riksdag's Second Chamber was the Rural Party, which favoured lower taxes on farms. It had no national organisation, however, did not run candidates in elections and split into free-trade and protectionist factions on the question of protecting domestic agriculture against the threat of an influx of cheap grain from the Americas, Romania and Ukraine.

All three Agrarian parties had varying degrees of regional support before the First World War, but they did not emerge as national parties until after it. In Sweden the Agrarians (Bondeförbundet) emerged at the regional level in 1910 as the organ of the small and medium-sized landowners in the south-west and, led by Carl Berglund, organised themselves on a national basis in 1913, replacing the Rural Party, which had been decimated at the general election two years earlier (Carlsson 1956). A separate Agrarian grouping, the National

Association of Swedish Farmers (Jordbrukarnas Riksförbund), was formed in Skåne in the 'deep south' in 1915, predominantly by larger landowners and assorted rural bigwigs (Jonnergård 1985). In the celebrated Farmers' March of February 1914, farmers from all over the country descended under their provincial banners on the yard of the royal palace, where King Gustav V (contrary to government policy) supported their demands for higher defence spending. Mirroring this upsurge in agrarian mobilisation, the two farmers' groupings won a combined 8.5 per cent in the general election of autumn 1917. A merger in 1921 between the two led to an initial loss of votes, although by the 1930s the Swedish Agrarians had achieved their best electoral result, of over 14 per cent of the vote.

The impetus for the Norwegian Agrarian Party (Bondepartiet) came in 1906 from the farmers in the east and centre (Trøndelag) of the country who were members of the pressure group Norsk Landsmansforbund (Greenhill 1965). However, in 1921 the Agrarians put up candidates everywhere except Oslo, Bergen and Finnmark, and managed a creditable 13.1 per cent of the vote, drawn fairly evenly from the small and medium-size farmers in the south-west, in the main former supporters of Venstre, and the larger producers in the east, who had favoured Høyre. By 1924 the Agrarians' support had declined in the south-west but they gained ground in the east (Aasland 1974). The Norwegian Agrarians achieved their best result, 15.9 per cent, in 1930.

So, too, did the Finnish party, although its support amounted to no less than 27.3 per cent. Prompted by the superimposition of mass democracy and uni-cameralism on a predominantly rural society, the Agrarian Party was formed in 1906 largely out of breakaway elements from the two nineteenth-century nationalist parties, the Old Finns and Young Finns (Hakalehto 1986: 61–194). It stressed socio-economic issues over and above matters of 'high politics' such as the constitution question – that is, the strategy to adopt towards Russification and czarist violations of Finland's basic rights – although on the constitutional question it was closer to the principled stance of the Young Finns than the more conciliatory line of the Old Finns. Whilst at 66 per cent in 1910 the proportion of the economically active population engaged in agri-culture was higher than in Norway and Sweden – that is, industrialisation was less advanced – far more pertinent for the emergence of the Finnish Agrarians were the concentrations of independent family-sized farms in the north-west (Oulu and Vaasa) and south-east (Karelia) of the country. Indeed, in recruit-ing support almost exclusively from the stratum of independent farmers, the Scandinavian Agrarian parties were more evidently class parties than the Social Democratic/Labour parties.

A broad picture of the significantly greater electoral strength of the Finnish Agrarian Party than its Norwegian and Swedish counterparts can be gained from table 4.2. In the ten Storting elections between 1921 and the party's change of name in 1959, the Norwegian Agrarians polled an average of 11.3 per cent, marginally the weakest of the three farm-specific parties. Their best

Table 4.2 *The average Agrarian Party poll in the Norwegian, Swedish and Finnish general elections, 1919–62 (%)*

Country	Best poll	Year	Period average
Norway	15.9	1930	11.3
Sweden	14.3	1936	12.2
Finland	27.3	1930	22.9

result, 15.9 per cent, was achieved in 1930 and the worst, 4.9 per cent, in 1949. The Swedish party's profile was not significantly different. In the eleven elections to the Riksdag's Second Chamber between 1920 and the adoption of the title Centre Party in 1957, the Swedish Agrarians averaged 12.2 per cent of the poll. Their best result, 14.3 per cent, was achieved in 1936, whilst, following a period of coalition with the Social Democrats, they plunged to a nadir of 9.4 per cent in 1956, a year before the change of name. The average poll of the Finnish Agrarians, in contrast, was more than double that of the Norwegian party and nearly double that of the Swedish Agrarians. In the fifteen Eduskunta elections between 1919 and 1962, the Finnish Agrarians averaged 22.9 per cent of the vote and they obtained a high of 27.3 per cent in 1930. Indeed, excluding the first post-independence general election, that in 1919, the Finnish Agrarians' vote did not fall below one-fifth of the total poll and it was the largest single party when it became the last of the Nordic Agrarian parties to change its name, in 1965.

In seeking to understand the greater electoral strength and, it might be added, all-round 'relevance' – in Sartori's sense of eligibility for government (Sartori 1976) – of agrarianism in Finland, the following points need emphasis:

1 the Finnish Agrarians' central role in the completion of state-building between 1917 and 1919 (the independent farmers fought on the victorious White side during the 1918 civil war) and in promoting a republican constitution for the new successor state (Arter 1979);
2 the party's promotion of a land reform programme in the 1920s, which was designed as a measure of social engineering and which, in providing independent holdings for the rural proletariat of crofters and farm labourers, strengthened the Agrarians' core class of supporters;
3 a vigorous resettlement programme in the late 1940s for refugees from that part of Karelia conceded to the Soviet Union after two lost wars, which served to maintain the family-size farm population at a time of accelerated industrialisation (Arter 2001: 63–5);
4 the role of the long-serving (and former Agrarian) president Urho Kekkonen (1956–81) in maintaining the Agrarians in office and the concomitant special relationship between the Agrarians and the Kremlin (see the section on Finlandisation in chapter 12) (Arter 1981);

5 divisions among the Social Democrats in the late 1950s, which kept them out of power for a decade and until 1966 made the Agrarians the natural governing party.

In addition to the 'capital A' parties in Finland, Norway and Sweden, the initial phase of party-building witnessed the emergence of agrarian parties with a small 'a' – that is, farm-based class parties in all but name – in Denmark and Iceland. Venstre (literally 'Left') has been a deviant case among the Nordic farmers' parties in that, as Jørgen Goul Andersen and Jan Bendix Jensen have noted, it has never changed its name, which at no point has carried any reference to farmers – it added the suffix 'Denmark's Liberal Party' in the 1960s – and yet it was a genuine farmers' party from the time of its foundation in 1870 and it remained essentially a farmers' party until the 1980s (Goul Andersen and Bendix Jensen 2001: 96). The Icelandic Progressive Party was formed in December 1916 by farmers in parliament and, as Gunnar Helgi Kristinsson has observed, it remained for over a decade 'a more or less pure farmers' party, representing only farmers and the rural areas, and not making systematic attempts to win support in the towns until the early 1930s' (Kristinsson 1991: 211). In 1931 about three-quarters of the agrarian vote went to the Progressive Party (Kristinsson 1991: 211), which in turn polled 35.9 per cent of the active electorate. The following year, Venstre in Denmark gained 24.7 per cent of the total poll. Both 'small a' agrarian parties, in short, won a significantly greater vote share than their 'capital A' counterparts in Norway and Sweden.

The strength of the radical left in Norden

Denmark, Norway and Sweden

In Denmark, Norway and Sweden until the 1960s the radical left comprised generally stable but small communist parties that exercised only marginal influence on the policy process. Thereafter, beginning with the entry of the Danish Socialist People's Party into the Folketing in 1960, reorientation and modernisation created 'new left parties', which in Denmark and Norway in turn led to fragmentation on the radical left (see chapters 5 and 6).

The Danish Communist Party (Danmarks kommunistiska parti, DKP), founded in 1919, averaged 2.6 per cent of the vote in the twenty-five Folketing elections it participated in between 1924 and 1988 (it was banned from participating in the 1943 election). Against the background of economic depression, the DKP polled 1.1 per cent of the vote and elected two Folketing members in 1932 but it attracted significant support, albeit in the event ephemeral, as a consequence of the prominent role it played in the Danish Resistance movement: in contrast to Norway, the Danish Communists enjoyed the prestige that came from being the first organised group to produce a large illegal newspaper – the national monthly *Land og Folk* (*Country and People*) first appeared in autumn 1941, some months after the Communist Party had been banned – and the first organised group to initiate sabotage. The date 9 April 1942 was fixed for the start of its sabotage campaign (Grimnes 1983: 213–14) and Communist representatives on the shop floor were behind the wave of street disturbances and strikes in August 1943 that came to be known as the 'August uprising' (Trommer 1983: 229, 233–6). At the 1945 Folketing election the DKP achieved a record vote of 12.5 per cent and eighteen seats and two Communists, including their leader, Aksel Larsen, participated in the first post-war coalition. Following Larsen's expulsion from the party in 1958, the DKP lost its toehold in parliament in 1960, returned briefly between 1973 and 1979, but has not been successful since.

The history of the Norwegian Communist Party (Norges kommunistiska parti, NKP) does not differ substantially from that of the Danish party. The NKP averaged 3.1 per cent in the Storting elections between 1924 and 1985, winning 11.9 per cent in 1945 following its efforts in the Resistance. The Communists constituted a distinct element within the Norwegian Resistance, with their own leadership and organisation, and they were much less well integrated into wider Resistance activity than in Denmark. Moreover, there was intense suspicion among other Resistance elements, which believed that the Communists' sabotage strategy was 'made in Moscow' rather than by the Norwegian Communists themselves (Trommer 1983: 255). None the less, their sabotage organisation, Saborg, executed a number of striking actions, most notably in November 1944, when six ships were sunk or damaged in two Oslo shipyards, and these acts of Communist sabotage increasingly appealed to the desire for direct action on the part of other Resistance elements and lent sabotage, and by extension the NKP, enhanced legitimacy (Trommer 1983: 255). The NKP claimed two ministers in the post-war coalition, but by 1949 its vote had been halved, to 5.8 per cent, and by 1969 it was down to 1.0 per cent (Ersson 2005). In 1973, in collaboration with the Left-Socialist Party and Socialist People's Party, the NKP formed part of the anti-European Community Socialist Electoral Alliance, which won 11.2 per cent of the vote. But thereafter its vote quickly dwindled to virtually nothing.

The Swedish Communist Party (Sveriges kommunistiska parti, SKP) averaged 4.9 per cent of the poll in the fourteen elections to the second Riksdag chamber between its creation in 1921 and 1968, achieving its best result, 10.3 per cent, in 1944. The party changed its name to Left Communists (Vänsterpartiet kommunisterna) in 1967, although this had little effect on the level of its support. In the nine elections to the unicameral Riksdag between 1970 and 1994, the Left Communists, and from 1990 their successor, the Left Party (Vänsterpartiet), polled an average of 5.3 per cent (see table 4.3). Unlike their counterparts in Denmark and Norway, the Swedish Communists never participated in government.

Table 4.3 *The average communist/'old left' poll in Nordic general elections since 1919 (%)*

Country	Party	Best poll	Year	Period average	Period
Denmark	Communists	12.5	1945	2.6	1924–88
Norway	Communists	11.9	1945	3.1	1924–85
Sweden	Communists	10.3	1944	4.9	1921–68
	Left Party Communists	5.8	1988	5.3	1970–88
Finland	Socialist Workers' Party	14.8	1922	12.7	1922–29
	Finnish People's Democratic League	23.5	1944	19.8	1945–83[a]
Iceland	United Socialists/People's Alliance	22.9	1978	16.1	1942–95

[a] By 1987 the Finnish radical left was split into two. The 'rump' Finnish People's Democratic League gained 9.4 per cent and the splinter Democratic Alternative (Demokraattinen Vaihtoehto) 4.3 per cent.

Finland

In Finland the radical left has enjoyed an historic electoral strength far in excess of its counterparts in Denmark, Norway and Sweden. In the form of the Socialist Workers' Party (Sosialistinen työväenpuolue), the radical left averaged 12.7 per cent in the four general elections between 1922 and 1929 – it was proscribed the following year – and the communist-dominated Finnish People's Democratic League (Suomen kansan demokraattinen liitto, SKDL) averaged 19.8 per cent of the poll in the twelve general elections between 1945 and 1983 (London 1975). It never fell below one-fifth of the vote until 1970, but internal division then began to take its toll and it declined to 14.0 per cent in 1983. Behind both the Socialist Workers' Party and the SKDL was the Finnish Communist Party (Suomen kommunistinen puolue, SKP), as discussed below.

Against the backdrop of the White (bourgeois) victory in the Finnish civil war over winter–spring 1918, the SKP was founded by Red exiles in Moscow in September 1918. The total number of Finnish Red Guard refugees was in the order of 6,000 (mostly ordinary soldiers, their wives and children); their living conditions were poor and the majority of them joined the Soviet Red Army simply to survive. Initially, therefore, the primary task of the SKP was to organise the lives of the refugees and, in consequence, the party's activities were concentrated in St Petersburg and Moscow (Iivonen 1986). None the less, its attention soon turned towards Finland, and throughout the 1920s the SKP operated in the guise of the Finnish Socialist Workers' Party (founded in June 1920), which developed a solid organisational base with the assistance of agents directed from Moscow. Illegal communist literature was easily smuggled in, whilst the network of social contacts formed by widows and orphans seeking information from the peripatetic Red agitators was also important in the diffusion of communism. Already by 1922 the Socialist Workers' Party had achieved a membership level of about 70 per cent of that of the Social Democrats and had laid a solid organisational foundation in the industrial areas of Turku, Vaasa and western Kuopio (Laulajainen 1979: 129–39).

A White backlash was quickly in evidence. In 1923 several Socialist Workers' Party MPs were arrested and charged with treasonable activities, and the same thing happened again in 1930. In the fiercely anti-communist climate generated by the radical rightist Lapua movement (Lapuan liike) and its successor, the Patriotic People's Movement (Isänmaallinen kansan-liike, IKL), the Socialist Workers' Party was able to field only seventeen candidates and gain only 1 per cent of the vote at the 1930 general election, compared with 175 candidates and 13.5 per cent respectively the previous year (Törnudd 1968: 74). At this time, 60 per cent of the economically active population still worked in the primary sector and, hit by the effect of the international depression and a dramatic fall in revenues from the sale of timber on their land, the large and medium-sized farmers were in the van of the anti-communist riots that marked the inception of the Lapua movement at the end of 1929. As Risto Alapuro has observed, 'in 1929–32 the Lapua movement understood the situation as a continuation of the civil war against the communists and to a lesser extent the Social Democrats and even against the Russians' (Alapuro 1980: 680). The Socialist Workers' Party was banned altogether in the elections of 1933, 1936 and 1939.

The SKP's success following its re-legalisation in 1944 was perhaps not altogether surprising in view of the relatively strong electoral showing of the radical left across western Europe in the first post-war elections – although the Communist front organisation, the SKDL, undoubtedly surpassed its own expectations in polling 23.5 per cent in March 1945. However, it seems curious *prima facie*, at least to a non-Finnish observer (this author) – and certainly not exhaustively explained by Finnish political historians – that in March 1945 nearly one-quarter of Finns voted for the communist-dominated SKDL when the Finns had just fought (and lost) two wars against the communist regime in the Soviet Union and, unlike Denmark and Norway, the communists did not attract respect as part of a patriotic Resistance movement against fascist occupation. Why did the communists exceed expectations and, in the guise of the SKDL, poll approaching a quarter of the vote?

In many ways the March 1945 Finnish general election was both remark-able and remarkably normal. It was remarkably normal in that it was a free, competitive election (only the neo-fascist IKL was banned), contested with an electorate expanded by the reduction of the voting age from twenty-four to twenty-one years and an election which mobilised a greater proportion of eligible voters than any previous Finnish general election. The turnout was nearly 75 per cent. However, the election was also remarkable on at least three counts.

First, although, against the odds, Finland had not been occupied, an Allied Control Commission, chaired by the Russian Andrei Zhdanov, had installed itself in Hotel Torni in central Helsinki shortly after the armistice with the Soviet Union of 19 September 1944. The Finns, moreover, were required (and had begun) to meet a reparations debt payable largely in terms of heavy goods and machinery – trawlers and other merchant shipping, pulp and paper refining equipment, metal products and so on – and by the end of the first repayment year, goods worth 51.5 million gold dollars had been sent to the Soviet Union (Hyvämäki 1978: 265).

Next, the election was held whilst Finland was still at war. The Soviets had demanded that the Finns drive (their former co-belligerents) the Germans out of Finland and on 1 March 1945, only two weeks before the general election, a unanimous cabinet in Helsinki reaffirmed – 'lest there be any misunderstanding with regard to Finland's position towards Germany' – that Finland had been at war with Hitler since 15 September 1944, the day the Germans attacked the island of Suursaari in the Gulf of Finland (Hyvämäki 1978: 260). At the time of the election the so-called 'Lapland War' was still in progress and the retreating Germans were pursuing a 'scorched earth' policy. About 104,000 persons were evacuated from Lapland – over half to Sweden – nearly 15,000 buildings, including houses, saunas and barns, were destroyed and roads, fields and forests were mined. It was September 1945 before Finland was free of German forces. According to a report from the United Nations Relief and Rehabilitation Administration (UNNRA), Lapland was the most devastated area in the whole of Europe and it was UNNRA funding which provided the lion's share of the reconstruction aid to the area. Incidentally, American Quakers played a significant part in restoring Lapland's infrastructure by setting up work camps in the worst-affected parts and they were joined by volunteers from Sweden, Denmark and Britain (Torkko 1995: 38).

Finally, in addition to the problems of providing for returning evacuees and demobilised soldiers, the armistice meant that Finland lost 12 per cent of its land area and about 420,000 displaced persons – including approximately 7,000 from the Porkkala enclave, which had been leased to the Soviet Union – had to be resettled. Symptomatically, the votes of the displaced Karelians were counted in the newly formed Kymi constituency, whilst about 15,000 northern Finns voted in the 'evacuation camps' in Sweden.

In preparation for the 1945 general election, the re-legalised Finnish Communists had in practice to start from scratch following their long underground years and, above all, they had to determine an appropriate strategy and mobilise a body of activists. To an extent guided by Zhdanov, they pursued a so-called 'popular front strategy' and eschewed revolutionary socialist objectives (at least in the short term) in favour of building a broad alliance of 'democratic forces' under the umbrella of the newly formed SKDL. A divided Social Democratic Party voted by a majority of only one to reject the approach to join the SKDL, although from the outset the latter embraced those left-wing socialists who had been expelled from the Social Democrats during the war. Eleven of the forty-nine parliamentary seats the SKDL gained in March 1945 went to non-Communists, although pre-election overtures to the Agrarians proved fruitless.

In terms of mobilising a body of activists, the SKDL's electoral success in March 1945 was grounded in the rapid development of an organisational base, which served to institutionalise the position of a substantial radical left in the post-war Finnish party system. At the end of 1944 the SKDL had 93 branch organisations and 8,500 members; at the end of the first quarter of 1945 this had risen to 348 branches and 22,000 members; and by the end of 1945 the SKDL had 976 branch organisations and 59,000 members. Pertti Laulajainen (1979) has noted that there was a fundamental correspondence between the organisational strength of the Socialist Workers' Party in the 1920s and the core SKDL areas after the Second World War. In other words, the areas of Communist strength and weakness remained essentially unchanged from the earliest years of independence onwards. Yet the SKDL's poll in March 1945 was nearly 10 percentage points greater than the Socialist Workers' best result in 1922. Why?

Clearly, the SKDL represented an entirely new organisation, which hit Finnish politics, in the words of the Agrarian Johannes Virolainen, like a 'violent autumn storm' (Hokkanen 1996: 180). It presented itself as an anti-war, anti-fascist alternative and as the champion of the casualties of conflict – those who had lost limbs, land and close relatives as a result of war. In still a predominantly agrarian society, the SKDL appealed to small farmers, war veterans and, not least, first-time voters. It is perhaps a measure of the success of its 'popular front' strategy that it seems many of its voters viewed the SKDL as being to the right of the Social Democrats (Hokkanen 1996: 186). A vote for the SKDL was emphatically not a vote for socialist revolution. According to the British historian David Kirby, 'much of the initial success of the Finnish Communist Party can be attributed to the broad-based appeal of the People's Democratic League, which seemed to offer a definite break with the past and the hope of a better future to many voters' (Kirby 1979: 168). Shortly after the election, Sylvi Kyllikki Kilpi's decision to leave the Social Democrats meant that, with fifty Eduskunta seats, the SKDL became the largest parliamentary group and it proceeded to head a broad left–centre coalition under Mauno Pekkala (earlier expelled from the Social Democratic Party) as prime minister.

That Finland did not become a communist-led 'people's democracy' was, according to Kimmo Rentola (1997), the result of three main factors: that Finland was not occupied during the two wars against the Soviet Union in 1939–44 and maintained its own army; that social democracy remained independent and was led by its right wing (the patriotic wing under Väinö Tanner); and that the 1948 Treaty of Friendship, Co-operation and Mutual Assistance (FCMA) with its big-power neighbour met the Soviet Union's minimum security needs.

The communist coup in Czechoslovakia in February 1948 prompted rumours of something similar in Finland, whilst the strong sense of personal insecurity felt by many 'bourgeois' politicians led to the period 1944–48 being characterised as the 'danger years' (*vaaran vuodet*) (Arter 1994: 284–8). Clearly prompted from Moscow, the SKP leadership believed that intimidating opponents, arresting prominent politicians and organising mass demonstrations would guarantee what Hertta Kuusinen described in a letter to her father, Otto Ville (a member of the Soviet Politburo), as 'a great election victory' in 1948 (Rentola 1997). In the event, however, fears of a Prague-style take-over, together with the tiresome presence of the Allied Control Commission under Zhdanov, all contributed to the SKDL's vote declining to 20 per cent in March 1948 and the Communists embarked on sixteen years in the wilderness of political opposition. Until the mid-1950s, a couple of years after Stalin's death, the Soviet Union and in particular the KGB used the SKP as a vehicle for espionage activities.

Against the background of a split in the Social Democratic Party and the emergence of the Social Democratic Opposition (the Työväen ja pienviljelijäin sosialidemokraattinen liitto, TPSL) – an estimated 100,000 social democratic votes were effectively wasted at the 1958 general election – the SKDL rose in the same year to become the largest Eduskunta grouping, only two years after the Soviet suppression of the Hungarian rising. Moreover, it participated in broad centre–left coalitions for much of the period 1966–82.

However, between its fourteenth congress, in 1966, and 1985, when two distinct communist parties came into being, there were two factions within the SKP. The base of the reformist majority was mostly in the trade union movement, whilst, as Jyrki Iivonen (1986: 5) has pointed out, the bastion of the minority wing comprised the old party apparatchiks who joined the party during the underground period before 1944. By the early 1980s, the Communist Party of the Soviet Union had taken sides and openly supported the minority. Nevertheless, this was expelled in 1985 and two years later contested the 1987 general election as an electoral alliance known as the Democratic Alternative (Demokraattinen vaihtoehto, DEVA). DEVA polled 4.2 per cent; the SKP (the former majority wing) polled 9.4 per cent.

The ecology of post-war Finnish communism, in simplified form, showed two core constituencies: the north-east and south-west of Finland (Berglund 1990). The SKP shared with its Swedish and Norwegian counterparts electoral strength in the rural communes in the geographical periphery. The Swedish Communists, for example, averaged 19.5 per cent of the vote at elections to the Riksdag's Second Chamber in the northern constituency of Norrbotten between 1932 and 1964. However, like the radical left in Iceland (discussed shortly), the SKP made considerably greater electoral inroads into the industrial working population, especially in the southern third of the country, than did its Swedish and Norwegian counterparts. Viewed from a comparative Nordic perspective, it was not so much the phenomenon of 'backwoods communism', in Erik Allardt's terms (1970), that was the primary electoral feature of the post-war Finnish radical left, as the strength of blue-collar 'industrial communism'. There was also a high level of partisan identification among SKP voters, which could be contrasted with the fortunes of the Swedish Communists, who ran into difficulties whenever the Soviet Union appeared in a bad light. As to the communist electorate, the lion's share of the SKP's vote came from the working class. In the late 1970s, for example, 61 per cent of its support was recruited from industrial workers, agricultural labourers and lumberjacks (the latter often owning a small amount of land) and the SKDL emerged as the most socially cohesive and class-based of the Finnish parties.

Iceland

To suggest that the strength of the radical left in Iceland might be compared to (or considered in the same breath, so to speak, as) its Finnish counterpart might seem to be stretching the point. True, the Icelandic radical left – the Communist Party 1930–38, United Socialist Party 1938–56 and People's Alliance 1956–99 – has been numerically stronger than the communist parties in Denmark, Norway and Sweden. But, unlike the SKDL in Finland, the Icelandic radical left has never been the largest party in either votes or seats and only once – in 1978 – has its poll exceeded 20 per cent of the active electorate.

The strength of the Icelandic radical left, then, is relative to the support for social democracy, which it surpassed at every election except one in the period 1942–83. Overall, the left wing in Icelandic politics has been weak by Nordic standards, mustering only about one-third of the electorate and never exceeding a combined 38 per cent. Historically, this may partly be explained by the fact that the Icelandic left, in contrast to Finland, Norway and Sweden, drew its initial support almost exclusively from the towns. In large measure this could be viewed as a legacy of the weak impact of industrialisation during the formative era of mass politics and the absence of a real base for class conflict in the countryside. The small size of the factories also tended to deter the development of adversarial owner–worker relations. Equally, in the 1930s there was a high incidence of class voting and about three-quarters of the manual working population supported one of the two left-wing parties, although they in turn were liable to factionalisation and fragmentation. Indeed, whereas the 'classical' Nordic party system model comprised a bifurcated left and a fragmented non-socialist bloc, Iceland has witnessed a bifurcated centre-right – the (largely farmer-based) Progressive Party and Independence Party – and a fragmented political left. Accordingly, two questions seem germane:

1 Why has the political left in Iceland been relatively weak?
2 Why have the various parties to the left of the Social Democrats exceeded the support of the latter?

In fact, as elsewhere in the region, the Social Democrats were the stronger of the two left-wing parties before 1939. Established in 1916, the Social

Democrats were the only party before the mid-1930s to have a membership organisation, albeit an indirect one, with the trade unions forming the basic units in the party. Moreover, the Social Democrats entered into the type of 'red–green' arrangement common to all the Scandinavian states at this time and between 1934 and 1939 formed a coalition government with the Progressive Party, which introduced a state-sponsored system of social security benefits, in addition to providing public backing to farmers and fishing-vessel owners hard hit by the recession.

The Icelandic Communist Party was not founded until 1930, although a communist group had been formed within the Social Democratic Party much earlier and the Icelandic communists and radical socialists began their affiliation with the Comintern in 1920. In 1924, for example, a Comintern representative was sent to Iceland to mediate between opposing groups in the Reykjavík party. On the advice of the Comintern, the communist faction remained in the Social Democratic fold until 1930, when, in the conducive conditions of recession, it seceded and formed a party in its own right. Actively exploiting unrest during the recession, the Communists claimed over 7 per cent of the vote in 1933 and the figure rose to 8.5 per cent in 1937, when they gained three of the forty-nine seats in the Alþingi. Incidentally, the depression in Iceland lasted longer than in the other Nordic countries, not least because of the outbreak of the Spanish civil war, which effectively closed the market for salt fish (Karlsson 2000: 311).

At the breakthrough 1937 election, the Comintern channelled money to the Communists to cover campaign costs; throughout the 1930s, a relatively large number of Icelandic students went to study at Comintern schools in Moscow, so providing the Communists with a solid elite base; and close personal relations were forged between the two leading Icelandic Communists, Einar Olgeirsson and Brynjólfur Bjarnason, and the Soviet Communist Party leadership (Ólafsson 1998: 89). After the 1937 election, the Communists, following the Moscow line, pursued a 'popular front' strategy, but when the Social Democrats rejected demands for a popular front coalition, a left-wing faction broke away and joined the Communists. In order to accommodate it, the Communist Party renamed itself the United Socialist Party in 1938. By the second Alþingi election, in 1942, the United Socialist Party polled 18.5 per cent of the vote – well over twice the Communists' poll five years earlier – and by 1946 it had gained the support of nearly one in five voters (only a little less than what the SKDL attained in Finland the previous year).

The communist imprint on the new radical leftist party was reflected in the fact that the United Socialist Party supported the Ribbentrop–Molotov Pact of August 1939 and the subsequent invasion of Finland (the Winter War) – support for the 'Moscow line' which undoubtedly led to widespread public hostility in Iceland. This in turn raises what might be called the '1942 question' in Iceland. We have earlier endeavoured to understand the apparently paradoxical situation of a strong showing for the communist-dominated

radical left in Finland in 1945, despite the loss of two wars against the communist regime in the Soviet Union between 1939 and 1944. But why did the
United Socialist Party gain a vote share at the second Alþingi election in 1942
more than 10 percentage points greater than the Icelandic Communist Party
in 1937, when it had adopted a slavishly pro-Moscow line in 1939, which had
caused widespread resentment among the Icelandic electorate? Three points
warrant emphasis.

First, the unpopularity incurred by the United Socialist Party's pro-Soviet
stance on the Winter War was, to an extent, 'cancelled out' when in 1941
Hitler launched Operation Barbarossa against the Soviet Union and the latter
joined the war against fascism. Popular sympathy for the Soviets increased.

Second, the British and subsequent American ('protective') occupation of
Iceland was skilfully exploited by the United Socialist Party, which integrated
elements of nationalism into its platform in a way that appealed to many
young intellectuals. It should be noted here, moreover, that the occupying
forces were huge in number compared with the local population and frictions
were almost inevitable. Gunnar Helgi Kristinsson has reminded the author
that fist fights broke out between Icelandic youths and the occupying forces in
Reykjavík when the Germans surrendered.

Finally, in an attempt to combat inflation, the Icelandic government in
January 1942 froze all wages at 1941 levels, a move prompting a wave of
wildcat strikes which were so successful that the wage freeze was abolished in
September that year (Karlsson 2000: 315). In other words, the first half of
1942 was marked by high levels of unrest on the labour market and this may
well have contributed to a heightened mood of working-class radicalism, from
which the United Socialist Party profited at the polls.

On the subject of the labour market, it is worth recalling that when the
Social Democratic Party split in 1938, it divided the trade union movement,
and a number of trade union leaders, notably Héðinn Valdimarsson, were instrumental in forming the United Socialist Party along with the Communists.
By the 1940s, the Social Democrats had become independent of, and had lost
their previously dominant position in, the Icelandic Trade Union Federation
and the radical left controlled several individual unions. Indeed, as early as
the 1930s, the Communist-led Workers' Union of Northern Iceland had been
recognised by the employers as a legitimate bargaining partner. The loss of
the Social Democrats' control of the trade union movement was a significant
factor in explaining the greater strength of the radical left in Iceland.

After its formation, the communists remained active and influential in the
United Socialist Party, although just how influential the group was is difficult
to gauge. Jón Ólafsson has argued that 'the astonishing unity among Icelandic
communists is without doubt a major reason for their longevity and ability to
maintain their influence within the socialist movement' (Ólafsson 1998: 21).
Whilst the importance of the 'Moscow connection' for the Icelandic radical left
is hard to estimate, it is clear that there was extensive consultation between the

leaders of the United Socialist Party and subsequently the People's Alliance and representatives of the Soviet Communist Party between the early 1950s and the 1970s. Furthermore, Soviet financial support was procured (albeit not without some persistence on the Icelandic side) for the party's publishing company, *Mál og menning*, and daily newspaper, *Þjóðviljinn*, and at least one of the elements of the barter trade arrangements with the Soviet Union between 1953 and 1976 – the USSR bought the bulk of Iceland's herring production and paid with oil – was to promote pro-Soviet sympathies among the wider public.

Although the communists exerted influence in the United Socialist Party, the latter was none the less predominantly reformist and nationalist, in the sense of being alive to the need to protect native industries, to deal with fundamental issues such as unemployment and to protect the indigenous culture against the cosmopolitan culture of the United States. The radical left stressed the importance of Icelandic neutrality and mobilised anti-NATO sentiment by focusing on the US military presence at the Keflavík base (see chapter 12). In 1956 the United Socialist Party formed an electoral alliance known as the People's Alliance and, following the latter's forthright condemnation of the Warsaw Pact invasion of Czechoslovakia in August 1968, it formalised itself as a political party. At the same time, the hardliners on the left departed the People's Alliance in 1969 and formed a party of their own, called the Union of Liberals and Leftists.

The merger of liberalism and conservatism in Iceland

Outside Iceland we have noted that three or four parties occupied the ground stretching from the centre to the moderate right of the Nordic political spectrum in the period before 1970. Non-socialist tripartism was a feature in Sweden and Denmark and quadripartism in Norway and Finland. In Sweden, the non-socialist bloc comprised the Agrarian/Centre Party, the Liberals and Conservatives, the first two regarding themselves as centre-based parties; in Denmark, the historic non-socialist configuration embraced two liberal parties – the Social Liberals to the left of centre, the Agrarian Liberals to the right of centre – plus the Conservatives. In both Norway and Finland, the non-socialist camps before 1970 numbered four parties: in Norway, three centre-based parties, the Agrarian/Centre Party, Liberals and Christian People's Party, plus the Conservatives; and in Finland, also three centre-based parties, the Agrarian/Centre Party, Liberals and Swedish People's Party, plus the Conservatives. In short, the Nordic party systems have traditionally been characterised by a number of non-socialist parties seeking to protect and promote their separate identities in a crowded electoral marketplace. Their relative strengths varied across the region. In Denmark and Finland the farmer-based parties were the largest non-socialist grouping between the end of the First World War and the late 1960s. In Norway and Sweden the Conservatives were the leading non-socialist party. The Agrarian parties and

Table 4.4 *The average vote for the Conservative and Liberal parties in Denmark, Finland, Norway and Sweden, 1919–2007*

Country	Party	Period average poll
Sweden	Conservatives	19.4
	Liberals	14.2
Norway	Conservatives	22.4
	Liberals	10.2
Finland	Conservatives	17.3
	Liberals	4.8
Denmark	Conservatives	16.1
	Liberals	21.8
	Social Liberals	8.1

The Norwegian Liberal Party (Venstre) average includes the vote of the splinter pro-EU Liberals (Det Liberale folkepartiet) between 1973 and 1985.

the Swedish People's Party have been considered earlier, but table 4.4 sets out the average poll for the Liberal and Conservative parties in Denmark, Norway, Finland and Sweden for the period 1919–2007.

In contrast to the fragmented nature of the non-socialist blocs on mainland Scandinavia, the merger of conservatism and liberalism in Iceland in 1929 meant that the resultant Independence Party became not only the largest single party – ahead of the agrarian Progressive Party – but also overwhelmingly the strongest non-socialist party in Scandinavia, comparable in relative electoral strength to the Social Democratic vote in Sweden. At its first parliamentary election, in 1931, the Independence Party gained 43.8 per cent of the vote.

Although, *à la* Lipset and Rokkan (1967), the main phase of party-building in Iceland was complete by 1930, there was, as Gunnar Helgi Kristinsson (1996) has observed, a gap of about two decades between the introduction of universal suffrage in 1915 and the mobilisation of modern party organisations. The 'politics of scale' was probably the crucial factor here, since the small size of most constituencies meant that individual candidates had relatively little need of formal organisations. In any event, it needs emphasis that the Icelandic party system until just before the Second World War was elitist in character rather than mass-based. In contrast to Norway and Finland, moreover, the national question had not been fully resolved by the time the basic quadripartite configuration of Communists–Social Democrats–Progressive Party–Independence Party had emerged. The national question in fact dominated the political agenda and there was broad cross-party consensus in favour of the achievement of complete independence when the twenty-five-year treaty of union with Denmark expired in 1944.

The Independence Party was founded in 1929, at a time when the Conservatives and Liberals were in opposition to a Progressive Party government backed by the Social Democrats. It proceeded to become the largest single party at the first general election it contested, in 1931, and achieved its greatest-ever success in 1932, when it obtained 48 per cent of the vote. Unlike the Progressive Party (co-operative movement) and the Social Democrats (trade union movement), the Independence Party did not emerge as the extended arm of, or have strong links to, a sectoral interest group. However, although an 'internally created party' formed by the marriage of two parliamentary parties, the Independence Party quickly developed a mass organisational base. Its local branch, called Vörður, in Reykjavík was highly effective and in 1940 twelve working-class societies – including Óðinn – a society of independent sailors and workers founded in the capital in 1938 – came together in a national organisation (Kristjánsson 1979). The Independence Party presented itself as a nationalist party – in contrast to what it claimed were the narrow class interests promoted by the other parties – and by 'highjacking' the national question it quickly succeeded in forging a unique alliance between the urban bourgeoisie – public officials, merchants, owners of fishing vessels and so on – the farmers and manual workers under the banner of full independence. Clearly, the Independence Party possessed the distinct character of a catch-all party of the centre-right *before* the achieve-ment of full independence in 1944. Indeed, writing in the late 1970s, Svanur Kristjánsson concluded that: 'In its heterogeneous voting support and ideology of nationalism and class unity, the Icelandic Independence Party resembles such political parties as the Christian Democratic Union in West Germany and the Conservative Party in Britain rather than the Liberal and Conservative parties in Scandinavia' (Kristjánsson 1979: 31).

The historic party systems from a voter perspective

When viewing the Scandinavian party systems during their 'frozen period' before 1970 from an electoral standpoint, the striking feature is the high inci-dence of class voting, a phenomenon which can be seen to follow logically from the traditional left–right placement of the political parties. The preponderance of class-based parties, in short, was reflected in the prevalence of class-based voting patterns. The supremacy of class parties, particularly in Denmark and Sweden, has already been noted. Torben Worre (1980) comments that the Swedish party system, as elsewhere in Scandinavia, was dominated by 'three big class parties' – the Social Democrats, the Agrarians and the Conservatives. John Fitzmaurice (1981) regards all the historic Danish parties, except the Radicals, as class parties. Class voting involves high levels of political cohesion among socio-economic groups. Thus, in Scandinavia, farmers voted in force for the Agrarian parties in Sweden, Norway and Finland and for the farming-oriented Agrarian Liberals and Progressive Party in Denmark and Iceland, respectively; the workers backed one of the parties of the left, and, in the

Table 4.5 *Percentage class composition of support for the Norwegian parties in 1957*

Party	Commun- ists	Labour	Liberals	Christian People's	Agrarians	Conser- vatives
Old middle class	0	7	16	14	5	26
New middle class	13	16	33	25	6	49
Workers	87	70	31	42	21	19
Farmers	0	7	21	19	68	6
Total	*100*	*100*	*100*	*100*	*100*	*100*
N	*15*	*637*	*101*	*115*	*100*	*165*

'Old middle class' = self-employed, business owners and independent professional people.
'New middle class' = salaried employees, clerical workers and civil servants.
The 'Workers' category includes farm labourers.
Source: Listhaug (1997: 87).

Danish, Norwegian and Swedish cases, it was mostly the Social Democrats; the middle classes supported the Conservatives or possibly the Liberals. According to Petersson and Särlvik (1975: 88), in 1964, 84 per cent of the Swedish blue-collar workforce voted for one of the two left-wing parties (78 per cent for the Social Democrats); 93 per cent of farmers voted for one of the non-socialist parties (over two-thirds for the Agrarians); and 83 per cent of professional people and the larger entrepreneurs (the 'old middle class') supported one of the non-socialist parties, mainly the Conservatives and Liberals. Seventy-two per cent of small-firm owners also voted for a non-socialist party, principally the Liberals. However, among the lower white-collar (clerical) workers and rural workers (farm labourers, lumberjacks, etc.) partisan allegiances were roughly equally divided between the socialist and non-socialist parties.

The high political cohesion of socio-economic groupings (classes) in Scandinavia had a counterpart in the high social cohesion of those political parties that possessed an accentuated class profile. Norway and Finland will illustrate the general point. In 1957, as table 4.5 demonstrates, 70 per cent of Norwegian Labour Party voters were working class, 68 per cent of the Agrarians' support derived from farmers and 75 per cent of the Conservative vote emanated from the middle classes. Table 4.6, which compares the social composition of support for the 'historic' parties in Finland in 1948 and 1966, paints a very similar picture. In 1948 81 per cent and in 1966 72 per cent of the Agrarians' support derived from farmers; in the same two years, an average of three-quarters of the Social Democrats' support came from the working class and the proportion rose to four-fifths in the case of the radical leftist SKDL. Between 1948 and 1966 the Conservatives received relatively less support from the larger farmers and became more clearly middle-class in composition.

In the late 1960s, Peter Pultzer (1967: 98) wrote that 'class is the basis of voting behaviour in Britain; all else is embellishment and detail'. This was

Table 4.6 *Percentage class composition of support for the Finnish parties in 1948 and 1966*

Party	Year	Farmers	Working class	Middle class
Agrarians	1948	81	16	3
	1966	72	18	10
Social Democrats	1948	14	76	10
	1966	7	74	19
Conservatives	1948	27	25	48
	1966	12	20	68
People's Democratic League (SKDL)	1948	19	78	3
	1966	11	82	7
Swedish People's Party	1948	35	33	32
	1966	43	22	35

Source: Pesonen *et al.* (1993: 105).

broadly the case in Scandinavia at the time, although class voting does not constitute an exhaustive picture of traditional modes of voting behaviour in the region. Indeed, the multidimensional character of the Finnish, Icelandic and Norwegian party systems and the historic role of non-functional cleavages dictated historic patterns of cross-class or deviant voting in these countries. At least four deviant patterns warrant emphasis:

1 The ability of the Independence Party to mobilise broad-based support in the 1930s around the final resolution of the national question created a distinctive tradition of working-class conservatism in Iceland. It has been estimated that between one-quarter and one-fifth of the Independence Party's vote in the period 1931–42 derived from the working class.
2 The strength of ethnic allegiance at the time of the introduction of mass democracy in Finland in 1907 prompted a majority of Swedish-speaking blue-collar workers to vote for the Swedish People's Party and in the process to create the closest approximation to the phenomenon of working-class conservatism in Finland. Among the Finland Swede minority, irrespective of occupation, ethnic voting prevailed over class voting.
3 In Norway, religiosity (active churchgoing and membership of one of the revivalist organisations) and the strength of moral opposition (including teetotalism) to the secularisation of the established (high) church and state united elements of both the working and middle classes in support of Christian democracy.
4 In addition to its working-class 'core' of blue-collar and farm workers, social democracy attracted elements of the salaried strata. Middle-class socialism was important in the growth of Danish social democracy in the 1930s. The

Table 4.7 *Percentage class composition of support for the Swedish Social Democrats in 1964*

Occupational group	Percentage of group supporting the party
Blue-collar workers	78
Lower white-collar workers	46
Professional/larger entrepreneurs	8
Small entrepreneurs	26
Rural workers	53
Farmers	7

Source: Berglund and Lindström (1978: 108).

same was true in Sweden by the late 1950s. As table 4.7 demonstrates, 46 per cent of the lower middle class supported the Swedish Social Democrats in 1964.

Summary

1.   An analysis of the relative electoral strengths of the Scandinavian party families has revealed four prominent features – the supremacy of social democracy in Denmark, Norway and particularly Sweden; the strength and resilience of the Agrarian Party in Finland and significant backing for 'small a' agrarian parties in Denmark and Iceland; significantly greater support for the radical left in Finland and Iceland than elsewhere in the region; and the merger of liberalism and conservatism to create a broad-based centre-right party in Iceland.

2.   Viewed from a voter perspective, during their 'frozen' period before 1970 the Scandinavian party systems exhibited three striking features: a high level of electoral stability; generally low levels of inter-bloc mobility; and, above all, the predominance of class-based voting. A number of deviant patterns of voting behaviour were none the less noted.

3.   Until 1970, the Scandinavian party systems proved largely capable of adapting to social and economic change. Parties moderated and modernised their programmes, modified their names and used the media (increasingly television) to project themselves to the electorate. Most notably, all the Agrarian parties had become Centre parties with a capital C by the mid-1960s. However, over nearly half a century the Scandinavian countries had progressed, albeit at uneven rates, from possessing significant primary sectors to standing on the threshold of the post-industrial phase of development. The 'containment capacity' of the Scandinavian party systems, in short, was being stretched all the time, and in the 1970s the old mould was shattered. It is to the question of party system change from about 1970 that we shall now turn our attention.

References

Aasland, Tertit (1974) *Fra landmannsorganisasjon til bondeparti. Politisk debatt og taktikk i Norsk landmansforbund, 1896–1920*, Universitetsforlaget: Oslo.

Alapuro, Risto (1980) 'Mass support for fascism in Finland', in Stein Ugelvik Larsen (ed.), *Who Were the Fascists?*, Universitetsforlaget: Bergen, pp. 678–86.

Allardt, Erik (1970) 'Types of protest and alienation', in Erik Allardt and Stein Rokkan (eds), *Mass Politics*, Free Press: New York, pp. 45–63.

Arter, David (1979) 'The Finnish Centre Party: profile of a "hinge group"', *West European Politics*, 2 (1), pp. 108–27.

Arter, David (1981) 'Kekkonen's Finland: enlightened despotism or consensual democracy?', *West European Politics*, 4 (3), pp. 219–34.

Arter, David (1994) 'Die bürgerlichen und konservativen Parteien Finnlands. Zentrumpartei, Nationale Sammlungspartei, Schwedische Volkspartei und Finnischer Christlicher Bund', in Hans-Joachim Veen (ed.), *Christlich-demokratische und konservative Parteien in Westeuropa*, vol. 4, Schöningh: Paderborn, pp. 231–326.

Arter, David (2001) 'The Finnish Centre Party: a case of successful transformation?', in David Arter (ed.), *From Farmyard to City Square? The Electoral Adaptation of the Nordic Agrarian Parties*, Ashgate: Aldershot, pp. 59–95.

Bergh, Trond (ed.) (1977) *Vekst og velstand*, Universitetsforlaget: Oslo.

Berglund, Sten (1990) 'The ecology of Finnish communism: a study of postwar data, 1945–83', in Jan Sundberg and Sten Berglund (eds), *Finnish Democracy*, Gummerus: Jyväskylä, pp. 65–86.

Berglund, Sten and Ulf Lindström (1978) *The Scandinavian Party System(s)*, Studentlitteratur: Lund.

Birgersson, Bengt Owe, Stig Hadenius, Björn Molin and Hans Wieslander (1981) *Sverige efter 1900*, BonnierFakta Bokförlag: Stockholm.

Carlsson, Sten (1956) *Bondens politiska storhetstid, 1867–1914, Bonden i svensk historia*, vol. 3, Bonniers: Stockholm.

Ersson, Svante (2005) 'Den yttre vänstern i Norge och Sverige', in Marie Demker and Lars Svåsand (eds), *Partiernas århundrade*, Santérus: Stockholm, pp. 51–77.

Esping-Andersen, Gøsta (1985) *Politics Against Markets. The Social Democratic Road to Power*, Princeton University Press: Princeton, NJ.

Esping-Andersen, Gøsta (1990) 'Single-party dominance in Sweden: the saga of social democracy', in T. J. Pempel (ed.), *Uncommon Democracies*, Cornell University: Ithaca, NY, pp. 33–57.

Fitzmaurice, John (1981) *Politics in Denmark*, Hurst: London.

Goul Andersen, Jørgen and Jan Bendix Jensen (2001) 'The Danish Venstre: liberal, agrarian or centrist?', in David Arter (ed.), *From Farmyard to City Square? The Electoral Adaptation of the Nordic Agrarian Parties*, Ashgate: Aldershot, pp. 96–131.

Greenhill, Gaylon H. (1965) 'The Norwegian Agrarian Party: a class party?', *Social Science*, 40 (4), pp. 214–19.

Grimnes, Ole Kristian (1983) 'The beginnings of the Resistance Movement', in Henrik S. Nissen (ed.), *Scandinavia During the Second World War*, University of Minnesota Press: Minneapolis, MN, pp. 182–220.

Hakalehto, Ilkka (1986) *Maalailiitto-Keskustapuolueen historia I, Maalaisliitto autonomian aikana, 1906–1917*, Kirjayhtymä: Helsinki.

Heidar, Knut (2001) *Norway. Elites on Trial*, Westview: Boulder, CO.

Hokkanen, Kari (1996) *Maalaisliitto sodan ja vaaran vuosina 1939–1950*, Maalaisliitto Keskustan historia 3, Otava: Keuruu.

Hyvämäki, Lauri (1978) 'Valtioneuvosto 2. maailmansodan jälkeen vuoteen 1957', in *Valtioneuvoston historia 1917–1966*, Valtionpainatuskeskus: Helsinki, pp. 253–470.

Iivari, Ulpu (2007) *Kansanvallan puolustajat. Sosialidemokraattinen eduskuntaryhmä 100 vuotta*, Otava: Keuruu.

Iivonen, Jyrki (1986) 'State or party? The dilemma of relations between the Soviet and Finnish Communist Parties', *Journal of Communist Studies*, 2 (1), pp. 5–30.

Jonnergård, Gustaf (1985) *Så blev Centerpartiet. Bonderförbunds – och centeridéerna från fyrtiotalet fram till 1960*, LT's Forlag: Stockholm.

Karlsson, Gunnar (2000) *The History of Iceland*, University of Minnesota Press: Minneapolis, MN.

Karonen, Vesa (1997) 'Uusi demokratia – vaalit, ääni ja viiva', *Helsingin Sanomat*, 16 March.

Kianto, Ilmari (1997) *Punainen viiva*, thirty-first edition, Otava: Helsinki.

Kirby, David (1979) *Finland in the Twentieth Century*, Hurst: London.

Kirby, David (1995) *The Baltic World 1772–1993*, Longman: London.

Kristinsson, Gunnar Helgi (1991) *Farmers' Parties. A Study in Electoral Adaptation*, Félagsvisindastofnun: Háskóla Íslands.

Kristinsson, Gunnar Helgi (1996) 'Parties, states and patronage', *West European Politics*, 19 (3), pp. 433–57.

Kristjánsson, Svanur (1979) 'The electoral basis of the Icelandic Independence Party, 1922–44', *Scandinavian Political Studies*, 2 (1), pp. 31–52.

Laulajainen, Pertti (1979) *Sosialidemokraati vai Kommunisti?*, Itä-Suomen instituutti: Mikkeli.

Lipset, S. M. and S. Rokkan (eds) (1967) *Party Systems and Voter Alignments*, Free Press: New York.

Listaug, Ola (1997) 'The decline of class voting', in Kaare Strøm and Lars Svåsand (eds), *Challenges to Political Parties*, University of Michigan Press: Ann Arbor, MI, pp. 77–90.

London, Gary (1975) *The End of an Opposition of Principle. The Case of the Finnish Socialist Workers' Party*, Institute of Political Science Research Reports 37, University of Helsinki.

Miller, Kenneth E. (1991) *Denmark. A Troubled Welfare State*, Westview Press: Boulder, CO.

Nilson, Sten Sparre (1958) 'The political parties', in J. A. Lauwerys (ed.), *Scandinavian Democracy*, Schultz: Copenhagen, pp. 107–26.

Ólafsson, Jón (1998) 'The Comintern experience: how it influenced the Icelandic left', paper at www.nato.int/acad/fellow/95-97/olafsson.pdf.

Pesonen, Pertti, Risto Sänkiaho and Sami Borg (1993) *Vaalikansan äänivalta*, WSOY: Porvoo.

Petersson, O. and B. Särlvik (1975) *The 1973 Election*, Central Bureau of Statistics: Stockholm.

Pultzer, Peter (1967) *Political Representation and Elections in Britain*, Allen and Unwin: London.

Rentola, Kimmo (1997) *Niin kylmää että polttaa*, Otava: Helsinki.

Sartori, Giovanni (1976) *Parties and Party Systems*, Cambridge University Press: Cambridge.

Thermanius, Edvard (1933) *Sveriges Politiska Partier*, Hugo Gebers Förlag: Stockholm.
Torkko, Markku (ed.) (1995) *Terästä ja karvalakkeja*, Painotuote: Rovaniemi.
Törnudd, Klaus (1968) *The Electoral System of Finland*, Hugh Evelyn: London.
Trommer, Aage (1983) 'Scandinavia and the turn of the tide', in Henrik S. Nissen (ed.),
    Scandinavia During the Second World War, University of Minnesota Press: Minneapolis,
    MN, pp. 221–77.
Worre, Torben (1980) 'Class parties and class voting in the Scandinavian countries',
    Scandinavian Political Studies, 3 (4), pp. 299–320.

Part III

Parties, voters and social change: w(h)ither the Scandinavian party system model?

5

The 'earthquake elections' of 1970–73 and the emergence of new party types

So long as there are high taxes and Muslims, we've got something to fight for.
(Mogens Glistrup, founder member of Danish Progress Party,
cited in Miller 1991: 75)

The so-called 'earthquake elections', first in Finland and then in Denmark and Norway between 1970 and 1973, constituted a root-and-branch challenge to the unidimensional Scandinavian party system model and the old mould appeared irrevocably broken. Since this seismic period, four developments stand out. First, electoral volatility has increased. The electorate is less stable and the incidence of 'vote switching' from one election to the next has risen. Second, as a by-product of heightened electoral volatility, there have been marked short-term fluctuations in support for the historic (pre-1970) parties. Third, the number of legislative parties has increased. Across the five Nordic states, well over twenty parties entered parliament for the first time between 1970 and 2007. Fourth, there has been a relatively high mortality rate among these new parties. The splinter parties in particular have proved short-lived, but also several of the anti-Establishment populist parties spawned by the earthquake elections have had a short life span. Accordingly, this and the next chapter seek answers to two closely related questions. Chapter 6 asks both how we should go about analysing and assessing the extent of party system change since 1970 and how much change there has been. This chapter presents essential background material and asks whether the ground-breaking elections of 1970–73 created lasting fissures in the Scandinavian party systems and, if so, what new party types have emerged.

The 'earthquake elections', 1970–73

Although the 'earthquake elections' in Denmark and Norway three years later are more widely known, the 'thaw' in the frozen edifice of the Scandinavian party systems began in earnest in Finland in March 1970, when the Finnish Rural Party (Suomen maaseudun puolue) polled a sensational 10.5 per cent of the vote. The party was synonymous with the name of Vennamo. It was founded and led by Veikko Vennamo, a former Agrarian, who created a splinter Smallholders' Party (Pientalonpoikain puolue) in 1959, which, in 1966, was rechristened the Finnish Rural Party. Vennamo's trademark was an original, highly colourful and trenchant anti-Establishment rhetoric. In 1970 he hammered home the cause of the 'forgotten nation' – that is, the interests of those poorer small farmers in the peripheral areas of northern and eastern Finland who were being hardest hit by the amalgamation of holdings undertaken as part of a programme of agricultural rationalisation by the broad centre-left governments of the late 1960s.

Vennamo's 'shock result' in 1970 proved a precursor of things to come elsewhere in the region. Most notably, on 4 December 1973, the Danish Progress Party (Fremskridtspartiet) claimed a staggering 15.9 per cent of the vote, making it at a stroke the second largest party in the Folketing. Its founder, Mogens Glistrup, a Danish tax lawyer with no political experience and few contacts with politicians, used the 118 seconds of his first television appearance in January 1971 to put his case against income tax:

> I used the two minutes to tell the public that no one had to pay more income tax than he wanted, that the tax evaders were as heroic as the resistance groups during the German occupation in World War II and that people suffering from tax disease ought to consult a tax doctor, just as they consult a dentist if they have toothache. (Quoted in Harmel and Svåsand 1993: 82)

When not adopted as a candidate by any of the non-socialist parties, Glistrup had announced the decision to found his own party in a restaurant in Copenhagen on 22 August 1972. The party's name and records were bought for a fairly nominal sum from its former leader, who had been attempting to form a pensioners' party. Glistrup cultivated a plain language for public speaking and spiced his message with matters of 'general human interest', such as eating marzipan and having a big private swimming pool. For him, the four 'old parties' were not simply old but senile, and his particular aversions were 'paper pushers' and 'desk popes' (bureaucrats). The party's simple programme, which Glistrup wrote himself, concentrated on the unholy trinity of income tax (which would be abolished over a five-year period), red-tape bureaucracy and the jungle of laws and regulations.

The forerunner of Glistrup's Norwegian namesake – the Progress Party launched in 1977 by Carl I. Hagen – was Anders Lange's Party for a Drastic Reduction in Taxes, Rates and State Intervention. It was founded in 1973 by Lange, a sixty-nine-year-old former Conservative and kennels owner, who used the vehicle of the dog breeders' newsletter to put across his political views. At the 1973 general election Lange's party gained 5.0 per cent of the vote and four

Storting seats. In the simple – indeed simplistic – style of Glistrup, Lange's plat- *1973*
form for the 1973 election campaign comprised a single sheet of paper setting *0.5 % PP*
out on one side the ten things the party was tired of and on the other side the *facile language*
ten things it stood for. Lange challenged not only high taxes but also some basic
tenets of the welfare state. Unlike Glistrup, Lange was not an accomplished *→ 10/10*
speaker, though he, too, had the merit of using plain, readily comprehensible *single sheet*
language and of being entertaining. His address at the inaugural party meeting, *like Glistrup*
in front of about 1,000 persons gathered in an Oslo theatre, included anecdotes
ranging from the price of coffee in the Storting cafeteria to personal experiences
(Harmel and Svåsand 1993: 77–82). Lange was more than willing to make a
spectacle of himself. Certainly, wearing a sword for a national television debate,
as he did in 1973, was hardly likely to go unnoticed.

The 'earthquake elections' were, by definition, *high-volatility elections.* *PENDERSEN*
Indeed, based on Mogens Pedersen's (1985) 'volatility index' – calculated *'volatility index'*
by reference to the cumulative gains of all the winning parties at the polls –
Finland registered a net volatility level of 14.8 per cent in 1970, Norway 19.3
per cent in 1973 and Denmark no less than 29.1 per cent in the same year.
The volatility levels at the earthquake elections were, of course, exceptional.
However, across mainland Scandinavia there has, since then, been an upward
trend in levels of electoral instability, based on the increased incidence of 'vote
switching' from one election to the next and, in addition, the birth, and indeed
death, of still more new parties.

Rising electoral volatility and more new parties

In the first Swedish election surveys, in the mid-1950s, about 93 per cent of
voters supported the same party from one election to the next; by 1970 this
had dropped to 84 per cent, by 1998 to 70 per cent and by 2006 to 66 per cent
(table 5.1). Restated, at the Riksdag election in 2006, 34 per cent of Swedes
voted for a different party than in 2002. In Norway the proportion of 'stable'
voters in 1969 was 82 per cent, but this had declined to 63 per cent by 2001

Table 5.1 *The proportion of party switchers in Sweden, 1988–2006*

Year	Percentage switchers
1988–91	25
1991–94	26
1994–98	27
1998–2002	30
2002–6	34

Source: Valu, 2006.

Table 5.2 *The proportion of party switchers in Norway, 1981–2005*

Year	Percentage switchers
1981–85	20
1985–89	30
1989–93	32
1993–97	33
1997–2001	37
2001–5	40

Source: Aardal and Stavn (2006: 2).

(Ersson 2005: 61–2) and 60 per cent in 2005. In other words, the proportion of party switchers was 40 per cent in 2005 (table 5.2), or 47 per cent if those shifting to abstaining are included. In Denmark the proportion of stable voters in 1971 was 83 per cent, which dropped to only 56 per cent two years later and by 2001 stood at 66 per cent. Plainly, twice as many – 34 per cent – changed party in 2001 as did so in 1971 (Nielsen and Thomsen 2003: 67). However, the upward trend in electoral volatility has been less continuous in Denmark and in 2005 (table 5.3) the proportion of voters changing parties had reduced to 25 per cent (Andersen *et al.* 2007: 67–9). In Finland electoral research has been less comprehensive than elsewhere in the region. However, in 1983, 54 per cent of Finns reported that they *always* voted for the same party, whereas twenty years later that figure had fallen to 36 per cent. In the 1970s between 70 and 75 per cent of the active electorate *generally* voted for the same party as in the previous election; by the 1990s that figure had fallen to just over 60 per cent and by 2003 it stood at about 60 per cent (Paloheimo and Sundberg

Table 5.3 *The proportion of party switchers in Denmark, 1981–2005*

Year	Percentage switchers
1981	18
1984	22
1987	23
1988	23
1989	20
1994	28
1998	29
2001	34
2005	25

Source: Nielsen and Thomsen (2003: 67); Andersen *et al.* (2007: 67–9).

2005: 196–201). In other words, in the 1970s about one-quarter of Finns were vote switchers whilst most recently about two-fifths have been.

In addition to increased electoral volatility, the number of legislative parties has increased since the early 1970s. In short, there has been a growth in the number of new parties entering parliament. Curiously, a number of them revived the names of historic parties that antedated the attainment of national independence and the completion of the building of party systems that occurred in connection with the achievement of mass democracy. For example, at the 1923 Icelandic general election, an alliance between the Home Rule Party and the Citizens' Party – the latter formed from the rump of the old Independence Party – gained 53.6 per cent of the vote and more than half the parliamentary seats (Karlsson 2000: 304). The Citizens' Party then formed part of the new Independence Party, created in 1929. However, it seceded and became an independent entity again in the late 1980s.

A month before the 1987 Alþingi election, Albert Guðmundsson, a leading figure in the Independence Party, was removed by the prime minister from his post as minister of finance, having been implicated, *inter alia*, in a large financial lawsuit involving a defunct shipping company, Hafskip. In protest, and with the Independence Party badly divided, Guðmundsson (re)formed the Citizens' Party (Borgaraflokkurinn), which proceeded to gain a notable 10.8 per cent of the vote and seven of the sixty-three parliamentary seats in that election. When, two years later, Guðmundsson resigned the leadership of his party and was appointed Icelandic ambassador to Paris, the Citizens' Party split, two MPs forming their own parliamentary group whilst the remainder joined a centre-left coalition under Steingrímur Hermansson. At the 1991 general election, the Citizens' Party managed only 1 per cent of the vote, failed to win a parliamentary seat and ceased to exist altogether three years later.

The Young Finns (*nuorsuomalainen puolue*) emerged in the 1880s as the liberal–republican wing of the Finnish nationalist movement and took a harder line than the Old Finns (*vanhasuomalainen puolue*) against czarist violations of the basic constitutional rights of the Grand Duchy. However, the party did not survive the realignment of the centre-right that followed independence and the subsequent divisions over the new form of government. The Young Finn Party owed much of its 'second coming' to Risto Penttilä, a special adviser in the Ministry of Defence who, having narrowly failed to win the post of Conservative Party secretary (he was a party member for only a day!), devoted his energies to a self-styled 'reformist centre' movement. Registering as a political party barely four months before the 1995 Eduskunta election – at which it gained 2.8 per cent of the vote and two parliamentary seats – the Young Finns sought particularly to appeal to younger, middle-class, urban voters, with rather nebulous rhetoric about the need to change the political culture. Its 'pick and mix' programme included sizeable budget cuts – including the abolition of party, agriculture and enterprise subsidies – a shift from income to consumer taxation and a pledge to teach Finns to use computer networks (Arter 1995: 201). By 1999 the Young Finns' vote had fallen to 1 per cent and it had only a single MP elected, and in 2003 it lost its parliamentary toehold altogether.

The new post-1970 parties have included 'lone rangers' – that is, parties that only ever had elected a single MP, albeit not necessarily only for a single term. For example, at the 1997 Norwegian Storting election, Steinar Bastesen, a flamboyant whaling skipper, who dressed routinely in sealskin gear, was elected as the single representative of a cross-party electoral list (Tverrpolitisk folkevalgte), which was strongly opposed to the European Union (EU), the International Whaling Commission, Green Peace and indeed any other authority wishing to impose restrictions on the hunting and export of whales and seals. The name Coastal Party (Kystpartiet) was adopted at a meeting in Løvolds Café in Bodø in Nordland and the party was formally founded in February 1999. Bastesen's brand of populism was able to mobilise elements in the periphery against the dictates of the centre – whether in Oslo, Brussels or beyond – and the Coastal Party's support was heavily concentrated in northern Norway. In the Nordland constituency it polled 10.9 per cent of the vote at the 2001 general election and in neighbouring Troms 10 per cent the same year. However, the prospect of electing three MPs in 2001 and holding the balance of power in the Storting did not materialise (Madeley 2002) and, despite running candidates in every constituency, at the 2005 general election (including those without a coastline!), the Coastal Party went empty-handed.

As the cases of the Citizens' Party, Young Finns and Coastal Party demonstrate, there has been a relatively *high mortality rate* among the 'post-1970' parties. Many of the *splinter parties* in particular proved short-lived. Thus, the Finnish People's Unity Party (Suomen kansan yhtenäisyyspuolue) broke away from the Finnish Rural Party in 1973 in protest against Veikko Vennamo's authoritarian management style. It returned a solitary parliamentarian between 1975 and 1979 and quickly ceased to exist thereafter.

The Liberal People's Party (De Liberale folkeparti) in Norway split from the Liberals (Venstre) shortly after the first EU referendum in 1972 and comprised (losing) 'pro-marketeers'. It disbanded in 1988 and reunited with the Liberal Party. More significantly, several of the anti-Establishment populist parties proved to have a limited life span. This was the case with the Finnish Rural Party, the Progress Party in Denmark and a third anti-Establishment party, New Democracy, which broke through in Sweden in 1991.

The Finnish Rural Party was very much a 'family enterprise'. Veikko Vennamo was succeeded by his son, Pekka, who led the party to its 'second coming' in 1983, when it polled 9.7 per cent of the electorate, having claimed during the campaign to be able to halve unemployment in six months! Pekka coined the pejorative term *rötösherrat* (which can loosely be translated as 'sleaze merchants') effectively to mobilise public indignation over several minor incidents of sharp practice, involving, for example, MPs overclaiming on daily allowances (Arter 1983), and by 1983 the weight of the Rural

Party vote had shifted to the towns. In that year the party proceeded to enter government, where it remained until 1990, when Pekka Vennamo resigned both his ministerial and party chair's duties to take up a lucrative post as head of the National Postal Board. Without either Vennamo, the Rural Party subsided rapidly, polling only 1.3 per cent at the 1995 general election and ceasing to exist altogether after that.

Much as in the Finnish Rural Party, internal division debilitated the Progress Party in Denmark and its support had fallen to 11.0 per cent in 1979 and only 3.6 per cent in 1984. The year before that, Glistrup was convicted of tax fraud, sentenced to three years' imprisonment and necessarily relinquished day-to-day control of the party. He bounced back and during the 1988 general election campaign called for tighter restrictions on immigration. 'So long as there are high taxes and Muslims, we've got something to fight for', he is reputed to have said (Miller 1991: 75). However, the party effectively ditched him prior to the 1990 general election and he moved on to found another party, which got absolutely nowhere. By 1998 the Progress Party polled only 2.4 per cent and competed on the radical right with the stridently anti-immigrant Danish People's Party, founded by Pia Kjærsgaard, who, ironically, had led the Progress Party during Glistrup's period of internment.

Sweden's earthquake election – perhaps better described as a 'mini-quake' – occurred two decades after the rest of mainland Scandinavia, but at the 1991 Riksdag election two new parties, the Christian Democrats and New Democracy (Ny demokrati), made a parliamentary breakthrough. New Democracy polled 6.7 per cent. Formed, like Glistrup's Progress Party and Anders Lange's Party, only months before the general election, by a count, Ian Wachtmeister, and a fairground owner, Bert Karlsson (who also owned a record company and had come to public prominence with his criticism of food prices), the New Democrats' diffuse anti-Establishment tirade possessed a wide appeal. Karlsson's dismissive reference to the 'crocodile politicians' in the other parties – 'all mouth and no ears'! – was typical of the sort of inflammatory rhetoric – compare here Lange's derogatory reference to 'the political boys of this century' – which sought to trade off a prevalent and insidious *Politikverdrossenheit*, that is, popular mistrust of parties and politicians, and to project the image of an 'anti-party'. The New Democrats had received support for their joint venture from Siewert Öholm in his much-viewed television programme *Svar direkt* (*Direct Reply*); the mood was ripe and New Democracy strove to establish itself as an *enfant terrible*, poking fun at the existing parties and carving out a niche as an irreverent, old brigade-niggling populist force. The word 'New' in its title was intended to denote that the 'old parties' were played out. In the event, it was the New Democrats who were soon played out. A familiar story of internal dissension and revolt against dictatorialism (Wachtmeister's) turned the 'joke party' into a laughing stock itself and at the 1994 Riksdag election it polled a mere 1.2 per cent – well below the 4 per cent of the national vote necessary to qualify for parliamentary seats.

Four new party types

We have noted that since 1970 the number of legislative parties has increased, but that among the new parties mortality rates have been high. The parliamentary life of the splinter parties, in particular, has been short and, despite significant polls at breakthrough elections, a number of the anti-Establishment populist parties have also ceased to exist. Yet four new types of party have emerged and, more importantly, institutionalised their positions since the electoral turbulence of the early 1970s. Two, the 'eco-socialist' parties to the left of social democracy and the populist parties on the radical right, can be placed fairly readily on a unidimensional party spectrum. However, it is more difficult to locate the other two new 'party families', the Greens and Christian Democrats, on a conventional left–right continuum.

Eco-socialist parties

This group of five main radical leftist parties (table 5.4) may be said to have sought in varying measure to marry non-doctrinaire socialism, environmentalism and elements of feminism. The eco-socialist parties either seceded from, and/or displaced communist parties from parliament (Denmark and Norway in the 1960s), or succeeded communist parties at the time of the Soviet Union's collapse (Finland and Sweden) or were created on a red–green platform as part of a broader realignment on the political left (Iceland in the late 1990s). The five eco-socialist parties founded the Nordic Green Left Alliance in Reykjavík in February 2004.

Denmark

The Danish Socialist People's Party (Socialistisk Folkeparti) was formed in 1959, when the Danish Communist Party expelled Aksel Larsen and a group of what were described as 'Titoist revisionists'. The new party set out to chart a 'Danish road to socialism' – a course that lay between 'the Social Democrats' reformism (which only shored up capitalism) and the Communist Party's empty revolutionary rhetoric (which produced no changes)' (Logue 1982: 105). Initially, the Socialist People's Party directed itself expressly at blue-collar

Table 5.4 *The Nordic eco-socialist parties*

Party	Country	Year founded
Socialist People's Party	Denmark	1959
Socialist Left	Norway	1975
Left	Sweden	1990
Left Alliance	Finland	1990
Left Greens	Iceland	1999

socialists disillusioned with both the Communists and the Social Democrats. Indeed, many leading figures in the new party saw little that was errant in the theory of the Danish Communist Party. They believed they were founding a new Danish communist party, different from the existing one primarily in not having to defend the Soviet Union as the socialist utopia (Logue 1982: 89–90). However, in 1963 the Socialist People's Party programme jettisoned strategic communist concepts and insisted that socialism be adapted to the politico-economic realities of Denmark as a modern welfare state. Particular emphasis was given to the notions of decentralisation and democratisation – that is, the provision of equality of opportunity to make decisions and its corollary, a radical redistribution of power at every level and in every sphere of society. In this, as John Logue has noted, the Yugoslavian model of workers' self-management was influential (Logue 1982: 95).

At its first Folketing election, in 1960, the Socialist People's Party's vote of 6.1 per cent was 5 percentage points greater than that of the Communists; its strength lay in the towns and Copenhagen in particular (Borre and Stehouwer 1970: 51–3). Four years later its vote fell marginally, to 5.8 per cent. Indeed, although now the leading radical leftist party – and a non-communist radical leftist party that had abandoned the dogmatic precepts of the Communists – the Socialist People's Party's strategy was somewhat convoluted and its implementation lacked conviction. In essence, the party accepted the liberal democratic multi-party system and the reality of a dominant Social Democratic Party and sought by a combination of 'stick' – mass pressure through the trade union movement – and 'carrot' – co-operation in a 'workers' majority' in parliament – to force the reluctant Social Democrats to act as socialists (Logue 1982: 195). Logue (1982: 265) describes the basic approach of Larsen as one of 'antagonistic co-operation'. Yet when the Socialist People's Party polled 10.9 per cent and a 'workers' majority' was achieved in 1966, the party's reluctance to join the Social Democrats in government led only to informal co-operation between the two parties. Even this created internal tensions and the left-wing majority was eroded when in 1967 six Socialist People's Party MPs, led by Erik Sigsgaard, voted against the government and subsequently split away to form a new party, the Left Socialists (Venstre Socialisterne). This precipitated a general election at which the Socialist People's Party declined to precisely the poll it obtained at its first election, in 1960.

The 1973 'earthquake election' marked the beginning of a watershed for the Socialist People's Party in at least two important respects. First, the election defeat – the party's 6.0 per cent was over 3 percentage points down on its result in 1971 – coupled with Social Democratic losses and increased fragmentation on the radical left, undercut the strategy of 'antagonistic co-operation'. The Social Democrats' vote collapsed and the Communists returned to the Folketing after an absence of fifteen years. By 1975, moreover, the Left Socialists regained parliamentary representation and, although by the 1977 general election the Social Democrats had recovered much of their lost vote, there was virtually an even three-way split on the radical left. Second, the 1973 'earthquake election' was a watershed in that a younger generation, attracted to the party more often than not by its stance against membership of the European Economic Community (EEC) – at the time of Danish accession to the EEC on 1 January 1973 the Socialist People's Party was the only Folketing party to oppose membership (Fitzmaurice 1981: 109) – infused the party with an increasingly eco-socialist ethos. There were fewer manual workers and much of this 'new blood' was active in issue-based groups such as the women's movement, environmental movement and anti-nuclear lobby. By the 1977 general election all the 'Larsenists' had disappeared from the parliamentary group – Larsen himself died in 1972 – and four years later the Socialist People's Party doubled its vote to become the third largest party, with 11.3 per cent of the poll.

The 1980s have thus far been the best electoral years for the Danish Socialist People's Party. In the four Folketing elections in that decade, it averaged 12.6 per cent and in 1987 polled its record 14.6 per cent. Ole Borre points to the crystallisation of a 'new politics' agenda in Denmark between 1979 and 1987 – that is, the existence in the electorate of a coherent non-economic policy dimension, which is separate from the economic left–right dimension and is relatively permanent. He also speculates that 'small and medium-sized parties that are not obliged to represent a national or religious minority may "mutate" into New Politics parties' (Borre 1995: 2003). His point is well taken. The Socialist People's Party was not born an eco-socialist party: it became one, partly as a consequence of the need to compete with the old class parties and the Social Democrats in particular. Party change was facilitated by the growing importance attached to environmental questions in the late 1980s and, symptomatically, when in 1987 the Socialist People's Party recorded its best-ever poll, a Green Party participated in a Folketing election for the first time (gaining 1.4 per cent of the vote).

In the six general elections between 1990 and 2007, the Socialist People's Party's average poll was 8.1 per cent and, significantly, until 2007 it had not contrived to benefit from the general volatility of the left-wing vote. The 1990s saw a general shift to the right in Danish politics and immigration became the dominant 'new politics' issue. However, at the 2005 general election, many voters, it seems, were unhappy with the relatively passive line of the Socialist People's parliamentary group when faced with measures before the Folketing designed to tighten the immigration legislation (Knudsen 2005). Within the party, moreover, there was entrenched division between the 'traditionalists', who were hard-line anti-Europeans, and the 'revisionists', who favoured the softer Eurosceptic line canvassed by the party chair, Holger K. Nielsen. He resigned the day after the 2005 general election, at which the party was reduced to 6.0 per cent of the vote and there were defections to the unequivocally anti-EU Unity List (Enhedslisten – De Rød–Grønne). In 2007, however, under the leadership of Villy Søvndal, the Socialist People's Party revived and recorded its best result (13.0 per cent) since 1987, clearly taking votes from the Unity List, Social Liberals and Social Democrats. All in all, the Danish Socialist People's Party is not a protest party: it attracts left-wing voters in general and has established itself as a stable addition to the historic Danish party system.

Norway

The Norwegian Socialist People's Party (Sosialistisk Folkeparti), created in 1961 by intellectual dissidents expelled from the Labour Party, was modelled on its Danish counterpart and shared with it the conviction that international non-alignment was a *sine qua non* of any attempt to articulate a Scandinavian 'third way to socialism'. Both the Danish and Norwegian Socialist People's parties, in short, were anti-NATO, anti-EEC, anti-military spending and anti-imperialist, whether it was US or Soviet imperialism. The Norwegian Socialist People's Party was not required to confront the challenges of adapting communist dogma to an affluent welfare society in the manner of the Danish party. True, it was also a proponent of decentralisation, but this was geographical decentralisation, or what was described as 'ecological socialism', meaning the preservation of rural communities in the peripheral parts of the country (Logue 1982: 261). Indeed, the Norwegian Socialist People's Party has perhaps the strongest claim to be considered the first of the Scandinavian eco-socialist family of parties. Thus, Knut Heidar has noted that, during the 1970s and 1980s, the party made environmental protection part of its platform, so evolving from a 'new left' party in the 1960s to become a 'green party' by the 1980s. But he adds that it still considered itself a socialist party, in that it advocated an active role for the state in the development of Norwegian society (Heidar 2001: 69).

In 1975 the Socialist Left Party (Sosialistisk Venstreparti) was formed from a merger of those groupings to the left of the Labour Party that had successfully opposed Norwegian membership of the EEC in the referendum of September 1972. The bulk of its members and voters, however, came from the Socialist People's Party. Survey work in the 1980s indicated that Socialist Left voters in particular had a post-materialist orientation and when at the 1989 Storting election voters regarded the energy and environmental question as the second most important campaign issue, the Socialist Left advanced to 10.1 per cent of the poll. A collapse in oil prices had obliged the minority Labour government to pursue an austerity programme – which included two twelve-month statutory wage freezes in the spring of 1988 and 1989 – and although the economy had been stabilised, unemployment stuck at the (by Norwegian standards) unacceptably high level of 4 per cent. Accordingly, led by the personable twenty-four-year-old Erik Solheim, the Socialist Left mounted a classical eco-socialist campaign. It attacked the national and international polluters of Norway's spectacular natural heritage, on the one hand, whilst criticising the failings of the government on unemployment and inadequate health care for the sick and elderly, on the other (Madeley 1990).

Support for the Socialist Left fell back in the 1990s – to 6.0 per cent in 1997 – but in 2001, as in 1989, it doubled its vote to record its best-ever result, of 12.5 per cent, at the same time as Labour registered its worst performance since the mid-1920s. This time the Socialist Left's eco-socialist mix incorporated an express element of feminism. Under a young and energetic female leader, Kristin Halvorsen, the party's election campaign combined the need for 'environmental responsibility' – it had earlier opposed the development of gas-fired power stations on the west coast on environmental grounds – with the traditional socialist concern for adequate welfare provision and a range of gender issues (Madeley 2002).

Finland and Sweden

The post-communist left parties founded in Finland and Sweden in the first half of 1990 were *successor parties* rather than new parties in the strictest sense. However, that the Left Alliance in Finland (Vasemmistoliitto) and the Left Party (Vänsterpartiet) in Sweden sought to project an eco-socialist appeal is evident from the title of the Finnish party's first programme, 'Red Politics for a Green and Just Future'. In the Finnish case, there was opposition to the construction of a fifth nuclear power station, a commitment to reduce energy consumption by 10 per cent by 2010 and the espousal of what was described as 'the social and ecological management of the market economy'. In Sweden, the model for party change and (what was hoped would be) electoral success was 'West Nordic'. Thus, in a motion to the twenty-ninth Left Party Communist congress in May 1990 (when the name 'Left Party' was adopted), the Kristianstad branch argued that the Communist Party's decision to amend its name to Left Party Communists in 1967 was a compromise dictated principally by the party leadership's desire to avoid a split in its ranks. It added that the Danish Socialist People's Party had grown strongly and that the Swedish party's development might have been similar if the refurbishment of its name in 1967 had not been so half-hearted (Arter 2002: 15–16).

In both parties, parliamentary group cohesion has been intermittently strained by the refusal of diehard communist elements to toe the party line. There have been tensions, too, between the trade union and environmental wings of the party. Furthermore, the feminisation of their leaderships and the advent of educated, middle-class women at the helm, promoting 'soft' eco-socialist values, generated an undercurrent of disquiet, particularly among the older generation of male, blue-collar activists mainly concerned with bread-and-butter matters such as jobs and wages. Gudrun Schyman became leader of the Swedish Left Party in 1993 and succeeded in 1996 in gaining conference approval for adopting the suffix 'feminist party'. Suvi-Anne Siimes, who, unlike Schyman, had no previous communist association, became Left Alliance leader in spring 1998. Both women, particularly Schyman in 1998, proved considerable electoral assets. Much as in Norway in 1989, the Swedish Left Party profited at the 1998 Riksdag election – when it polled a record

12 per cent – from the fact that, in managing Sweden out of recession, the minority Social Democratic government had perforce to pursue policies of fiscal conservatism and trim the sails of the welfare state. This enabled the Left Party to champion welfare spending – that is, to steal the Social Democrats' clothes – and to exceed the poll of the Finnish radical left (the Left Alliance and earlier the communist-dominated Finnish People's Democratic League) for the first time ever. It benefited principally at the expense of the Social Democrats, but profited too from party switchers from the Greens (Holmberg 2000: 20).

It seems fair to assert that the Swedish Left Party has enjoyed more of a 'new politics' profile than its sister party in Finland, which appears to be in slow but irreversible decline. Today, the Finnish party is anchored in economically marginal (the low-paid and elderly) and geographically peripheral (the constituencies in northern and eastern Finland) groups and it has been largely displaced by the Greens in the populous economic and geographical centre in the 'deep south' (Arter 2002: 20). When comparing the Left Alliance and Greens in the 1990s, Kim Zilliacus concluded that 'the Greens fulfill all the criteria of new politics.... It is a female-dominated party of the highly educated, new middle class of the younger generation.' The Left Alliance, on the other hand, 'remained the working class-dominated party with a low educational profile, even if working class domination became weaker' (Zilliacus 2001: 43). The blue-collar core of the party has, however, remained strong. In a 2003 election study, 53 per cent of Left Alliance supporters saw themselves as working class, compared with 20 per cent for the Greens (Paloheimo and Sundberg 2005: 179). In the 1999 and 2003 general elections, moreover, Left Alliance support from voters aged under twenty-five years was almost 50 per cent less than that from middle-aged voters (Paloheimo and Sundberg 2005: 179). In short, the attempt to build a niche eco-socialist party has not been reflected in the significantly more diversified composition of its support base.

In contrast, the Swedish Left Party in recent times has boasted an eclectic support base. In 2002, for example, when its vote slipped to 8.4 per cent, it gained higher than average backing from women, young voters, students and both blue- and white-collar trade unionists. Since 1994, the Left Party has consistently derived greater support from women than from men – 10 per cent and 7 per cent respectively in 2002. It has had a notably increased appeal to first-time voters and those aged under thirty years. Nineteen per cent of the former and 12 per cent of the latter backed the Left Party in 2002, compared with 2 per cent in both categories in 1991. In addition, almost one-fifth of students, 13 per cent of those in the lowest 15 per cent income bracket and above average levels of blue-collar and white-collar trade unionists voted for the Left Party in 2002.

Yet the Left Party's 2002 Riksdag result was down 3.6 percentage points on its performance in 1998 and fell further, to 5.8 per cent, in 2006. This was well down on the 8.8 per cent the Left Alliance polled in the 2007 Eduskunta election, itself a 1 percentage point drop on four years earlier. Both female leaders have resigned – Schyman under a cloud in 2003 following tax irregularities and Siimes in 2006, exasperated by opposition from former hardline communists in the parliamentary group.

Oddbjørn Knutsen has brought out a '1968 effect' with regard to left socialist support in Scandinavia and notes that it is strongest among the 1950s cohort. Support among the youngest post-war cohorts, he adds, is lower than that among the 1950s cohort (Knutsen 2003: 280). The need for generational renewal is particularly acute in the case of the Left Alliance in Finland – faced with strong competition from the Greens for young voters – whilst following its dramatic rise in the late 1990s, the Swedish Left Party vote has returned to virtually its Cold War, Left Party Communist levels. In sum, the place for ecosocialism on the party political spectrum in Finland and Sweden is less readily demarcated than in Denmark and Norway, which have lacked parliamentary Green parties with a capital 'G'.

Iceland

The most recent addition to the Scandinavian eco-socialist family of parties is the Icelandic Left Greens (Vinstrihreyfingin – grænt framboð), which was founded in February 1999 as part of a broader realignment on the political left. Gaining 14.3 per cent at the 2007 Alþingi election, the Left Green Party is presently the largest of the Nordic eco-socialist parties and its poll has been exceeded only once, and then very narrowly, by a sister party, the Danish Socialist People's Party, in 1987. An opinion poll in March 2007 put the Left Greens on 27.7 per cent, the second largest party and less than 7 percentage points behind the Independence Party. That this was virtually halved at the general election two months later suggests a high degree of volatility among the Left Green electorate.

The Left Green Party embraces the 'classical elements' of eco-socialist parties. Its anti-militarist, anti-imperialist stance is reflected in the long-term opposition of its leader, Steingrímur J. Sigfússon, formerly in the People's Alliance, to the US base at Keflavík. Its environmentalism has manifested itself, *inter alia*, in opposition to the giant aluminium-smelting plants powered by geothermal and hydroelectric resources – this was perhaps the dominant issue at the 2007 election. The Left Greens also espouse feminism and have incorporated several of those previously active in the Icelandic women's party or, more exactly, Women's List (Kvenna Listin). The political mobilisation of women in Iceland began dramatically with a 'women's general strike' in 1980 – ironically, the year the first female head of state, Vigdís Finnbogadóttir, was elected – and the following year a radical feminist party (Kvennaframboðið) was founded by about twenty women previously active in the Red Stockings. It elected two representatives of the Reykjavík city council in 1982 but decided by the narrowest margin against fielding candidates at the 1983 Alþingi election (Dominelli and Jonsdottír 1988: 47). However, a breakaway Women's List put up candidates in three constituencies and returned three MPs. In 1987 the Women's List polled

10.1 per cent and won nine seats. Then, one-quarter (26 per cent) of those in skilled tertiary employment – nurses, teachers, social workers and so on – supported it, the highest backing for any of the parties from this occupational sector (Harðason 2005: 618). Moreover, over one-fifth of women backed the Women's List in 1987, more than for any other party except the Independence Party. However, eight years later, support for the Women's List had fallen to 4.9 per cent (Styrkarsdottír 1990) and, thereafter, several of those active in feminist causes joined the nascent Left Greens. The Left Greens attracted above average support from the farmers in 1999 and 2003 and from unskilled workers and the lower middle class in 2003 (Harðason 2005: 623). In the latter year, they attracted most support from the youngest age cohort – 12 per cent of those aged between eighteen and twenty-two years voted for the Left Greens – although nearly half the party's support (44 per cent) came from persons aged between thirty-one and fifty years. In both 1999 and 2003 there was a gender bias – more women supported the Left Greens than men.

Denmark's Unity List

As a postscript to eco-socialist parties, mention should be made of the Unity List in Denmark, which was formed as an electoral alliance in 1989 comprising Left Socialists, Communists and the Socialist Workers' Party. It developed into an independent party, with an individual membership, and entered the Folketing in 1994. At the general election in 2007, the Unity List gained 2.2 per cent of the poll. Distinctively, it has no chair but is led by an executive committee of twenty-five members, whilst MPs contribute part of their parliamentary salary to the party so that their net income is broadly comparable to that of a skilled worker.

New radical rightist parties

The emergence in the early 1970s of a group of radical rightist parties for really the first time in Scandinavian politics was predicated on a diffuse anti-Establishment *poujadisme* – a tirade against the oppressive and inequitable rules and regulations imposed by the 'democratic Leviathan' that was the central state. The anti-Establishment parties that emerged in Finland, Denmark and Norway between 1970 and 1973 were 'entrepreneurial issue parties' (Harmel and Svåsand 1993), founded and led by political entrepreneurs, with a strong populist instinct, who deployed a rich and original rhetoric to rail against the 'old parties' and so generate a wide-ranging, anti-elitist, anti-consensus appeal. By the late 1980s, however, the Scandinavian radical right had evolved to incorporate an assertive strain of ethno-nationalism – from anti-tax and anti-bureaucracy, it became expressly anti-immigrant. A further mutation had occurred by the late 1990s, when the anti-immigrant radical right populist parties sought to combine opposition to multiculturalism – especially Islam – with welfare chauvinism and a concern to provide comprehensive

Table 5.5 *Classification of the new Scandinavian radical right*

Anti-Establishment parties	Anti-immigrant parties
Finnish Rural Party	New Democracy (Sweden)
Anders Lange Party (Norway)	Progress Party (Norway)
Progress Party (Denmark)	People's Party (Denmark)
True Finn Party	Sweden Democrats

care (social policy) for their 'own people'. Only in Norway did the shift from an anti-Establishment to an anti-immigrant orientation occur within the same party – the Progress Party. Elsewhere, the *poujadiste* parties of the 1970s had atrophied or ceased to exist by the mid-1990s. They were replaced by new parties of the radical right, dominated by, or at least containing, significant racist elements. Table 5.5 is inevitably somewhat impressionistic – the True Finns contain racist elements whereas New Democracy embraced much of the anti-Establishment populism of the 1970s parties. None the less, it is designed to capture the evolution of the new Scandinavian radical right over the four decades since its breakthrough. In order to provide an exhaustive listing, the Sweden Democrats (Sverigedemokraterna) are included in the group of anti-immigrant parties, although they failed to gain Riksdag representation in 2006. Moreover, since the rise *and fall* of anti-Establishment parties has already been discussed, the present section will concentrate on the anti-immigrant parties.

Of the new radical rightist parties, the Danish People's Party (Dansk Folkeparti) has been the most stridently anti-immigrant. Founded in October 1995, when four MPs left the Progress Party, its support had risen from 7.2 per cent in 1998, to 12.0 per cent in 2001, 13.2 per cent in 2005 and 13.9 per cent in 2007 at the Folketing elections. According to Jens Rydgren, it is 'a *pure* radical right-wing populist party in the sense of embracing the notion of ethno-nationalism' (Rydgren 2004: 483 – my italics). He has brought out the close links between the nascent People's Party and the Danish Association (Den Danske Forening), which was founded in 1987 and in turn adopted many of the ideas of the Front National in France. Two prominent members of the Danish Association, Søren Krarup and Jesper Langbelle, were elected People's Party MPs in 2001 and again in 2005. In a controversial episode in 2006, moreover, another People's Party parliamentarian, Louise Frevert, wrote on her Internet page that Muslim men with criminal convictions should be locked up in Russian jails, with a daily allowance of only twenty-five crowns, since Danish law prevented their public execution. She added that 'this is only a temporary solution, however, because, once released, they will return to Denmark and become ever more eager to murder Danes'. When a storm broke out in the media, the party leadership dissociated itself from Frevert's remarks and she subsequently apologised, although, significantly, the popularity of the

People's Party rose dramatically in the opinion polls during the controversy in 2006 over the newspaper *Jylland-Posten*'s publication the previous year of the Muhammad cartoons.

Indeed, there can certainly be no doubt that the anti-immigrant stance of the People's Party has resonated with the anti-immigrant sentiments of a section of the electorate. Using data from the 2001 Danish election study, Susi Meret constructed a *tolerance index* based on responses to six statements:

1 Immigrants constitute a threat to our national identity.
2 Muslim countries pose a threat to Danish security.
3 Islam represents a threat to Danish culture.
4 The right of immigrants to be reunited with other family members should be severely restricted.
5 Refugees/immigrants should have the same rights to social security as Danes even if they are not Danish citizens.
6 The integration of immigrants/refugees could be achieved if they got jobs/work.

She found that over half (54 per cent) of Danish People's Party voters displayed *extremely low tolerance* towards immigrants – a figure three times greater than the cross-party average of those responses that fell into the 'extremely low tolerance' category (Meret 2003: 380–1).

Equally, survey data indicate that the party's attempt to combine a particularly hardline ethno-nationalism and a softer welfare chauvinist appeal has been successful in so far as a substantial proportion of its electorate comprises former Social Democrats, concerned about a decline in the welfare state. A study by the SiD trade union following the 2001 general election revealed that among unskilled workers aged under forty years, 30 per cent voted for the People's Party and only 25 per cent for the Social Democrats. Extensive survey work in the first half of 2002, moreover, indicated that the workers' share of the Danish People's Party electorate was 61.2 per cent compared with 48.2 per cent in the case of the Social Democrats (see Andersen and Andersen 2003: 217). Incidentally, in similar fashion, the Social Democrats in Sweden lost votes at the 2006 Riksdag election to the radical rightist Sweden Democrats, especially in the southern part of the country. The Sweden Democrats gained 2.9 per cent of the national vote (under the 4 per cent necessary for parliamentary representation) on a ticket of advocating Sweden's withdrawal from the EU and ending immigration on grounds that it threatened Swedish identity. The party advocates ethnic segregation, wanting, in the words of a leading figure, 'a multicultural world, not a multicultural society' (Rydgren 2007).

The Norwegian Progress Party (Fremskrittspartiet), which was founded in 1977 as the successor to Anders Lange's Party, was led from 1978 to 2006 by the charismatic Carl I. Hagen. It was the third largest party at the 2001 Storting election, with 14.6 per cent of the vote, and the second largest in 2005, with

22.1 per cent. Importantly, the Progress Party was not an ethno-nationalist party from the outset and developed an anti-immigrant stance only in the late 1980s, polling 13.0 per cent at the 1989 Storting election. By 1995, however, when immigration was a major question in the local government election campaign, 47 per cent of Progress Party supporters held that immigration was *the most important issue* in their voting behaviour (Hagelund 2003: 48). Thereafter, with governments placing North Sea oil and gas revenues into a 'rainy day fund', the Progress Party combined its anti-immigrant appeal (the cost of immigrants and the problems of managing multiculturalism) with welfare chauvinism and a demand for spending on the elderly, young-parent families, hospitals and so on. In short, there was a not unsuccessful attempt to steal the traditional clothes of the Labour Party. Survey research in 2001 showed that 26 per cent of respondents (the highest for any of the parties) believed that Hagen's party was best equipped to deal with the needs of the elderly, while 38 per cent held that it had the best immigration policy.

As in most populist parties, the Progress Party has experienced periods of factionalism and fragmentation. In 1994 four of its MPs broke away to found a libertarian group called the Free Democrats – although this rapidly came to naught – and before the 2001 general election, the second vice-chair's involvement in a sex scandal triggered internal unrest relating, among other things, to Hagen's authoritarian management style. There were defections, suspensions and expulsions and the formation of a splinter party called 'The Democrats'. Hagen's popularity survived remarkably unscathed, although in 2003 he announced his decision to stand down from the party leadership in 2006 and was then replaced, as in Denmark, by a female chair, Siv Jensen.

In recent years, the Norwegian Progress Party has appeared less blatantly anti-immigrant than the Danish People's Party, although at the 2005 general election its campaign brochure, which focused on criminal immigrants and carried the text 'the perpetrator is of foreign origin', attracted extensive criticism from the other parties. In defending his party's position, Hagen stated that 'there are many immigrants and law-abiding citizens that do a fantastic job for Norway. But, unfortunately, there are too many who do not. Statistics clearly show that criminality is growing among immigrants.'

Incidentally, there are undoubtedly racist elements in the True Finn Party (perussuomalaiset), the successor to the defunct Finnish Rural Party, which has been led since 1997 by Timo Soini and gained its best result, 4.0 per cent, in the 2007 general election. However, modelling himself on his mentor, Veikko Vennamo, Soini has eschewed an anti-immigrant message and promoted the type of 'responsible populism' which places the party far more in the anti-Establishment category of radical rightist parties than the anti-immigrant camp (Arter 2007).

In common with the Greens (discussed shortly), the Norwegian Progress Party had at the outset a marked generational and gender profile, developing as a protest party comprising mainly young adult males. At the 1981 general election, approximately 10 per cent of young men under thirty years backed the Progress Party and this was more than twice the party's national vote (Pettersen and Rose 2004: 11). When the Progress Party's vote rose sharply to 13.0 per cent at the 1989 Storting election, 18.2 per cent of its supporters were young males (Pettersen and Rose 2004: 31). The Progress Party continues to attract disproportionately high levels of support from first voters and adults under thirty years, although the 'gender differential' in the youngest age cohort is less pronounced than earlier. In 2005, the Progress Party gained the greatest support of all the parties from first voters: 30 per cent of them backed the party in that year – exceeding its previous best of 20 per cent, in 1989 – and that was 2 percentage points more than opted for Labour. Moreover, 25 per cent of those aged eighteen to twenty-nine years voted for the Progress Party in 2005, compared with between 15 and 19 per cent in the other age cohorts (Aardal and Stavn 2006: 6). However, a growth in young female support effectively removed the gender differential among the youngest age group of Progress Party voters.

In 1981, 10 per cent of those on the lowest incomes supported the Norwegian Progress Party. Indeed, by the 1990s it was more a working-class party – in terms of the composition of its support base – than the Labour Party. At the 2001 Norwegian general election, blue-collar workers made up only 14 per cent of the Labour Party's electorate, compared with 22 per cent of those voting for the Progress Party (Bjørklund and Andersen 2002: 119). At the same time, the Progress Party has clearly benefited from the long-term trend towards increased electoral volatility, which began in Norway in the late 1980s. Voters who had backed the Progress Party in 2001 made up only 37 per cent of its support four years later, compared with 29 per cent who had voted for the Conservatives, 11 per cent the Christian Democrats and 15 per cent who had abstained.

Greens with a capital 'G'

There were local environmental parties in Sweden in the 1970s – the Party for Environmental Protection and Consultation (Partiet för miljöskydd och medstämmande), founded in Ängelholm in 1972, was probably the first (Wörlund 2005: 242) – whilst in Finland Greens ran independent lists of candidates at the Helsinki city council elections in 1976. However, it was the 1980s before Green parties with a capital 'G' gained legislative status in Finland and Sweden (table 5.6). They originated in various extra-parliamentary movements, many so-called 'alternative movements', and, more so than the eco-socialist group of parties, they were grounded in a post-materialist value system. From the anti-party organisations of the 1980s, the Greens evolved the following decade into more or less conventional political parties, with office-seeking viewed as a legitimate, indeed primary means of influencing policy. To this end, the two Green parties developed broader-based

Table 5.6 *Nordic Green parties*

Country	Year founded	First entered parliament
Sweden	1981	1988
Finland	1987	1983 (Green lists)
Denmark	1983	–
Norway	1988	–

programmes designed to have a vote-winning, catch-all appeal, whilst not, of course, losing sight of their basic principles.

Only two of the Scandinavian states, Finland and Sweden, have witnessed the parliamentary breakthrough of Green parties with a capital 'G'. In Norway, Greens ran candidates in two counties – Oslo and Akerhus – where they gained 0.4 per cent and 0.8 per cent of the vote, respectively – at the 1987 local government election and the following year a Green Party (Miljöpartiet De Grønne) was set up. However, its vote has never exceeded 1 per cent in a parliamentary election (Wörlund 2005: 242–3). The Danish Greens (De Grønne), founded in 1983, joined a grouping of small parties opposed to the EU called Democratic Renewal (Demokratisk Fornyelse) in 1996, but at the general election two years later polled only a little over 20,000 votes and the party has not contested Folketing elections thereafter. In contrast, the Finnish Greens have been continuously represented in the Eduskunta since 1983, whilst the Swedish Greens entered the Riksdag for the first time in 1988 and have held seats unbrokenly since 1994.

The Finnish Greens started out very much as a capital city movement and many of the pioneering figures were active in the so-called 'Helsinki 1976' movement, which campaigned for fewer cars, pedestrianisation and a solution to the capital's traffic problems. The heterogeneous mix of persons who became active in the environmental movement had as their common denominator a reaction against the stultifying political climate of the 1970s, which suffocated the open debate of issues. Two direct civil action campaigns in the later part of that decade, however, served to radicalise the mood and place environmental protection issues firmly on the political agenda. In 1979 there was highly publicised action to prevent the draining of Koijärvi lake – an important breeding ground for birds – which the local farmers demanded so as to avoid the regular flooding in spring. Then, the so-called Hattuvaara movement emerged in eastern Finland to prevent the aerial spreading of pesticides in the area (Borg 1991: 270). In 1980 Ville Komsi became the first Green to be elected to the Helsinki city council. Curiously, leading Greens such as Komsi and Osmo Soininvaara had been candidates of the 'Helsinki 1976' movement whilst still active in the Liberal People's Party. The effective demise of the

Liberals in the 1980s – it briefly merged with the Centre Party – opened up a space in the political centre, which the Greens could occupy.

The Green lists, which ran a total of forty-six candidates in eight constituencies at the Finnish 1983 general election, were not the work of a political party but embraced various so-called 'alternative movements', among them the environmental, peace and women's movements, together with the disabled lobby. Two Greens were elected to the Eduskunta, one of them, the invalid Kalle Könkkölä, becoming the first MP to enter parliament in a wheelchair. The decision of Kalevi Sorsa's Social Democrat-led coalition, taken in the wake of the Chernobyl disaster, not to proceed with a fifth nuclear power plant deprived the Greens of a possible trump card four years later. However, despite the lack of a cohesive programme and conspicuous division in the ranks, the Greens almost trebled their vote, to 4.0 per cent, in 1987 and elected four members of parliament. Shortly thereafter, they (or at least the 'lighter Greens') organised as a political party (Sundberg and Wilhelmsson 2007). By 1991 the Greens (Vihreän liitto) had advanced to 6.8 per cent of the national vote and they became the third largest party in Helsinki, with nearly 14 per cent. By 2007, the Finnish Greens had polled 8 per cent of the national vote and boasted parliamentary seats in half the fourteen mainland constituencies.

The Centre Party's failure, as the established anti-nuclear party, to achieve a radical change in energy policy whilst leading a succession of non-socialist coalitions between 1976 and 1982 was a primary factor in the creation of a Green Party in Sweden in 1981 (Jamison *et al.* 1990: 13–65). The moving force in the project was a disgruntled Liberal, Per Gahrton, although the embryonic party was opposed by most of the leading lights in the extra-parliamentary environmental groups, many of whom were active (or would soon become active) in other parties. Björn Gillberg, for example, the Uppsala microbiologist who had dominated the National Organisation of Environmental Groups from its inception in spring 1971 and achieved national celebrity status in his campaign against food colouring and additives, stood unsuccessfully for the Riksdag as a Christian Democrat (Jamison *et al.* 1990: 59–60). The Green Party thus comprised a new young generation of environmentalists who had only limited contacts with the 'old guard'.

At their first general election in 1982 and again three years later, the 4 per cent electoral threshold proved too high a hurdle for the Swedish Greens to surmount. In the run-up to the 1988 general election, however, an astonishing three out of four voters stated that environmental questions were the most important electoral issues (Arter 1989) and, against this backdrop, the Greens entered parliament with 5.5 per cent of the vote. By 1991 the mood was very different: the Berlin Wall had collapsed; the Swedish economy had plunged into recession; the Social Democratic government had applied to join the EU; and, in an election dominated by bread-and-butter issues, especially unemployment, taxes and food prices, the Greens managed only 3.4 per cent of the vote and lost their toehold in the Riksdag (Sainsbury 1992). They returned in 1994 and have boasted parliamentary representation continuously since then. At the 2006 Riksdag election the Greens polled 5.2 per cent, their best performance since their breakthrough in 1988, although well down on the support their Finnish counterparts gained the following year (Aylott and Bolin 2007).

In terms of their support, the Finnish and Swedish Greens have displayed three common characteristics. First, both parties have had an accentuated generational profile, appealing predominantly to young adults. Thus, in 2003, 80 per cent of Finnish Greens were under forty-four years of age, and students were far more likely to vote for the Greens than for other parties. Four years earlier, the Greens attracted 18 per cent of the vote in the eighteen- to thirty-year age group and this was the third highest of all the parties. In the five Riksdag elections over the period 1991–2006, between 8 per cent (1991) and 14 per cent (1994) of first voters opted for the Swedish Greens. The 2006 exit poll data made the Greens the third most popular party among first voters, with 11 per cent backing from this cohort. As in Finland, the Swedish Greens were popular among students. In 2006, 15 per cent of Swedish students voted Green, making it the third most popular party among the student population.

Second, both Green parties have exhibited a pronounced gender bias. In Sweden in 2006, 7 per cent of women backed the Greens, compared with 4 per cent of men. Four years earlier, the Green electorate comprised 57 per cent women and 43 per cent men (Wörlund 2005: 248). In recent general elections, the Finnish Greens have been the only party in which over half their Eduskunta candidates have been women and in 2003, for example, Green female candidates gained exactly two-thirds of the party's vote. The Greens, in short, claim a higher proportion of female voters than the three 'pole parties' and in the 2007–11 Eduskunta two-thirds of the Greens' parliamentary group are women.

Third, the Green electorate has been characterised by its relative instability and both the Finnish and Swedish parties have profited from 'last-minute voters', those with only a weak partisan identification and those prone to abstention. For example, in 1999, the Finnish Greens were the most popular party (23 per cent of respondents) among those lacking a firm party allegiance. They have also been the most 'popular' party among young non-voters. Forty-six per cent of those in the eighteen- to thirty-year age group who abstained in 1999 thought the Greens might have been a viable option (Borg 1999: 35). In 2006, 52 per cent of Swedish Green voters (the highest of any of the parties) had decided to back the Greens either on election day or during the last week of the campaign. In general, moreover, over half of Swedish Green voters switch allegiance from one election to the next.

In one particular the support for the two Green parties displays a measure of difference – the Finnish party has a more marked urban profile than its Swedish sister party. The strength of the Finnish Greens has been in the larger university towns and cities, particularly, although not exclusively, those in southern Finland. In recent elections, about half the Greens' vote has been concentrated in the capital, Helsinki – where in 2007 they polled just over one-fifth of the vote – and the hinterland constituency of Uusimaa. In contrast, the Greens have never won a seat in the Lapland constituency. In Sweden the Greens have also had a strong position in the towns but latterly they have also polled well in non-urban areas (Wörlund 2005: 247).

New Christian parties

Although mono-religious protestant countries, where the impact of the Reformation was total and the confessional cleavages of other west European systems have been absent, the Scandinavian states have none the less been characterised by extensive pietistic pluralism within the state Lutheran church. Accordingly, historic linkages developed across the region between high-church clericalism and the political right, on the one hand, and low-church pietism and parties of the 'old' non-socialist left, on the other. In Norway the fundamentalist Christian lay movement, with its core strength in the rural west and south-west coastal districts (Malmström 2005: 135), formed part of the loose 'coalition of interests' that was the Liberals (Venstre) in the 1880s (Leipart and Svåsand 1988: 305). Soon after the unifying cause of parliamentarism had been achieved in 1884, the fundamentalists were excluded from the Liberals' parliamentary group and formed their own party, the Moderate Left (Moderate Venstre), which subsequently fused with the Conservatives (Høyre). In Finland Revivalism and Laestadianism, both rooted in northern Finland (the latter in the northern parts of Norway and Sweden too), forged lasting bonds with the nascent Agrarian Party. The Agrarians' successor party, the Centre, still today has its strongholds in Lapland and the neighbouring Oulu constituency.

There were historic links, too, between nonconformism (dissident groups outside the Lutheran church) and liberalism. Thus, in Sweden, the so-called 'northern frees' (norrlandsfrisinnet) – the Free Church groups in central and northern Sweden, which canvassed prohibition, free trade and pacificism – formed their own liberal splinter party in 1924 (frisinnade partiet) following a narrow referendum vote against the introduction of prohibition the previous year. Its strength, in addition to the northern parts of the country, was in the counties of Kristianstad and Jönköping (Birgersson *et al.* 1981: 100–4). All in all, then, a complex pattern of connections had developed between fundamentalist religious groups, both within and outside the Lutheran church, and the Scandinavian political parties around the time of the completion of mass democracy.

However, with the exception of the Norwegian Christian People's Party, religious political mobilisation, triggered in particular by teetotalism and the case for prohibition, was contained within the historic party system and the 'prohibition parties' proved short-lived. This was the case with the Finnish Christian Workers' Party, which modelled itself on English and especially German

Table 5.7 *Nordic Christian parties*

Country	Year founded	Year first entered parliament
Norway	1933	1933
Finland	1958	1970
Sweden	1964	1985
Denmark	1970	1973

Christian socialism and initially boasted large numbers of clergy in positions of leadership (Salokas 1916). It gained a maximum 2.8 per cent of the valid poll in 1909 and ceased its party political activities in 1922, shortly after its primary goal of prohibition had been achieved. Similarly, the nonconformist Free Liberals, which had pressed for prohibition in Sweden, reintegrated with the minority-wing Liberals in 1934 to form the People's Party (Folkpartiet).

John Madeley has argued that, outside Norway, there were an insufficient number of dissenters and an insufficient body of common interests to precipitate the formation of a religious party. In his words, 'throughout Scandinavia conflicts between clerical conservatives, 'churchly revivalists', radical revivalists and dissenters among religious activists, each with their own particular interests, undermined any attempt to set up a successful religious party' (Madeley 1982: 168). Interestingly, the stronghold of the fundamentalist revivalists that initiated the Norwegian Christian People's Party in 1933 was the same 'Bible belt' in the south and west of the country that had been the core area of the short-lived Moderate Left Party in the late 1880s. The Christian People's Party was created to campaign against the demon of drink, the perceived laxity of the high-church clergy and the secularism of the Liberal and Labour parties. On the last point, particular exception was taken to the National Theatre's staging – in the run-up to the 1933 Storting election – of *God's Green Angels*, which Christians viewed as blasphemous (Richard and Demker 2005: 192). The Norwegian Christian People's Party remained a relatively small-scale regional party before the Second World War and developed a national organisation only in 1945.

Whilst the Norwegian Christian People's Party (Kristelig Folkeparti) expanded from its regional base in Hordaland to become a national party after the Second World War – in line with the general surge in Christian democracy in post-war western Europe – Christian parties on the Norwegian model were formed in Finland in 1958, Sweden in 1964 and Denmark in 1970 (table 5.7). All three based their programmes on the Norwegian 'mother party' and took as their 'Bible' the pamphlet on Christianity and politics *Kristendom og politik*, by the Norwegian pastor Karl Marthinussen. In turn, the Norwegian party played a material role in encouraging the sibling Christian parties. The new parties were committed to protecting Christian ethics and standards against the pervasive licentiousness and moral turpitude of the period. They cast themselves in the role of 'moral vigilantes', in Lauri Karvonen's (1993) phrase, working indefatigably to restore the Christian order in increasingly secular and hedonistic societies and, initially at least, the threshold created by their hardline stance on such issues as abortion, alcohol, sex and pornography was too high for the average voter.

The first of the new Christian parties to be established outside Norway, the Finnish Christian League (Suomen kristillinen liitto), was founded in May 1958, the year in which the communist-dominated Finnish People's Democratic League became the largest parliamentary grouping (see chapter 4). The electoral advance of an atheist political credo, the related increase in the number of persons withdrawing from their membership of the state Lutheran church and the ensconced position of the Communist Party in the trade union movement all contributed to an increasingly secular, anti-religious mood in which a separate Christian party was deemed necessary. The 1960s were an 'incubation period' – although the Christian League gained a seat on the Helsinki city council in 1964 – but there was a growing conviction of the need for parliamentary seats in the wake of legislation permitting the sale of middle-strength beer in grocers' shops, the approval of abortion on social grounds and the legalisation of homosexual relations. Indeed, at the 'earthquake election' of 1970, after four years of so-called Popular Front government (including the Communists), which became synonymous with liberalisation and secularisation, the Finnish Christians had a solitary MP elected and have been represented in the Eduskunta continuously ever since.

The formation of the Christian Democratic Union (Kristen demokratisk samling) in Sweden in 1964 was prefaced by two petitions. One, the 'Petition of the 140 Doctors', expressed professional concern about increased promiscuity, the spread of venereal diseases and the growth in the number of abortions; the other, opposing the planned reduction in the level of religious education in schools, was signed by over 2 million persons. Active Christians also opposed the general release (albeit in censored form) of the film *491*, which had explicit sex scenes. The government's decision to lift an initial ban on the film was in fact important in the decision to launch a Christian party in 1964 (Karvonen 1993). For the first two decades, the Swedish Christian Democrats failed to obtain 2 per cent of the national poll, but in 1985 it gained a solitary MP and it has been continuously represented in the Riksdag since 1991 (Attefall 2004).

The Danish Christian People's Party (Kristeligt folkeparti) was created on 13 April 1970 specifically to oppose laws, introduced by the non-socialist coalition under Hilmar Baunsgaard, which liberalised pornography and abortion. As in Sweden, there were also plans afoot to reduce the time allowed for religious education in the school curriculum. At the party's inaugural meeting, the revivalist Inner Mission was strongly represented, as were both the low-church Grundtvigians and the high-church wings of the Evangelical Lutheran Church. At the 1971 Folketing election, the Christian People's Party fell tantalisingly 606 votes short of the 2 per cent threshold for parliamentary representation, but it entered parliament in 1973 and remained there with the exception of the periods 1994–98 and from 2005 onwards.

The parliamentary breakthrough of the Finnish and Swedish Christian parties – in 1970 and 1985, respectively – was indebted to the conclusion of electoral alliances with the Centre parties in both countries. In the Finnish case, moreover, the existence of a strong personal preference voting system – requiring voters to opt for an individual and not simply a party list (Arter 2006: 26–45) – enabled Christian League voters to concentrate their support on the party's 'lead candidate'. Thus, Raino Westerholm was elected on a joint list in the Kymi constituency – the Christian League gained only 1.1 per cent of the national poll – and it was testimony to the capacity of the party's supporters to unite behind Westerholm that his tally of 28,547 votes was the highest individual total of all the candidates on the joint list in Kymi (Almgren 1998). Similarly, in Sweden, the Christian Democrats' first Riksdag member, Alf Svensson, was elected in 1985 from a joint list with the Centre in Jönköping constituency. Discussions on the electoral alliance, which did not have the wholehearted support of the Centre, began the previous year and, since the outcome turned out to be more advantageous to the Christian Democrats, the Centre did not renew the arrangement three years later. Svensson was not re-elected and the Christian Democrats went empty-handed. The parliamentary breakthrough of the Danish Christian People's Party, which polled 4 per cent in 1973, its second-best result to date – ironically after a period of deep division in the party's ranks – is best viewed perhaps as part of the wider fall-out from the 'earthquake election', which saw a proliferation of protest parties.

The core supporters of the new Christian parties in Scandinavia have been highly religious persons – attending church at least once a week – and *religiosity*, defined in the same way, has been a fairly reliable predictor of a Christian democratic vote. A 1991 Finnish election study (albeit on the basis of only thirty-eight respondents) revealed that two-thirds of Christian League supporters reported that they were 'very religious' (at least monthly church attenders) and that was almost six times greater than in any of the other parties (Pesonen *et al.* 1993: 155–7). The 'Valu 2006' exit poll survey in Sweden indicated that 32 per cent of regular worshippers (the same criterion as above) voted for the Christian Democrats and that was 10 per-centage points more among the actively religious than supported the Social Democrats. However, among the more occasional churchgoers, the Social Democrats were the best-supported party.

Among the religiously active core supporters of the new Christian parties, moreover, there has been a significant proportion of persons belonging to nonconformist organisations – Pentecostalists, Methodists, Baptists and so on – within the state Lutheran churches. An investigation of active members of the Finnish Christian League (conference delegates) in 1979 revealed that 55 per cent identified with a revivalist organisation within the Lutheran church – the vast majority of whom belonged to the National Mission (Kansanlähetys), founded in 1967 – whilst 12 per cent adhered to nonconformist organisations (Arter 1980). More recent data on the religious affiliation of Christian League supporters are not available. In the Swedish case, however, it is clear from a 2002 election study that 26 per cent of Christian Democrat voters gave their religious allegiance as 'free church' – that is, nonconformist – although the various 'free churches' were not separately identified. In his comparative, longitudinal analysis of party choice and religious denomination in western Europe between 1970 and 1997, based on Eurobarometer survey data, Oddbjørn Knutsen reports that 7.3 per cent of 'other denominations' – that is, nonconformists – in the sample supported the Danish Christian People's Party, compared with 2.1 per cent of Lutheran state church members who did so. He adds that supporters of the new Christian parties in Scandinavia 'are not primarily active members of the dominant State churches but belong most frequently to the more fundamentalist sects, partly found within and partly outside the Lutheran Church' (Knutsen 2004: 116).

All three new Christian parties sought in time to broaden their support base and appeal to voters who were not necessarily religious but none the less subscribed to basic Christian values. New programmes were accompanied by new party names. In Sweden the Christian Democratic Union became the Christian Democratic Social Party in 1987 and simply Christian Democrats in 1996. The Finnish Christian League became Christian Democrats in 1999, albeit after much internal resistance. Indeed, for opponents of the refurbishment of the name in both parties, modernisation appeared tantamount to secularisation and a reneging on fundamental principles. In 2003 the Danish Christian People's Party followed suit and became simply the Christian Democrats. The attempt to become a broad-based, German-style Christian Democratic Party has met with a degree of success (albeit not sustained) in the Swedish case. Significantly, in 1991 the Swedish party became the leading party among regular churchgoers – 36 per cent of whom backed the party – but the extent of its gains (it won 7.1 per cent) in the national poll meant that regular churchgoers no longer comprised a majority of its voters (46 per cent, compared with 68 per cent three years earlier).

In Finland the Christian League/Democrats has recorded its best general election results – in 1979 and 2003 – following presidential elections at which its leader has been a candidate for the post of head of state. For small parties in particular, presidential elections are a means of raising their profile, and a solid performance from their candidate can cement his/her reputation as a national politician. Raino Westerholm, the Christian League's first MP and the party chair between 1973 and 1982, polled a creditable 8.8 per cent at the 1978 presidential election – all the larger parties were backing the re-election of the long-serving Urho Kekkonen – and the Christians profited from a modest 'Westerholm effect' at the 1979 general election, polling their (then) best result, of 4.8 per cent. It also seems plausible to suggest that the Christian

League (now Christian Democrats) benefited from a 'Kallis effect' when it polled a record 5.3 per cent at the 2003 Eduskunta election. Bjarne Kallis, the party chairman between 1995 and 2004, had been an effective presidential candidate in 2000, had been instrumental in the party's change of name and concern to attract a wider electorate, and was also a fully bilingual 'Finland Swede', able to draw votes from the Swedish People's Party, as well as some Finnish-speaking Conservative and Centre voters.

In Sweden the Christian Democratic Party became virtually synonymous with its long-serving chair Alf Svensson (1973–2004) and could with some justification be included in the category of an 'entrepreneurial issue party' or, better, two-issue party. Thus, Gilljam and Holmberg (1995) note that the Christian Democrats could be described in 1991, when in a mini-quake election it polled 7.1 per cent, as a one-man, two-issue party – family policy, religion and Alf Svensson were the three main factors, according to voters, that catapulted the party into the Riksdag. Svensson also led the party to its highest-ever poll, of 11.8 per cent, in 1998, although, curiously, a Sifo poll in *Svenska Dagbladet* in May 1998 had given the Christian Democrats under 5 per cent and they appeared in danger of falling below the 4 per cent threshold and losing their status as a parliamentary party. The importance of Svensson's leadership during the campaign cannot, therefore, be underestimated. Since multiple candidacies are still permitted in Sweden, Svensson stood in all twenty-nine constituencies. Moreover, whilst not a populist in the Vennamo, Glistrup and Hagen mould, Svensson shared their ability to use simple, direct language to convey simple messages. He contrasted basic standards, family values and Christian ethics against the arid jargon, interminable facts and 'smokescreen' statistics of the other party leaders. Ultimately, polls showed that Svensson's personal appeal surpassed even that of the Conservative leader, Carl Bildt (Arter 1999: 298–9).

Summary

PENDERSEN(1985) 1.   The so-called 'earthquake elections' of 1970–73 were 'high-volatility elections' and the incidence of 'party switching' has risen since then, albeit neither continuously nor universally across the Nordic region. In general, though, levels of electoral stability have been significantly higher since 1970 than in the earlier period.

2.   Since the early 1970s, the number of legislative parties has increased and in most of the Nordic states support for parties in the 'others' category has grown. The new parties have included modern revivals of defunct historic parties (the Young Finns, the Icelandic Citizens' Party), splinter groups born of factionalisation (the New Alliance founded in Denmark in May 2007) and ultimately fragmentation (the Liberal People's Party in Norway) and several single-issue parties, among them the pro-whaling Coastal Party in Norway.

3. However, the mortality rate among the post-1970 parties has been relatively high. Among the parties that have gone 'out of business' have been most of the splinter parties but, more significantly, two of the *poujadiste*, anti-Establishment parties that were at the heart of electoral protest in the 1970–73 period – the Finnish Rural Party and the Danish Progress Party.

4. The increase in legislative parties was not confined to the seismic early 1970s. Indeed, the chapter has concentrated on profiling four new 'party families' that since then have both institutionalised their position and lent the party political spectrum added 'dimensionality'. The eco-socialist parties and new radical rightist parties have been relatively easy to locate on a left–right continuum, whereas the placement of the Greens and new Christian parties, embodying post-materialist and anti-secularist values, respectively, has been more problematical.

5. The following brief chapter seeks to pull the threads of our discussions together by focusing on the 'so what?' question. It asks how we should go about analysing and assessing the extent of party system change in Scandinavia since the early 1970s.

References

Aardal, Bernt and Guro Stavn (2006) 'Enda flere skifter parti', *Samfunnsspeilet*, 20 (3), pp. 2–8.

Almgren, Esko (1998) *Villenpoika*, Gummerus: Jyväskylä.

Andersen, Johannes and Jørgen Goul Andersen (2003) 'Klassernes forsvinden', in Jørgen Goul Andersen and Ole Borre (eds), *Politisk Forandring*, Systime Academic: Århus, pp. 207–21.

Andersen, Jørgen Goul, Johannes Andersen, Ole Borre, Kasper Møller Hansen and Hans Jørgen Nielsen (eds) (2007) *Det nye politiske landskab Folketingsvalget 2005 i perspectiv*, Academic: Århus.

Arter, David (1980) 'The Finnish Christian League: party or "anti-party"?', *Scandinavian Political Studies*, 3 (2), pp. 143–62.

Arter, David (1983) 'The 1983 Finnish election: protest or consensus?', *West European Politics*, 6 (4), pp. 252–5.

Arter, David (1989) 'A tale of two Carlssons: the Swedish general election of 1988', *Parliamentary Affairs*, 42 (1), pp. 84–101.

Arter, David (1995) 'The March 1995 Finnish election: the Social Democrats storm back', *West European Politics*, 18 (4), pp. 194–204.

Arter, David (1999) 'The Swedish general election of 20th September 1998: a victory for values over policies?', *Electoral Studies*, 18 (2), pp. 296–300.

Arter, David (2001) 'Conclusion', in David Arter (ed.), *From Farmyard to City Square? The Electoral Adaptation of the Nordic Agrarian Parties*, Ashgate: Aldershot, pp. 162–83.

Arter, David (2002) 'Communists we are no longer, Social Democrats we can never be: the evolution of the leftist parties in Finland and Sweden', *Journal of Communist Studies and Transition Politics*, 18 (3), pp. 1–28.

Arter, David (2006) *Democracy in Scandinavia*, Manchester University Press: Manchester.

Arter, David (2007) 'The end of the Social Democratic hegemony and the "normalisation" of centre-right government? The March 2007 Finnish general election', *West
European Politics*, 30 (5), pp. 1148–57.

Attefall, Cecilia Hjort (2004) *Partiet som lyfte: 40 år med svenska kristdemokrati 1964–
2004*, Samhällsgemenskap: Stockholm.

Aylott, Nicholas and Niklas Bolin (2007) 'Towards a two-party system? The Swedish parliamentary election of September 2006', *West European Politics*, 30 (3), pp. 621–33.

Birgersson, Bengt Owe, Stig Hadenius, Björn Molin and Hans Wieslander (1981)
Sverige efter 1900, BonnierFakta: Stockholm.

Bjørklund, Tor and Jørgen Goul Andersen (2002) 'Anti-immigrant parties in Denmark
and Norway: the Progress Parties and the Danish People's Party', in Martin Schain,
Aristide Zolberg and Patrick Hossay (eds), *Shadows Over Europe: The Development and
Impact of the Extreme Right in Western Europe*, Palgrave Macmillan: Basingstoke,
pp. 107–36.

Borg, Olavi (1991) 'The green movement in European politics', in Matti Wiberg (ed.),
The Political Life of Institutions, Finnish Political Science Association: Jyväskylä,
pp. 264–79.

Borg, Sami (1999) 'Nuorten äänestyspäätökset vuoden 1999 eduskuntavaaleissa', in
Eduskuntavaalit 1999, Tilastokeskus: Helsinki, pp. 31–6.

Borre, Ole (1995) 'Old and new politics in Denmark', *Scandinavian Political Studies*, 18
(3), pp. 187–205.

Borre, Ole and Jan Stehouwer (1970) *Fire Folketingsvalg 1960–68*, Akademisk
Boghandel: Århus.

Dominelli, Lena and Gudrun Jonsdottír (1988) 'Feminist political organisation in
Iceland: some reflections on the experience of Kwenna Frambothid', *Feminist Review*,
autumn, pp. 36–61.

Ersson, Svante (2005) 'Den yttre vänstern in Norge och Sverige', in Marie Demker and
Lars Svåsand (eds), *Partiernas århundrade*, Santérus Forlag: Stockholm, pp. 51–77.

Fitzmaurice, John (1981) *Politics in Denmark*, Hurst: London.

Gilljam, Mikael and Sören Holmberg (1995) 'Väljarnas val', in *Valundersökningar 15*,
Statistiska Centralbyrå: Stockholm.

Hagelund, Annika (2003) 'A matter of decency? The Progress Party in Norwegian immigration politics', *Journal of Ethnic and Migration Studies*, 23 (1), pp. 47–65.

Harðason, Ólafur (2005) 'Kjósendur og stéttir á Íslandi 1983–2003', in Úlfar
Hauksson (ed.), *Rannsóknir í félagsvísindum VI, félagsvísindadeild*, Reykjavík: Félagsvísindastofnun.

Harmel, Robert and Lars Svåsand (1993) 'Party leadership and party institutionalisation: three phases of development', *West European Politics*, 16 (2), pp. 67–88.

Heidar, Knut (2001) *Norway. Elites on Trial*, Westview: Boulder, CO.

Holmberg, Sören (2000) *Välja parti*, Norsteds Juridik: Stockholm.

Jamison, Andrew, Ron Eyerman and Jacqueline Cramer, with Jeppe Læssøe (1990)
The Making of the New Environmental Consciousness, Edinburgh University Press:
Edinburgh.

Karlsson, Gunnar (2000) *The History of Iceland*, University of Minnesota Press:
Minneapolis, MN.

Karvonen, Lauri (1993) 'In from the cold? Christian parties in Scandinavia', *Scandinavian Political Studies*, 16 (1), pp. 25–48.

Knudsen, Ann-Christina (2005) 'The Danish general election of February 2005',

Election Briefing No. 19, at www.sussex.ac.uk/sei/documents/epern_eb_19_denmark.pdf.

Knutsen, Oddbjørn (2003) *Generations, Age-Groups and Voting Behaviour in the Scandinavian Countries. A Comparative study*, Research Report 4, Faculty of Social Sciences, University of Oslo

Knutsen, Oddbjørn (2004) 'Religious denomination and party choice in western Europe: a comparative longitudinal study from eight countries, 1970–97', *International Political Science Review*, 25 (1), pp. 97–128.

Leiphart, Jørn Y. and Lars Svåsand (1988) 'The Norwegian Liberal Party: from political pioneer to political footnote', in Emil J. Kirchner (ed.), *Liberal Parties in Western Europe*, Cambridge University Press: Cambridge, pp. 304–25.

Logue, John (1982) *Socialism and Abundance. Radical Socialism in the Danish Welfare State*, University of Minnesota: Minneapolis, MN.

Madeley, John (1982) 'Politics and the pulpit: the case of Protestant Europe', *West European Politics*, 5 (2), pp. 149–71.

Madeley, John (1990) 'Norway's 1989 election: the path to polarised pluralism?', *West European Politics*, 13 (2), pp. 287–92.

Madeley, John T. S. (2002) 'Outside the whale: Norway's Storting election of 10 September 2001', *West European Politics*, 25 (2), pp. 212–22.

Malmström, Cecilia (2005) 'Folkpartiet och Venstre-liberala partier i Sverige och Norge', in Marie Demker and Lars Svåsand (eds), *Partiernas århundrade*, Santérus Förlag: Stockholm, pp. 133–58.

Meret, Susi (2003) 'Højrepopulisme', in Jørgen Goul Andersen and Ole Borre (eds), *Politisk Forandring*, Systime Academic: Århus, pp. 375–89.

Miller, Kenneth E. (1991) *Denmark. A Troubled Welfare State*, Westview: Boulder, CO.

Nielsen, Hans Jørgen and Søren Risbjerg Thomsen (2003) 'Vælgervandringer', in Jørgen Goul Andersen and Ole Borre (eds), *Politisk Forandring*, Systeme Academic: Århus, pp. 61–73.

Paloheimo, Heikki and Jan Sundberg (2005) 'Puoluevalinnan perusteet', in Heikki Paloheimo (ed.), *Vaalit ja demokratia Suomessa*, WSOY: Porvoo-Helsinki, pp. 169–201.

Pedersen, Mogens (1985) 'Changing patterns of electoral volatility in European party systems, 1948–77: exploration in explanations', in Hans Daalder and Peter Mair (eds), *West European Party Systems*, Sage: London, pp. 29–66.

Pesonen, Pertti and Sten Berglund (1991) 'Puolueenvalinnan pysyvyys ja vaihdokset, 1987–9', in *Kansanedustajain vaalit*, Tilastokeskus: Helsinki, pp. 29–36.

Pesonen, Pertti, Risto Sänkiaho and Sami Borg (1993) *Vaalikansan äänivalta*, WSOY: Porvoo.

Pettersen, Per Arnt and Lawrence E. Rose (2004) 'Høyrebølgene – de stora og små: Velgerprofilene til Høyre og Fremskrittspartiet i flo og fjære', *Norsk Statsvitenskapelig Tidskrift*, 20 (3), 3–37.

Richard, Helen and Marie Demker (2005) 'Religion och politik i Norge och Sverige: Kd och KrF', in Marie Demker and Lars Svåsand (eds), *Partiernas århundrade*, pp. 191–217.

Rydgren, Jens (2004) 'Explaining the emergence of radical right-wing populist parties: the case of Denmark', *West European Politics*, 27 (3), pp. 474–502.

Rydgren, Jens (2007) 'Sweden: the Scandinavian exception', in Daniele Albertazzi and Duncan McDonnell (eds), *Twenty-First Century Populism. The Spectre of Western European Democracy*, Palgrave: London.

Sainsbury, Diane (1992) 'The 1991 Swedish election: protest, fragmentation and the shift to the right', *West European Politics*, 15 (2), pp. 160–6.

Salokas, P. (1916) 'Kristillis-sosialinen puolue Saksan poliittisessa elämässä', *Yhteiskuntataloudellinen aikakauskirja*, pp. 21–30.

Styrkarsdottír, Audur (1990) 'From social movement to political party: the new women's movement in Iceland', in Drude Dahlerup (ed.), *The New Women's Movement. Feminism and Political Power in Europe and the USA*, Sage: London.

Sundberg, Jan and Niklas Wilhelmsson (2007) 'Moving from movement to government: the transformation of the Finnish Greens', in Kris Deschouwer (ed.), *New Parties in Government*, Routledge: London.

Wörlund, Ingemar (2005) 'Miljöpartier i Sverige och Norge', in Marie Demker and Lars Svåsand (eds), *Partiernas århundrade*, Santérus Förlag: Stockholm, pp. 241–52.

Zilliacus, Kim O. K. (2001) 'New politics in Finland: the Greens and left wing in the 1990s', *West European Politics*, 24 (1), pp. 27–54.

6

Party system change since 1970

The structure of party competition can persist even when the protagonists involved in its promotion change out of all recognition.

(Mair 1997)

When playing the role of *advocatus diaboli*, it could be argued that the notion of 'party system change' is not only grammatically ponderous but also conceptually imprecise, operationally problematical and, ultimately, of limited utility in understanding the nature of policy-making in pluralist polities. If this seems harsh, it is none the less the case that, despite the extensive political science literature on party system change, there is surprisingly little agreement on what to measure, how to measure it and how to characterise the extent of change in the collective dynamics – that is, the action and interaction – of the individual parties that make up the party system. It is not clear either that the 'so what?' question has been adequately addressed. In other words, assuming that it is possible to establish that party system x has 'changed' from y to z, what are the wider implications of this change for political decision-making? In light of these remarks, it would seem perverse perhaps to concentrate in this brief chapter on party system change in Scandinavia since 1970. In addition to the above-mentioned caveats, moreover, there is an inherent risk in the 'periodisation' of party system change. The process cannot be pinned down to a rigid 'start date' of 1970 and, as noted, some members of the new party families – the Danish Socialist People's Party, for example, pre-dated that year.

However, in view of the increased levels of electoral volatility, the increased number of legislative parties and the emergence and consolidation of new party types, it seems important to tie together the threads of our discussion in the previous chapter by seeking to assess the extent of party system change in Scandinavia since the 'earthquake elections'. Has the five-party Scandinavian party system model changed out of all recognition? How much 'change' and how much 'persistence' has there been? In the following analysis, a distinction is drawn between the *electoral party system* and the *legislative party system*. The two may be treated separately, although in reality they are likely to be inter-twining. For example, an individual party may, during an election campaign, promote a set of policies intended to maximise its vote but which may in prac-tice reduce its prospects of achieving government office. As Michael Laver has noted, 'a change in policy position designed to increase electoral weight may in fact reduce bargaining power', and he adds that, in particular, 'movements away from the centre of the system have this effect' (Laver 1989: 306). Parties will, of course, give different priority to vote-seeking and office-seeking.

Changes in party system size

In considering the extent of change, whether in the electoral and/or legisla-tive arenas, it seems useful to separate out three analytically distinct elements of party systems – their *size, structure* and *dynamics*. The extent of change in the *size* of the Scandinavian electoral party system since 1970 can be assessed using two measures. First, there is change in the *effective number of electoral parties* (ENEP) using the Laakso–Taagepera index $1 \div \sum p^2 i$, where p is the proportion of votes received by party i. This will yield a measure of vote frag-mentation. Table 6.1 presents data on the effective number of electoral parties in all five Nordic states since the Second World War.

Table 6.1 *The average of the effective number of electoral parties (ENEP) in the five Nordic states in the pre- and post-1970 periods*

Country/period	ENEP	Period differential
Denmark		
1945–71	4.08	
1973–2005	5.37	+1.29
Norway		
1945–69	3.63	
1973–2005	4.68	+1.05
Iceland		
1946–67	3.64	
1971–2003	4.17	+0.53
Finland		
1945–66	5.17	
1970–2003	5.88	+0.71
Sweden		
1948–68	3.31	
1970–2006	3.91	+0.60

Source: Calculations based on data on www.tcd.ie/Political_Science/Staff/Michael.Gallagher/ ElSystems/Docts/ElectionIndices.pdf.

Two broad conclusions are in order. First, in all five Nordic states the ENEP has been higher – and the size of the electoral party systems may therefore be said to have increased – since the 'earthquake elections'. The increase has been greatest in Denmark and Norway and smallest in Iceland and Sweden. Second, there has not been a pattern of consistent increase in the ENEP; rather, periods when the effective number of parties has risen have been followed by periods of relative decline. In Norway, for example, there has been a marked upward trend in the ENEP since 1989 and the figures for the two general elections in the new millennium (2001 and 2005) have exceeded those following the seismic 1973 election. In Finland, in contrast, the ENEP has declined from the 1987 and 1991 levels and the size of the Finnish electoral party system has not increased in recent elections.

A second way of measuring change in the size of the electoral party systems in the Scandinavian countries – or, alternatively, the degree of 'core persistence' (Smith 1989) – is to calculate variations in the vote share of the 'three pole parties' before and after 1970. Thus, Jan Sundberg (1999) distinguishes between the vote share of:

1 the three pole parties – the Social Democrats, Agrarian/Centre and Conservatives;
2 the two remaining parties in the basic five-party model – the Liberals and Communists;
3 the 'other parties'.

In Denmark there has been a significant decline in the combined vote share of the three pole parties – the Social Democrats, Liberals (Venstre) and Conservatives – since the early 1970s (table 6.2). True evidence of 'core persistence' can be found in the fact that over the entire post-war period, nearly 70 per cent of Danes have supported these three historic 'class parties'. However, their vote share dropped by an average of 15 percentage points in elections between 1973 and 2005 compared with those between 1945 and 1971. In other words, since the 1973 election, an average of two-thirds of Danes have backed the three pole parties whereas four-fifths did so between 1945 and 1971. Equally, support for the parties in the 'others' category – parties formed after the initial period of party-building and mostly since the 1970s – more than tripled after the 'earthquake period' to reach an average approaching 30 per cent.

The 'core persistence' level of the post-war Norwegian electoral party system has been very similar to that in Denmark, with the vote share for the three pole parties running at 69.0 per cent between 1945 and 2005. Much as in Denmark too, however, that figure masks a marked decline since 1973 – from 73.6 per cent between 1945 and 1969 to 65.3 per cent between 1973 and 2005. Moreover, whilst three elections are scarcely sufficient to confirm a trend, the pole parties' share has not exceeded 54 per cent since 1997 and in 2001 only a little over half the Norwegian electorate supported them – the lowest anywhere in the region. Also, as in Denmark, the parties in the 'others' category have nearly tripled their support since 1973 compared with the 1945–1969 period.

Sweden has registered the highest post-war vote share for the three pole parties of all the mainland Nordic states. Almost three-quarters of Swedes voted for the pole parties in the period 1948–2006. Distinctively, moreover, their average vote share has been remarkably stable – 74.6 per cent between 1948 and 1968, and 74.8 per cent between 1970 and 2006. However, it dropped sharply in the late 1990s. Indeed, in the three Riksdag elections between 1998 and 2006 the pole parties' vote share averaged only 64.9 per cent. The parties in the 'others' category increased sevenfold over the post-1970 period, albeit from a low base. In fact, the 'others' did not reach a double-figure poll until 1991!

As in Sweden there was an *increase* in the average support for the three pole parties in Finland in the post-1970 period. Over the entire post-war period, an average of 63.5 per cent of Finnish voters have backed the pole parties. Between 1945 and 1966, 62.5 per cent did so and this rose to 64.2 per cent between 1970 and 2007. Indeed, at the two elections in the new millennium – 2003 and 2007 – over two-thirds of Finns backed the 'big three'. Parties in the 'others' category more than doubled their vote share in the post-1970 period,

Table 6.2 *Vote share of the 'pole parties', Liberals and Communists and 'others' in general elections in Denmark, Finland, Norway and Sweden, 1945–2007 (%)*

	Three pole parties: Social Democrats, Agrarian/ Centre, Conservatives	Two remaining parties in the basic five-party model: Liberals, Communists	Others
Denmark			
1945–2005	69.9	9.6	20.5
1945–1971	78.0	12.4	9.6
1973–2005	63.0	7.2	29.8
Finland			
1945–2007	63.5	20.0	16.4
1945–1966	62.5	27.7	9.8
1970–2007	64.2	15.1	20.7
Norway			
1945–2005	69.0	9.3	21.8
1945–1969	73.6	15.3	11.1
1973–2005	65.3	4.6	30.1
Sweden			
1948–2006	74.7	19.2	6.1
1948–1968	74.6	24.2	1.2
1970–2006	74.8	16.3	8.9

largely at the expense of the Liberals and Communists (and post-communist successor party).

Summing up, examining support for the pole parties reveals a mixture of persistence and change. Evidence of what Sundberg (1999) refers to as 'the enduring Scandinavian party system', or significant 'core persistence' in Gordon Smith's (1989) phrase, can be found in the post-war vote share of the three pole parties – the Social Democrats, Agrarian/Centre (in Denmark, the Liberals – Venstre) and Conservatives – which has ranged from nearly three-quarters in Sweden, seven-tenths in Denmark and Norway and under two-thirds in Finland. However, when comparing the periods before and after the 'high volatility' elections of 1970–73, it is evident that there has been a substantial decline in the pole parties' vote share in Denmark and Norway – 15 and 8 percentage points, respectively – effective parity of performance in Sweden and a modest increase in Finland. Restated, since the seismic elections of 1970–73, an average in the order of two-thirds of Danes, Finns and Norwegians and three-quarters of Swedes have backed the pole parties. At the same time, there has been a sizeable increase in the vote for parties in the 'others' category. Since the early 1970s approximately 30 per cent of Danes and Norwegians, 20 per cent of Finns and nearly 9 per cent of Swedes have opted for parties that did not form part of the historic five-party Scandinavian party system model.

Structural change in the electoral party systems since 1970

Turning now from changes in the size to examining the extent of change in the *structure* of the Scandinavian electoral party systems since 1970, it seems reasonable to explore the impact of both the institutionalisation of new party types and the long-term trends affecting the historic parties and the pole parties in particular. After the 'frozen period' in the west European and in our case Scandinavian party systems, which Lipset and Rokkan (1967) noted lasted from the late 1920s to the late 1960s, the post-1970 period witnessed, in addition to several short-lived splinter parties, the emergence of four new types of party. These were profiled in the previous chapter. Two, the eco-socialist groupings to the left of social democracy and the populist parties on the radical right, can be located fairly readily on a unidimensional party spectrum. However, two new 'party families', the Greens and Christian Democrats, have been more difficult to place on a conventional left–right continuum. Knut Heidar has argued that 'it is difficult to sustain the notion of a particularly Nordic or even Scandinavian party system' (Heidar 2004: 59). It would certainly appear that the Greens and Christian Democrats have vested the Scandinavian party systems with a multidimensionality they did not previously possess. Nor has there been any 'structural rationalisation' among the 'old' parties. Despite ephemeral talk of merging, the Social Democrats and the radical left have 'kept their distance' and there has been no conflation of the tripartite configuration of non-socialist forces to create a catch-all party of the centre-right. True, the Liberals briefly merged with the Centre in Finland in the mid-1980s – similar plans in Sweden in the early 1970s proved stillborn – but the emergence of new Christian, new radical rightist and miscellaneous short-lived splinter parties has contributed to an accentuated fragmentation in the Scandinavian non-socialist camp. In short, the structure of the party systems in the region is more complex and less obviously unidimensional.

It could, of course, be countered that it was not so much the unidimensionality of the pre-1970 Scandinavian party systems that was distinctive – outside Sweden it was probably exaggerated – as the high political cohesion of the three main social classes – the workers, farmers and middle class. But this no longer appears the case. Indeed, long-terms trends affecting the two main 'pole parties' have conspired to make the structure of the Scandinavian party systems less class-based (Listhaug 1997). First, there has been a steady erosion in support for the mainland Scandinavian Social Democratic/Labour parties, something captured already in the mid-1980s in Gøsta Esping-Andersen's reference to the phenomenon of 'social democratic party decomposition' (Esping-Andersen 1985). Second, despite their change of name to Centre parties, the former farmers' parties in Norway and Sweden have been reduced to the status of 'small parties' (defined as those with under 10 per cent of the vote). The impression is of class parties, or at least parties with an accentuated class profile, in slow decline, not parties boasting a stable catch-all status.

It is important to distinguish short-term fluctuations in support – both upwards and downwards – from long-term structural change. Mirroring the increased levels of electoral volatility since 1970, the old as well as new parties have been the beneficiaries of large swings in support, suggesting that, collectively, they have not only recovered lost ground – as we noted earlier when analysing the pole parties' vote share – but also on occasions served as an effective channel for the expression of diffuse political protest. A few examples must necessarily suffice. The largest individual party gain in Norway since 1970 was the Centre Party's 10.2 per cent increase in 1993 – when it polled 16.7 per cent – which it achieved in the run-up to the second referendum on the European Union (EU) on a stridently anti-membership stance (Aardal and Valen 1997). By 2005, in contrast, the Centre managed only 6.5 per cent. In 1995, against the backdrop of economic recession, the opposition-based Finnish Social Democrats gained 6.2 percentage points on four years earlier to achieve 28.3 per cent of the poll, the party's best result since the Second World War. The 21.4 per cent it managed in 2007, however, was its worst performance in nearly half a century. In Sweden in particular there has been striking voter switching between the 'old' non-socialist parties. In 1985 the Liberals gained 8.3 per cent to claim 14.2 per cent – shortly after Bengt Westerberg became the new leader – dropped to only 4.7 per cent at the 1998 Riksdag election, shot up to 13.3 per cent four years later, but registered only 7.5 per cent of the vote in 2006, when the Conservatives made the highest individual gain of any post-war Swedish party. Spearheading the so-called 'Alliance for Sweden' – the four-party, non-socialist bloc seeking to displace the Social Democrats – the Conservatives, under their new leader, Fredrik Reinfeldt, gained no less than 10.9 percentage points on their performance four years earlier, albeit it from the abnormally low base of 15.3 per cent in 2002.

Aside from these 'temporary fluctuations' (Smith 1989), there is evidence of a long-term erosion in the core support for the two principal class parties in Scandinavia. In the Social Democrats' case, the *prima facie* evidence would not suggest as much. In only seven Scandinavian general elections since 1945 have Social Democratic/Labour parties not emerged as the largest party. Yet the heyday of social democracy in the region appears well and truly over. Between 1945 and 1969, the Norwegian Labour Party's average support of 45.4 per cent was only 1.5 percentage points below that of its more celebrated Swedish counterpart in the same period. However, in the nine Storting elections since 1973, its average had fallen to 35.4 per cent. The Swedish Social Democrats, moreover, no longer appear a '40 per cent party', whilst in the first five general elections in the new millennium in Denmark and Finland, the Social Democrats had not emerged as the largest party and in Finland in 2007 slipped to third place for the first time in their history. In her doctoral study *Class Voting in Sweden*, Maria Oskarsson (1994) poses the rider question – 'rationality, loyalty or simply habit?' Borrowing her terms, there appear to be four elements in the long-term downward trend in the Social Democratic/Labour vote on mainland Scandinavia.

First, the proportion of 'habitual social democratic voters' is greatest among the older cohorts and there is variable evidence of what Oddbjørn Knutsen refers to as 'age decomposition' among the social democratic electorate (Knutsen 2003: 135–6). Put another way, generational turnover has left the Scandinavian Social Democratic parties with an increasingly senescent support base and the challenge of electoral rejuvenation. Second, there are fewer 'habitual social democrats' among younger voters and one manifestation of the heightened volatility among this group has been the extent of young working-class support for the new radical rightist parties. Although the point should not be exaggerated, there has been a decline in core class voting for social democracy. Third, the number of 'loyal social democratic voters' has declined, as class identification has weakened and social and geographical mobility increased. Social structural change, in short, has undercut the relative size of the Social Democrats' 'natural' electoral constituency. Finally, and more speculatively, the number of 'rational social democratic voters' – that is, those motivated to support a social democratic party primarily out of considerations of economic self-interest – may well have fallen as the Social Democrats have pursued fiscal policies more closely associated with the political right and appeared to abandon the traditional politics of redistribution.

The fortunes of the Nordic Centre parties, with a capital 'C' – formerly class-based agrarian parties – have fluctuated considerably since 1970 and the Swedish and Norwegian parties in particular have experienced periods of strong electoral growth associated with a specific issue stance. The Swedish Centre polled over one-quarter of the vote in 1976 as *the* party opposed to the expansion of a nuclear energy programme. The Norwegian party in turn gained its best-ever result, of nearly 17 per cent, in 1993 on the basis of its unequivocal opposition to EU membership (although, ironically, an exit poll conducted in conjunction with the EU referendum in November 1994 indicated that only 55 per cent of Centre voters were against the EU, with 45 per cent in favour). Since these high points, support for both parties has dropped sharply. For example, by 1998 the Swedish Centre polled only 5.1 per cent and only 37 per cent of farmers supported it. Indeed, at a time when the agricultural population is in irreversible decline (despite huge state subsidies to farmers in Norway) and constitutes only a tiny fraction of voters, the former farmers' parties have struggled to stabilise non-agrarian support and to build lasting alliances with significant sections of the predominantly urban electorate. They have attracted at times considerable support from outside the *classe gardée* but, importantly, not on a regularised basis (Arter 2001: 182–3).

Building a stable body of support in the capital city and its environs has proved especially problematical for the former farmers' parties. Whereas the Swedish Centre had its first MP elected, for Stockholm, in 1964, it was not until 1993 (and its 'big election') that the Norwegian Centre had an MP for Oslo elected, when, on a 4.4 per cent poll in the capital, Arne Haukvik, was returned to the Storting. The Finnish Centre is the striking exception to the long-term electoral decline of the former Scandinavian farmers' parties, although it was indebted to a (short-lived) merger with the Liberals for its first Helsinki MP, in 1983, and only once, in 2003, has it gained more than a single parliamentarian for the capital city. Yet at the 2007 Eduskunta election, the Centre emerged as the largest party in votes and seats for the second successive election – the first time in its history it has achieved this feat. For a former farmers' party to be the largest party in the 'high-tech', information-based, Nokia-driven Finland of the new millennium is remarkable indeed. It is a unique case of a class party of small and medium-sized farmers that has adapted to acquire a broad-based 'small town' and 'small business' appeal without the 'hot-house' single-issue growth of its Swedish and Norwegian sister parties.

Summing up on the structural changes to the Scandinavian party systems since 1970, three points warrant emphasis. First, there has been the establishment of new 'party families' articulating post-materialist (Greens and eco-socialists) and anti-secularist values (new Christians), which cannot readily be located on a conventional left–right continuum and which may be said to have lent the party systems added *dimensionality*. Second, a numerically significant radical right has emerged in Scandinavian politics for really the first time. Predicated on such 'new politics' issues as immigration, it has lent the party systems – particularly in Denmark and Norway – a greater degree of *polarisation*. Third, there has been the recovery – after the vote haemorrhaging of the 'earthquake elections' – and so persistence of the essentially class-based, left–right pole parties (Elff 2007), support for which has, in the short term, been subject to considerable fluctuation but which, in the case of the Social Democrats and Agrarian/Centre parties, are experiencing long-term electoral decline. The success of the Finnish Centre is clearly a deviant case and the exception to the phenomenon of *class party decline* – it has been the largest party in four post-war elections including the last two, although its astonishing resilience was doubtless facilitated by the collapse of the 'Vennamo enterprise' (the Finnish Rural Party), which in the 1970s in particular attracted small farmers in the Centre's core areas.

From size and structure to the changing dynamics of the electoral party systems

Work on classifying party systems has tended to focus on the so-called 'drives' or basic dynamics – whether centripetal or centrifugal – of the legislative party system or, in other words, how parties act and interact in parliament. However, the electoral party system – the action and interaction of the parties 'in the country' – will generate its own dynamics and these will reflect the strategic calculations of the parties, severally and collectively, in respect of vote-winning and office-seeking. The various and varying patterns of inter-party co-operation and competition are likely to effect change in the *dynamics* of the electoral party system.

Vote-winning strategies are, of course, legion. For example, where a preferential voting system exists (as in Finland, Denmark and Sweden), a party may decide to run a particularly strong slate of candidates in one of its core areas, calculating that the intense rivalry between its candidates will mobilise a high turnout of party supporters and produce an aggregate list vote big enough to claim an extra seat or seats. The basic logic is that parties will compete more effectively when intra-party candidate competition is fierce. In such cases, it is not uncommon for policy differences between candidates from the same party to exceed those between that party and the candidates of its rivals.

Electoral systems may facilitate formal co-operation between parties in the form of electoral alliances, that is, the provision for running joint (multi-party) lists. These may be arrangements of pure expediency, serving the perceived interest of parties that may have very different policy views. Equally, they may reflect common goals. In the Finnish case, where electoral alliances have been commonplace, they are today purely technical arrangements and the lifeblood of the small parties. However, famously, in the 1930 general election, two pole parties, the Agrarians and Conservatives, made an electoral alliance and then built a plywood tank bearing the slogan 'Filthy Communists Out of Finland', which they dragged around during the campaign.

Formal electoral alliances aside, elections may involve varying degrees of informal co-operation between parties when office-seeking is their collective goal.

Minimally, this might involve the largely cosmetic exercise of papering over policy differences and the achievement of what might be called consensus of the lowest common denominator. The brief interludes of non-socialist electoral co-operation in Sweden in 1976 and again in 1991 come into the latter category and had as their overriding logic the displacement of the Social Democrats from government. Equally, electoral co-operation may involve the drafting of a joint manifesto by a 'government in waiting'. Recently, unprecedented electoral co-operation on the centre-left in Norway in 2005 (involving the Labour, Left Socialist and Centre parties) and on the centre-right in Sweden (the four non-socialist parties) created a choice between rival blocs – that is, the appearance of bipolar rather than multipolar electoral competition – and led in both cases to the formation of majority governments. At this point there is a convergence between electoral party system and legislative party system change.

Legislative party system change since 1970

The legislative party system can be analysed very briefly by reference to the same three variables of size, structure and dynamics as for the electoral party system. The *size* of the legislative party system has increased in the obvious sense that there are more 'relevant parties' in the Scandinavian parliaments. Virtually all the post-1970 parties may be regarded as 'relevant' *à la* Giovanni Sartori in the sense that they have either participated in governing coalitions or formed part of *legislative coalitions* supporting the governing party or parties. Thus, all the new Christian parties, the eco-socialist Left Alliance in Finland and Socialist Left in Norway and the Finnish Greens have entered government at least once. At the same time, the Swedish Greens and the new radical rightist parties have acted as *support parties* when minority governments (very much the norm in Denmark, Norway and Sweden) have been in office. Of the 'new parties' only the Icelandic Left Greens and the True Finns appear less relevant in Sartori's sense of the term ('coalition potential' or 'blackmail potential').

Somewhat paradoxically, whilst from an electoral standpoint the Scandinavian party systems have exhibited heightened dimensionality, the *structure* of the legislative party systems has been predominantly unidimensional. In other words, despite espousing values that are not readily placed on a traditional left–right continuum, most of the post-1970 parties have acquired a clear *bloc association* in legislative terms – that is, they are regarded as part of the so-called 'socialist' or 'non-socialist' grouping of parties. For example, none of the new Christian parties, although to the left on social policy matters, has participated in a Social Democrat-led cabinet, whilst the Swedish Greens have consistently aligned themselves with the political left. The exception has been the Finnish Green Party, which between 1995 and 2002 was a member of the Social Democrat-led 'rainbow coalitions' and presently forms part of a Centre-led non-socialist government.

The *dynamics* of the legislative party system are likely to be affected by at least three factors:

1 Changes may be made to the institutional rules relating to decision-making, among other things whether qualified majorities (and not only simple majorities) are required/no longer required for particular decisions. Clearly, the existence of minority veto provisions would also be likely to have implications for the 'chemistry' of legislative party systems. Upper chambers might also function as 'institutional veto players' (Tsebelis 2002), although in the Scandinavian case, the last vestige of bicameralism, the Norwegian Lagting, will be abolished in 2009.

2 Changes in the size and/or structure of the legislative party system might also have repercussions for the cohesion of policy-making at the parliamentary stage. For example, a small, new party might behave unpredictably in the standing committees on which it has representation or, if too small to command committee seats, might be disruptive on the floor of the chamber. It might filibuster (where, as in Finland, there have been no time limits on plenary speeches), table interpellations or use other available institutional mechanisms to complicate the enactment of legislation.

3 The variable electoral strength of the parliamentary parties will, or at least may, influence their strategic considerations – office-seeking ambitions – both severally and collectively.

In short, exploring the changing dynamics of the legislative party system involves focusing on three things above all – the interaction of the parliamentary parties, the nature of legislative majority-building and the structure of party competition.

Peter Mair (1997) has noted that the structure of party competition can persist even when the protagonists involved in its promotion change out of all recognition. Equally, the structure of party competition can change significantly even when the protagonists involved in its promotion remain effectively the same. For example, in 1976 Sweden acquired the bipolar dynamics of Sartori's *moderate multipartism* and the transition from a *one-party dominant* system occurred within the existing framework of the five-party system model, underpinned by relatively minor electoral shifts between the competing blocs. Put another way, it was possible to speak of 'crunch co-operation' between the non-socialist parties (Arter 1998). When it came to the crunch, the non-socialists finally combined forces against the Social Democrats and broke their monopoly of power. Collectively, the Conservatives, Centre and Liberals advanced by only 2 percentage points compared with the 1973 Riksdag election, whilst the two left-wing parties lost a mere 1.4 percentage points, but the structure of party competition was decisively altered.

Making much the same point that the structure of legislative party competition can change significantly without significant changes in the core electoral features of the party system, Knut Heidar has noted in respect of Norway that 'the significant changes have not occurred in format – that is, in the number of significant parties – but rather in their changing strategies for seeking power – mostly triggered by external events' (Heidar 2005: 829). He proceeds to identify three major strategic developments that have affected the structure of party competition in Norway. First, there has been the emergence of a 'centre alternative' – the Christian Democrat Kjell-Magne Bondevik led a series of numerically weak, centre-based coalitions over 1997–2000 and 2001–5. In this connection, Tim Bale has suggested that where there is a substantial radical right, as in Norway, the centre-right has exploited its existence to gain office and, once there, to implement policies (notably on immigration) tradi- tionally associated with the radical right (Bale 2003: 84–5). Second, Heidar notes, there has been the growing ambition of the Progress Party to enter government. Under its new leader, Siv Jensen, the Progress Party has empha- sised social policy and the 'caring side' of its nature and, by seeking to present itself as a responsible alternative, has aspired to government office. Finally, the 'coalition potential' of the Socialist Left has increased. As early as 1993, when the Socialist Left stood at over 15 per cent in the opinion polls, the party's then leader, Erik Solheim, gained the backing of party congress for a strategy of challenging the Labour and Centre parties to co-operate in government. However, by 2001, when, under Kristin Halvorsen, the Socialist Left polled its best result and the Labour Party its worst, governmental co-operation between the two became a realistic option and, before the 2005 Storting general elec- tion, a pre-electoral alliance was formed between the Labour, Centre and Socialist Left parties, which proceeded to win power (Sitter 2006: 579).

Space prevents a detailed analysis of the changing dynamics of the legis- lative party systems in each of the five Nordic states. There will be further discussion of the matter in chapter 9, which considers whether there is a distinctively Scandinavian form of parliamentarism. However, perhaps the closest thing to a general trend, at least in Denmark, Norway and Sweden, is that legislative majority-building has involved increased governmental co- operation between the historic non-socialist parties, and this has denoted an end to one-party-dominant systems and the shift to a two-bloc structure of party competition. Government coalitions and legislative coalitions, in short, have had a 'bloc character'. Not for the first time, Finland is a deviant case in that it does not conform to the trend towards bipolar systems. Although a non-socialist (plus Greens) government was in power at the time of writing (2008), coalitions 'across the blocs' have been the norm and the core of govern- ments has comprised any two of the three larger parties – Social Democrats and Conservatives (1987–91 and 1995–2003), Centre and Social Democrats (2003–7) and Centre and Conservatives (1991–95 and from 2007 onwards). Since all the new parties (except the True Finns), as well as the old, have par- ticipated in government in recent years and have elevated office-seeking above all else, the 'drives' of the legislative party system in Finland have been highly centripetal and, in this context, the present author (Arter 2007) has referred to the transition from a 'contingent party system' – parties and government dependent on the acquiescence of the Finnish president and Kremlin – to an 'imploded party system', in which 'all the major parties become centre parties capable of governing with one another' (Green-Pedersen 2004: 324). In Iceland, too, governments have been routinely formed 'across the blocs' and, after a period of centre-right Progressive Party–Independence Party coalition between 1995 and 2007, the Alþingi election in the latter year brought an Independence Party–Social Democrat coalition to power.

Mair (1997) has argued that electoral change should be seen to lead to party system change only when it brings about a shift from one type of party system to another. The problem, however, lies in the limitations imposed by Sartori's typology (Sartori 1976). Outside Finland, the Nordic party systems display a sufficient degree of left–right bipolarity – that is, two-bloc competition – to justify being described as moderate multi-party systems. Yet certain issues – EU membership and nuclear power are obvious cases – can have a polarising effect, realigning the parties and creating what Heidar refers to as 'two modes of party system mechanics'. One, referring to Norway, he suggests is 'moderate, pluralist and consensual' (Heidar 2005: 829), with the parties located along a left–right spectrum; the other is polarised, with pro- and anti-issue permutations of parties which do not fit left–right lines. In other words, the blanket characterisation of the Scandinavian party systems as 'moderate multi-party' both is of limited value in a comparative west European perspective and also conceals dimensions and dynamics that differentiate one Nordic party system from another.

Summary

1. Whilst acknowledging the limitations inherent in the periodisation of party system change, this chapter has focused on the extent of party system change since the 'earthquake elections' of 1970–73.

2. Four general features were noted: the increased levels of electoral volatility, the increased number of legislative parties, the relatively high mortality rate among new parties, and the significant short-term fluctuations in support for the historic parties.

3. A distinction was drawn between the electoral party system and the legislative party system and three analytically distinct elements of party systems identified – their size, structure and dynamics.

4. When measured using the Laakso–Taagepera index, the effective number of electoral parties – and by extension the size of the electoral party system – has increased, albeit not consistently, since the early 1970s. Alternatively, if changes in the size of the Scandinavian party systems are assessed in relation to the vote share of the three 'pole parties' – the Social Democrats, Agrarian/Centre and Conservatives – there has been a mixture of 'core

persistence' and change. In Denmark and Norway there has been a substantial decline in the combined support for the pole parties since the early 1970s, but in Sweden and particularly Finland an increase.

5.   Long-term trends affecting the pole parties have included an erosion of the support for Social Democratic/Labour parties, a decline in the core support for the former farmers' parties in Norway and Sweden and extensive intra-bloc mobility, particularly on the non-socialist side.

6.   It is probably fair to argue that the size of the Scandinavian party systems has changed less than their basic structure. The structure of the electoral party systems has changed as a consequence of the emergence of four new types of party – the eco-socialists, the new radical right parties, Greens with a capital 'G' and new Christian parties. Together they have vested the Scandinavian party systems with added dimensionality and heightened polarisation.

7.   Work on classifying party systems has focused on the so-called 'drives' or basic dynamics of the legislative party system. However, new patterns of inter-party co-operation and competition are likely to effect change in the dynamics of the electoral party system. The novel pre-electoral alliances on the centre-left in Norway in 2005 and the centre-right in Sweden in 2006 are cases in point.

8.   Changes in the size, structure and dynamics of the electoral party systems in Scandinavia – in sum, the 'core features' – have probably been less important for the nature of government and policy-making than changes in the structure of party competition in the parliamentary arena – that is, legis-lative party system change.

9.   The size of the legislative party system has increased and there are more 'relevant' legislative parties.

10.   Equally, notwithstanding the consolidation of parties that, in terms of their basic values and policies, are difficult to locate on a left–right continuum, the Scandinavian legislative party systems have remained essentially uni-dimensional in structure. The new parties have acquired a 'bloc association'.

11.   Whilst outside Finland there is evidence of a shift towards the dynamics of two-bloc party competition, realignment across left–right lines can and does occur on high-saliency questions. In other words, a degree of issue polarisation has been evident.

12.   In response to the 'party system change – so what?' question, it is obvious that changes in the dynamic relations between the parliamentary parties will have implications for legislative majority-building (facilitating or complicat-ing it) and, by extension, the cohesion of policy-making at the parliamentary stage in the process. We shall return to this matter in chapter 9 in particular.

References

Aardal, Bernt O. and Henry Valen (1997) 'The Storting election of 1989 and 1993: Norwegian politics in perspective', in Kaare Strøm and Lars Svåsand (eds), *Challenges to Political Parties. The Case of Norway*, University of Michigan: Ann Arbor, MI, pp. 61–76.

Arter, David (1998) 'Sweden: a mild case of "electoral instability syndrome"?', in David Broughton and Mark Donovan (eds), *Changing Party Systems in Western Europe*, Pinter-Cassell: London, pp. 143–62.

Arter, David (2001) 'Conclusion', in David Arter (ed.), *From Farmyard to City Square? The Electoral Adaptation of the Nordic Agrarian Parties*, Ashgate: Aldershot, pp. 162–83.

Arter, David (2007) 'From a contingent party system to party system implosion? Party system change in Finland, 1945–2007', paper presented at the Political Studies Association, Annual Conference, University of Bath, April.

Bale, Tim (2003) 'Cinderella and her ugly sisters: the mainstream and extreme right in Europe's bipolarising party systems', *West European Politics*, 26 (3), pp. 67–90.

Elff, Martin (2007) 'Social structure and electoral behavior in comparative perspective: the decline of social cleavages in western Europe revisited', *Perspectives on Politics*, 5 (2), pp. 277–94.

Esping-Andersen, Gøsta (1985) *Politics Against Markets. The Social Democratic Road to Power*, Princeton University Press: Princeton, NJ.

Green-Pedersen, Christoffer (2004) 'Center parties, party competition and the implosion of party systems: a study of centripetal tendencies in multiparty systems', *Political Studies*, 52 (2), pp. 324–41.

Heidar, Knut (2004) 'Parties and party systems', in Knut Heidar (ed.), *Nordic Politics. Comparative Perspectives*, Universitetsforlaget: Oslo, pp. 40–59.

Heidar, Knut (2005) 'Norwegian parties and the party system: steadfast and changing', *West European Politics*, 28 (4), pp. 807–33.

Knutsen, Oddbjørn (2003) *Generations, Age Groups and Voting Behaviour in the Scandinavian Countries, A Comparative Study*. Research Report 4, Faculty of Social Sciences, University of Oslo.

Laver, Michael (1989) 'Party competition and party system change', *Journal of Theoretical Politics*, 1 (3), pp. 301–24.

Lipset, S. M. and S. Rokkan (eds) (1967) *Party Systems and Voter Alignments. Cross-National Perspectives*, New York: Free Press.

Listhaug, Ola (1997) 'The decline of class voting', in Kaare Strøm and Lars Svåsand (eds), *Challenges to Political Parties*, University of Michigan: Ann Arbor, MI, pp. 77–90.

Mair, Peter (1997) *Party System Change*, Clarendon Press: Oxford.

Oskarsson, Maria (1994) *Klassröstning i Sverige: rationalitet, lojalitet eller bara slentrian?*, Nerenius och Santérus förlag: Stockholm.

Sartori, Giovanni (1976) *Parties and Party Systems*, Cambridge University: Cambridge.

Sitter, Nick (2006) 'Norway's Storting election of September 2005: back to the left?', *West European Politics*, 29 (3), pp. 573–80.

Smith, Gordon (1989) 'Core persistence: system change and the "People's Party"', *West European Politics*, 12 (4), pp. 157–68.

Sundberg, Jan (1999) 'The enduring party system', *Scandinavian Political Studies*, 22 (3), pp. 221–41.

Tsebelis, George (2002) *Veto Players: How Institutions Work*, Russell Sage Foundation: New York.

Part IV

The Nordic model

7

A Nordic model of government?

Capitalism in the north, it seems to me, has been modified and, in a sense, controlled; the profit motive in many fields drastically curbed or abolished – subjugated
might be a better word. To a considerable degree ... the domestic economy has
been made to serve the greatest good of the greatest number.

(Childs 1936: 18)

When in the 1930s the Swedish Social Democrats began to build their
celebrated welfare state, it was based on two strong pillars – *neutrality* and
industry. Neutrality provided the means of avoiding the economic dislocation
involved in war and gave Swedish industry a competitive advantage, which it
exploited to the full. Indeed, export industry generated the wealth on which
the security of the 'people's home' was built, whilst the symbiotic relationship
which developed between social democracy and big business marginalised
the political right. For three decades after the Second World War, Sweden
enjoyed an international reputation for being a small, stable and progressive
democracy and one which stood in sharp contrast to the instability and extremism of Italy and the French Fourth Republic (which collapsed in 1958)
and, indeed, the adversarial approach of British politics. Sweden was the jewel
in the Scandinavian crown and high-level delegations of politicians and interest group representatives made the 'pilgrimage' north in search of the secret.
Andrew Schonfield (1965: 199) described amusingly how in the 1950s a
group of senior British trade unionists visited Sweden to discover the panacea
for industrial peace:

At the least sign of trouble '*We has a meeting,*' related one shop steward. 'Huh!
"We has a meeting"!' was the incredulous but unspoken reaction of the British
team. Try telling that to the lads back home, they thought to themselves.

The first part of this chapter explores the building of Sweden's reputation as a successful small democracy. The second seeks to identify the main

characteristics of the 'Swedish model' in its heyday in the 1960s. The third section considers the extent of the deviation from the model elsewhere in the Nordic region. Finally, it is asked whether the model has become little more than a receding memory. In the following discussion, a distinction is drawn between an ideal-type *model of government*, which refers to the political institutions, structures and policy processes, and an ideal-type *welfare model*, the latter representing in large part the legislative product of the former. The Nordic welfare model will be described and analysed in chapter 8.

Sweden – the anatomy of a 'harmonious democracy'

Sweden's international reputation as a 'harmonious democracy' (*den lyckliga demokratien*) in Herbert Tingsten's (1966) phrase – successful at resolving political conflict and stimulating a high economic growth rate – has been indebted in no small measure to the commentaries of foreign journalists and academics. Thus, when in spring 1936 the young American journalist Marquis Childs published a short volume on the reform policies of the Swedish Social Democratic Party entitled *Sweden. The Middle Way* it became a surprising best-seller. It was penned at the time of the Great Depression, when over 20 million Americans were out of work and faith in the capitalist system had been severely shaken. In sharp contrast, in the totalitarian systems of fascist Germany and communist Russia, Hitler and Stalin claimed that everybody had a job. It was against this background of capitalism in crisis, on the one hand, and the pretensions of the illiberal regimes of right and left, on the other, that Sweden's 'third way' appeared to offer salvation by demonstrating that it was possible to create a society in which full employment, social security and equality could be combined with democracy and respect for individual rights. Following Childs' analysis, Sweden became not just another state but a model for other states, its solidary 'people's home' respected as a shining example of consensus politics and the product of an historic compromise between capital and labour. Sweden became the epitome of an egalitarian culture and pragmatic style of politics that many yearned to emulate. As Childs concluded, the Swedes are 'the ultimate pragmatists, interested only in the workability of the social order' and they have found 'a moderate solution ... in a world torn by every sort of extreme' (Childs 1936: 213–15). The foundations of the reputation had been laid.

On the theme of pragmatic politics, the American political scientist Thomas Anton in the late 1960s and early 1970s identified several quintessential properties of Swedish policy-making and emphasised the way institutions were designed to avoid open conflict at all costs (Anton 1969). First, he noted that the policy preparation process was *extraordinarily deliberative*. There were long periods in which more or less constant attention was given to a problem by well trained experts; indeed, Anton argued that policy-making was dominated by experts and expert roles, and the principal site for the extended deliberation of policy initiatives was the pre-legislative commission of inquiry (*utredning*). An important structural reason for the dependence on commissions in Sweden, it might be added, was that government departments were small and ministers exercised no direct authority over the implementation of policy. Rather, a network of independent and relatively autonomous central boards and agencies – the Social Welfare Board, the National Labour Market Board, the National Pensions Board and so on – oversaw policy directives (Linde 1982).

Second, policy-making was *highly rationalistic*. By this Anton (1969: 98) meant that the maximum amount of information on a subject was amassed and the exercise of analysing it was approached in a pragmatic, intellectual style. He stressed the 'problem-focused' rather than 'theory-focused' orientation of Swedish policy-makers. Broadly, the view was that the government was established to do things, not to talk about doing things or think about doing things. There was a 'politics as work' rather than 'politics as game' ethic, and commissions were the perfect expression of the work orientation, in being very long and thorough. Specialisation might also be seen as a mechanism of conflict avoidance.

Third, the policy process was *very open*, in two senses. All interested parties were consulted before a decision was finally made. The *remiss procedure* involved referring draft commission proposals for major policy change to all parties and organisations likely to be affected by them or likely to have any interest in responding to them. Anton (1969: 94) claimed that although remiss procedures did not eliminate conflict, they 'domesticated' it, by reducing the possibility of public conflict. He observed that there was a tendency for affected organisations to talk themselves into agreement. Policy-making was open in a second sense, too: namely, that all government documents, except those dealing with national security or defence questions, were readily available for public scrutiny. The library shelves of (say) the University of Stockholm are stacked with commission reports, although the deliberations of commissions are secret.

Finally, policy-making was *consensual*. Anton (1980) contended that decisions were seldom taken without the agreement of virtually all the parties to them and that even 'reservations' (dissenting statements to commission reports) did not challenge the consensus, since groups could be in disagreement without being in conflict.

Effusive analyses of Sweden can also be found in the work of, *inter alia*, the American Donald Hancock (1972) and Canadian Henry Milner (1989, 1994). In the early 1970s Hancock (1972: 11) wrote that Sweden 'appears to have entered the post-industrial era as a leading empirical example of system transforming change'. At the end of the following decade, against the backdrop of the ascendancy of Thatcherite neo-liberalism and Reaganomics, Milner (1989: 16) insisted in relation to Sweden that 'up-to-date statistics and common-sense observation depict a society that has found a viable mean between equitable distribution and solid economic performance'. Sweden, it seems, continued to be special.

The Swedish model

The United States that Anton left for a Fulbright year in Stockholm in the late 1960s was marked by racial violence and campus unrest and the decade witnessed the assassination of such leading public figures as President John F. Kennedy, Martin Luther King and Malcolm X. Moreover, whilst the United States was a big federal system, Sweden was small, unitary and centralised, and US political scientists could perhaps be expected to fall ready prey to the 'small is beautiful' syndrome. Yet more or less contemporaneously, the Swedish political scientist Herbert Tingsten was describing the transition 'from ideas to idyll' and how Sweden was a 'harmonious democracy', managed in a consensual way by politicians not blinkered by all-pervasive ideologies. Ideology was dead and Sweden, to borrow from the British prime minister Harold Macmillan (1957–63), 'had never had it so good'. In view of the broad consensus among academics (both Swedish and non-Swedish) that Sweden was a successful consensual democracy (Lijphart 1969, 1975, 1999), it is plainly important to seek to identify the essential elements of the 'Swedish model' in its heyday two decades or so after the Second World War. As an ideal type, four components may be enumerated:

1 a dominant Social Democratic Party that monopolised government office but not political power;
2 a polity that accorded primacy to representative over accountable government;
3 a polity predicated on an historic compromise between capital and labour which, facilitated by a Social Democratic executive, permitted the development of close working relations with the major economic interest groups in the management of the economy and society;
4 the existence of a political culture based on consensus.

Monopoly of government office but not political power

The Social Democrats' cabinet hegemony extended, except for a few months in 1936, over four decades. Put another way, their forty-four-year domination of government office began before Adolf Hitler came to power in Germany and lasted until the third general election to the new unicameral Riksdag in 1976. Moreover, apart from participation in a wartime coalition (1940–44) and a coalition with the Agrarians from 1951 to 1957, and in both cases the prime minister was a Social Democrat, the Social Democrats governed alone. Yet, in contrast to the 'Westminster model', where opposition parties can only oppose and office is a prerequisite for policy influence, the Swedish model approximated Wolfgang Müller and Kaare Strøm's notion of an *inclusionary democracy* – that is, a system in which policy influence may be gained without control of the executive branch (Müller and Ström 1999).

Primacy accorded to representative government

Proponents of the Westminster model laud the virtues of 'responsible govern-ment', that is, a system of single-party majority governments that govern as they see fit – albeit rarely with absolute majority backing in the country – and are then held accountable for their actions at regular general elections. Voters adjudicate on the record of the government and the alternatives offered by Her Majesty's Opposition. However, in Sweden, as Leif Lewin has pointed out, 'by sharing power with the parties in opposition and including them in the rule of the country, the government is supposed to be regarded as representative of the people as a whole and consequently one that all can feel loyal to' (Lewin 1998: 203). The notion of accountability, by contrast, is weak. As the former Swedish Liberal Party parliamentarian Daniel Tarschys (2002) has observed, there is no good word for it in Swedish. Approximations include *ansvar, redovisning, rappor-tering* and – from a British viewpoint the most readily intelligible – *kontroll*.

Close working relations with the major economic interest groups

Significantly, when revisiting Sweden some fifty years on in *The Middle Way on Trial*, Childs notes that the 1938 Saltsjöbaden Pact between industry and labour was the vital component of the 'middle way' (Childs 1980: 19). Importantly, the prime minister and cabinet liaised with both sides of industry and not simply the trade union movement. Thus, from 1939 onwards, Social Democratic govern-ments periodically invited representatives of business to confer on economic and financial questions and, accordingly, a good relationship developed between industry and ruling social democracy – a rapport strengthened through infor-mal discussions in the so-called 'Thursday Club' in the early 1950s. By the end of that decade, the talks between the government and representatives of the so-called labour-market organisations, held at the country residence of the prime minister, Tage Erlander, gave rise to the phenomenon of 'Harpsund democracy'. In November 1958 the Social Democratic daily *Stockholms Tidningen* wrote that 'the recurring discussions at Harpsund between the government and repre-sentatives of the business sector and working life are one of several signs that a new spirit of co-operation is being created. Wise people both within enterprises and the labour movement are working to gain a more comprehensive perspec-tive on economic policy issues' (Lewin 1988: 204). In short, neo-corporatism was at the heart of policy-making in the Swedish model.

Political culture based on consensus

This has been an aspect of the Swedish model over which there has been widespread agreement between Swedish and non-Swedish commentators. Among the former, Olof Petersson (1994: 34) has written that 'the aim of political decision-making has been to avoid divisive conflicts; an emphasis on compromise and pragmatic solutions has led to a political culture based on consensus'. In similar vein, the Americans Eric Einhorn and John Logue (1986: 207) comment that 'formal Scandinavian political institutions are not very exceptional: they are typical parliamentary democracies. The less formal aspects – corporatist interest organization and strong parties – and informal aspects – political culture – are more unique.'

Consensus is, of course, the outcome of bargaining, negotiation and ultimately accommodation. Indeed, among the characterisations of the Swedish system used most frequently by Swedes in recent years has been the label *negotiating democracy*. When I interviewed the former Riksdag Speaker, Birgitta Dahl, she insisted that, in their heyday in the 1960s, the pre-legislative commissions of inquiry constituted 'the first stage in Sweden's negotiating democracy' (Arter 2000: 110). On the first page alone of the introductory chapter of their edited volume, Lars-Göran Stenelo and Magnus Jerneck refer to Sweden as a 'negotiating democracy', 'bargaining democracy' and 'consensual democracy' and to the Swedish model of the 'politics of compromise' (Stenelo and Jerneck 1996: 11). They define a 'bargaining democracy' as one in which 'negotiations as a method of conflict resolution predominate over voting but naturally do not exclude it' (Stenelo and Jerneck 1996: 12). The contrast is with a 'voting democracy'. In his introduction to a special issue of the journal *West European Politics* on 'Understanding the Swedish Model', Jan-Erik Lane asserts that 'the Swedish model ... comprises a set of concepts and ideas about what good government is' (Lane 1991: 1). It can reasonably be inferred from this that if negotiation is a central concept in a notion of good government in Sweden, it should be viewed as both process and norm – what does happen and what should happen. Equally, the process of bargaining and negotiation has an obvious functional logic in a country where minority government has been commonplace. As the (then) veteran Social Democratic parliamentarian Jan Bergqvist put it tellingly to the author, 'majority-building is the whole point of Swedish politics'.

Deviations from the Swedish model?

The extent of Social Democratic domination of government, albeit not power; the scale, scope and rigour of the consultation process at the pre-legislative stage of policy-making; the tradition of neo-corporatist practices involving both sides of industry in strategic economic decisions; and a political culture imbued with consensual norms appears a distinctive, if not necessarily unique, syndrome of features. But how far did the other Nordic countries deviate from the Swedish model in its prime in the 1960s?

Norway

Norway appears to have been the closest 'fit'. Except for a few weeks in 1963, the Labour Party held government office continuously for the first two post-war decades, unlike its Swedish sister party never in coalition, and did so until 1961 with a majority of its own in the Storting. In the way the Swedish party was dominated by Tage Erlander, who was prime minister continuously between 1946 and 1969, the Norwegian Labour Party was almost synonymous with the name of Einar Gerhardsen, who led no less than four governments between 1945 and 1965 (Bergh and Pharo 1977). Whilst the dominant governing party, the Labour Party none the less involved a range of non-executive actors in the legislative process and, though a majority government for most of the first two post-war decades, its *policy style* (Gustafsson and Richardson 1980; Richardson 1982) differed considerably from that of majority governments in the Westminster model.

Indeed, as in Sweden, the commission system afforded an institutionalised mechanism for consultation between the executive and relevant policy actors in the gestation of public policy. In the Norwegian case, the commission system is notably old, pre-dating the emergence of political parties and mass politics (Solvang and Moren 1974). Between 1814 and 1900 there were 894 at work – an average of about ten new commissions annually, compared with a mean of about twenty new ones yearly in the period 1900–36 (Arter 1984: 54). However, the real expansion of the commission system coincided with the growth of welfarism after the Second World War and the increased role of the state in social and economic management. Significantly, Robert Kvavik (1976) drew on Norwegian experience to produce his 'co-optive polity model' – a system in which interest groups are routinely 'co-opted' on to the preparatory network of commissions, committees and working groups. As in Sweden, in short, pre-legislative consultation has been extensive, the remiss system relatively formal and, as one Norwegian under-secretary of state put it frankly, 'if there were more consultation than there is today, nothing would ever be done!' (Olsen 1980: 249).

In Norway, as in Sweden, there has been a tradition of neo-corporatist negotiation involving actors from both sides of industry in the process of macro-economic decision-making. The biennial incomes policy deliberations inspired Stein Rokkan's celebrated model of *corporate pluralism*, in which he brings out the decisive influence exercised by the leading sectoral interest groups. In his ground-breaking work, Rokkan identified two distinct channels of influence in the policy process. First, there is voter influence through the ballot box – what he calls *the electoral channel* – which determines the partisan balance in parliament and by extension the composition of the government. This is *numerical democracy*, although it should be added that in practice in proportional electoral systems votes do not always determine the composition of the post-election government. Second, there is the influence exerted by organised interests through their routinised involvement in the policy-making process. Rokkan refers to this as *the corporate channel* and in a celebrated axiom he makes it clear that in the Norwegian case it is the corporate channel that has exercised the decisive influence: 'votes count ... but resources decide'

(Rokkan 1966: 167). By 'resources' Rokkan meant the economic resources, as well as resources of expertise, possessed by the major sectoral interests and their strategic role, especially in the generation and management of economic policy. In sum, Rokkan maintained that the bargaining and consultation process between the government, on the one side, and the trade union movement, business and the farm and fisheries' organisations, on the other, had come to affect the lives of ordinary citizens more than general elections.

Denmark

The Danish case is less well served by the literature, but there appear to have been sufficient common denominators between Denmark, Norway and Sweden to justify reference to a 'Scandinavian model of government' – though not a Nordic one – in the 1960s.

The Danish Social Democrats, to be sure, did not dominate government in the first two post-war decades in the manner of their Nordic sister parties and either shared power (usually in coalition with the Social Liberals – Radikale Venstre) or operated as a single-party minority administration, dependent on opposition-based 'support parties' for a legislative majority. The structure and dynamics of the legislative party system, in short, placed a premium on representative government and the achievement of broad-based policy solutions. None the less, as in Norway and Sweden, the Danish Social Democrats enjoyed a hand-in-glove relationship with the peak blue-collar federation and, while 'social democratic state' (Rothstein 1992) would probably be an exaggerated description in the Danish case, the Social Democrats could none the less be said to have exercised decisive influence on the policy agenda.

As in Norway and Sweden, moreover, the extensive consultation between the government and organised interests on the preparatory committees of the Danish central administration substantially antedated the growth of the welfare state after the Second World War. In the period 1913–27 at least two-thirds and as many as eight-tenths of the policy-formulating committees had interest group representation. Between 1946 and 1975 interest groups were represented on about three-fifths of the significantly increased number of Danish commissions preparing laws (*lovforberedende kommissioner*) and approximately half the commissions of inquiry (those with a wider investigative function – *utredningsopgaver*). Peter Munk Christiansen and Asbjørn Sonne Nørgaard in fact refer to the period from the late 1950s to the late 1960s as 'the golden era of classical Danish corporatism' (Christiansen and Nørgaard 2003: 46).

Corporatist practices in economic policy-making have been particularly long-standing in Denmark and the 'September Compromise' in 1899 between the trade union confederation and employers was the first agreement of its kind in the world (Kjellberg 1992: 89). This 'historic compromise' came over three decades before similar arrangements in Norway and Sweden. Over the years there has been a tradition of centralised wage-bargaining and, whilst the government has not formally been involved, the Social Democrats on occasions introduced ancillary legislation (in the form of increased housing subsidies, for example, or extra statutory holiday entitlements) to 'sugar the pill' for the labour movement when an agreement was hard to reach.

All in all, although less obvious from the literature than in Norway and Sweden, Denmark in the 1960s may be said to have had a consensual political culture. Thus, John Fitzmaurice has written that Denmark 'produced a particular form of "co-operative parliamentarism" in which pragmatism, tolerance, willingness to negotiate and competence are key behavioural norms' (Fitzmaurice 1981: 89). He adds that 'it is a basic principle of Danish politics that as wide a consensus as possible of parties and organisations should be arrived at before decisions are taken' (Fitzmaurice 1981: 93).

Finland

By the end of the 1970s it had become commonplace to speak of 'consensus politics' in Finland and in 1978 all the main parties, from the radical left to the Conservatives, supported the re-election of the long-serving president Urho Kekkonen and the so-called Paasikivi–Kekkonen line of maintaining amicable relations with Moscow. The previous year there was a Finnish variant of 'Harpsund democracy' when the government convened a meeting of representatives of all the leading interest groups and a wide range of experts in a motel outside Helsinki with a view to agreeing a strategy for stimulating the economy. This spawned the so-called 'Korpilampi spirit', which subsequently became a symbol for corporate-channel consensus in the national interest. In the 1960s, however, Finland deviated in several essentials from the 'Scandinavian model'.

First, there were two numerically significant and broadly equally sized parties of the left, both of which experienced significant periods out of office. The communist-dominated Finnish People's Democratic League was in opposition continuously from 1948 to 1966, whilst the Social Democrats, weakened by the formation of a splinter party, were 'out in the cold' between 1958 and 1966. The 'pivotal' governing party in Finland, in short, was the Agrarians, the largest Eduskunta grouping between 1962 and 1966, and it was not until the latter year that the Social Democrats became a perennial governing party.

Second, whilst the evidence is limited, pre-legislative consultation appears to have been less open and probably also less comprehensive than elsewhere on mainland Scandinavia, the preference being for the creation of intra-departmental working groups. Not enough is known to be definitive but in the heyday of the Scandinavian model there was no comparable tradition in Finland of public commissions of inquiry with formalised or, indeed, informal remiss procedures. It was the early 1970s before there was a significant growth in both the staff and the representation of the main employee federations on the expanded network of executive committees (Tiihonen and Tiihonen 1983: 248; Helander 1979).

Third, the historic class compromise between workers and employers was born in very different circumstances in Finland and the centralised collective wage-bargaining system can be traced back to the climate of solidarity generated by the nation's military struggle against the Soviet Union in the Winter War of November 1939–March 1940. On 23 January 1940 a first agreement between the central trade union federation and employers' organisation – the so-called 'January Engagement' – was concluded. The commitment of these two organisations to resolve differences in a spirit of mutual understanding was renewed in the form of a General Agreement in May 1946 (Arter 1987: 204–5). That spirit of mutual understanding quickly dissipated in the changed climate after the Second World War. The Finnish Social Democrats did not enjoy the special bond with the trade union movement of its Scandinavian counterparts. Rather, with the labour movement divided along ideological lines and with the re-legalised Communists controlling a number of unions in the heavy industrial sector – notably the Metal Workers and Construction Workers – attempts to forge centralised incomes policy agreements stalled in the early 1950s. It was not until 1968, in the wake of a devaluation of the currency, that an incomes policy package – the so-called Liinamaa 1 (Stabilisation) Agreement – was concluded and a neo-corporatist approach to economic management began to develop (Hetemäki 1979: 58).

It follows from the preceding points that during the 'golden era' of the Scandinavian model, in the 1960s, Finland did not have a political culture based on consensus. At that time, indeed, Giovanni Sartori viewed Finland as a possible case of polarised pluralism (Sartori 1966) and, in his recent defence of Sartori, Jocelyn Evans assumes that Finland was a polarised system and he detects evidence for this in the core (centre-based) parties losing ground 'in bursts' (Evans 2002: 163). Yet the Communists' reincorporation into government in 1966 meant that Finland did not manifest the essential characteristics of polarised pluralism. Instead, broad-based 'surplus majority' coalitions embracing the three centre-left 'pole parties' marked the advent of an era of so-called 'consensus politics' – as did a series of central incomes policy agreements – and a numerically weak parliamentary opposition consisted primarily of the fourth pole party, the Conservatives, who were excluded from government for 'general reasons' (the code for 'unacceptable in Moscow'). Yet 'consensus politics' should not be equated with a consensual political culture. Both broad-based government and the nascent incomes policy system owed much to the proactive engagement of a strong, long-serving president. In a real sense, it was a 'compulsory consensus'.

Iceland

Iceland deviated from the Scandinavian model in its prime more than Finland. As Sigurdur A. Magnússon observed in the 1970s, 'political life in Iceland is traditionally rather turbulent and unstable, in contrast to the three Scandinavian countries' (Magnússon 1977: 144). Unlike in the last-mentioned, the Social Democrats in Iceland have been a relatively minor party in electoral terms, although they have entered coalitions with the dominant Independence Party, notably in the so-called Restoration Government of 1959–71. Many governing coalitions, moreover, particularly those of the centre-right, have faced opposition from the trade unions, not least when seeking to control inflation by preventing index-linked wage increases. In contrast to the 'we has a meeting' ethos of industrial relations in Sweden during the peak years of the model, frequent and often lengthy strikes affecting mostly unskilled workers – with the Dagsbrún union in Reykjavík often in the van – blighted the Icelandic economy in the 1950s and 1960s (Karlsson 2000: 352).

The 'Scandinavian model' – a distant memory?

It has been argued that there was a Scandinavian (though not Nordic) model of government, which was consultative and consensual in approach and saw a strong Social Democratic Party dominate office without monopolising power. The ruling Social Democrats incorporated a wide range of actors, including parliamentarians from the opposition parties, into the policy-formulation process and mediated between the peak interest organisations in the negotiation of a central incomes policy. The party was in a real sense the 'glue' to which the various elements in the 'model' adhered. The tangible increment of the Scandinavian model was a body of welfare legislation (the 'welfare model' is discussed in the next chapter) which was facilitated by high-growth economies that the corporatist management style was designed to maintain. The model, in short, emerged as a 'fair weather phenomenon', but could it withstand the 'foul weather' (economic crises) of the last part of the twentieth century? When viewed from the standpoint of 2007, has the 'Scandinavian model' become little more than a distant memory? Is Michele Micheletti (1991: 154) correct in asserting that 'compromise and consensus in political decision-making are less emphasised today than in the past and Sweden is gradually becoming decorporatised'? To approach an answer to these questions, we must review developments by reference to the four components of the 'Swedish model' set out earlier in this chapter.

The first relates to the strategic importance of social democracy. Here the contrast is sharp. Unlike in the first two post-war decades, the Social Democrats can no longer be regarded as dominant cabinet parties in the 'Scandinavian model' countries, and in Denmark in particular there have been extended periods of non-socialist government. At the time of writing the Social Democrats were in opposition in Denmark and Sweden and returned to office in Norway in 2005 only after two recent periods in opposition (1997–2000, 2001–5). The increased incidence of non-socialist government has been probably the most significant aspect of legislative party system change in

Scandinavia in recent decades. Nor have the Social Democrats enjoyed the same empathetic relationship with the labour movement as earlier. In some cases formal links have been severed – in Sweden since the early 1990s, for example, members of the central blue-collar federation, the Landsorganisation, are no longer automatically party members – but, more widely, the force of the special relationship between social democracy and the labour movement has been undermined by the emergence of competing organisations based on the huge growth in white-collar unionisation. Put another way, the political cohesion of the trade union movement has been substantially reduced and the picture considerably more pluralistic than in the prime years of the model.

Rune Premfors (1989) has noted how the Swedish model of decision-making has been 'front-loaded' – that is, it has attached disproportionate importance to the preparation of decisions at the expense of their execution, evaluation and feedback. However, there is persuasive evidence of a contraction in the scale and scope of the *formal* pre-legislative consultation process in connection with the preparation of measures. The decline and declining importance of the Swedish commission system (Johansson 1992) will illustrate the point. First, the number of commissions has fallen – from 409 in 1981 to 277 in 1997, for example. Second, the number of one-person 'civil servant commissions', which began to rise in the 1970s, has increased steadily over the years. In 1981 one-person commissions constituted two-fifths of the total number of commissions; by the mid-1990s the figure had risen to about two-thirds. Third, the number of 'parliamentary commissions' – classified as those with at least two serving MPs as members – fell from one-third of the total in 1981 to just under one-fifth in 1997. The proportion of commissions with interest groups represented on them has remained stable at about one-third over the last quarter of a century, although, in view of the smaller number of Swedish commissions, this has meant a real decline in formal pressure group involvement in policy formulation. Significantly, moreover, the commissions have a narrower remit than earlier and focus on more technical questions.

The number of committees and commissions has been scaled down in Norway, too, and one result has been that interest groups have built up a more professional information and communications apparatus, with a view to targeting decision-makers and the mass media (Haugsvær 2003). As the co-optation of groups has declined, so they have increasingly directed themselves at the Storting standing committees, seeking to exert influence at the parliamentary stage of the policy process – what Christiansen and Rommetvedt (2003) have described as a shift from corporatism to 'lobbyism' (Rommetvedt 2005). Equally, it is important to emphasise that across the region there have been marked differences between policy areas with respect to the extent of routine pressure group involvement in decision-making. As Per Lægreid and Paul G. Roness (1997) note in the Norwegian context, the departments concerned with economic policy have developed the most elaborate co-optive structures and sectoral interest groups have dominated the representation on preparatory committees and the remiss system. In contrast, a prominent characteristic of the petroleum sector, for example, has been the weakness of interest group representation and the leading economic organisations have played a minor role compared with other sectors. Contrary to the conventional wisdom, Richard Hoefer (1996) insists that interest groups have maintained their level of involvement in the Swedish social welfare sector.

It is certainly not clear that less formal co-optation of outside interests has meant reduced pressure group influence in the policy process (Blom-Hansen 2000; Heidar 2001: 76). For example, it was evident from the conclusions of the Danish Democracy and Power Commission, which reported in 2003, that, from the 1970s onwards, groups were no longer included to the same extent in the preparation of legislation. Fewer policy-formulating committees were set up and even the larger groups were not invited to be represented on them. Importantly, decisions on labour market matters were increasingly taken without including the central trade union confederation and the central employers' organisation. However, *informal* contacts between groups and civil servants and groups and the Folketing appear to have become very extensive. Moreover, groups have ample opportunity to mobilise resistance to proposals that deleteriously affect their members' interests and have on occasions defeated such proposals. As the Democracy and Power Commission concluded, 'interest groups continue to enjoy close relations with the authorities and in many cases they have significant influence on legislation' (Togeby *et al.* 2003: 25).

Neo-corporatism was an essential element in the Scandinavian model, especially in relation to macro-economic policy management. Yet the evidence pinpoints a number of factors that have conspired to strain the previously close working relationship between the peak economic interest groups and the state and, by extension, to undercut the basis for institutional tripartism. The literature has made widespread reference to the *post-corporate state* (Eriksen 1990: 346) and to a 'decline in the neo-corporatist model of interest representation' (Lewin 1994: 78). In contrast to the strong growth years in the 1960s, first Denmark in the 1980s and then Finland and Sweden in the first half of the 1990s experienced periods of economic recession. Indeed, in February 1990, the Swedish minister of finance, Kjell-Olof Feldt, resigned, bemoaning Landsorganisation's refusal to co-operate with its 'own government' in securing a crisis package of measures. He predicted the imminent collapse of the 'Swedish model' (Arter 1994).

Before proceeding further, it is important to bring out the multi-level character of corporatist practice and to distinguish between what I have termed 'peak corporatism', or 'summit corporatism', on the one hand, and 'routine corporatism', on the other. 'Routine corporatism' – Trond Nordby describes it simply as 'corporatism linked to the administration' (Nordby 2004: 104–6), which is infinitely preferable to the obscure terms 'sectoral' or 'meso' corporatism – involves the routine participation of organised interests in the preparation and formulation of public policy initiatives. We have already noted evidence of a decline in 'routine corporatism' and the co-optation of interest groups on to executive committees and commissions. It may be, in any event, that claims about the scale of routine corporatism in Scandinavia have been exaggerated. Thomas Pallesen (2006), for example, has challenged the conventional wisdom by suggesting that routine corporatism in the United States – or at least Washington state – has approximated Danish levels.

'Peak corporatism' refers to a regularised and culturally entrenched system of macro-economic management, which involves the government working closely with the peak sectoral interest groups to achieve national incomes policy settlements that are compatible with the government's overall fiscal policy objectives (Arter 2006: 111). Peak corporatism flourished in the high-growth 1960s in Denmark, Norway and Sweden (and by the 1970s and 1980s in Finland too) based on what Peter Katzenstein (1985) refers to as an 'ideology of social partnership' and the absence of a 'winner-takes-all mentality'. However, substantially reduced economic growth in the 1980s (Denmark) and early 1990s (Sweden and Finland) challenged the 'consensual incomes policy system' (Marks 1986) and created pressure to shift from centralised collective wage-bargaining towards more flexible, decentralised *enterprise bargaining*.

In the Danish case, economic necessity was in large part the mother of moves towards plant-level bargaining and an increase in the number of locally negotiated work contracts in the 1980s. Put another way, the problems of the Danish economy pointed up the need to adapt a peak corporatist system that had become dysfunctional in promoting excessive wage increases when there was only a weak capacity to export and high (import) consumption. The twin maladies of a long-term current-account deficit and severe debt-servicing problems (on foreign loans) were integrally bound up with an economy with a distinctively large and 'low-tech' small- and medium-sized firms sector, which did not engage in long production runs of standardised goods. As Herman Schwartz has noted colourfully, 'Denmark entered the 1980s on a fast train to macro-economic hell, albeit it in the first class coach' (Schwartz 2001: 136).

In Sweden from the early 1980s, the export-oriented employers in the engineering sector pressed for more devolved forms of wage-bargaining (Kunkel and Pontusson 1998: 3). Anti-corporatist attitudes also hardened among strategic (middle-level) decision-takers in the central employers' organisation, Svenska arbetsgivareförening (Swedish Employers' Association). There was particular opposition to the 'solidary wage policy' promoted by the Social Democrats and Landsorganisation, since, in principle, this required wage increases across the board, regardless of differential output and productivity. At the time of substantially reduced economic growth (Sweden was heading from an overheating economy in the late 1980s into the deepest recession in its history by the early 1990s) and a widening imbalance between private and public sectors, this was felt to be simply unsustainable.

In Finland, a centralised collective bargaining system developed relatively late, at the end of the 1960s, but over the following two decades an incomes policy system (known by the acronym TUPO) and incomes policy culture became integral elements of the new 'consensus politics'. However, when in 1991 the advent of a (rare) non-socialist coalition under the Centre chair Esko Aho coincided with a rapid slide into a slump – with wholesale bankruptcies, mass unemployment and bank closures – the TUPO system collapsed. An attempt to reach a broad-based 'social contract' between the main sectoral interests, spearheaded by the governor of the Bank of Finland (and former long-serving Social Democratic prime minister), Kalevi Sorsa, failed in November 1991, the currency was devalued and relations deteriorated rapidly between the government and the central blue-collar federation, Suomen am-mattiliittojen keskusjärjestö (Finnish Federation of Trade Unions). There were two threats of general strikes during the Aho cabinet of 1991–95.

Yet when the Social Democrat Paavo Lipponen replaced Aho and led a so-called 'rainbow coalition' between 1995 and 2003, the incomes policy system was revived and in 2004 an unprecedented three-year central agreement was signed. Indeed, the decline of peak corporatism should not be exaggerated. The Norwegian Power and Democracy Commission concluded in 2003 that 'the economic and labour-market groups remain strong and there are still central decisions, which are made in organs of corporatist co-operation' (Haugsvær 2003: 5). Clearly, a more nuanced picture is required. For instance, the Danish Power and Democracy Commission reported that the larger interest groups have come to enjoy privileged access at the expense of smaller ones. In the Commission's words, 'corporatism in Denmark has always favoured the large and strong organizations, but the weakening of corporatism seems to have magnified this tendency' (Togeby et al. 2003: 26).

In the Icelandic case, only modest steps have been taken in a corporatist direction. The formula of a large centre-right party, the Independence Party, opposed by a divided left and a fragmented trade union movement hugely complicated the task of macro-economic management. The creation in 1999 of the (Social Democratic) Alliance and its concomitant, greater cohesion in the labour movement have facilitated a form of 'embryonic corporatism', al-though this remains fragile.

In the heyday of the Scandinavian model of government, in the 1960s, politics and economics were essentially national in orientation. Fiscal and monetary policy operated within national parameters and devaluation was the standard mechanism for stimulating the crucial export sector. Much has changed. Today, the twin processes of Europeanisation and globalisa-tion – the latter defined as the growth of multinational companies and their share of world trade, the growth of money markets beyond government control and the increased mobility of capital – have transformed the context in which cabinets operate. Space prevents a discussion of the extent to which governments remain *dirigiste* policy actors or rather have become essentially reactive agencies, increasingly obliged to recognise the fact of the growing internationalisation of decision-making. However, it seems a fair conclusion that the 'social democratic state' of the Scandinavian model – in which the party–labour movement combination worked with other salient groups to set the agenda – has given way to a more improvisational state, in which cabinets increasingly respond 'on their feet', so to speak, to activities in wider international arenas. Elements of the Scandinavian model have survived, but the syndrome of features that defined the model was the product of an era long past.

Summary

1.   There has been widespread reference in the political science literature to a/the 'Swedish model', but the tendency has been to assume its existence, and definitions have been hard to come by.

2.   It is important when exploring the 'Swedish model' or evidence of a possible 'Nordic model' to distinguish between an ideal-type 'model of government' and an ideal-type 'welfare model'. In the literature on Scandinavia there has been a tendency to conflate the two.

3.   The basis of Sweden's reputation as a successful and 'harmonious' democracy is discussed and traced to both Anglo-American and Swedish writing, ranging from Marquis Childs in the late 1930s to Herbert Tingsten in the mid-1960s and Henry Milner in the late 1980s.

4.   The central argument in the chapter is that whilst there has not been a Nordic model of government (Finland and particularly Iceland have been deviant cases) it seems legitimate to refer to the existence of a 'Scandinavian model of government', with the 1960s as its heyday.

5.   The distinctive, though not necessarily entirely unique, syndrome of features marking out the 'Scandinavian model' involved: the Social Democratic domination of government, although without a concomitant monopoly of power; the scale and scope of the government's pre-legislative consultation process; a neo-corporatist approach to macro-economic decision-making; and the existence of a consensual political culture.

6.   The final section of the chapter considers whether today the model is simply a receding memory. In the new millennium, it is argued, it is no longer possible to speak of a 'Scandinavian model of government'. The 'decline factors' are examined briefly. In particular, it is suggested that the Social Democrats' ability to set the political agenda has declined as the parameters of political decision-making have become increasingly internationalised.

References

Anton, Thomas J. (1969) 'Policy-making and political culture in Sweden', *Scandinavian Political Studies*, 4, pp. 88–102.

Anton, Thomas J. (1980) *Administered Politics. Elite Political Culture in Sweden*, Nijhoff: Boston, MA.

Arter, David (1984) *The Nordic Parliaments. A Comparative Analysis*, Hurst: London.

Arter, David (1987) *Politics and Policy-Making in Finland*, Wheatsheaf: Brighton.

Arter, David (1994) 'The war of the roses: conflict and cohesion in the Swedish Social Democratic Party', in David S. Bell and Malcolm Shaw (eds), *Conflict and Cohesion in Western European Social Democratic Parties*, Pinter: London, pp. 70–95.

Arter, David (2000) 'Change in the Swedish Riksdag: from a part-time parliament to a professionalised assembly?', *Journal of Legislative Studies*, 6 (3), pp. 93–116.

Arter, David (2006) *Democracy in Scandinavia*, Manchester University Press: Manchester.

Bergh, Trond and Helge Pharo (1977) *Vekst og velstand*, Universitetsforlaget: Oslo.

Blom-Hansen, Jens (2000) 'Still corporatism in Scandinavia? A survey of recent empirical findings', *Scandinavian Political Studies*, 23 (2), pp. 157–81.

Childs, Marquis W. (1936) *Sweden. The Middle Way*, Faber & Faber: London.

Childs, Marquis W. (1980) *Sweden. The Middle Way on Trial*, Yale University Press: New Haven, CT.

Christiansen, Peter Munk and Asbjørn Sonne Nørgaard (2003) *Faste Forhold – Flygtige Forbindelser. Stat og Interesseorganisationer i Danmark i det 20 århundrade*, Århus Universitetsforlag: Århus.

Christiansen, Peter Munk and Hilmar Rommetvedt (2003) 'From corporatism to lobbyism? Parliaments, executives and organised interests in Denmark and Norway', in Hilmar Rommetvedt (ed.), *The Rise of the Norwegian Parliament*, Frank Cass: London, pp. 134–58.

Einhorn, Eric and John Logue (1986) 'The Scandinavian democratic model', *Scandinavian Political Studies*, 9 (3), pp. 193–208.

Eriksen, Erik Oddvar (1990) 'Towards the post-corporate state?', *Scandinavian Political Studies*, 13 (4), pp. 345–64.

Evans, Jocelyn A. J. (2002) 'In defence of Sartori', *Party Politics*, 8 (2), pp. 155–74.

Fitzmaurice, John (1981) *Politics in Denmark*, Hurst: London.

Gustafsson, Gunnel and Jeremy Richardson (1980) 'Post-industrial changes in policy style', *Scandinavian Political Studies*, 3 (1), pp. 21–37.

Hancock, M. Donald (1972) *Sweden. The Politics of Postindustrial Change*, Dryden Press: Hindsale, IL.

Haugsvær, Steinar (2003) Maktutredningar, www.sv.uio.no/mutr/aktuelt/ maktutredningens_hovedkonklusjoner_kort.html.

Heidar, Knut (2001) *Norway. Elites on Trial*, Westview: Boulder, CO.

Helander, Voitto (1979) *Etujärjestöt ja komitealaitos*, Åbo Akademi: Åbo.

Hetemäki, Päiviö (1979) *Itse Asiassa Kuultuna*, WSOY: Porvoo.

Hoefer, Richard (1996) 'Swedish corporatism in social welfare policy, 1986–94', *Scandinavian Political Studies*, 19 (1), pp. 67–80.

Johansson, J. (1992) *Det Statliga Kommittéväsendet. Kunskap, Kontroll, Konsensus*, Akademitryck: Edsbruk.

Karlsson, Gunnar (2000) *The History of Iceland*, University of Minnesota Press: Minneapolis, MN.

Katzenstein, Peter J. (1985) *Small States in World Markets. Industrial Policy in Europe*, Cornell University Press: Ithaca, NY.

Kjellberg, Anders (1992) 'Sweden: can the model survive?', in A. Ferner and R. Hyman (eds), *Industrial Relations in the New Europe*, Blackwell: Oxford, pp. 88–142.

Kunkel, Christoph and Jonas Pontusson (1998) 'Corporatism versus social democracy: divergent fortunes of the Austrian and Swedish labour movements', *West European Politics*, 21 (2), pp. 1–31.

Kvavik, Robert B. (1976) *Interest Groups in Norwegian Politics*, Universitetsforlaget: Oslo.

Lægreid, Per and Paul G. Roness (1997) 'Political parties, bureaucracies and corporatism', in Kaare Strøm and Lars Svåsand (eds), *Challenges to Political Parties*, University of Michigan: Ann Arbor, MI, pp. 167–90.

Lane, Jan-Erik (1991) 'Interpretations of the Swedish model', *West European Politics*, 14 (3), pp. 1–8.

Lewin, Leif (1988) *Ideology and Strategy. A Century of Swedish Politics*, Cambridge University Press: Cambridge.

Lewin, Leif (1994) 'The rise and decline of corporatism: the case of Sweden', *European Journal of Political Research*, 26 (1), pp. 59–79.

Lewin, Leif (1998) 'Majoritarian and consensual democracy: the Swedish experience', *Scandinavian Political Studies*, 21 (3), pp. 195–206.

Lijphart, Arend (ed.) (1969) *Politics in Europe*, Prentice Hall: Englewood Cliffs, NJ.

Lijphart, Arend (1975) *The Politics of Accommodation*, University of California Press: Berkeley, CA.

Lijphart, Arend (1999) *Patterns of Democracy. Government Forms and Performance in Thirty-Six Countries*, Yale University Press: New Haven, CT.

Linde, Claes (1982) *Departement och Verk. Om synen på den centrala statsförvaltningen och dess uppdelning i en förändrad offentlig sektor*, Statsvetenskapliga institutionen, Stockholms universitet.

Magnússon, Sigurdur A. (1977) *Northern Sphinx*, Hurst: London.

Marks, Gary (1986) 'Neocorporatism and incomes policy in Western Europe and North America', *Comparative Politics*, 18 (3), pp. 71–83.

Micheletti, Michele (1991) 'Swedish corporatism at a crossroads: the impact of new politics and new social movements', *West European Politics*, 14 (3), pp. 144–65.

Milner, Henry (1989) *Sweden. Social Democracy in Practice*, Oxford University Press: New York.

Milner, Henry (1994) *Social Democracy and Rational Choice. The Scandinavian Experience and Beyond*, Routledge: London.

Müller, Wolfgang C. and Kaare Strøm (1999) 'Conclusions: party behaviour and representative democracy', in Wolfgang C. Müller and Kaare Strøm (eds), *Policy, Office or Votes? How Political Parties in Western Europe Make Hard Decisions*, Cambridge University Press: Cambridge, pp. 279–309.

Nordby, Trond (2004) 'Patterns of corporatist intermediation', in Knut Heidar (ed.), *Nordic Politics. Comparative Perspectives*, Universitetsforlaget: Oslo, pp. 98–107.

Olsen, Johan P. (1980) 'Governing Norway: segmentation, anticipation and consensus formation', in Richard Rose and Ezra N. Suleiman (eds), *Presidents and Prime Ministers*, American Enterprise Institute for Public Policy Research: Washington, DC, pp. 203–55.

Pallesen, Thomas (2006) 'Scandinavian corporatism in a trans-Atlantic comparative perspective', *Scandinavian Political Studies*, 29 (2), pp. 131–45.

Petersson, Olof (1994) *The Government and Politics of the Nordic Countries*, Fritzes: Stockholm.

Premfors, Rune (1989) *Policyanalys*, Studentlitteratur: Lund.

Richardson, J. (ed.) (1982) *Policy Styles in Western Europe*, Allen & Unwin: London.

Rokkan, Stein (1966) 'Numerical democracy and corporate pluralism', in R. A. Dahl (ed.), *Political Oppositions in Western Democracies*, Yale University Press: New Haven, CT, pp. 70–115.

Rommetvedt, Hilmar (2005) 'Norway: resources count, but votes decide? From neo-corporatist representation to neo-pluralist parliamentarism', *West European Politics*, 28 (4), pp. 740–63.

Rothstein, Bo (1992) 'Explaining Swedish corporatism: the formative moment', *Scandinavian Political Studies*, 15 (2), pp. 173–91.

Sartori, Giovanni (1966) 'European political parties: the case of polarized pluralism', in J. LaPalombara and M. Weiner (eds), *Political Parties and Political Development*, Princeton University Press: Princeton, NJ, pp. 137–70.

Schonfield, Andrew (1965) *Modern Capitalism. The Changing Balance of Public and Private Power*, Oxford University Press: London.

Schwartz, Herman (2001) 'The Danish "miracle": luck, pluck or stuck?', *Comparative Political Studies*, 34, 131–55.

Solvang, Bernt Krohn and Jorolv Moren (1974) 'Partsrepresentasjon i Komitéer: Litt om utvicklingen over tid', in Jorolv Moren (ed.), *Den Kollegiale Forvaltning. Råd og utvalg i sentraladministrasjonen*, Universtitetsforlaget: Oslo, pp. 33–6.

Stenelo, Lars-Göran and Magnus Jerneck (1996) 'Introduction', in Lars-Göran Stenelo and Magnus Jerneck (eds), *The Bargaining Democracy*, Lund University Press: Lund, pp. 11–16.

Tarschys, Daniel (2002) *För tomma hus. Om Riksdagen som vår politiska nationalscen*, Bertil Ohlin-Institutet: Stockholm.

Tiihonen, Seppo and Paula Tiihonen (1983) *Suomen hallintohistoria*, Valtion painatuskeskus: Helsinki.

Tingsten, Herbert (1966) *Från idéer till idyll. Den lyckliga demokratien*, Norstedts: Stockholm.

Togeby, Lise, Jørgen Goul Andersen, Peter Munk Christiansen, Torben Beck Jørgensen and Signild Vallgårda (2003) *Power and Democracy in Denmark. Conclusions*, University of Århus: Århus.

8

The Nordic welfare model

> In Sweden, social security remains an issue constantly praised and held up for public worship.... It is celebrated without end in the mass media as if it were some hallowed religious dogma that it was vital to assimilate for peace of mind. It is taught at school like a religion. Above all, it is presented as a vital possession that, ever threatened, must constantly be defended, for its loss is the worst of all possible dangers.
>
> (Huntford 1975: 190)

Where there is a reputation, there are invariably detractors and, as the opening citation makes abundantly clear, Roland Huntford was certainly no admirer of the Swedish welfare state. His iconoclastic view was that welfare served as an instrument of social control designed to subjugate the citizen to the state and discourage political change. 'The Swedish government has consciously exploited welfare to control the population', Huntford insists, and he adds that 'welfare in Sweden has taken a militant form, used in order to exert a kind of tyranny of insistent benevolence, to make the state appear all-seeing and all-caring'. 'It has been employed to forestall political change', he concludes (Huntford 1975: 186–7). In contrast to Huntford, most observers have seen Sweden – and the other mainland Scandinavian states – as exemplars of a *specific type of welfare system* and one that is an advanced, de luxe, top-of-the-range model. According to Peter Abrahamson, 'the Social Democratic or Scandinavian model is the luxury edition of the Liberal or Beveridge model and the Catholic model is the discount edition of the Bismarck or Conservative model' (Abrahamson 1992: 10).

Classifications of welfare systems have been legion. Gøsta Esping-Andersen (1990) identifies three sub-types – the liberal regime of Anglo-Saxon nations, the corporatist regime of central European nations and the social democratic regime of the Scandinavian states. Esping-Andersen's typology, of course, ante-dated the end of the Cold War. Pekka Kosonen (1993) defined no less than four welfare state models in Western Europe alone, based on the distinctive pattern of connections between the labour market, social security and gender relations. The *peripheral model* was found in poor Catholic countries like Portugal, Spain and Ireland, where the church and extended family were central welfare producers. The *continental model* developed, Kosonen noted, in economically advanced states in which social spending was high and social benefits were good. He claimed the continental model could be found with varying degrees of fit in eight West European countries: Germany, Austria, Belgium, France, Italy, Luxembourg, Switzerland and the Netherlands. It was the standard, not de luxe edition: female participation in paid employment was low, especially among married women; social security was tied to labour-market position; and, in the area of social spending, cash benefits dominated over public services provided by the state. Kosonen also spoke of a *crisis model*, typified by Britain in the 1980s, in which the basic premises of the welfare state were challenged by market-oriented, neo-liberal governments. Finally, there was the *Scandinavian model*, which is the focus of this chapter.

The first part briefly examines the origins of the Nordic model and the process of welfare state-building in the region. Despite widespread reference in the literature to a generic 'Nordic welfare model' (albeit variously defined), it is clear, as Kautto *et al.* (2001a: 2) have pointed out, that the Scandinavian countries 'have qualitatively different types of social policies that to a large extent have resulted from diverse social structures and historical and political processes'. The Scandinavian welfare state, in short, developed at a different pace and embraced differing policies in the individual countries, with Sweden in the van, Norway and Denmark not far behind, Finland a 'late developer' and Iceland a 'back marker'.

The second part presents a nine-point, ideal-type Nordic welfare model, which incorporates three analytically distinct components – the core welfare principles constituting the normative foundations of the model, the main features of the practical operation of the welfare state and the identification of desired policy outcomes – that is, the type of welfare state being sought. Of course, there are objections to welfare modelling – welfare systems are not static and may develop along different lines, so reducing the practical utility of the model. Moreover, instead of a single model, some scholars have described several Nordic models, pointing to intra-regional disparities in, among other things, social policy programmes, the balance between cash transfers and services, and the balance between public and private solutions (Kautto *et al.* 2001a: 5). Yet the value of the ideal-type model is that it represents a standard against which empirical cases can be analysed and compared. No one Nordic country will exhibit all the characteristics of the model – still less, all the time.

The third section concentrates on the performance of the Nordic welfare model and the extent to which desired policy outcomes have been realised. Whilst the principles and goals of policies may be clear enough, legislation by no means guarantees the achievement of intended objectives. For example, the Swedish Social Democrats' 1944 programme on education had two primary aims: the creation of a single type of comprehensive school providing nine or ten years of compulsory education; and the elimination of the financial obstacles to secondary and higher education. The idea was to produce greater social equality, not just in the education system but, more importantly, in society as a whole – to take, in the words of diplomat, politician and writer Alva Myrdal, a driving force in the creation of the Swedish welfare state, 'a gigantic step away from the old class society' (quoted by Rothstein 1996: 68). The comprehensive school reform was finally introduced in 1960. Yet, three decades later, it seems, the percentage of students of working-class background entering university was lower than in the early 1960s (Rothstein 1996: 136–8).

The concluding part of the chapter considers the challenges facing the Nordic welfare model in the years ahead. Stein Kuhnle (2000a: 224–5) relates how the recession in the early 1990s led, outside Norway, to a *less generous welfare state*. Benefit levels were reduced – particularly in Finland and Sweden – across all social security schemes; benefit periods were shortened; eligibility for benefits was tightened up; much greater emphasis was placed on rehabilitation and training; and structural reforms in the pensions systems were introduced. Yet he insists the basic structure of the welfare systems was preserved. Similarly, Jaakko Kiander (2005) notes that adjustments were made by raising taxes and restricting the growth of public expenditure, but the basic structure of the Nordic welfare model was not changed. However, since the 1990s, user charges have become common – instead of welfare services being funded through the taxation system – as, too, have private and occupational insurance schemes. Are we witnessing a convergence between the Nordic welfare model and those elsewhere in continental Europe, and will the challenges ahead further reduce the distinctiveness of the Nordic model?

Welfare state-building in the Nordic region

The origins of the Nordic welfare state can be traced to the recessionary 1930s and the historic class co-operation between the party of the workers (Social Democrats) and that of the farmers (Agrarians). The red–green coalition in Sweden in 1936 – formed the same year as the Popular Front in France – is a case in point. It enabled the ruling Social Democrats to raise taxes in order to increase unemployment benefits and housing subsidies, whilst affording the farmers protection during a slump in food prices. The leading Social Democrats and trade unionists of the day were enthusiastic disciples of Keynesianism; indeed, they were in a sense Keynesian before Keynes. Economists such as Gunnar Myrdal and Bertil Ohlin advocated counter-cyclical policies – a 'spend your way out of recession' approach – *before* the publication in 1936 of Keynes' *General Theory*. There were similar red–green deals elsewhere in the Nordic region. Three years earlier in Denmark, following setbacks for the Liberals at the 1933 Folketing (lower house) election, a package deal between the Social

Democrats, Radicals and Liberals – the so-called *Kanslergadeforliget* – was worked out in which the Liberals got increased aid for agriculture and provisions to maintain food prices, and the Social Democrats gained protection against cuts in workers' wages and the promise of Liberal support for social reforms.

If the red–green cabinets represented an historic compromise between consumer and producer interests in the parliamentary–electoral channel, there were parallel developments in the corporate channel. The Saltsjöbaden agreement in Sweden in 1938 provided a framework of procedures for collective bargaining between the two sides of industry, although the major ingredient in the historic class compromise between capital and labour in Sweden was probably the Industrial Efficiency Inquiry, which reported in June 1939. The central trade union federation, Landsorganisation, agreed not to hamper the ongoing rationalisation of industry, whilst the employers' organisation, the Svenska arbetsgivareförening (Swedish Employers' Association), would support assistance to workers hit by unemployment as a result of the restructuring process (Rothstein 1996: 92).

Although rudimentary social legislation pre-dated the Second World War, the modern Scandinavian welfare state was not shaped as a reaction to the economic crisis of the 1930s. Most of the major welfare reforms were initiated in the era of relative economic prosperity after 1945 and were predicated on an assumption of economic growth, not of poverty and recession. Indeed, two contextual factors in post-war welfare state-building in the Nordic region stand out in importance. First, there was *market-based economic growth*: accelerated capitalism generated the wealth to pay for welfare and, importantly, this process of wealth accumulation went unchallenged by the state. For a quarter of a century after the Second World War, the Scandinavian states, Sweden in particular, experienced rapid and uninterrupted economic growth and exceptionally low levels of unemployment. Poor countries in the late nineteenth century, they were transformed into prosperous, affluent societies by the second half of the twentieth. Sweden between 1870 and 1970, for instance, grew more quickly than any other country except Japan and giants such as Volvo, Ericsson and Electrolux became genuine multinationals, selling (and increasingly manufacturing) in every corner of the world. In 1970 Sweden's gross domestic product (GDP) *per capita* in purchasing power terms ranked fourth among the member states of the Organisation for Economic Co-operation and Development (OECD). The creation of the modern Nordic welfare state, in short, was facilitated by a period of strong economic growth, although the timing of this growth varied somewhat across the region. Finland was referred to as 'Europe's Japan' in the 1980s, by which time the economies of Norway and Sweden had slowed and Denmark was emerging from the crisis of the 1970s.

Whilst economic growth created the means, there would not have been an advanced welfare state in post-war Scandinavia without the political will. Thus, a second factor in understanding the post-war surge of welfarism in the region was the *strategic role of social democracy*, its close links with the trade union movement and, in Sweden in particular, its good working relationship with business and industry. The phenomenon of 'Harpsund democracy' during Tage Erlander's premiership in the late 1950s was described in the previous chapter. Indeed, the Swedish Social Democrats rejected a policy of collective ownership at their 1932 party conference and nationalisation was never seriously on the agenda after that; the emphasis was placed on planning, not state ownership. A case in point was the so-called Rehn–Meidner model – after the leading Landsorganisation trade union economists who devised it – which was adopted at the Social Democrats' party conference in 1955 and implemented in full from the 1960s onwards. The central idea was wage solidarity, which, it was assumed, would tend to weed out the least efficient and competitive firms in low-wage sectors not able to afford the negotiated national wage rates. Equally, profitable firms would be in a position to expand because the negotiated rates would leave them with a fairly large margin. Under Social Democratic direction, the industrial policy contained in the Rehn–Meidner model served the interests of both capital and labour and, importantly, needed the support of both.

Outside Sweden, the development of an advanced welfare system was perhaps less exclusively a Social Democratic project, although the party's role was none the less vital. In Norway the expansionist years of the welfare state spanned the period 1945–80, during which time such major social reforms as a compulsory health insurance scheme for the whole population (1957) and state-run unemployment benefit (1959) were introduced. The initial influences were Social Democratic practice in Sweden and the British experience in the wake of the 1942 Beveridge report. Knut Heidar emphasises the diffusional impulses from Sweden: 'During the war, neutral Swedes had been able to continue their efforts at building a welfare state, closely watched by exiled Norwegian politicians and trade unionists who had fled from the German occupation. The wartime experience is crucial in understanding the post-war consensus on welfare issues' (Heidar 2001: 119). On the point of the consensual basis of post-Second World War welfare reform, Anton Steen emphasises that, precisely because of the cross-party consensus, the welfare state in Norway should not be viewed as exclusively a social democratic achievement (Steen 2004: 209). Indeed, the wide-ranging Social Security Act, which was passed by the Storting in 1966, was introduced into parliament by the four-party, non-socialist coalition led by Per Borten.

Steen argues that, because of the existence of sizeable Liberal (Venstre) and Conservative parties on the centre-right, 'the Danish welfare state was never a typical social democratic welfare regime' (Steen 2004: 209). This seems harsh, although it might draw attention to the challenge of building a consensus for social policy reforms faced by Social Democrat-led minority coalitions and this might in turn contribute to explaining why Denmark lagged some way behind Sweden and Norway in the pace of welfare development. For example, it was not until the 1971 Health Security Act that health care in Denmark was 'nationalised', the sickness benefit associations were abolished and the state assumed responsibility for the provision of comprehensive health insurance. Yet although the rationalisation and reorganisation of welfare which took place in the 1960s and 1970s were supported in their essentials by all the political parties, the strategic role of social democracy in driving it forward should be acknowledged.

The Finnish case differs in several essentials from Denmark, Norway and Sweden, although it could plausibly be argued that the catalyst for a phase of accelerated welfare expansion was the reunification of a divided social democratic movement and the reincorporation of the party into a broad coalition of the centre-left in 1966. Finland was a 'late developer' as a welfare state. True, child benefits were introduced in 1948, but it was not until the late 1950s and early 1960s – general sickness insurance was introduced in 1964, for example – that Finland began to catch up with the other mainland Nordic countries. Finland also manifested a number of aberrational welfare features when viewed from a developmental perspective (Alestalo *et al.* 1985). Industrialisation was relatively late and was driven in the late 1940s and early 1950s by the need to pay a reparations debt to the Soviet Union, mainly in terms of heavy goods and machinery; the 'hinge group' within government coalitions until 1966 was the Agrarian and not the Social Democratic Party; until the late 1980s the trade union movement was divided between the left and the radical left, whilst the Social Democrats were themselves split in the late 1950s and early 1960s. The Agrarians' dominance may explain, among other things, why urban housing policy in Finland remained undeveloped by wider Nordic standards. Yet by the time the left – the Social Democrats and Communist-dominated Finnish People's Democratic League – won a majority in the Eduskunta in 1966, a period of welfare expansion was already underway and this expansion gained pace throughout the 1970s. Indeed, following an increase in welfare spending in the 1980s much greater than in other OECD countries, and a rise in the share of public employment matched only by Norway, the size of the welfare state in Finland in 1990 (i.e. expenditure on income transfers, health care and education) was broadly comparable to that of the other mainland Nordic states.

It seems reasonable, in relation to our discussion of welfare state-building in the Nordic region, to speak of 'Icelandic exceptionalism'. By the 1960s, despite a coalition between the Independence Party and the Social Democrats that spanned the entire decade, Iceland trailed well behind the other Nordic countries in terms of social expenditure and dragged its feet on public welfare provision. Initially, Iceland followed the red–green course of the other Scandinavian countries and in 1936 legislation introducing a general workers' insurance scheme was enacted by a Progressive Party–Social Democrat coalition that was widely known as 'the government of the working classes'. Although a relatively small party in electoral terms, particularly when compared with its fraternal parties elsewhere in the region, the Icelandic

Social Democratic Party was possibly as influential in laying the foundations of the welfare state – in the pre- and immediate post-independence years – as its counterparts on mainland Scandinavia. Thus, Stefán Ólafsson brings out the strong political influence exercised by the Social Democrats in the negotiations leading up to the formation of a new coalition in 1944. Having been rejected by the Progressive Party, the Independence Party sought a coalition with the Social Democrats and Socialists – the latter split from the Social Democrats in 1939 – but the Social Democrats, not willing to risk being outflanked by the breakaway group, agreed to participate only on condition that new social security legislation, comparable to the best in the world, was introduced. As Ólafsson (1989: 12) comments: 'A rather unusual situation of bargaining strength for the Social Democrats explains why Iceland took a big step towards a modern type of welfare state at nearly the same time as the Scandinavian countries and the UK'. After the Second World War, however, the Icelandic Social Democrats failed to dominate government and it was this different balance of power – with a cohesive centre-right and fragmented left – which in large part may be said to explain 'welfare exceptionalism' in Iceland (Ólafsson 1989: 30).

Outside Finland, the expansionist years of the mainland Nordic welfare systems were over by the 1980s – and in Denmark and Sweden earlier than that. In the Danish case, the Yom Kippur war and subsequent oil crisis of 1973–74 led to a rise in unemployment from 2 per cent to 8 per cent in under two years, at precisely the time the welfare reforms spawned of the prosperous 1960s had to be paid for. The prevailing 'welfare consensus' was challenged, not least by Mogens Glistrup's anti-tax Progress Party, which led the flurry of new parties at the 1973 'earthquake election'. Retrenchment became the order of the day. In Norway, although public support for the welfare state remained solid, the flatter growth of the early 1990s saw a political debate about rising welfare costs, particularly those incurred by the health and social service sector, which accounted for approximately one-fifth of GDP. Individuals were urged to assume greater economic responsibility for their own lives and the Conservatives (Høyre), although far from Thatcher-style neo-liberals, began to deploy the term 'welfare society' rather than 'welfare state'. On the radical right, the rhetoric was more vituperative and the Progress Party leader, Carl I. Hagen, inveighed against welfare state parasites.

The Finnish economy hit the buffers with a shuddering jolt in the early 1990s and the country plunged into the deepest recession in its history. The slump was as severe as it was unexpected, since in 1990 the ratio of welfare spending to trend GDP had climbed from 26 per cent in 1979 to 35 per cent in 1991 and this compared with a 2.3 per cent rise for Denmark, Norway and Sweden and only 1 per cent for European OECD states as a whole. Similarly, the share of public employment throughout the 1980s increased from 18 per cent to 22 per cent in Finland compared with 17 per cent to 18 per cent across the rest of the OECD. In short, the 1980s were the growth years of the Finnish welfare state but they came abruptly to an end in the early 1990s, when un-employment rose to mass proportions and the economy effectively stalled.

There was a comparable economic crisis in Sweden, although the structural problems ran deeper than in Finland. Lane and Ersson (1997: 205) have noted that the Swedish welfare model began to decline about 1970 and the root cause of the problem lay in the shifting balance between the public and private sectors. In 1960 private sector employment accounted for 80 per cent of all employment, but in 1990 the figure stood at only 56 per cent. In their terms, Swedish developments involved the public sector driving out the private sector. The impact of recession compounded matters, so that by the mid-1990s Sweden was running the largest budget deficit in the OECD group of countries and interest payments, the single most expensive item in the national budget, amounted in 1996 to 80 per cent of GDP. When, before 1970, the Swedish model worked well, there was steady growth and a strong growth orientation, priority was given to the private sector and there was full employment, low inflation and few strikes. Thereafter the emphasis shifted to the public sector and redistribution, and there was high unemployment, high inflation, high nominal wage increases and high levels of economic volatility (Lane and Ersson 1997: 204).

Building the model

It follows from this brief account of welfare state-building in the region that the Nordic welfare model, facilitated by the twin impact of strong economic growth and strong Social Democratic or Social Democrat-led government (albeit backed by a broad cross-party consensus), took shape in the 1950s and 1960s. The model has been variously presented. One approach has been to depict it as based on a series of fundamental contracts between state and society:

1 The *corporatist contract* has involved the close relationship between the state and the main economic interest groups and in particular the tradition of class co-operation between employers and workers.
2 The *gender contract* has involved the public sector assuming many of the caring functions previously undertaken by women.
3 The *generation contract* has vested the state with the legal obligation to guarantee acceptable and appropriate care for the elderly.
4 The *disadvantage contract* has involved the state safeguarding the basic rights of the worst-off in society – that is, setting a clearly defined minimum standard of living for everybody, irrespective of the reasons why external help may be needed.

The corollary of these 'social contracts' is, of course, a growth in the scale and scope of government as the state assumes a series of commitments with a view to creating a 'better society'.

An alternative to the 'contract approach' is simply to enumerate the main features of the Nordic welfare model. Stein Kuhnle lists twelve 'fairly distinct characteristics', including 'a comparatively high level of trust between citizens and governments'. 'Nordic societies are more "state-friendly" than other European societies', he insists (Kuhnle 1998). But is this trust to be regarded as a condition of welfare policy or more a consequence of a perception of its success? Is it primarily output- or outcome-related or rather to be viewed as a basic pre-condition for welfare state-building? Plainly, the distinguishing features of a Nordic welfare model – and they become distinct only when taken together – need to be accorded clear analytical and explanatory status.

The Nordic welfare model enumerated below is constructed in three parts. The first seeks to identify the *basic principles* that provide the normative foundations of the model. In a recent volume edited by Nanna Kildal and Stein Kuhnle (2005) the authors refer to three fundamental principles of the Nordic welfare state – 'universalism', 'public responsibility for welfare' and 'work for all'. My triad of welfare principles varies somewhat, at least in its formulation. Second, there is the generation of social policies that are informed by, and in turn reflect, the practical application of the core principles. The focus here is on the role of political actors – parties, groups, local and central government and so on – and the operation of the *welfare state in practice*. Finally, there is the impact of welfare legislation – that is, welfare policy outcomes – and the search for evaluative criteria with which to assess the *performance of the welfare state* and the extent to which basic objectives have been achieved. For instance, Kangas and Palme (2005: 2–3) argue that 'the clearest achievement of the Scandinavian welfare state has been in poverty reduction programmes'. Which other areas have been prioritised? The nine-point Nordic welfare model that follows, then, is based on the distinction between the fundamental principles of Nordic welfarism, the practical operation of the Nordic state and its performance in terms of the achievement of express policy objectives.

The Nordic welfare model

Welfare state principles
1 *Universalism as the basic principle of welfare distribution* – that is, welfare is viewed as a civic right. Social rights are based on citizenship and citizens are entitled to basic social security and services regardless of their position in the labour market.
2 *Comprehensiveness as the basis for public welfare provision* – that is, state-directed welfare, which covers, among other things, social security, social services, health, education, housing and employment, is designed to cater for the entire citizenry based simply on perceived need.
3 *Equality, equality of opportunity and, above all, equality of outcomes as the basic policy goals* – that is, the state seeks actively to overcome as far as possible

the basic inequalities in the conditions and life prospects of individuals. Equality as an explicit welfare policy objective has been integrally linked with a social democratic dominant governing party, particularly in Sweden, and in the late 1960s reference came to be made to the 'social democratic model of equality'.

Welfare state in practice

4 *The state (central government) plays an active role in the direction of all aspects of welfare policy* and measures to obtain the cardinal goal of full employment have embraced macro-economic policy, social policy and a proactive labour-market policy. In the Nordic countries, there is a right – as well as an obligation – to work, and this was given powerful symbolic expression in the form of a constitutional amendment in Finland in 1972.

5 *Local authorities play a prominent role in the provision of social services.* Traditionally, the Scandinavian states have been viewed as 'service heavy' (providing a breadth of care services) compared with the 'cash heavy' income transfer countries of continental Europe; the local authorities provide the services and, more often than not, produce them as well.

6 *Welfare services are funded primarily through the taxation system, making the Nordic countries 'high-tax states'*, in which tax revenues as a proportion of GDP have been well above the European average. In Denmark, Norway and Sweden in particular about half of GDP has been collected in taxes and redistributed in the form of transfers and services.

Welfare state performance

Of the many policy outcomes in the Nordic welfare model, three may singled out as having foremost importance:

7 *The realisation of low income inequality* – that is, the relatively even distribution of disposable incomes and the reduction of differences in living standards. A vital factor here is the poverty-reducing capacity of the state in the Nordic countries and its provision of generous benefits to mitigate the gap between rich and poor.

8 *The realisation of low health inequality* – that is, the adoption of measures designed to reduce differences in morbidity and mortality between groups of people who occupy different positions in the social structure. The aim is to improve living conditions.

9 *The realisation of gender equality* – that is, the creation of equal opportunities for women in the labour-market, the elimination of gender disparities in wages and the provision of a range of measures enabling women to be financially independent of their partners.

The Nordic welfare model set out above draws on a range of sources (Kosonen 1993; Rothstein 1996: 65; Kautto *et al.* 2001a: 1–7; Nielsen 2006: 273–4) and should be regarded as an ideal type. Clearly, however, welfare systems (rather than 'the model') are dynamic and adaptive and respond to a range of challenges, albeit without necessarily abandoning their core features. For example, the welfare systems have had to accommodate two striking features of Nordic society in the first decade of the new millennium – the high level of the feminisation of labour (in part a function of the gender contract) and the relatively high number of single parents (particularly mothers).

The high level of female participation in the labour market has obviously increased the need for childminding options during the parents' working hours. Not all women, of course, go out to work. Indeed, although the rules vary slightly, parents in Denmark, Finland and Norway may be granted a cash allowance in order to mind their children in their own homes, on either a part-time or full-time basis. However, the vast majority of pre-school children attend day-care institutions provided by the local authorities. In 2004, 92 per cent of Danish local authorities provided a guarantee of a day-care place for children of nine years and under. In Sweden local authorities are required to provide pre-school activities or family day care to: children whose parents work or study; children whose parents are unemployed or on parental leave (in such cases, the children must be offered at least three hours per day or fifteen hours per week); and children who are in need of the activities. Places must be provided within three to four months and the local authorities must take into due consideration the parents' wishes about the type of minding, whilst the place should be provided as close to the child's home as possible (Nielsen 2006: 60).

A child allowance, which is tax-free and independent of the parents' income, is available across the region except Iceland (where it is means-tested). In Norway, a supplement is available for children living in the most northerly county of Finnmark and in certain communes in neighbouring Troms. Moreover, in all the Nordic countries except Sweden, a special child allowance is payable to single providers, so that the allowance per child is higher for single parents than for two-parent families (Nielsen 2006: 55). It might be mentioned, incidentally, that benefits in connection with childbirth (and adoption) have been extended to fathers. In Denmark, Finland and Sweden, fathers are entitled to cash benefits for a number of days immediately following the birth of a child – that is, at the same time as mothers receive maternity benefit. In Iceland since 2003 fathers have been entitled to thirteen weeks' paternity leave quite independently of the maternity allowance – it can be taken at the same time as the mother's leave – whilst in Norway since 1993 the so-called 'father's quota' has granted men the right to four weeks' leave plus daily cash benefits (Nielsen 2006: 45–50).

Rules, of course, alter, policies are adapted and welfare systems evolve. Moreover, whilst small cuts in benefit levels and/or the introduction of (new) eligibility criteria may appear minor matters at the time, they may cumulatively represent significant change in a welfare system. The Scandinavian welfare systems have been obliged, albeit at different times in the individual countries, to adjust to a less propitious economic climate and to make changes. Is there evidence, as some have suggested, of a measure of convergence between the Scandinavian welfare regimes and those in continental Europe? Rephrasing the question in more concrete terms: How successful has the Nordic welfare state been in achieving the three primary outcomes specified in our model – that is, low income inequality, low health inequality and gender equality?

Objectives and outcomes – evaluating the performance of the Nordic welfare state

Using data from the 1990s, Johan Fritzell could find no evidence that, in terms of *income equality*, the Nordic states (Iceland was not included) had become more 'European' (the three non-Nordic countries used for comparison were the UK, Germany and the Netherlands) and he notes that, despite mass unemployment in Finland and Sweden and substantial increases in unemployment in Denmark and Norway, there was no evidence of convergence. True, Fritzell observes that the recession in the early 1990s had led to a relatively substantial increase in inequality of *market income*. However, when cash benefits were included, there was a significant reduction in inequality (Fritzell 2001: 27). Kautto *et al.*, looking at Fritzell's study, concluded that 'relative poverty rates among typically vulnerable groups still appear to be lower than in other countries', although it has been noted by others that young persons seemed to have experienced a more negative development in their incomes than other age groups (Kautto *et al.* 2001b: 264, 267).

If the objective of low income inequality has been achieved relatively more successfully in Scandinavia than elsewhere in western Europe, the same cannot be said for the second outcome of the Nordic welfare model, *low health inequality*. Health inequalities may be defined as systematic differences in morbidity and mortality between groups of people who occupy different positions in the social structure and, as Olle Lundberg and Eero Lahelma note, it might be expected that 'such major welfare outcomes as health and death would not only show better levels in the Nordic countries, but also be more equally distributed than elsewhere' (Lundberg and Lahelma 2001: 43). Indeed, in the Black report in the UK, which was based on data from the 1970s, Norway and Sweden were singled out as countries with significantly smaller mortality inequalities than others (Lundberg and Lahelma 2001: 51). However, Lundberg and Lahelma found that the size and pattern of health inequalities in the Nordic states were very similar to those found in most west European countries when health inequalities are studied as differences in health between social classes and educational groups.

The achievement of the third desired outcome of the Nordic welfare model (and probably the most researched), *gender equality*, would involve women and men having equal power to shape society and their own lives, and this in turn would imply the existence of the same opportunities, rights and obligations in all walks of life. In its study *Women and Men in Sweden*, Statistics Sweden distinguishes between the qualitative and quantitative aspects of the notion of gender equality. Qualitative gender equality presupposes that the knowledge, experience and values of both women and men are given equal weight and used to enrich and direct all spheres of society (Statistics Sweden 2006: 5). Quantitative gender equality presumes an *equal distribution between women and men* in all aspects of society and areas such as education, work, recreation and positions of power in particular. The briefest note on the gender balance in higher education, the labour market and positions of power is in order.

The gender distribution of students in universities is undoubtedly more favourable to women, but there is none the less an uneven gender distribution across subject disciplines. Since the 1980s there have been more female students than male in Swedish universities and, in the academic year 2004–5, 60 per cent of those enrolled on undergraduate programmes were women. Similarly, in Norway in 2004, 35 per cent of women aged between nineteen and twenty-four years were in higher education, compared with 24 per cent of men in that age group. The previous year, for the first time, as many women as men graduated in Norway and in the cohort aged twenty-five to twenty-nine years, 45 per cent of women had been in higher education, compared with 30 per cent of men. Yet there is gender segregation in the subjects studied. For example, in Denmark in 2004, women made up 94 per cent of students on social and health education programmes. In Norway 80 per cent of students in health, welfare and sports subjects were women, whereas the gender ratio in the natural sciences, vocational and technical subjects was 70–30 in favour of men. It might, of course, be argued that these differences simply reflect the segregated nature of the job market and the likelihood that women will find employment in public sector 'care' posts.

Access to work for women has grown and female participation in the labour force has been the higher in Scandinavia than among the other OECD countries. In 2007, in the fifteen- to sixty-four-year age group, across the region between just over two-thirds of women (in Norway) and just over four-fifths (in Iceland) were in work (table 8.1). Women, in short, no longer have to choose between paid work and having children. Equally, however, the

Table 8.1 *Participation in the labour force in the Nordic countries, by gender, 2007 (%)*

	Women	Men
Denmark	71.9	82.0
Finland	77.6	81.3
Iceland	80.7	89.1
Norway	68.6	75.2
Sweden	78.0	83.1

labour market is still gender-segregated and salary differences remain. On the first point, the minister for gender equality in Denmark (2006: 5) has written strikingly that 'a total of 60 per cent of all Danes are employed in jobs dominated almost exclusively by women or by men' and adds that this is one of the most important individual factors bearing on the wage differentials between men and women. Throughout the region women are 'overrepresented' in the 'care sector', teaching, office-related jobs and cleaning. In Sweden in 2005, 85 per cent of those employed in social work and 83 per cent of those working in health care were women.

There remain gender differences in salaries, although these have generally narrowed. In the third quarter of 2004, for example, women's salaries in Norway were 87 per cent of men's and this compared with 60 per cent in 1960 (women's salaries were 88 per cent of men's, but when additional allowances and bonus/commissions were included, women's salaries worked out at 87 per cent of men's) (Statistics Norway 2006: 14). Part of the gender gap in salaries was the consequence of significant differences in pay between the public and private sector. Indeed, across the region there is considerable sectoral variation in the extent of the pay differential between men and women. In Norway the largest relative difference is in the financial services industry (banking, insurance, etc.), where the earnings of full-time female employees is only 74 per cent of men's, whereas among school teachers women's earnings are 96 per cent of those of their male colleagues. In Sweden there is a situation of parity in women's and men's salaries in school teaching and also in personal care and related work. However, the general point is that there remains a gender pay gap in the Nordic states. The Danish National Institute of Social Research calculated that in the period 1997–2001 the *gross* difference in women's and men's pay ranged between 12 and 19 percentage points and that when adjusted for educational level, work experience and so on it worked out at 2–6 percentage points (minister for gender equality 2006: 9).

In terms of women in *positions of political power*, the picture in the Nordic countries looks *prima facie* quite impressive. The Norwegian Gro Harlem Brundtland (Labour) became the first female prime minister in the region in 1981 and held the post on several occasions until 1996. Anneli Jäätteenmäki became the first female Finnish prime minister in 2003, although she was obliged to resign in controversial circumstances only three months later. The divorcee and single mother Vigdís Finnbogadóttir became Icelandic president in 1980 and held the post for sixteen years, whilst in Finland a former foreign minister, Tarja Halonen, became the country's first female head of state in 2000 and was re-elected to a second term of office six years later. The Nordic parliaments, moreover, have some of the highest levels of female representation in the world, the 2007–11 Finnish Eduskunta comprising two-fifths women and the 2006–10 Swedish Riksdag approaching one-half female MPs. Only in the Icelandic Alþingi (2007–11) does the proportion of women legislators number less than one-third (table 8.2).

Table 8.2 *Female representation in the Nordic parliaments, 2007*

	Parliamentary session	Percentage women
Denmark	2007–11	37.4
Finland	2007–11	42.0
Iceland	2007–11	31.7
Norway	2005–9	37.9
Sweden	2006–10	47.3

Table 8.3 *Female ministers in Nordic governments, 2007*

	Number of women	Total number of ministerial posts	Percentage women
Denmark	7	19	36.8[a]
Finland	12	20	60.0
Iceland	4	12	33.3
Norway	9	19	47.4
Sweden	9	22	40.9

[a] Following the appointment of the third coalition under Anders Fogh Rasmussen on 23 November 2007.

Women are currently also well represented in three of the five governments in Scandinavia (table 8.3). Two-fifths of the Swedish cabinet comprises female ministers and the figure approaches one-half in Norway. For the first time in Finnish history the government (the second coalition, of non-socialists and Greens, under Matti Vanhanen), formed after the March 2007 general election, comprises a *majority* of female ministers. There are ministers for equality/gender equality in all but Finland and Iceland, although, ironically, in one of them, Denmark, only a little over one-third of ministers are female, in Anders Fogh Rasmussen's Liberal-led non-socialist coalition formed after the 2007 general election.

Although the picture suggests that women do occupy positions of political power in Scandinavia, two caveats need entering. First, there still appears a degree of gender segregation in the distribution of ministerial portfolios. True, women presently hold the 'heavy' posts of minister of foreign affairs in Iceland, minister of industry in Sweden and both the minister for defence and (uniquely in the region) minister of finance in Norway (the Socialist Left leader Kristin Halvorsen). More typically, however, in Denmark, women hold the 'soft' portfolios, *inter alia*, of development co-operation, welfare and equality, climate and energy, refugee, immigration and integration affairs, and family and consumer affairs. Second, whilst the evidence is limited, it does appear that there

Table 8.4 *Female representation on company boards in Scandinavia*

	Percentage
Denmark	7.2
Sweden	15.1
Norway	24.2

Source: Randøy *et al.* (2006: 18).

is a gender imbalance in the senior echelons of the civil service. For example, 'top administrators in government offices' in Sweden in 2006 were reported to comprise 36 per cent women and 64 per cent men (Statistics Sweden 2006: 6).

In terms of holding *positions of economic power*, women appear to fare less favourably than in the political arena: they are heavily underrepresented in senior management positions in both the public and private sectors. There are problems of data comparability but, suggestively, in Denmark in 2005, women comprised only 20 per cent of 'top executives' and 21 per cent of 'executives' in the state sector and 4.4 per cent and 7.0 per cent, respectively, in the private sector (minister for gender equality 2006: 19–20). The proportion of female 'executive managers' in Norway in 2004 was 23 per cent and women 'middle managers' 32 per cent. In Sweden in 2005 only 22 per cent of female private sector managers were women and a mere five out of 291 enterprises listed on the stock exchange employed women in permanent positions as managing directors. There has also been low female representation on company boards – only 7.2 per cent in Denmark in 2005 (table 8.4). In Iceland the same year, 22 per cent of members of boards of enterprises comprised women, but the figure for boards of listed companies was only 4 per cent. Even allowing for the problems of comparing like with like ('top executives' in Denmark, 'executive managers' in Norway, etc.), it is clear that men dominate positions of economic power in the Nordic countries and that, as Randi Kjeldstad has asserted, 'the very low proportion of female managing directors in the largest private enterprises reveals a severe shortcoming of Nordic gender equality policies' (Kjeldstad 2001: 93–5). Incidentally, new Norwegian legislation, which came into force in January 2006, has led to a significant increase in female representation on the boards of publicly owned enterprises and privately owned public limited companies (PLCs). It requires, among other things, that when a board comprises ten or more members both genders must have at least 40 per cent representation.

In the conclusion to their study of the Nordic welfare states in a European context, Mikko Kautto and colleagues note that 'a systematic pattern of more pronounced gender equality was found in almost all aspects studied' (Kautto *et al.* 2001b: 264). Women in the Nordic states, they argue, are less concentrated at the lowest end of the earnings scale and are less economically dependent on their husbands, whilst being a mother of small children has less impact on her economic independence in the Nordic countries. The authors conclude that the Nordic countries have the lowest gender gap in earnings, as a result of higher labour force participation rates and lower gender disparities in wages. In contrast, we have noted the existence of gender segregation in the labour market and in the subjects studied at university, along with a glaring imbalance between men and women in positions of 'economic power'. Clearly, despite considerable progress having been made, there is still some way to go to achieve the goal of gender equality in the Nordic states.

The future of the Nordic welfare model

The Nordic welfare model appears to have emerged relatively unscathed from the economic crisis of the early 1990s, when public deficits and unemployment rose to record levels. Taxes were increased and government expenditure cut back but the basic structure of the welfare model was preserved largely intact. The welfare state, moreover, has retained its basic legitimacy at both mass and elite levels, although, in the Norwegian case, as Gulbrandsen and Engelstad's (2005: 907) elite survey shows, private sector business leaders favour more privatisation and a halt to increased welfare spending. But what does the future hold for the Nordic welfare model? Will the relative role of the state as a welfare provider decline, in line with Kuhnle's hypothesis (2000b: 231) that greater individual resources – that is, more wealth in society and higher earnings for the vast majority of the population – make it more likely that alternative providers will emerge as a reaction to a perception of poor quality, a real decline in the quality of services or unmet demand in the public welfare system? In short, will greater diversity in the provision of welfare services and the increased imposition of user charges to fund them lead to a negation of the basic principles of universality and comprehensiveness and the effective demise of the distinctive Nordic welfare model?

Plainly, the Nordic welfare system will face further challenges, foremost among which, it is widely accepted, will be Europeanisation, globalisation and demographic change. *European economic integration*, and its concomitant, the free movement of capital, labour, goods and services, has generated pressure on governments to create competitive tax regimes. The Scandinavian states have already responded by reducing corporate tax rates and taxes on capital income and raising other taxes, especially on private consumption. If there is further pressure to reduce taxation, it is difficult to see how the Nordic welfare model – especially with reference to the rising costs of pensions and health care – can be maintained.

From a national welfare state perspective, it makes little sense to seek to analyse the processes of globalisation and European integration separately. They are interwoven exogenous forces, which have transformed the setting of national policy-making in general and welfare policy decisions in particular.

In the case of *globalisation*, the argument, put simply, is that firms are increasingly exposed to global competition in an era characterised by the increasing mobility of factors of production. Given the increased mobility of capital and the possibility (sometimes threat) of firms relocating production, and bearing in mind, too, that a country's wealth and welfare are essentially dependent on a thriving private sector, governments, it is argued, need to protect and promote the competitiveness of nationally based enterprises through the appropriate fiscal measures. This conventional wisdom that globalisation will have a deleterious impact on welfare regimes by delimiting the overall level of taxation that can be imposed and the rate at which different taxes can be levied (Kangas and Palme 2005: 13) has, however, been challenged. There is a school of thought which maintains that globalisation does not inevitably lead to the disintegration of the welfare system, because the state has the necessary adaptive capacity. Equally, others would insist that, contemporaneous with globalisation, the state has lost power and no longer exercises total control over macro-economic policy. All in all, it is difficult to estimate the overall significance of external factors such as Europeanisation and globalisation, although it may be fair to conclude that 'while the control of expenditure remains in the hands of the government, the revenue side is increasingly affected by factors beyond the control of nation states' (Kautto *et al.* 2001b: 236).

Clearly, too, the 'revenue side' is directly affected by such internal factors as employment trends, policy choices and, not least, demographic change. As to the last, it is obvious that an increasingly senescent population will raise the costs of welfare provision whilst at the same time reducing the 'tax take', and the projections are that a significantly higher proportion of the overall population will comprise elderly persons in the future. In Sweden the population at sixty-five and over is predicted to increase by 55 per cent from the present 1.6 million to about 2.5 million by 2050. In Finland the proportion of persons over sixty-five years is estimated to rise from the present 16 per cent to 26 per cent by 2030. By then the *demographic dependency ratio* – that is, the number of children and elderly people per 100 of working age – will have risen from the present 50 to 74.6. In Denmark, where the economically active population is calculated as those within the twenty to fifty-nine years age group, the demographic dependency ratio in 2007 was 87, signifying that for every 100 persons who were economically active, eighty-seven needed support. The projections were for the demographic dependency ratio to increase to 91 in 2010 and 110 by 2030. Clearly, then, reducing unemployment – even in oil-rich Norway this stood at 2.7 per cent in summer 2007 – increasing employment levels and keeping people economically active longer will be essential if a wholesale rationalisation of welfare services is to be avoided. In Finland a flexible retirement age of between sixty-two and sixty-eight has recently been introduced, with an enhanced pension for those working to the latter year. In Norway the proportion of persons aged between sixty-seven and seventy-four in the labour force increased from 6.9 per cent in the first quarter of 2006 to

10.9 per cent (of the total population in that age group) in the first quarter of 2007, largely as a result of persons who combine short-term, part-time jobs with their pensions. Many people, it seems, want to work longer and should be encouraged to do so since, as Olli Kangas and Joakim Palme have written, 'the sustainability of the Nordic model of social policy hinges on the number of taxpayers that can be mobilised' (Kangas and Palme 2005: 15).

At least twice in this chapter the question has been posed as to whether there is evidence of a convergence between the Nordic welfare model and welfare systems elsewhere in continental Europe. Not surprisingly perhaps, there is no consensus on the matter among social policy specialists. The 'Kautto school', as noted, has emphasised the retention of basic structures. Peter Abrahamson, in contrast, is of a different mind and points, among other things, to the growth in Denmark since the 1980s of employer-funded private hospital insurance schemes and the tendency of local authorities, particularly in Denmark and Sweden, to contract out various social services. He argues that the Nordic welfare systems are still distinct but less so than twenty years ago and that welfare in the region is undergoing a process of *Europeanisation*. In his words, 'elements of individualization, decentralization, more reliance on family and kin and market solutions are pushing Scandinavia closer to the principles governing the other European Union welfare models' (Abrahamson 2003).

Summary

1.   The origins of the Nordic welfare state were traced to the recessionary 1930s and 'historic compromises' between organisations representing the conflicting interests of capital and labour. The essence of the deal involved [minimal disruption to the wealth-generating process in return for a redistribution of wealth for welfare.]

2.   The major welfare surge in Scandinavia occurred in an era of relative prosperity after 1945 and was grounded in an assumption of economic growth, not poverty and recession. In addition to market-driven economic growth, welfare development was linked to the strategic role of a social democratic governing party, its close links with the trade union movement and its good working relationship with business and industry. None the less, the Nordic welfare state developed at a different pace and embraced differing policies in the individual countries, with Sweden leading the field, Norway and Denmark in close attendance, Finland well behind and Iceland a 'back marker'.

3.   A nine-point, ideal-type Nordic welfare model was outlined, comprising three analytically distinct elements – the core welfare principles, the proactive role of the state as a welfare provider and a specification of desired outcomes.

4.   The performance of the Nordic welfare model was examined with reference to three primary objectives – income equality, health equality and gender equality. Although much has been achieved with respect to the last, evidence

of gender segregation in the labour market and a glaring imbalance between men and women in positions of 'economic power' were noted.

5. Some of the main challenges facing the Nordic welfare states in the future were considered, with particular reference to the exogenous forces of Europeanisation and globalisation and the internal pressures generated by demographic change.

6. There is no clear consensus among social policy specialists on the question of a possible convergence between the Nordic welfare model and those in continental Europe, something reflected in the contrasting views of Kautto and Abrahamson. However, there is undeniable evidence of a growing diversity of provision, with private firms and private, employer-funded hospitals offering alternatives to public sector services.

References

Abrahamson, Peter (1992) 'Europe: a challenge to the Scandinavian model of welfare', paper delivered at the first European Conference of Sociology, University of Vienna, August.

Abrahamson, Peter (2003) 'The end of the Scandinavian model? Welfare reform in the Nordic countries', paper at http://individual.utoronto.ca/RC19_2003/papers.html.

Alestalo, Matti, Peter Flora and Hannu Uusitalo (1985) 'Structure and politics in the making of the welfare state', in Risto Alapuro *et al.* (eds), *Small States in Comparative Perspective*, Norwegian University Press: Oslo, pp. 188–210.

Esping-Andersen, Gøsta (1990) *The Three Worlds of Welfare Capitalism*, Polity: Oxford.

Fritzell, Johan (2001) 'Still different? Income distribution in the Nordic countries in a European comparison', in Mikko Kautto *et al.* (eds), *Nordic Welfare States in the European Context*, Routledge: London, pp. 18–41.

Gulbrandsen, Trygve and Fredrik Engelstad (2005) 'Elite consensus on the Norwegian welfare state model', *West European Politics*, 28 (4), pp. 898–918.

Heidar, Knut (2001) *Norway. Elites on Trial*, Westview: Boulder, CO.

Huntford, Roland (1975) *The New Totalitarians*, Allen Lane: London.

Kangas, Olli and Joakim Palme (2005) 'Social policy and economic development in the Nordic countries: an introduction', in Olli Kangas and Joakim Palme (eds), *Social Policy and Economic Development in the Nordic Countries*, Palgrave: London, pp. 1–16.

Kautto, Mikko, Johan Fritzell, Bjørn Hvinden, Jon Kvist and Hannu Uusitalo (2001a) 'Introduction: how distinct are the Nordic welfare states?', in Mikko Kautto *et al.* (eds), *Nordic Welfare States in the European Context*, Routledge: London, pp. 1–17.

Kautto, Mikko, Johan Fritzell, Bjørn Hvinden, Jon Kvist and Hannu Uusitalo (2001b) 'Conclusion: Nordic welfare states in the European context', in Mikko Kautto *et al.* (eds), *Nordic Welfare States in the European Context*, Routledge: London, pp. 262–72.

Kiander, Jaakko (2005) 'Growth and employment in the "Nordic welfare states" in the 1990s: a tale of crisis and revival', in Olli Kangas and Joakim Palme (eds), *Social Policy and Economic Development in the Nordic Countries*, Palgrave: London, pp. 210–40.

Kildal, Nanna and Stein Kuhnle (2005) 'The principle of universalism: tracing a key idea in the Scandinavian welfare model', in Stein Kuhnle and Nanna Kildal (eds), *Normative Foundations of the Welfare State: The Nordic Experience*, Routledge: London.

Kjeldstad, Randi (2001) 'Gender policies and gender equality', in Mikko Kautto *et al.* (eds), *Nordic Welfare States in the European Context*, Routledge: London, pp. 66–97.

Kosonen, Pekka (1992) 'European welfare state model: converging trends', paper delivered at the first European Conference of Sociology, University of Vienna, August.

Kosonen, Pekka (1993) 'The Scandinavian welfare model in the new Europe', in Thomas P. Boje and Sven E. Olsson Hort (eds), *Scandinavia in a New Europe*, Scandinavian University Press: Oslo, pp. 39–70.

Kuhnle, Stein (1998) 'The Nordic approach to general welfare', paper at www.nnn.se/n-model/approach.htm.

Kuhnle, Stein (2000a) 'The Scandinavian welfare state in the 1990s: challenged but viable', *West European Politics*, 23 (2), pp. 209–28.

Kuhnle, Stein (2000b) 'Reflections on the Nordic welfare state', in Lauri Karvonen and Krister Ståhlberg (eds), *Festschrift for Dag Anckar on his 60th Birthday on February 12, 2000*, Åbo Akademis förlag: Åbo, pp. 225–39.

Lane, Jan-Erik and Svante Ersson (1997) *Comparative Political Economy*, second edition, Pinter: London.

Lundberg, Olle and Eero Lahelma (2001) 'Nordic health inequalities in the European context', in Mikko Kautto *et al.* (eds), *Nordic Welfare States in the European Context*, Routledge: London, pp. 42–65.

Minister for gender equality (2006) *Facts and Gender Equality 2006*, Department of Gender Equality: Copenhagen.

Nielsen, Johannes (ed.) (2006) *Social Protection in the Nordic Countries 2004*, Nordic Social Statistical Committee: Copenhagen.

Ólafsson, Stefán (1989) *The Making of the Icelandic Welfare State. A Scandinavian Comparison*, University of Iceland: Reykjavík.

Randøy, Trønd, Steen Thomsen and Lars Oxelheim (2006) *A Nordic Perspective on Corporate Board Diversity*, Nordic Innovation Centre: Oslo.

Rothstein, Bo (1996) *The Social Democratic State. The Swedish Model and the Bureaucratic Problem of Social Reforms*, University of Pittsburgh: Pittsburgh, PA.

Statistics Norway (2006) *Women and Men in Norway*, Statistics Norway: Oslo.

Statistics Sweden (2006) *Women and Men in Sweden. Facts and Figures 2006*, Statistics Sweden: Stockholm.

Steen, Anton (2004) 'The welfare state – still viable?', in Knut Heidar (ed.), *Nordic Politics. Comparative Perspectives*, Universitetsforlaget: Oslo, pp. 207–27.

Part V

Legislative–executive relations in the Nordic region

9

The Nordic parliaments:
an alternative model?

> It is characteristic of this classical agricultural country and of the great impor-
> tance of the farming community in Danish political affairs that the rear seats in
> the assembly should be known earthily as the 'dung channel' or *grebningen* – that
> is, the gutter behind cattle in a cow-shed!
>
> (Andersen 1974: 5)

Any television producer charged with making a series of half-hour programmes on the Nordic parliaments without inducing a soporific switch-off
among the viewing public should have no shortage of material with which to
work. For example, Finland in 1906 was the first country in the world to grant
women the right to stand as parliamentary candidates and at the 1907 general
election, when the country was still a Grand Duchy of the Czarist empire, nine
female MPs were elected to the 200-seat Eduskunta. Norway in 1928 became
the first nation in the world to introduce a system of parliamentary deputies
to serve when regular members are prevented from attending meetings of
the Storting. Iceland followed suit in 1945, Denmark in 1953 and Sweden in
1974. Seating in the semi-circular assemblies is not by the conventional party
but by region in Norway and Sweden and by drawing lots in Iceland. Moreover,
despite the introduction of highly sophisticated voting equipment, there is no
provision to abstain in the Storting and no provision either for an early dissolution of parliament in Norway. In short, there are distinctive features in both the
history and the contemporary legislative practice of the Nordic parliaments,
but are they really any (that) different from other legislatures?

In their rigorously comparative volume *Beyond Westminster and Congress*,
Peter Esaiasson and Knut Heidar put the question: Do the Nordic parliaments
represent an alternative model to parliaments in the style of Westminster and
the US Congress? Do the Nordic parliaments, in other words, form a homogeneous and distinct unity within the universe of democratically elected
legislative assemblies? They conclude (Esaiasson and Heidar 2000: 418) that
'the particular mix of influential party groups, not-so-strong group hierarchies

and fairly strong standing committees is shared by neither Westminster nor the US Congress'. Accordingly, chapter 10 examines that 'particular mix' with reference to the role of standing committees and parliamentary party groups (PPGs). The present chapter sets the scene by mapping a series of common denominators – that is, properties and practices that are shared by the parliaments across the region.

Ultimately, Esaiasson and Heidar conclude that the particular Nordic mix does not make a strong enough case for an alternative Nordic model of legislatures because it differs at best in degree rather than in kind from the continental parliamentary model typified by the likes of the German, Dutch and Austrian parliaments. However, none of the aforementioned countries has witnessed the preponderance of minority governments that has been a feature of politics in Denmark, Norway and Sweden in recent decades and where, as a consequence, the executive (policy-making) has routinely proceeded on the basis of various types of legislative coalitions with particular opposition groups. In this connection, Anders Sannerstedt has referred to a distinctively *Scandinavian form of parliamentarism*, precisely because in Denmark, Norway and Sweden minority cabinets have been obliged to engage in dialogue with parties in opposition. In his words, 'negotiations between the political parties in the parliament are more common in the "Nordic model" than in other types of democratic systems' (Sannerstedt 1996: 54). Chapter 11 explores the phenomenon of so-called 'minority parliamentarism' and the multifarious modes of majority-building in the Danish, Norwegian and Swedish legislatures. Finland and Iceland may be regarded as deviant cases, with majority governments, and often broad-based majority governments, the norm. They will also be considered in chapter 11, which includes a discussion of the dual executive in these two countries.

The Nordic parliaments: the common denominators

1. Unicameral legislatures

Outside Finland, which has had a single-chamber Eduskunta since 1906, all the Nordic parliaments have become unicameral legislatures since the Second World War. Constitutional reform saw the abolition of upper chambers in Denmark in 1953 (Arter 1991) and Sweden in 1970 (von Sydow 1989, 1991), although right-wing opposition to the move prompted the incorporation into the new Danish constitution of a provision (article 42) permitting one-third or more of Folketing members (i.e. sixty or more) to submit to a referendum a measure that has already completed its third reading and only awaits the royal assent (Qvortrup 2000). No comparable minority safeguards were built into the new Swedish constitution. Unlike Denmark, it was the non-socialists in Sweden who were in the van of a campaign to abolish the First Chamber. Criticism of the First Chamber, which was elected by the county and larger city councils (members served for eight-year terms) and had had a 'permanent' Social Democratic majority since 1941, intensified in the 1950s, especially when in 1956 the non-socialists gained a majority in the popularly elected Second Chamber. Probably influenced by the introduction of unicameralism in Denmark three years earlier, Bertil Ohlin in particular, the leader of the largest opposition party, the Liberals, sought the abolition of the First Chamber. Indeed, by 1964 the Conservatives, Centre Party, mass media and most of the general public concurred with Ohlin's view that there were strong democratic arguments in favour of the electorate having 'the chance to determine the composition of the Riksdag and the government of the country in one and the same election' (Stjernquist 1987: 238). The divided Social Democrats had prevaricated but by 1966 there was cross-party agreement on a directly elected unicameral Riksdag.

The transition to unicameralism in Iceland and Norway has been more recent and it marked the demise of highly distinctive legislative arrangements. Thus, between 1934 and 1991 the Alþingi was structurally unique in that it was elected as a single unit but functioned as a tricameral assembly. Two 'internal divisions', the Efri Deild (upper chamber) and Nethri Deild (lower chamber), constituted after the election, enjoyed co-equal legislative powers. The budget, however, was considered in the United Alþingi. Each division, together with the United Alþingi, had its own standing committee system. Article 15 of the 1874 constitution envisaged the Alþingi's work proceeding first and foremost in the two legislative chambers but, after the Second World War, an increasing volume of business, including reports from ministers, questions to ministers, votes of no confidence and general debates, was conducted in the United Alþingi and, as Þorsteinn Magnússon has written, this amounted to a transition from *de facto* bicameralism to *de facto* tricameralism (Magnússon 1990). The system was unwieldy and inefficient and in a constitutional reform in 1991 the Alþingi became a unicameral assembly, although the decision in favour of legislative modernisation was far from unanimous.

It took more than a decade and a half before Norway followed the Icelandic example. The 1814 Eidsvoll constitution, drafted during the brief interregnum in the aftermath of the Napoleonic wars, prescribed a parliament (Storting) that would be elected as a single body but function as two 'internal divisions' when considering 'law proposals'. Unlike Iceland, the two chambers were not to possess equal powers and bills could be introduced only in the larger division, the Odelsting, comprising three-quarters of all elected MPs. There were in fact many members of the Constituent Assembly (*riksforsamlingen*) that met at Eidsvoll who favoured a single-chamber assembly, whilst others (the likes of Christian Magnus Falsen) advocated bicameralism and the need to create the sort of 'healthy' checks and balances built into the US constitution and conventional practice in Britain. Valentin Sibbern's diary, however, reveals a more pragmatic and prosaic reason for ultimately opting for the compromise position of a system of internal divisions. It was feared that the (for the time) liberal franchise would lead to the Storting being dominated by landowning peasants and the smaller division, the Lagting, was conceived as an elitist counterpoise to a possible tyranny of the farming majority in the Odelsting (Kaartvedt 1964: 174). It was designed as a specialist body of lawyers (although it never became one), which would vet, amend and generally tighten up legislative proposals emanating from the larger division. The ability of the Lagting (which comprises one-quarter of Storting MPs) to serve as a brake on ill-considered and/or unduly hasty government legislation – the principle of parliamentarism was established in Norway in 1884 – was vitiated by the rise of highly cohesive parties, since this meant the composition of the Lagting simply replicated the partisan balance in the Storting as a whole. The status of the Lagting has been relatively low and books on Norwegian government have barely afforded it a mention (Berggrav 1994). None the less, it proved remarkably resilient – largely on the basis of 'we've always had it, so why abolish it?' – but, finally, in 2007 it was decided by a unanimous parliamentary vote that the Lagting would be abolished after the 2009 general election and Norway would shift to a unicameral legislature.

Finland became a unicameral system in 1906, when parliamentary and electoral reform replaced an antiquated, quadricameral Diet of Estates with a single-chamber Eduskunta elected on the basis of universal suffrage. However, modelled, like the internal divisions of the Alþingi, on Norwegian practice, the 1906 reform created a forty-five-member Grand Committee (*suuri valiokunta*) to act as a type of Council of Elders. Much as for proponents of the Lagting at Eidsvoll, the creation of a Grand Committee was viewed by the non-socialists as a mechanism for preserving the privileged position of influential social groups at a time of radical political change and, at the first session of the unicameral Eduskunta in 1907, was strongly criticised by the largest parliamentary party, the Social Democrats (Nousiainen 1977: 397–9). In contrast to the Lagting, moreover, the overwhelming majority of bills (though not the budget) were to be considered in the Grand Committee, after first going to one of the specialist standing committees (Helander 1976). In practice, however, the Grand Committee never attracted senior politicians, rapidly became party politicised and in 1990 was reduced in size to twenty-five, when its primary remit became the monitoring of European 'legislation'.

Today, the size of the Nordic parliaments ranges from the sixty-three members of the Icelandic Alþingi, making it one of the smallest national assemblies in Europe, to the 349 members in the Swedish Riksdag. When Iceland gained independence from the Danish crown in 1944, there were only fifty-two Alþingi members; this rose to sixty in 1959 and to its present level in 1984. With a population of only a little over 300,000 this has meant a very low voter–MP ratio and a highly personalised form of representative democracy. Icelanders are much more able to cite the name of their local MP than are other Nordic citizens. Constitutional reform in Sweden created a 350-strong unicameral Riksdag but, between 1973 and 1976 in the so-called 'lottery

Riksdag', this resulted in a dead heat between the socialists and non-socialists, obliging the Speaker on occasions to draw lots to determine the result of tied ballots. The number of MPs was subsequently reduced to 349, although there has been ephemeral talk of the need to reduce the number still further. In the 1988/89 Riksdag session, a motion from the Liberal Daniel Tarschys simply read: 'There are too many of us. From the 1994 general election, the number of Riksdag members should be 299'!

The number of Finnish parliamentarians (200) has remained constant since 1906, whilst the size of the Danish Folketing has remained at 179 since the adoption of the constitution in 1953. Both the Finnish and Danish parliaments allocate seats to their Home Rule territories. In the Folketing both Greenland and the Faeroes are represented by two MPs. In the Eduskunta, the Åland islands elect a single member and, throughout, he or she – for the first time in 2007 a woman was elected for Åland – has joined the Swedish People's Party's PPG. The Norwegian Storting had 155 members from the time of the Eidsvoll constitution in 1814 to 1985, when the number was increased by two, and it rose again, to 165, in 1989. The Storting currently comprises 169 members. In both Norway and Sweden there is an 'incompatibility rule' preventing cabinet ministers from being at the same time MPs – they are replaced by a substitute – and the full compliment of legislators is thus maintained. Moreover, outside Finland, as mentioned, deputy members replace MPs who are granted leave of absence on health grounds or for parliamentary business that necessitates their absence from the chamber.

2. Professional assemblies

All the Nordic parliaments are professional assemblies in the sense that the facilities and resources available to members have been significantly improved, whilst the role of legislator is now viewed as a full-time profession rather than a part-time occupation. Shared rooms, the requirement to pay for telephone calls, minimal or no support staff – these were all an integral part of the parliamentarian's experience until relatively late in the last century. A veteran, radical leftist Icelandic MP has related how, between 1971 and 1974, he was chairman of his PPG, chair of the standing committees of finance and education and was in addition a member of a third committee. Yet, at the beginning, he had no office, no committee staff and was obliged to write the committee reports himself (Arter 2000a: 51–2)! As to the professionalisation of the legislator's role, a long-serving Conservative parliamentarian commented that, in the 1960s, 'the Riksdag was a part-time parliament', the demands on an MP were less than today and the background of members was far more varied. (This was particularly the case, it might be added, in the First Chamber.) To paraphrase his sentiments, the Riksdag comprised gifted amateurs – members of a socio-political elite – who could combine being an MP with a range of other responsibilities (Arter 2000b: 106). A few were senior academics and business leaders, whilst many spent much of their time on local government duties; attendance at PPG meetings was generally poor.

Today, the facilities and resources available to legislators have been individualised (with the provision of their own rooms, personal assistants, etc.) and computerised (with the concomitant access to ever-greater information banks), and the role of parliamentarian has been professionalised (with a clearer career structure and pension arrangements – and in many cases, too, a more careerist approach to the job). In the digital democracy of the new millennium, the legislators' world has been transformed: they have become readily accessible by email and in turn increasingly communicate with voters through personal websites and daily 'blogs'. Mention might be made here of the distinctively Finnish phenomenon of 'candidate selection machines' (*vaalikoneet*), which were first used in the European Parliament election of 1996. The candidate answers a series of web questions, the voter does likewise, chooses a constituency and is then matched up with the candidate(s) closest to his/her own views. The number of selection machines has exploded. By the 2003 Eduskunta election there were approximately a dozen and one in four Finns is estimated to have used them; by 2007 their number had doubled and so had the number of users. True, citizens relatively seldom vote for the candidate they are 'matched' with. A parliamentarian who was elected in the Kymi constituency in 2007 recorded amusingly how, on meeting her in person, an elderly man, paired with her by the selection machine, declared bluntly that 'you are fatter and older than I thought'! However, for parliamentary candidates, candidate selection machines provide a cheap way of communicating their views and of targeting younger voters in particular.

3. Policy deliberations outside plenary sessions

All the Nordic parliaments can be considered 'working parliaments' in that the significant policy deliberations take place outside plenary sessions, which are mostly poorly attended and at which contributions are governed by strict time limits on members' speeches. Of course, it might be countered that in most, if not quite all, modern parliaments, the significant parleying takes place away from the chamber – in the standing committees, PPGs and the various committees inside the PPGs. Yet in the 'debating parliament', importance is attached to 'set-piece' full-sitting debates – such as the second reading of a government bill in the House of Commons – and MPs tend to be 'show horses', advertising themselves through their rhetorical skills, rather than 'work horses' (in Donald Matthews' celebrated terms) labouring on the small print of legislation in standing committee (Matthews 1960).

The Nordic parliaments are emphatically not debating parliaments; rather, plenary debates are generally sparsely attended, hierarchical and liturgical. Speeches are mostly read verbatim and there is not the 'cut and thrust' of Westminster, where speakers react to what has earlier been said. Chamber debates are dominated by ministers and the various policy spokespersons of the parties who will present the government/party line. MPs are generally specialists in a particular policy area and if the debate is on another topic there is little opportunity and/or incentive to participate. In Norway and Sweden, moreover, the plenary discussion will in all likelihood relate to the standing committee's report on a government measure, since bills go directly to the relevant standing committee. In any event, members can observe plenary proceedings from television monitors in their own rooms and those dotted around the parliament building – and they can see just how few MPs there are in the chamber itself. Indeed, as the Danish adage has it: 'If you've got a secret, tell it in the Folketing – there will be nobody there to hear it'!

True, plenary proceedings are not always liturgical. Small parties, especially populist parties, often with very limited representation on the standing committees, may well use speeches on the floor of the chamber as a profiling mechanism – and often do so with considerable gusto. In the first two years of the 2003–7 Eduskunta, the chair of the True Finns, Timo Soini, made over 300 plenary speeches. There are, in any event, more debates on topical issues, executive white papers and reports from government ministers. None the less, a majority of Nordic parliamentarians are oriented towards the detailed work of legislation, excel in examining the minutiae of government proposals and often feel most at home in the usually informal environment of the standing committees. The Nordic parliaments, in sum, may be considered 'working parliaments' in that there is a strong legislative culture and members are both recruited with, and subsequently consolidate, an area of policy expertise. Where MPs are members of more than one standing committee, as in Finland and Iceland, a 'committee culture' is probably less well developed and absenteeism is entrenched. But, still, a solid performance in the prioritised committee will do the legislator's career prospects no harm at all.

4. Growth in workload

All the Nordic parliaments have experienced a massive growth in their workload in recent years, partly because of the growth in the scale and scope of government and the growing complexity of executive bills, but mainly because individual MPs have become more proactive in tabling a greater volume of legislative initiatives and questions to ministers than ever before. Sweden will illustrate the point. The number of government bills has remained relatively constant over the last fifty years. In the 2002–6 Riksdag they averaged 181 per annual session, compared with 190 government bills submitted in 1960, 168 in 1986/87 and a high of 246 in the 1992/93 Riksdag. However, the activity of individual members has increased enormously. In 1960, 944 motions were tabled, compared with 4,824 in 2005/6 – a rise of 511 per cent – whilst the number of written questions, which can be submitted even when the Riksdag is not in session over the summer, spiralled from a mere 83 in 1960 to 2,144 in 2005/6 – an increase of 2,583 per cent. Among other factors, the introduction of personal assistants for MPs, along with the growth in the size of the PPG staff, have materially assisted in the production of motions and questions.

5. Feminisation of membership

All the Nordic parliaments have witnessed a significant feminisation of their memberships in recent decades and the proportion of women MPs is high by international standards. By the new millennium, the average proportion of female legislators across the world was 13 per cent, whereas in the Nordic countries it stood at 37 per cent (Wängnerud 2000: 132). This was not always the case. The proportion of female MPs did not exceed 10 per cent in the bicameral Riksdag until 1957 and Kerstin Hesselgren, who became the first female member of the First Chamber in 1922, was in fact the only woman there until 1934. Similarly, the number of women serving in the Storting never exceeded 10 per cent from 1921 – the year the first female MP was elected – until the 1970s, when the proportion of female legislators shot up. By 1977, 24 per cent of Storting members were women and by 1989 the figure had risen to 36 per cent (Matthews and Valen 1999: 136–7).

Perhaps the most striking rise in female representation has occurred in Iceland, where, until the advent of the Women's List in 1983, the Alþingi was a veritable male bastion. In the ten electoral terms of the Alþingi between 1916 and 1946 the average proportion of female MPs was a mere 1.6 per cent; between 1946 and 1983 it averaged 3 per cent; but in the seven Alþingi terms between 1983 and 2011 the number of women parliamentarians has risen sharply, to an average of 26 per cent. These figures are based on the composition of the Alþingi immediately after a general election but on many occasions the proportion of female MPs has subsequently risen. For example, in the 1999–2003 Alþingi, the initial figure was 34.9 per cent but, following various resignations, this had risen to 36.5 per cent by 2001.

The impact of the feminisation of the Nordic parliaments is hard to assess. Helle Degn, a Social Democrat MP, who in autumn 1998 became the first woman to celebrate a quarter of a century in the Folketing, emphasised how the heightened visibility of women had led to a 'different tone, style and prioritisation' (Arter 2000a: 62). Lena Wängnerud has noted that 'if we are to judge from the experiences of MPs themselves, the impact of women's representation has been greatest in policy areas closely connected to the development of the Nordic welfare state' (Wängnerud 2000: 146). Certainly in the first two post-war decades, female Riksdag members were concentrated in the standing committees dealing with family and social policy matters, whilst still in the 1970s very few women had seats in committees dealing with taxation, finance, transport, industry and defence. Recently, however, there is evidence of a more equal gender distribution of committee seats. In the 2006–10 Riksdag, seven of the fifteen standing committees are chaired by women and they include the committees on transport, industry and finance.

The feminisation of the Nordic parliaments, however, should not be seen in isolation from more general changes in their composition. Matthews and Valen's statement (1999: 100) would hold broadly true of all five legislatures in the region: 'more teachers, professionals and managers and fewer farmers, fishermen, lumberjacks and workers; younger and more highly educated members; and a rapidly increasing number of women have been elected to the Storting since World War II'.

6. Simple majority rules, absence of minority vetoes

All the Nordic parliaments operate on the basis of simple majority rules for the enactment of legislation and there is an absence of minority veto provisions with which to bolster the position of the opposition. Until relatively recently, Finland was a notable exception. An historic complex of qualified majority rules needed for the enactment of measures 'at the constitutional level' – in other words, most important economic legislation – ensured that opposition groups (at least the largest one) were usually consulted, even during periods of majority government. Because of the strict defence of individual property rights enshrined in the (earlier) 1919 constitution – and originally conceived by the political establishment as a bulwark against socialism – essential powers to regulate the economy, such as changes to the tax laws that were intended to apply for longer than a year, were achieved through 'Exceptional Laws', which temporarily set aside the provisions of the constitution. Exceptional Laws were dealt with in precisely the same way as constitutional amendments: either they had to be supported by a simple plurality of delegates and then, in precisely the same form, by a two-thirds majority following a general election, or (more usually) they required a five-sixths majority to be declared 'urgent' – and so could be passed in the lifetime of a single parliament – and then a two-thirds majority for approval. In short, one-sixth of Eduskunta members (thirty-three) could prevent major economic policy becoming law in a single parliamentary session and one-third of delegates (sixty-six) could vote 'urgent' financial legislation over an election (Arter 1987: 49–50; Mattila 1997). Clearly, these rules prevented the government from governing in a significant sense and the qualified majority rules were abolished in respect of economic policy in 1992. Faced with the deepest economic recession in Finnish history, the non-socialist coalition led by Esko Aho (1991–95) had majority support in the Eduskunta but not the qualified majority to push through austerity measures.

Although legislation proceeds through its three 'readings' in the Folketing on the basis of simple majorities of MPs, article 42 of the 1953 Danish constitution permits a minority of one-third of members (sixty) to refer to a referendum a bill that has completed its parliamentary passage and only needs the royal stamp of approval. To overthrow the legislation, over half of those voting and at least 30 per cent of all eligible voters must have voted against in a referendum. Article 42 was strongly influenced by the Finnish 'suspensive veto' practice of 'putting bills to rest' (*panna lepäämään*) over a general election. Indeed, when it appeared that the battle for modified unicameralism along Norwegian lines had been lost in the 1946 Constitutional Commission, similar provisions to those of article 42 became a leading demand of the Conservative Party and its commission representatives (Arter 1991: 113). The idea was to create a barrier against radical legislative change at the hands of a future left-wing majority in the new single-chamber assembly. Ultimately, the specifics of article 42 reflected a compromise between the centre-right parties and the Social Democrats: the former got a vetoing threshold of 30 per cent of the total electorate (the Social Democrats had wanted no less than 40 per cent) but the budget, taxes, salaries, pensions and expropriation measures were excluded, ensuring, as the left-wing parties desired, that a government's capacity to govern and in particular to manage the economy would not be seriously threatened. The minority safeguards were in fact a pale shadow of those available to Eduskunta members in Finland and the Communist commission member, Aksel Larsen, held that article 42 would prove to be little more than a 'toothless tiger' in providing effective safeguards for legislative minorities (Arter 1991: 115).

Significantly, a referendum under article 42 has been called only once since the new constitution came into force – on the last day of the 1962–63 Folketing session (Arter 1984: 275–6) – although there have been several unsuccessful attempts to use it. In his analysis of the impact of article 42, Mads Qvortrup insists that 'the significance of the provision should not be measured solely by the single occasion – in 1963 – when it was brought into use. Rather, its infrequent use serves to emphasise that the provision has encouraged the search for consensus in Danish politics' (Qvortrup 2000: 18). Qvortrup's interviews with opposition party spokespersons, however, reveal that only the major opposition parties have found article 42 an efficient alternative to the upper chamber (Landstinget), which was abolished in 1953. For the smaller opposition parties, the threshold of one-third of parliamentarians has simply been too high.

7. Specialist and permanent standing committee systems

All the Nordic parliaments have moved to specialist and permanent standing committee systems, which, outside Norway, broadly reflect the structure of government departments. Since the following chapter will deal in some detail with the Nordic parliamentary standing committees and their changing work practices, it will suffice to note at this stage that all the standing committee systems in the region were modernised in the last decades of the last century. Denmark in 1972 abandoned its *ad hoc* Westminster-style bill committees; Sweden, in connection with cameral change in 1970, streamlined the Riksdag committees, granting of all them, *inter alia*, powers of legislative initiative; Finland in 1991 overhauled the Eduskunta committees, not least by strengthening their information-gathering rights; Iceland in the same year restructured its committees as part of the shift to a unicameral Alþingi; and Norway in 1993 reformed the Storting committees – the Agriculture Committee was abolished, a Committee on Energy and the Environment created, the workload between committees evened out and the committees 'emancipated' from the structure of government ministries (Rommetvedt 1998: 69–72). In addition, all the Nordic parliaments have created 'European committees', with varying powers, to consider regulations and directives from Brussels.

The standing committees number twelve in the Icelandic Alþingi, thirteen in the Norwegian Storting, fifteen in the Finnish Eduskunta, the same in the Swedish Riksdag and twenty-four in the Danish Folketing. The number of Riksdag standing committees was reduced from sixteen to fifteen in the 2006–10 term, following the merger of the Legal Affairs and Housing Committees. It was argued, among other things, that there was no minister for housing and no department for the committee to 'shadow'. Conversely, in Finland in 2007, a new Audit Committee (*tarkastusvaliokunta*) was created, to monitor state spending and ensure value for money. Exceptionally, in Norway MPs serve on one of the specialist Storting committees and one only. In contrast, in Sweden, with 349 MPs and fifteen seventeen-member standing committees – that is, 255 committee seats to fill – not all parliamentarians gain full membership of a committee. Most newcomers serve an apprenticeship as a substitute member of one or more standing committees. In Finland from the 1920s onwards, an MP who is nominated to serve on two standing committees has had the right to refuse membership of more. In Iceland, multiple committee membership has led to ephemeral demands to reduce the number and increase the size of Alþingi committees, albeit thus far without success.

'Strong committees, it appears', Kaare Strøm has noted, 'are at least a necessary condition for effective parliamentary influence in the policy-making process. Whether they are also sufficient is less obvious' (Strøm 1998: 47). Whether the powers of the Nordic standing committees (discussed in the next chapter) make them 'strong committees' is a moot point. What is not in doubt is that the recent concern has been to strengthen the position of standing committees, especially in respect of obtaining information and scrutinising the executive. The provision for public committee hearings, introduced in Sweden in 1988, is a case in point. All things being equal, a collective body of expertise should endow committees with considerable strength *vis-à-vis* the executive – with members who have the capacity to be actors in their own right. But this, of course, is to overlook the fact that standing committees comprise members of political parties, who must account to their PPGs.

8. Political cohesion

All the Nordic parliaments are characterised by cohesive political parties and meetings of the PPGs form an integral part of the legislative week. As with the standing committees, the role of the PPGs will be examined more fully in the following chapter. It is sufficient now to note that members of a political party in parliament form a PPG – 'an organised group of members of a representative body who belong to the same political party' is how Heidar and Koole (2000: 8) define one. The PPG will have its own rules, decision-making structures and indeed legislative culture, although, clearly, size will have implications for its internal organisation. PPGs may meet daily when parliament is in session, as in Denmark, or at least once weekly, as in Sweden – on Tuesday evenings between meetings of the standing committees and the Wednesday plenary debates. However, attendance will be expected at PPG meetings and the party line will be expected to be observed. For example, in the rules of the Danish Social Democrats' PPG, it is stated that if, during a plenary reading of a bill, a member wishes to express a view which deviates from the party line, this has to be discussed at a prior PPG meeting (Bille 2000: 134–5). The Nordic PPGs do have whips – the British term is translated directly into the Scandinavian languages and Finnish – but they are generally relatively junior MPs and group cohesion rests essentially on sentiments of collective loyalty rather than the threat of disciplinary measures. PPGs are central parliamentary actors: they participate in the formation and policy-making of governments (Heidar and Koole 2000: 4), whilst for the opposition PPGs are policy sub-systems in their own right, generating policy alternatives, not least in the form of a 'shadow budget' (Arter 2006: 196–216).

9. Growing internationalisation of their activities

All the Nordic parliaments have witnessed a growing internationalisation of their activities in recent years. Restated, the Nordic parliaments work in an internationalised environment and a growing number of MPs today have developed international contacts and networks (until recently only a relatively small elite of legislators would have done so). A study of the Riksdag revealed that in the 1990s approximately one in five Swedish MPs had frequent inter-national contacts, when the latter are defined as at least once or twice monthly (Brothén 2002: 59). True, cross-national survey data indicate that members of the Danish Folketing are more international in their orientation than their counterparts across the region, whereas Alþingi members are strongly Nordic in their focus (Brothén 2000: 326). Clearly, opportunities for international contacts are likely to be greater for senior politicians, some standing com-mittees have a stronger international bias and facilitate greater international contacts than others, and some MPs have a greater linguistic proficiency than others. Indeed, according to Martin Brothén, parliamentarians with the most developed international networks have 'high seniority; a leading position in the party group; a place on the Committee on Foreign Affairs; or a place in a delegation to the Nordic Council, Council of Europe or Interparliamentary Union' (Brothén 2000: 336). He concludes, however, that *committee placement* and *linguistic proficiency* have the greatest impact on the degree of international orientation in an MP's contact networks, whilst the centre-right parties have developed the most extensive links abroad.

It is consonant with the thrust of Brothén's analysis – namely, that most Nordic parliaments have *not* developed international connections – that in June 2006 the Speaker, Paavo Lipponen, founded an 'international affairs forum' in the Eduskunta designed to promote the international work of the standing committees and their role in profiling themes of relevance to Finland. None the less, over the course of 2006, over one-third of Finnish MPs (seventy-four) took an active role, either as members or substitutes, in delegations to international parliamentary meetings. These included the Nordic Council, Inter-Parliamentary Union, the General Assemblies of the Council of Europe and the Organisation for Security and Co-operation in Europe, the Arctic and Baltic Sea Councils and the interparliamentary network of the World Bank. The international profile of the Eduskunta itself was raised by the centenary exhibition which was on show in a number of national parliaments, as well as the European Parliament in Strasbourg.

Whilst the internationalisation of the environment in which the Nordic parliaments operate has stimulated a range of international contacts and networks among a (growing) minority of parliamentarians, the broader internationalisation of decision-making – not least through membership of the European Union or European Economic Area in the case of Norway and Iceland – has reduced the effective legislative ambit of the national parliaments. This is implicit in a special issue of *Scandinavian Political Studies* in which Torbjörn Bergman and Kaare Strøm distinguish between a parliament's position in relation to the executive and its position in the wider external environment. They conclude that 'reforms have strengthened the constitutional parliamentary chain' – a parliament's position *vis-à-vis* the domestic executive – but that there has also been a 'general deparliamentarisation of modern politics' (Bergman and Strøm 2004). Three broad strands in the 'deparliamentarisation thesis' may be noted briefly. The first points to a sense of reduced subjective competence among parliamentarians and the basic truth of the maxim that if situations are defined as real, they are real in their consequences; the second makes a case for the displacement of parliament as an effective agenda-setting arena; the third is premised on the increased political power of judges.

On the first point, the *internationalisation of politics* (broadly defined) has appeared to generate a diffuse feeling among parliamentarians that there has been a decline in the legitimacy and legislative capacity of the national assembly. It was this sense of loss of power to outside bodies which led the Folketing in 1997 to back the creation of a commission entitled 'An Analysis of Democracy and Power in Denmark'. Second, it is argued that the *medialisation of politics* – that is, the increasing importance of the mass media as arenas for political discourse and as a means of communicating political messages – has contributed to a 'loss of domain' for parliament. This was one of the main findings of the Norwegian Power and Democracy Commission, which reported in 2003. In essence, the parleying that matters takes place not in parliament but on radio, television and in the press. Finally, the *juridicialisation of politics* – that is, decisions increasingly being taken by domestic and international courts – it is claimed has led to an erosion of parliamentary sovereignty. In short, the separation of power between law-makers and law-interpreters has become blurred, to the detriment of the elected representatives of the people. Significantly, phrases such as the 'general deparliamentarisation of modern politics' have not been clearly defined in the literature, nor has the extent of the supposed marginalisation of parliaments in their wider external environment been subjected to systematic empirical testing. The Nordic parliaments have to an extent sought to adapt, especially through the creation of the machinery with which to 'monitor' European initiatives. Whilst the European committees have struggled in the face of the sheer volume of paperwork stemming from Brussels and the limited time available to the committee in which to scrutinise it, there has at least been a concern to design mechanisms of accountability.

Summary

1.   By 2009 (when the Lagting division of the Norwegian Storting is abolished) all the Nordic parliaments will have become unicameral 'working parliaments', based on simple majority rules for the enactment of legislation. The role of the parliamentarian is viewed as a full-time profession. A professional staff is attached to the individual MP, as well as to the standing committees and parliamentary party groups. The number of 'staffers' has grown, although it does not compare with that in the US Congress.

2.   Nordic MPs are generally recruited with a particular expertise and they function in parliament primarily in the role of policy specialists. An individual MP's principal networks will comprise actors from the same *policy community* – the policy spokespersons from the other parliamentary parties, interest groups and members of the executive, particularly officials from the government department corresponding to the MP's standing committee.

3.   Nordic MPs have become proactive in generating legislative initiatives and asking a range of questions of the executive, with the result that the workload of the Nordic parliaments has increased markedly and sittings and sessions have become longer.

4.   The Nordic parliaments now comprise fewer primary- and secondary-sector representatives (farmers, blue-collar workers, etc.), more members with a university education and, not least, more women. The feminisation of the Nordic parliaments has led more recently to some weakening of the traditional gender-based allocation of committee placements, although the point should not be overstated.

5. The two main components in the organisational infrastructure of the Nordic parliaments have comprised the system of specialist and permanent standing committees and the network of PPGs.

6. The internationalisation of the working environment of the Nordic parliaments has not been accompanied by the commensurate development of an international orientation on the part of a *majority* of MPs. Rather, the internationalisation of politics has tended to create feelings of loss of power and a concern to investigate a possible 'deparliamentarisation of politics'.

References

Andersen, Gert (1974) *Folkestyrets arbejdsplads*, Folketingets Præsidium: Beckers Papirindustri.

Arter, David (1984) *The Nordic Parliaments*, Hurst: London.

Arter, David (1987) *Politics and Policy-Making in Finland*, Wheatsheaf: Brighton.

Arter, David (1991) 'One ting too many: the shift to unicameralism in Denmark', in Lawrence D. Longley and David M. Olson (eds), *Two into One*, Westview: Boulder, CO, pp. 77–142.

Arter, David (2000a) 'From a "peasant parliament" to a "professional parliament"? Change in the Icelandic Althingi', *Journal of Legislative Studies*, 6 (2), pp. 45–66.

Arter, David (2000b) 'Change in the Swedish Riksdag: from a "part-time parliament" to a professionalised assembly?', *Journal of Legislative Studies*, 6 (3), pp. 93–116.

Arter, David (2006) *Democracy in Scandinavia*, Manchester University Press: Manchester.

Berggrav, Dag (1994) *Slik styres Norge*, Schibsted: Oslo.

Bergman, Torbjörn and Kaare Strøm (2004) 'Shifting dimensions of citizen control', *Scandinavian Political Studies*, 27 (2), pp. 89–113.

Bille, Lars (2000) 'A power centre in Danish politics', in Knut Heidar and Ruud Koole (eds), *Parliamentary Party Groups in European Democracies*, Routledge: London, pp. 130–44.

Brothén, Martin (2000) 'International networking', in Peter Esaiasson and Knut Heidar (eds), *Beyond Westminster and Congress: The Nordic Experience*, Ohio State University Press: Columbus, OH, pp. 313–43.

Brothén, Martin (2002) *I kontakt med om världen. Riksdagsledamöterna och internationaliseringen*, SNS Förlag: Stockholm.

Esaiasson, Peter and Knut Heidar (2000) 'Learning from the Nordic experience', in Peter Esaiasson and Knut Heidar (eds), *Beyond Westminster and Congress: The Nordic Experience*, Ohio State University Press: Columbus, OH, pp. 409–37.

Heidar, Knut and Ruud Koole (2000) 'Approaches to the study of parliamentary party groups', in Knut Heidar and Ruud Koole (eds), *Parliamentary Party Groups in European Democracies*, Routledge: London, pp. 1–22.

Helander, Voitto (1976) *Kamari vai kirjaamo?*, Political Science Reports 32, Turku University: Turku.

Kaartvedt, Alf (1964) 'Fra Riksforsamlingen til 1869', in *Det Norske Storting gjennom 150 år*, Gyldendal Norsk Forlag: Oslo, vol. 1, pp. 49–513.

Magnússon, Þorsteinn (1990) 'Fra tre til ett kammer', *Nordisk Kontakt*, 3, pp. 38–42.

Matthews, Donald (1960) *U.S. Senators and their World*, University of North Carolina Press: Chapel Hill, NC.

Matthews, Donald and Henry Valen (1999) *Parliamentary Representation. The Case of the Norwegian Storting*, Ohio State University Press: Columbus, OH.

Mattila, Mikko (1997) 'From qualified majority to simple majority: the effects of the 1992 change in the Finnish constitution', *Scandinavian Political Studies*, 20 (4), pp. 331–45.

Nousiainen, Jaakko (1977) 'Valiokuntalaitos', in *Suomen kansanedustuslaitoksen historia*, Kymmenes osa Valtion painatuskeskus: Helsinki, pp. 217–497.

Qvortrup, Mads (2000) 'Checks and balances in a unicameral parliament: the case of the Danish minority referendum', *Journal of Legislative Studies*, 6 (3), pp. 15–28.

Rommetvedt, Hilmar (1998) 'Norwegian parliamentary committees: performance, structural change and external relations', in Lawrence D. Longley and Roger H. Davidson (eds), *The New Roles of Parliamentary Committees*, Frank Cass: London, pp. 60–84.

Sannerstedt, Anders (1996) 'Negotiations in the Riksdag', in Lars-Göran Stenelo and Magnus Jerneck (eds), *The Bargaining Democracy*, Lund University Press: Lund, pp. 17–58.

Stjernquist, Nils (1987) 'From bicameralism to unicameralism: the democratic Riksdag, 1921–1986', in Michael F. Metcalf (ed.), *The Riksdag. A History of the Swedish Parliament*, Bank of Sweden Tercentenary Foundation: Stockholm, pp. 223–303.

Strøm, Kaare (1998) 'Parliamentary committees in European democracies', in Lawrence D. Longley and Roger H. Davidson (eds), *The New Roles of Parliamentary Committees*, Frank Cass: London, pp. 21–59.

von Sydow, Björn (1989) *Vägen till enkammarriksdagen*, Tidens förlag: Stockholm.

von Sydow, Björn (1991) 'Sweden's road to a unicameral parliament', in Lawrence D. Longley and David M. Olson (eds), *Two Into One*, Westview: Boulder, CO, pp. 143–201.

Wängnerud, Lena (2000) 'Representing women', in Peter Esaiasson and Knut Heidar (eds), *Beyond Westminster and Congress. The Nordic Experience*, Ohio State University Press: Columbus, OH, pp. 132–54.

10

'Fairly strong standing committees' and 'influential party groups' – a distinctively Nordic mix?

> There are quite simply many more similarities than differences between the Nordic parliaments on the one hand and non-Nordic parliaments operating in representative democracies on the other.
>
> (Esaiasson and Heidar, 2000: 422)

The roles and relative influence of the specialist standing committees and the parliamentary party groups (PPGs) have been the focus of increased research by Nordic legislative scholars in recent years, although their conclusions have at times appeared rather contradictory. Matthews and Valen state in respect of Norway that 'the standing committees are the most important work groups in the Storting; a large majority of the members spend most of their time and energy within the single standing committee upon which they serve' (Matthews and Valen 1999: 157). In contrast, Ingvar Mattson comments in relation to Denmark and Sweden – on the 'actor or arena?' debate – that 'committees are arenas for representatives of the parliamentary party groups, rather than unitary and integrated actors' (Mattson 1996: 138). At least these statements have the merit of being unequivocal. However, attempts to characterise the relative influence of standing committees and PPGs have also spawned phrases involving rather imprecise qualifying adverbs. Thus, as noted in the previous chapter, not untypically, Esaiasson and Heidar refer in the region as a whole to '*fairly* strong standing committees' and '*not-so-strong* group hierarchies', as well as 'influential party groups' – features which they claim distinguish the Nordic parliaments from Westminster and the US Congress (Esaiasson and Heidar 2000: 418, my italics).

This chapter is not concerned to resolve the question of the relative policy influence of standing committees and party groups. Clearly, however, conclusions cannot simply be based on surveys in which MPs have compared and rated the importance of the two. Rather, the chapter examines the main powers and functions of the Nordic standing committees, the changes in their work practices and the contribution of PPGs as autonomous policy sub-systems. Three points are to be emphasised. First, it is difficult to disagree with Esaiasson and Heidar's conclusion that 'fairly strong standing committees' and 'influential party groups' scarcely constitute a unique Nordic legislative mix. Even allowing for the problems of precise quantification, they seem typical features of many continental parliaments. Second, the role and influence of standing committees and PPGs should not simply be studied bilaterally but rather considered in the wider, dynamic context of the legislative–executive relationship. It is obvious that in situations of minority government, both standing committees and PPGs will manifest significantly greater 'actor potential' than when majority governments are in power. Third, the legislative role of standing committees and PPGs should be viewed *segmentally* – that is, in relation to the broad *policy community* of which both form part, along with other relevant actors, including interest group representatives, various experts and officials from government departments.

We noted in chapter 9 that all the Nordic parliaments have specialist and permanent standing committees, ranging in number from twelve in Iceland to twenty-four in Denmark. The standing committees vary in size from nine in Iceland (the exception is the eleven-strong Budget Committee) to seventeen in Sweden, twenty in the Norwegian Finance Committee and twenty-five in the Finnish Grand Committee. Outside Norway, the standing committee systems mirror the structure of the government departments. Bills go directly to standing committee in Norway and Sweden; in Denmark and Iceland there is a First Reading before the committee stage; and usually in Finland there is a pre-committee 'dispatch debate' (*lähetekeskustelu*). The rules relating to standing committees – the appointment of their chairs, quorate numbers, basic procedures and so on – are set out either in the constitution or in the parliamentary standing orders, or both. But what are the basic powers and functions of the Nordic parliamentary standing committees?

The powers and functions of the Nordic standing committees

Parliamentary standing committees are multi-purpose bodies that may possess any combination of five basic powers and functions. In the Nordic context their traditional – and still primary – task has been to consider government proposals (bills); their legislative and investigative functions have been at best a poor second. In recent years, however, the picture has changed somewhat and parliamentary reform has vested the standing committees with new responsibilities and a wider role, as agenda-setters and as mechanisms for holding the executive (both ministers and civil servants) to account. In what follows, a general checklist of standing committee powers and functions is applied (albeit necessarily selectively) to the parliaments in the Nordic region.

1. Legislative initiative

Standing committees may initiate legislative change independently of the executive, either by formulating legislation of their own in the shape of a *committee bill* or by requesting parliament as a whole to instigate the process of legislative change. The Swedish and Icelandic standing committees have the power of legislative initiative. The 1974 Swedish constitution vests all the Riksdag standing committees with an 'initiative right', whereas earlier this had been confined to the Constitution Committee, the Committee on Ways and Means and the Bank Committee. A report from the second Commission on the Constitution (*Grundlagberedningen*) in 1969 favoured extending the right of initiative to all standing committees. It argued that committee members had acquired a broad expertise in and understanding of a particular policy field and were thus well placed to play a more active legislative role. The Commission conceded, however, that the 'committee initiative' provision was likely to have its greatest impact during periods of minority government or when a government had only a weak parliamentary majority. It also acknowledged that the likelihood of a standing committee proposing major legislation would be small, since committees lacked the necessary resources. Committee initiatives would thus mostly be requests for commissions of inquiry to be set up on urgent and important matters.

When the Riksdag's Constitution Committee subsequently considered the government bill incorporating the committees' right of initiative, it was supportive but cautious. It presumed that the new powers would be exercised with the same degree of prudence that was displayed by the three committees previously possessing the right. For a time this was indeed the case. Jan Fredrik Richardson has noted that the committee initiative was deployed only three to four times a session between the shift to unicameralism in 1971 and the 1983/84 Riksdag (Richardson 1988: 75). He concluded that 'in the power play between the government and Riksdag, the committee initiative does not have any significance', and added that 'the more active role for parliament envisaged by the 1969 commission during periods of weak government has been channelled through the political parties, not the committee system' (Richardson 1988: 78).

Today, however, Richardson's ready dismissal of committee initiatives seems questionable, at least in so far as they have been relatively commonplace and by no means insignificant, although the vast majority have not taken the form of committee bills. Committee bills must be legally watertight and approved by the Law Council (Lagrådet) and committees do not possess the staff or legal expertise to formulate them. Moreover, the growth in the number of initiatives from individual MPs (motions) has imposed a high workload on committees and reduced the time available for generating committee bills. But if independent committee bills (still more so successful ones) have been relatively rare, other forms of committee initiatives (which require majority backing in committee) have been routine. In some cases, a unanimous committee will seek to remedy technical deficiencies in the formulation of a government proposal. At other times, committee initiatives have been used by opposition-based majorities to twist the arm of the executive on political questions. Indeed, during typical periods of minority government, the threat, or even simply the discussion, of a committee initiative may be sufficient – when brought to the minister's attention through the committee chair or via the ruling party's 'committee group' – to trigger the desired action. Failing that, opposition MPs can at least claim in the media that they have sought unstintingly but unavailingly to persuade a recalcitrant committee to proceed with a desired initiative. All in all, Sannerstedt and Sjölin's conclusion (similar in many ways to Richardson's) that 'Swedish committee initiatives [that] have concerned the technical amendment of laws and bills on "political issues" have been relatively scarce', although strictly correct, may well miss an important wider point (Sannerstedt and Sjölin 1992: 117). Committee initiatives may be designed precisely to politicise and publicise issues that *prima facie* are of an essentially technical nature, but which may well have given rise to widespread public concern. The relocation of a town from one county to another, the law on the re-trial of Swedes for offences committed abroad and the granting of residence permits to economic migrants (from Kosovo) are recent cases in point.

Unlike their Swedish counterparts, Icelandic standing committees do not possess a formal right of initiative. There is no mention of this either in the constitution or in the Alþingi standing orders. It is simply presumed that, because individual MPs have the right to propose legislation, so, too, do groups of parliamentarians in committees. However, committee bills have been relatively common, averaging about ten in each of the five annual Alþingi sessions between 1999 and 2004. Moreover, the proportion of enacted committee bills relative to the number proposed has been exceptionally high since the shift to a unicameral assembly. In the first decade of the single-chamber parliament, that is, between 1991 and 2002, the Alþingi committees proposed ninety-eight bills, of which ninety-one became law, a success rate of 92.1 per cent. Committee bills routinely reflect cross-party consensus in the committees and command unanimous backing at the third reading plenary stage. Nearly 92 per cent of the forty-eight committee bills introduced between 1999 and 2004 were passed and 89 per cent of those enacted were passed unanimously, a figure which represented a higher success rate for committee bills than for government bills (Hardarson 2005: 7).

In a large number of cases, committee bills propose the amendment of existing legislation rather than the enactment of an entirely new law. Committee bills also routinely proceed with the active co-operation and sometimes at the request of the minister and relevant government department rather than independently of the political executive. Ólafur Hardarson has even viewed committee bills as a special type of executive bill. Committee bills are in some cases a response to rules, decisions and agreements involving actors outside the parliamentary–governmental arena. For example, the Alþingi committees may propose legislative amendments following neo-corporatist agreements between the main economic interest groups. Finally, some committee bills propose conferring Icelandic citizenship on named individuals since, distinctively, separate legislation is required for each foreigner granted Icelandic citizenship.

There is no committee bill provision in Denmark and Norway but Finnish standing committees were granted a restricted right of legislative initiative as part of a proposal containing comprehensive reforms of the standing committee system introduced into the 1990/91 Eduskunta session. However, committees can initiate a 'linked committee bill' only on matters closely related to the content of a government and/or private member's bill being considered by the committee. The contiguity principle (*asiayhteysvaatimus*) is a condition of proceeding with a committee bill. Thus far, linked committee bills have been very rare.

2. Deliberation of bills and preparation of reports

Standing committees deliberate on government and (occasionally) private members' bills and prepare a committee report for consideration by the chamber. The Swedish constitution enshrines the principle of 'obligatory preparation' (*beredningstvång*) and all matters in the Riksdag must be prepared in a parliamentary standing committee before a definitive decision is taken in the chamber. Bills go directly to one of the specialist standing committees and there is no equivalent of the second reading debate in Westminster. The principle of 'obligatory preparation' is also set out in paragraph 32 of the standing orders of the Finnish Eduskunta, although most bills are given a preliminary debate in the chamber before being sent to the relevant committee. In Denmark, however, the preparation of legislation in a standing committee is not mandatory – although a bill will normally be sent to a committee after the first of three readings on the floor of the Folketing – nor is the submission of a standing committee report obligatory, although this is standard practice.

The procedures for considering proposed legislation vary from one country to the next, as do the length of committee meetings. Finnish standing committees give two 'readings' to bills. The first reading, the so-called 'expert stage', involves hearing expert witnesses from interest groups, academia and the professions. Each committee has a somewhat different approach but in the Constitution Committee, for example, about three experts (usually lawyers) are called to give evidence, although on occasions a so-called 'broad hearing' (*laaja asiantuntijakuuleminen*) involving ten or more evidence-givers is staged. Whilst across the region the deliberations of standing committees take place behind closed doors – that is, the discussions in connection with the content of the bill and committee report take place in private – in Norway and Sweden hearings *for the purposes of information-gathering* may be staged in public. In Sweden open hearings are usually a 'set-piece event' lasting two or three hours and no more. In Norway, however, multiple hearings are commonplace. Between March and May 2004, the Storting Transport Committee staged seven hearings on the 'National Transport Plan 2006–2015' and these lasted a total of 22 hours 40 minutes.

The production of the committee report is the task of the committee staff working with the committee chair. Committee reports, of course, are not necessarily unanimous and the product of cross-party consensus. Indeed, there is some evidence that, subsequent to the rise of small radical parties, minority reports and dissenting statements have become more common (Rommetvedt 2003).

3. Holding the executive to account

Standing committees hold the executive to account by monitoring the work of the government, regularly calling ministers to explain their actions and, where necessary, seeking remedial action. Interestingly, Daniel Tarschys has observed that there is no good word in Swedish for 'accountability'. Yet in Sweden, as indeed in Norway, 'control' of the executive – or at least the cross-examination of ministers – has been effectively confined to a standing committee – the Riksdag Constitution Committee's 'political review' of the government and the 'scrutiny hearings' of the Storting's Scrutiny and Constitutional Affairs Committee, respectively. Ministers only rarely appear before other committees, indicating the existence of an 'accountability deficit' when compared with the US or Westminster models of 'executive control'. Indeed, Tarschys has noted that holding the executive to account is 'very unSwedish' and adds that 'Sweden has a weak control power and a weak outcome orientation' (Tarschys 2002: 2). In Denmark, in contrast, the growing practice of so-called 'committee questions' has involved ministers routinely being called to answer questions and appearing before any of the standing committees.

The Riksdag Constitution Committee's task of inspecting the government was written into the 1809 constitution. The present 1974 constitution does not prescribe limits on the nature of the Constitution Committee's annual review (*granskningsbetänkande*), although in practice the Committee has tended to restrict itself to examining government activities from a constitutional standpoint (Arter 1984: 381–8). Since 1996 the Constitution Committee has produced two review reports annually. The first in the parliamentary year, in December, is on 'general matters' (*allmänna ärenden*). This is concerned to ensure that the procedures and norms relating to the administration of government have been faithfully observed. The matters in this *administrative review* are taken up by the Committee staff and typically lead to criticisms of such things as dilatory ministerial responses to parliamentary questions and the length of the period between the enactment and implementation of laws. The Constitution Committee's second report, in May, deals with 'special matters' (*särskilda ärenden*). The 'special matters' in this *political review* involve investigating the action of ministers – largely on the basis of 'review requests' (*anmälningar*) from legislators – often through staging open hearings (Arter 2004: 173–4). In principle the Constitution Committee has the right to decide whether to consider a review request; in practice, the convention has been that a parliamentarian is entitled to a reply in the Committee's annual report (however brief).

The remit of the nine-member Scrutiny and Constitutional Affairs Committee is broad, although in practice the bulk of its relatively heavy workload has involved investigations based on the reports of the Office of the Auditor General (*Riksrevisjonen*). Of the twelve 'scrutiny hearings' staged in the 2001–5 Storting, exactly two-thirds emanated from the reports of the Auditor General. Unlike the Riksdag Constitution Committee, its Norwegian sister committee does not undertake investigative activity on the basis of 'review requests' from parliamentarians. However, the Scrutiny and Constitutional Affairs Committee is the only Storting committee to have the right to instigate a hearing on matters within the public administration, that decision being taken by one-third of its members. Other standing committees may investigate only those matters referred to them by the Storting. The sole exception to this rule is the Defence Committee, which, exceptionally, may initiate a hearing in respect of its task of 'continuously monitoring the preparedness' of the armed forces.

Claims that the investigative ('political control') function of the Swedish and Norwegian parliaments has become endemically party politicised – and by extension undermined – have centred on the hearings that form part of the Riksdag Constitution Committee's 'political review' of the government and the 'scrutiny hearings' of the Storting's Scrutiny and Constitutional Affairs Committee. In the Norwegian case, Fredrik Sejersted has asserted that 'it is an illusion to believe that a Storting committee comprising party politicians can exercise politically neutral control' (Sejersted 2000: 183). In Sweden, Olof Petersson has pointed to the classical structural dilemma of achieving effective parliamentary control of the executive in a strongly party politicised legislature. 'Constitution Committee members are placed in an impossible dual role. On the one hand, they are responsible for a statesman-like inspection of constitutional democracy. On the other, they are party politicians who are driven by a wholly legitimate desire to maximise their votes in the coming election' (Petersson 2006).

The party politicisation of the Constitution Committee's 'political review' has been an intermittent complaint of governing parties, no more so than between 1991 and 1994, when Sweden was led by a four-party, non-socialist minority coalition and, exceptionally, the Social Democrats found themselves in opposition. Plainly, when the conduct of ministers, and particularly the prime minister, is being investigated, media interest will be aroused and opposition groups will seek to gain a tactical advantage. Many of the Riksdag Constitution Committee's investigative hearings, moreover, have been prompted by 'review requests' and in the 2002–6 Riksdag these emanated exclusively from opposition legislators and were intended to discomfort the government.

Broadly speaking, the greater the level of public sensitivity to an issue, the more likely it is that the opposition will seek to make political capital out of it. This was certainly true of the seven public hearings which the Riksdag Constitution Committee staged in spring 2006 in connection with its investigation into the minority Social Democratic government's handling of the Asian *tsunami* disaster (in which 543 Swedes lost their lives). Furthermore, when in February–March 2005 the Norwegian Scrutiny and Constitutional Affairs Committee probed budget irregularities in the defence ministry, the hearings were politicised to such an extent that there was talk of the opposition moving a vote of no confidence in the minister, Kristin Krohn Devold.

Yet, whilst the proceedings of high-profile investigative hearings played out in public have invariably been party politicised, the committee may behind closed doors produce a unanimous report – as in the *tsunami* case. Moreover, whilst opposition parties will normally share the goal of discrediting the government, tactical differences between them may dictate that a minister under pressure will survive. In the Devold case, the two main opposition parties, Labour and the Progress Party, ultimately disagreed on the use of a no-confidence motion and the Labour leader, Jens Stoltenberg, was unwilling to unseat the government so close to an election.

The Riksdag Constitution Committee's review of the government's handling of the Asian *tsunami* aftermath – an inquiry it initiated itself – is particularly interesting in so far as it appeared to reveal the existence of twin cultures. There was a 'party culture' evident in the adversarial nature of the hearings and a parallel 'committee culture' evident from the production of a unanimous committee report, which criticised the government (and ultimately the prime minister) for not having a functioning crisis-management apparatus. The public hearings had involved political points-scoring but, in the end, experienced committee members, including those representing the governing Social Democrats, combined forces in the face of the harsh realities of the tragedy.

'Committee questions' (*samrådsspørgsmål*) in Denmark provide a means of obtaining information from ministers on any matter falling within his/her area of responsibility and not just a bill currently being considered in standing committee. The Folketing standing orders state that 'a committee can request a minister to answer a question put by the committee'; the question is to be submitted in writing and the committee can request either a written response or a reply in person from the minister and a 'consultation' (*samråd*) with the committee. The number of these 'consultations' varies considerably between the committees. Committee questions are usually tabled by an individual committee member on behalf of the committee, but they must, of course, be approved by the committee and are vetted by the committee secretary to ensure, among other things, that they do not express partisan viewpoints that are not acceptable to the committee, or at least its majority.

In fact, far from reflecting a common committee position, as the term suggests, Henrik Jensen (1994) has shown how 'committee questions' are mainly tabled by opposition members in the role of 'partisan'. When the question put is particularly technical and/or detailed, some ministers may request civil servants to accompany them to the 'consultation'. Other ministers have been opposed in principle to involving civil servants (Hess and Thøgersen 2001: 76–7). Consultations may be held in public and the incidence of open committee consultations has risen sharply in recent years. In the 2001–5 Folketing term, the number of (closed) 'committee consultations' climbed year on year, from 611 in the 2001/2 session to 689 in 2004/5. At the same time, the number of 'open consultations' increased over tenfold, from 28 in 2001/2 to 293 in 2004/5. In the last-mentioned year, 30 per cent of all 'committee consultations' were held in public. In the routine Danish situation of minority government – since 2001 non-socialist minority coalitions led by the Liberal Anders Fogh Rasmussen have been in office – public 'committee consultations' represent a means by which opposition parties can put a minister 'on the spot' and in the spotlight in relation to politically sensitive and controversial questions. In any event, the figure of 982 'committee consultations' in the 2001–5 Folketing testifies to the vastly greater extent to which cabinet ministers are rendered accountable to Danish standing committees compared with the practice in Norway and Sweden.

4. Post-legislative scrutiny (follow-up and evaluation work)

Standing committees may engage in post-legislative scrutiny in the form of follow-up and evaluation work. Thus far, this has been an exclusively Swedish practice and has reflected the growing emphasis placed on the need to shift the orientation of committee work away from legislative scrutiny – the deliberation of executive bills – towards inquiries and analyses undertaken on the committee's own initiative. In June 1993 the report of a commission entitled *Reform the Riksdag's Work* held that committees should undertake what was described as 'follow-up and evaluation' work in their particular area of jurisdiction. Seven years later, a parliamentary committee of inquiry, chaired by the Riksdag Speaker, Birgitta Dahl, reasserted this case and in 2001 the Riksdag Act was amended to require standing committees to undertake post-legislative scrutiny. This was less than enthusiastically received for the most part. In its main report, entitled *Parliament in a New Era*, completed in December 2005, a new parliamentary committee noted that follow-up and evaluation had not become an integral part of committee work and that a much greater emphasis on it was needed.

In the main, follow-up and evaluation projects, and the policy review hearings that often constitute (the public or private) part of them, have involved holding to account those charged with the administration of legislation – the general directors and senior officials in the vast network of central boards and agencies (Labour Market Board, Transport Board, Nature Protection Agency, etc.). The policy review hearings held in public have been the tip of the iceberg, since the bulk of follow-up activity takes place behind the scenes. There has in fact evolved a variety of ways of undertaking review work, notably the creation of cross-party evaluation sub-groups assisted by committee staff and possibly, too, outside experts on short-term contracts. A degree of follow-up and evaluation activity operates through the informal contacts between the committee secretariats and government officials, public bodies and pressure groups. Moreover, committee staff may be asked by the committee to explore the bases for embarking on an evaluation project. Alternatively, the staff may itself initiate a review project. Plainly, whilst follow-up and evaluation work has largely involved delegation rather than action by the full committee, the policy review function, earlier performed through the commission system, may be said to have passed in at least modest measure to the Riksdag committees.

A possible criticism of the functioning of the follow-up and evaluation process is that the selection of witnesses, a task primarily undertaken by the committee staff, may, to an extent, have undermined the capacity of the committees to generate the independent information necessary really to undertake effective policy review. Restated, the evidence obtained through the process of policy review derives in significant measure from officials in the very central boards the committees are supposed to be reviewing. Well over one-quarter (27.5 per cent) of all witnesses attending public committee hearings in the 2002–6 Riksdag were employed in central boards and agencies. None the less, several committees have used open policy review hearings to highlight prioritised themes and to draw the attention of the government and the relevant organised interests to them.

5. Agenda-setting

Standing committees may well perform an agenda-setting role. There are a variety of ways in which this can be done – either through regular standing committees operating in essentially non-legislative mode or through the work of expressly non-legislative committees. The specialist standing committees may, for example, organise *ad hoc* events – seminars in the chamber and so on – designed to profile particular themes. The Finnish Social Affairs and Health Committee organised two such events in 2006 – one, organised in conjunction with the Lions and Child Protection League, focused on child protection, whilst the other, opened by the social affairs and health minister, dealt with adoption. In the 2002–6 Riksdag, the Speaker, Björn von Sydow, launched two events specifically designed to prompt the standing committees to reflect on their activities and to think beyond their immediate workload, to future priorities. The first, a so-called 'research day' (*forskningsdag*) in March 2004, probed the interaction between research and policy, whilst the second, the 'future days' (*framtidsdagar*) in March 2005, followed the recommendation of a commission entitled Riksdag on the Threshold of the New Millennium (*Riksdag inför 2000-talet*), which held that committees should plan their work more thematically and adopt a longer-term perspective. There has in fact been some support among Swedish parliamentarians for a designated Finnish-style Committee for the Future (*tulevaisuusvaliokunta*).

The latter is a good example of an expressly non-legislative committee designed to set a future agenda and the Finnish Eduskunta was in 1993 the first parliament in the world to create a committee specifically mandated to deal in scenario-building and the projection of the likely course of developments over the decade or so ahead. The Committee for the Future was given permanent standing committee status in 2000 (Arter 2000) and today its primary remit is to consider the *Report on the Future* which the government is obliged to submit to parliament at least once in the four-year electoral cycle. In addition, the committee identifies a number of leading themes at the beginning of each new Eduskunta term. In the 2003–7 Eduskunta, the main theme was 'A Good Society for all Ages', which involved analysing the challenges of adapting to demographic change and in particular the realities of declining fertility and increased life expectancy. A continuing theme of the Committee for the Future has been the impact of technology, especially but not exclusively information technology, on society. The Committee routinely commissions analyses from research institutes and other external bodies and consults widely with experts both at home and abroad. The Committee's most recent output was a study entitled *Russia 2017: Three Scenarios*, which was distributed widely outside Finland. Indeed, the Committee for the Future is the most 'internationalised' of the Eduskunta's standing committees and in 2007 it played host to the Fifth General Assembly of the International Parliamentarians' Association for Information Technology, on the theme 'Human Competency Development in the Information Society'.

The changing work practices of the Nordic standing committees

It is ironic that, for all the reputation of the Nordic countries for open, transparent government, the work of their parliamentary standing committee systems has been until recently as closed and secretive as the Vatican! The conventional wisdom has been that closed meetings discourage 'grandstanding' and conduce towards consensus-building. The committees have been closed, too, in lacking structured contact with the population at large. For example, there is no German-style Petitions Committee, which, with its sizeable staff, takes up a range of matters raised by citizens, whilst in the case of the Scottish Parliament access to its Petitions Committee is also possible through an electronic petitions procedure. It is not common, either, in the Nordic parliaments for *rapporteurs* to be working 'in the field' on tasks assigned to them by the committee or, indeed, for sub-committees to be created (the Finance/Budget committees are the exception). Rather, as the workload of committees has grown, so too has the dependency on their limited staff resources. The standing committees, of course, conduct study trips and fact-finding visits, both at home and abroad. But the principle of representative democracy is strictly observed and the standing committees have not been designed to serve as an essential link between the state (at least its legislative arm) and civil society. There has been no attempt to incorporate elements of participatory democracy. However, perhaps the most notable change in the work practices of the standing committees in Sweden and Norway – signalling a modest shift towards more open procedures – has been the introduction of open hearings.

Moves to introduce public committee hearings in Sweden originated in opposition party circles in the late 1960s, which was when Giovanni Sartori first described Sweden as a *one-party dominant system*, governed continuously since 1932 (except for a few months in 1936) by the Social Democrats (Arter 2008). In a private member's bill in 1967, two senior, opposition-based, non-socialist politicians, Per Ahlmark (Liberals) and Torbjörn Fälldin (Centre), proposed the introduction of public committee hearings, but the initiative was summarily rejected. They responded the following year by producing an unusually long private member's bill on the same topic, which was in fact written by the Liberal Daniel Tarschys. Tarschys had witnessed Congressional hearings during visits to the United States in the 1960s and became an active campaigner for open hearings when a member of the Riksdag Constitution Committee between 1976 and 1982. Indeed, the follow-up Ahlmark–Fälldin bill contained an extensive preamble describing in very basic terms the nature of US committee hearings at the time of the so-called 'textbook Congress'. The bill was rejected, although the question of public hearings was taken up by the Constitutional Law Commission, which reported in 1972. The Commission was divided, the majority being particularly concerned about what it saw as the inevitable party politicisation of proceedings if committee hearings became public events. This, it was believed, would undermine the consensual culture of Riksdag committees. It was also feared that committees would emerge as rival actors to plenary meetings and divert interest away from full-sitting debates. The risk that a committee's scrutiny of measures could suffer as a result of the 'party politics factor' was the primary reason why the majority on the Constitutional Law Commission came out against public hearings. In sharp contrast, the Democracy Commission (*Folkstyrelsekommitté*), which reported in 1987, was united in favouring open hearings.

The Swedish model of public committee hearings is a far cry from the US Congressional practice on which it is loosely based. In a so-called 'special statement' (*särskilt yttrande*) appended to the Trade and Industry Committee's response to the Constitution Committee's report on the 1987 government bill proposing public hearings, the seven non-socialist members expressed the view that a minority of at least five members should have the right to demand a public hearing. In fact, however, the decision to stage an open hearing requires a majority of committee members. It may be organised only for the purposes of 'obtaining information' and a committee has no authority to summon witnesses, conduct proceedings under oath or impose sanctions. When in spring 2006, in connection with the Constitution Committee's public hearings on the government's handling of the Asian *tsunami* disaster, the Christian Democrat leader, Göran Hägglund, proposed cross-examining witnesses under oath, the suggestion was widely opposed.

Interest in public committee hearings in Norway could be dated back to 1973 and a request from the Storting member Tønnes Andenæs for information about how hearings worked in other countries. Thereafter, a number of individual legislators acted as *issue entrepreneurs*, most notably the Progress Party leader Carl I. Hagen, who in 1977 proposed open hearings – with committees broadly empowered to require witnesses to attend – and he took the matter up again in an approach to the Storting Presidium in January 1985. But it was the proposal from Petter Thomassen, the chair of the revamped Scrutiny and Constitutional Affairs Committee, which prompted the Committee in 1994 to visit its counterpart in the Swedish Riksdag, where it was impressed with what it heard. The subsequent decision in October 1995 to introduce public committee hearings on a two-year experimental basis – extended for a further two years in 1997 – was taken by a majority of only one (eighty to seventy-nine) in the Storting. Five years later, however, there was an overwhelming consensus among Norwegian legislators in favour of making the experiment permanent. The 2001 Norwegian model of public committee hearings shared several of the features of the 1988 Swedish blueprint. There was to be no compunction on the part of witnesses to attend and answer questions and there was to be no exchange of views between members during a public hearing. Yet in other respects there was evidence of *institutional mutation* – the Norwegian model of public committee hearings displayed features which differentiated it from that of its Swedish neighbour.

The point of departure in Norway – enshrined in article 21 of the Storting's Rules of Procedure – was the principle that *all* 'committee hearings' were to be open, although meetings held wholly or partly in camera required only a majority decision of the committee. Paradoxically, however, there also appeared the presumption that public records of the proceedings of hearings in Norway would not be routinely kept, since a committee's decision to take stenographic minutes required the consent of the Storting Presidium. Special detailed rules, incorporated into the Storting's Rules of Procedure in June 2001, were to apply to the so-called 'scrutiny hearings' conducted by the Scrutiny and Constitutional Affairs Committee. Significantly, unlike the Swedish Constitution Committee, one-third of members of the Scrutiny and Constitutional Affairs Committee were entitled to demand a 'scrutiny hearing'. All in all, the introduction of public committee hearings in Scandinavia involved a process of two-step legislative diffusion – one step away from the US Congressional model in Sweden and one step away from the Swedish model in Norway.

The early proponents of public committee hearings came primarily from the non-socialist opposition parties, but their case was not predicated (openly at least) on the need to consolidate the 'control function' of the legislature or increase the accountability of executives long dominated by the Social Democrats. Rather, the manifest rationale for the change in work practice of committees was the need to increase public interest in, and popular understanding of, the legislature and in particular the work of its specialist committees. Giving greater transparency to the legislative process would enhance the legitimacy of parliament and reduce the 'democratic deficit'.

There has been a significant increase in the frequency of public committee hearings in both Sweden and Norway. Between February 1988 and the September 2006 general election, the Riksdag committees staged 507 public hearings. There were 360 between the 1988/89 and 2001/2 Riksdag sessions – an average of 25.7 per annum – and 147 public hearings in the 2002–6 Riksdag term – an average of 36.8 per annum. The number of open hearings fell to 28 in the pre-election 2005/6 session but rose to 37 in the 2006/7 session (including those staged by the European Affairs Committee). In the Norwegian Storting just over 30 public committee hearings were held during the experimental period between 1996 and 2000, but no less than 422 in 2001/5.

In the Swedish case, much of the recent rise in the number of public committee hearings can be attributed to the implementation of the follow-up and evaluation directive in 2001 obliging Riksdag committees to engage in post-legislative scrutiny, whilst stimulus for non-legislative hearings was provided by von Sydow's research and future days. In the Norwegian case, at least four factors appear to account for the escalation in the number of hearings in the 2001–5 Storting. First, Norwegian hearings are public by definition – there is no provision for closed hearings. Second, the number was inflated by the practice of holding multiple hearings on the same topic, a procedure dictated in part by such practical considerations as the ruling that committee hearings may not take place when the plenary is in session. Third, Kjell Magne Bondevik's second non-socialist coalition between 2001 and 2005, although a minority cabinet, pursued a bold, at times controversial programme – including the privatisation of state companies and the buying and selling of fish quotas – and, accordingly, hearings were used (especially by the opposition) to debate both the principles and the practice of these far-reaching proposals. Finally, the relative frequency of Norwegian hearings has reflected their perceived value for interest groups. Groups often press committees to stage hearings, so giving neo-corporatism in Norway a curiously parliamentary dimension.

Just how far the change in work practice with the introduction of open hearings has increased public interest in, and popular understanding of, the legislative process must remain an open question. If public interest can be measured by television viewing figures (admittedly a crude indicator) their record seems mixed. Millions of Swedes watched the Constitution Committee hearings over the summer of 1988 into the publisher Ebbe Carlsson's highly controversial private investigation into the murder in February 1986 of the prime minister, Olof Palme. In contrast, an open hearing on the new pensions system staged by the Riksdag's Social Insurance Committee in March 2001, which was televised in the afternoon and, exceptionally, included questions to the responsible minister attracted an audience of about 30,000 – and the minister was impressed by that number of viewers!

The parliamentary party groups at work

Esaiasson and Heidar's reference to 'influential party groups' in the Nordic parliaments warrants some qualification. Clearly, there is a difference in influence – or at least the manner in which influence is exerted – between party groups on the governing side and those in opposition. The former will have direct contact with the minister, who will need the backing of the PPG to proceed with planned legislation. Party groups in opposition, in contrast, will seek to influence primarily by generating and promoting alternative policies.

A distinction also needs to be drawn between large and small PPGs. The larger the parliamentary party, the more the substantial growth in its financial capacity will lead to a *professionalisation* of its PPG. In the Nordic context, the introduction of state subsidies to PPGs (Denmark in 1965, Finland in 1967, Norway in 1970 and Sweden in 1975) gave them the resources to buy in expertise, create policy research units and develop press agencies. The level of secretarial assistance and, by extension, the overall staff of the larger PPGs have increased significantly. In Sweden in 2004 the staff of the largest party, the Social Democrats, numbered eighty, compared with twenty-one for the smallest group, the Greens. Moreover, the larger the party the more the internal organisation of its PPG will be characterised by *specialisation and segmentation* and the absence of a hierarchical power structure. Simplifying somewhat, whilst the PPG leader and an elected group board will bear responsibility for the general management of the group, policy matters will devolve in significant measure to the network of 'committee groups'. Committee groups mirror the structure of the parliamentary standing committee system and comprise those backbench members of the PPG who belong to a particular standing committee (or sometimes related group of standing committees). Committee groups form policy communities in their own right and lead to the *de facto* segmentation and decentralisation of decision-making referred to above.

Restated, in the larger parties, PPG decision-making will follow horizontal rather than simply vertical lines of authority. The committee groups are strategic actors and individual members may be assigned important duties as *rapporteurs*, reporting back to the whole PPG on the matter at hand. Magnus Isberg's work on Swedish PPGs indicated that, in substantive policy terms, it was the horizontal axis that was decisive and that full PPG meetings generally rubber-stamped the line formulated in the committee groups (Isberg 1999). Findings from the other Nordic countries point in a similar direction. Commenting on Norway, Hilmar Rommetvedt has noted that 'on a day-to-day basis I would expect the committee groups (*komitefraksjoner*) to be more influential in relation to most specific issues than the group boards' of the Storting parties (Arter 2006: 261). All in all, the larger the PPG the greater the scope (and need) for the dispersal of policy roles among members and the greater the potential for individuals and sub-groups to specialise in particular policy fields. There will be a two-way flow of authority, downwards from the group executive, but also laterally from the sub-groups that present proposals to the full PPG meeting. The committee groups will also in all likelihood have extensive contacts with experts and outside organised interests.

More or less independent of size, the PPGs of parties in opposition will comprise autonomous policy sub-systems engaged in the process of generating and articulating policy alternatives. These policy alternatives (outputs) will typically range from the production of an 'alternative budget' and the determination of a 'party line' on a specific issue to the decision to table an interpellation or submit a party motion. Parliamentary opposition parties will, of course, possess variable staff and financial resources and different policy capacities. The process of formulating and finalising opposition policy will involve the interplay of a variety of actors – individual MPs, committee groups, *ad hoc* working groups and members of the group secretariat – within the PPG. In other words, the parliamentary group will be both a policy actor *and* policy arena – an arena for the process of generating policy alternatives and an actor in promoting the outputs (increment) of the process in parliament at large.

Whilst PPGs are for the most part a highly secretive world closed to outside scrutiny, each will have its own culture and style. When Katarina Barrling Hermansson investigated the party culture in the Swedish PPGs – based on interviews and direct observation during the 1998–2002 Riksdag – she emphasised, among other things, the cultural differences between the opposition non-socialist groups. The Conservatives' group, for instance, was hierarchical and collectivist, whereas the Liberals comprised a group of individuals without an unthinking sense of conformity (*jantelag*). She concluded that the PPG culture can impinge on policy-making and both facilitate and complicate communication between parties (Barrling Hermansson 2004).

Independent of the PPG's size and internal organisation, its position in government or opposition, the 'group chemistry' will be affected by a host of factors, including ideological schisms (new or old), generational tensions, regional allegiances, the continuity of group membership, personal ambitions and antagonisms, and the quality of group leadership. In general, however, group cohesion has been high and the larger parties have only occasionally experienced a measure of factionalisation (or, perhaps more exactly, the existence of conflicting 'tendencies'). Norms of group loyalty are strong and Westminster-style whipping is alien to Scandinavian practice. As Torben K. Jensen has noted, 'in all the Nordic countries, only a miniscule share of all individual votes cast on parliamentary roll calls break with the party position', whilst 85 per cent of Nordic parliamentarians have indicated that they are satisfied with the norm of adhering to the party line (Jensen 2000: 232, 222).

Jensen attaches considerable importance to the growth in the workload of parliamentarians in explaining a long-term increase in group cohesion. The increased workload has resulted in specialisation and a more elaborate division of labour among MPs, which, in turn, has made it impossible for individual group members to follow each and every legislative issue closely. They are obliged to rely on the expertise of their colleagues.

The conventional wisdom is that the PPGs are the dominant actors in the Nordic parliaments. Matti Wiberg writes in respect of Finland that 'the status of the PPGs is not legally regulated, but in practice the groups have the most important role in decision-making inside the Eduskunta' (Wiberg 2000: 173). Knut Heidar, referring to the Nordic countries as a whole, has hypothesised that 'multiparty systems and frequent coalition governments have nurtured strong party groups in all five countries' (Heidar 2000: 184). He does not define what is meant by 'strong' but it is clear it is strong in the sense that parliamentarians believe the PPGs are powerful. In all the Nordic parliaments except the Swedish, it seems, PPGs are considered by parliamentarians to be more powerful than the standing committees and in Denmark the differential is as much as 20 percentage points (Heidar 2000: 202). MPs also believe PPG debates are important and try to make an impact at meetings (Heidar 2000: 205). Heidar seeks to explain strength in the PPGs in terms of the absence (any longer) of a dominant party, which has meant that 'the Nordic parliaments are in high degree negotiating parliaments' (Heidar 2000: 208). The programmatic compromises and operational priorities are determined in the PPGs.

In his analysis of the Danish PPGs, Henrik Jensen argues that decision-making in the groups, as in the legislative process as a whole, is dispersed in both time and space. It is an atomised process where the work and influences moulding a PPG's day-to-day decisions are spread out and devolve first and foremost to individual policy spokespersons and (when the party is in government) ministers. They, in turn, will invariably have contact with a network of external actors – the party in the country, interest groups, experts, journalists and so on – and there will be a multilateral flow of communication between them. Consequently, decision-making should be viewed as an incremental process, fashioned in a variety of forums such as the full chamber, Folketing standing committee rooms, PPG rooms and government ministries. The implicit thrust of Jensen's submission is that the genesis of majority-building in Denmark should be sought in the relevant policy community, where a variety of cognate actors, including parliamentarians, work to construct the necessary support for legislative change (Jensen 2002: 216–18).

Summary

1. All the Nordic parliaments have multi-purpose, policy-based standing committees, constituted for the full electoral term, which facilitate and

promote the individual and collective expertise of their members. The standing committees, in short, have considerable 'actor potential' – the capacity to be unitary, integrated and autonomous players in the legislative process. In fact, the (limited) evidence suggests that the Nordic standing committees appear to function more as arenas for the registration of differing party standpoints than actors in their own right, although parliamentarians undoubtedly attach much importance to their work in the standing committees.

2.   Specialist standing committee systems are the norm outside the House of Commons and the French National Assembly, and the Nordic parliaments, although boasting distinctive committees, such the Finnish Committee for the Future, are not distinctive in having policy-based committees. The investigative role of the Nordic standing committees has been strengthened and their agenda-setting capacity reinforced, but their primary task remains the traditional one of deliberating and reporting on executive bills.

3.   The Nordic parliaments have varying numbers of PPGs to which members (outside Sweden) attach primary importance. The PPGs have differing rules, organisational features and legislative cultures, but they have one thing in common – it is in the PPG that the 'party line' is determined, whilst norms of loyalty ensure that, for the most part, it is observed without Westminster-style whipping. PPGs are, of course, an integral element in the legislative process across continental Europe. It is difficult, therefore, to dissociate from Esaiasson and Heidar's conclusion that the combination of 'fairly strong standing committees' and 'influential party groups' (even allowing for the adverbial imprecision) does *not* constitute a 'distinctively Nordic mix'.

4.   Attempts to compare and characterise the relative influence of the standing committees and PPGs in the Nordic parliaments have been (too) narrow in focus and the supposition of the pre-eminence of the party groups has lacked firm empirical grounding. The role of both standing committees and PPGs needs to be placed in the wider context of the legislative–executive relationship and, indeed, the dynamics of the policy process as a whole.

5.   As Henrik Jensen's analysis of the Danish party groups implies, the PPGs (or at least the relevant committee groups and individuals within them) are members of a particular policy community, to which MPs from other parties, interest group representatives, miscellaneous experts and executive officials also belong. In other words, the legislative role of standing committees and PPGs should be viewed segmentally – each policy-specific segment bringing together relevant parliamentary and non-parliamentary actors, who act and interact to produce legislative change.

6.   In accounting for the influence of the Nordic PPGs in terms of the absence of a dominant party, Knut Heidar implies the need to view the role of PPGs – and, it might be added, standing committees – in the broader perspective of the legislative–executive relationship. In situations of minority government, both standing committees and PPGs will possess significantly

greater 'actor potential' or at least will serve as important negotiating sites for government–opposition consensus-building.

7. Minority government has become routine in Denmark, Norway and Sweden in recent decades, prompting Anders Sannerstedt to claim that 'negotiations between the political parties [in these three legislatures] are more common than in other types of democratic system' (Sannerstedt 1996: 54). The following chapter investigates this assertion whilst focusing on the executive at work.

References

Arter, David (1984) *The Nordic Parliaments*, Hurst: London.

Arter, David (2000) 'The model for parliaments in the future? The case of the Finnish Committee for the Future', *Politiikka*, 42 (3), pp. 149–63.

Arter, David (2004) *The Scottish Parliament: A Scandinavian-Style Assembly?*, Frank Cass: London.

Arter, David (2006) *Democracy in Scandinavia*, Manchester University Press: Manchester.

Arter, David (2008) 'From "parliamentary control" to "accountable government"? The role of public committee hearings in the Swedish Riksdag', *Parliamentary Affairs*, 61 (1), pp. 122–43.

Barrling Hermansson, K. (2004) *Partikulturer. Kollektiva självbilder och normer i Sveriges riksdag*, Acta universitatis upsaliensis: Uppsala.

Esaiasson, Peter and Knut Heidar (2000) 'Learning from the Nordic experience', in Peter Esaiasson and Knut Heidar (eds), *Beyond Westminster and Congress. The Nordic Experience*, Ohio State University Press: Columbus, OH, pp. 409–37.

Hardarson, Ólafur Th. (2005) 'The Icelandic Althingi – a strong parliament?', paper presented at the ECPR Joint Sessions of Workshops, Granada, 14–19 April.

Heidar, Knut (2000) 'Parliamentary party groups', in Peter Esaiasson and Knut Heidar (eds), *Beyond Westminster and Congress. The Nordic Experience*, Ohio State University Press: Columbus, OH, pp. 183–209.

Hess, Mikkel Hagen and Andreas Fugl Thøgersen (2001) *Folketingets Arbejdt*, Høst: København.

Isberg, Magnus (1999) *Riksdagledamoten i sinn partigrupp*, Gidlunds Förlag: Södertälje.

Jensen, Henrik (1994) 'Committees as actors or arenas', in Matti Wiberg (ed.), *Parliamentary Control in the Nordic Countries*, Gummerus: Jyväskylä, pp. 77–102.

Jensen, Henrik (2002) *Partigrupperne i Folketinget*, Jurist- og Økonomsforbundets Forlag: København.

Jensen, Torben K. (2000) 'Party cohesion', in Peter Esaiasson and Knut Heidar (eds), *Beyond Westminster and Congress. The Nordic Experience*, Ohio State University Press: Columbus, OH, pp. 210–36.

Matthews, Donald R. and Henry Valen (1999) *Parliamentary Representation. The Case of the Norwegian Storting*, Ohio State University Press: Columbus, OH.

Mattson, Ingvar (1996) 'Negotiations in parliamentary committees', in Lars-Göran Stenelo and Magnus Jerneck (eds), *The Bargaining Democracy*, Lund University Press: Lund, pp. 61–144.

Petersson, Olof (2006) 'KU:s uppgift att granska regeringen fungerar inte', *Dagens Nyheter*, 21 February.

Richardson, Jan Fredrik (1988) 'Riksdagsutskottens initiativrätt i den nya enkammarriksdagen', *Statsvetenskapliga Tidskrift*, 91 (1), pp. 75–9.

Rommetvedt, Hilmar (2003) *The Rise of the Norwegian Parliament*, Frank Cass: London.

Sannerstedt, Anders (1996) 'Negotiations in the Riksdag', in Lars-Göran Stenelo and Magnus Jerneck (eds), *The Bargaining Democracy*, Lund University Press: Lund, pp. 17–58.

Sannerstedt, A. and M. Sjölin (1992) 'Sweden: changing party relations in a more active parliament', in Erik Damgaard (ed.), *Parliamentary Change in the Nordic Countries*, Universitetsforlaget: Oslo, pp. 99–149.

Sejersted, Fredrik (2000) 'Stortingets kontrollfunksjon', *Nytt Norsk Tidskrift*, 2, pp. 173–85.

Tarschys, Daniel (2002) *För tomma hus. Om Riksdagen som vår politiska nationscen*, Stockholm: Bertil Ohlin-Institutet.

Wiberg, Matti (2000) 'The partyness of the Finnish Eduskunta', in Knut Heidar and Ruud Koole (eds), *Parliamentary Party Groups in European Democracies*, Routledge: London, pp. 161–76.

11

Nordic government(s): parliamentary, presidential or prime ministerial?

> It is evident that Finland has been moving closer to the parliamentary states of Western Europe and that there are hardly any grounds for the epithet 'semi-presidential.
>
> (Nousiainen 2001: 108)

This chapter focuses on the *executive–parties dimension* (Lijphart 1999) and in particular on two striking differences in the nature of the political executive across the Nordic region. First, there is the contrast, in Lijphart's terms, between the *executive–legislative balance* systems of the 'metropolitan' Scandinavian states of Denmark, Norway and Sweden and the *executive dominant* systems of Finland and Iceland. Bjørn Erik Rasch (2004: 131) has noted that the two distinctive features of the Scandinavian form of parliamentarism have been the prevalence of minority governments and the frequency of single-party cabinets. The last majority coalition in Denmark, for example, left office in 1994, having survived barely twelve months. In Finland and Iceland, however, broad-based, majority governments have been the norm, the first so-called 'rainbow coalition' in Finland between 1995 and 1999, under Social Democrat Paavo Lipponen, commanding the backing of nearly three-quarters of the Eduskunta seats. Second, there is the contrast, in Duverger's (1980) terms, between the *semi-presidential systems* of Finland and Iceland and the *parliamentary governments* in Denmark, Norway and Sweden. In Finland, in particular, the 1919 constitution vested the head of state with significant veto powers in respect of government formation, the dissolution of parliament and the ratification of legislation. During the last decade in power of the long-serving Urho Kekkonen (1956–81) it might not have been wholly inappropriate to refer to the existence of 'presidential government' in Finland.

The adoption of a new constitution on 1 March 2000, however, reduced the role of the head of state and meant that Finland was no longer a case of semi-presidential government other than in the minimalist sense of a 'situation where a popularly-elected, fixed-term president exists alongside a prime minister and cabinet who are responsible to parliament' (Elgie 2004: 317). The head of state no longer possesses 'quite significant powers' (Duverger 1980); rather, the new constitution has elevated the role of the prime minister. Since the recent Scandinavian political science literature has pointed to the growing importance of the office of the prime minister, the final section of the chapter examines whether a fundamental convergence across the region has witnessed the emergence of prime minister-dominant parliamentary executives.

'Executive–legislative balance' and 'executive dominant' systems

A striking feature of the political executive in the Nordic region has been the diversity of coalition types and the frequency of minority governments. Cabinets have ranged from numerically weak, single-party minority administrations with less than one-ninth of the legislative seats behind them – as in Sweden between 1978 and 1979 – to 'surplus majority' coalitions with the backing of between two-thirds and three-quarters of the seats in parliament – as in Finland between 1995 and 2003. The contrast between the size of cabinets in metropolitan Scandinavia and elsewhere in the region has been marked. Of the forty-three governments in Denmark, Norway and Sweden between 1970/71 and the 2005 general elections in the first two of those countries, thirty-three (88 per cent) were minority governments. In Iceland, however, majority governments have been in power for over 90 per cent of the period since the achievement of independence in 1944 and since 1979 there have been only two minority coalitions. There has been only one minority cabinet in Finland in the same period and since 1983 every government has been either a majority or 'surplus majority' coalition. In short, the distinction would appear to be between 'executive–legislative balance' systems, on the one hand, and 'executive dominant' systems, on the other.

Minority governments are in many ways a counter-intuitive phenomenon, especially when viewed from a Westminster perspective. They tend to be seen as weak, aberrant and, therefore, undesirable. Yet, as Erik Damgaard has noted: 'Minority governments are not as rare and abnormal as hitherto assumed, but on the other hand they do appear to be concentrated in a limited number of West European countries, not least the three Scandinavian countries' (Damgaard 2000: 365). Of these three (see table 11.1), Denmark has legitimately been described as the 'home of minority governments'. The last majority cabinet was a Social Democratic, Radical, Centre Democrat and Christian People's Party coalition under the Social Democrat Poul Nyrup Rasmussen, formed in January 1993, which had the slenderest majority, of 90 seats in the 179-member Folketing. It formally lost this when, the same year, a Centre Democrat deserted to become an independent.

Whereas minority governments have characterised Danish politics throughout the post-war period (albeit becoming increasingly frequent since the early

Table 11.1 *Minority governments in the metropolitan Scandinavian states, 1970/71–2007*

	Total number of governments	Number of minority governments	Number of single-party minority governments
Denmark	14	13	5
Norway	16	13	9
Sweden	16	13	11
Total	*46*	*39*	*25*

1970s), the shift to minority governments in Norway has been essentially a phenomenon of the last four decades. In the four general elections between 1945 and 1957, the Labour Party gained over half the Storting seats and between 1961 and 1965 the party maintained its domination of power with the help of two Socialist People's Party delegates. True, in mid-1963 the latter voted against the minority cabinet led by Einar Gerhardsen and this permitted a three-week spell of non-socialist minority coalition under the Conservative John Lyng. But the 1965 election brought a reversion to majority government, albeit in the guise of a four-party, non-socialist coalition under the Centre prime minister Per Borten, which survived until the debate over membership of the European Community led to its collapse in 1971. The shift in power to the non-socialists in 1965 prompted Jan Henrik Nyheim (1967: 257) to declare that 'the regularity – almost monotony – of majority [Labour] party rule was broken'. Whilst this was true, the wider point is that between 1945 and 1971 majority governments were in power in Norway for all but four years (at least if the Labour governments of 1961–63 and 1963–65 are viewed, *à la* Nyheim, as enjoying *de facto* majorities). In marked contrast, there have been only two majority governments in Norway since 1971. A three-party non-socialist coalition under the Conservative Kåre Willoch was in office for twenty-seven months between 1983 and 1985 and a three-party Labour, Socialist Left Party and Centre coalition under the Labour leader Jens Stoltenberg was formed after the 2005 general election. This, incidentally, was the first time the Norwegian Labour Party had entered a coalition government.

There has been a similar paucity of majority government in Sweden since the shift to unicameralism in 1970. Prior to the 2006 Riksdag election, the last majority government was a three-party non-socialist coalition between the Centre, Liberals and Conservatives from 1979, which had an overall majority of only a single seat. It collapsed in 1981, when the Conservatives withdrew over differences in taxation policy. However, in October 2006, increasingly close co-operation between the four non-socialist parties (the three aforementioned plus the Christian Democrats) led to the formation of a Conservative-led majority coalition under Fredrik Reinfeldt, which had a majority of seven. This broke a twelve-year period of Social Democratic minority government.

Minority government is, of course, a generic term embracing a variety of different types. *Single-party minority governments* have predominated in Norway and Sweden: 73 per cent of all governments in Sweden between 1971 and October 2006 and 60 per cent of governments in Norway between 1971 and the 2005 general election were single-party minority cabinets. In Denmark, nearly three-fifths of all governments between 1971 and 2007 were *minority coalitions*. Minority governments, moreover, operate in varying political circumstances. Anders Sannerstedt and Mats Sjölin (1992) refer in the Swedish context to 'cabinets in a majority-like situation' and Sannerstedt (1996) to 'minority governments with a bloc majority'. When minority governments have the backing of stable parliamentary majorities, they may in practice differ relatively little from majority cabinets. None the less, whether minority governments have commanded a *de facto* majority or not, policy-making in Denmark, Norway and Sweden in recent decades has typically proceeded on the basis of *legislative coalitions* (agreements between one or more parties in government and one or more 'support parties' in opposition).

In contrast to metropolitan Scandinavia, majority governments have been the norm in Iceland throughout the independence period and in Finland, too, since the mid-1960s. Majority governments have been in power in Iceland for over 90 per cent of the time since 1944 and since 1979 there have been only two minority coalitions. There has been only one minority cabinet in Finland in the last-mentioned period, whilst a number of majority cabinets have been *outsize*. Even between 1945 and 1966, 18 per cent of all Finnish governments comprised *surplus majority coalitions*, that is, with the backing of over two-thirds of Eduskunta seats – as opposed to the '50 per cent + 1' or 'minimal winning coalition' lauded in the literature as the most rational coalition type. However, from the so-called Popular Front, broad-based, centre-left coalitions of the late 1960s onwards, this type of government has become increasingly common and, for example, the first 'rainbow coalition' of 1995–99 commanded 145 or nearly three-quarters of the Eduskunta seats (Arter 2006: 90–7; Jungar 2002). Minority governments have been said to work best where they are most common and the same could probably be said for outsize coalitions. Restated, surplus majority coalitions function best where they are most common and in Finland they have been relatively common in recent decades (Arter 2006: 96).

Whilst the contrast in the size of governments in the Nordic region has been striking, there appears no clear connection between their size and stability – that is, the length of their stay in office. Equally, George Tsebelis would seem to overstate his case when arguing that 'minority governments are equipped with significant positional and institutional weapons that enable them (most of the time) to impose their will on parliament, just as majority governments do' (Tsebelis 2004: 175). Indeed, some numerically weak minority governments may fairly be described as 'caretaker cabinets', conceived primarily as stop-gap measures to facilitate a possible route out of a political crisis (Denmark

1973–75) and/or to prevent recourse to an early general election (Sweden 1978–79). In Finland until the mid-1970s such caretaker cabinets, appointed by the president, often comprised ministers from outside parliament – civil servants, experts, local government politicians and so on. Not all caretaker cabinets have proved short-lived. Similarly, minority governments with only limited parliamentary backing have at times proved durable and perfectly capable of implementing a legislative programme. In Norway, Kjell Magne Bondevik's centre-right minority coalition of Christian Democrats, Liberals and Conservatives, formed after the 2001 general election, held only 62 of the 165 Storting seats. But legislative majority-building did not prove particularly difficult and the government, where necessary, used the twenty-six seats of the radical rightist Progress Party to pass vital legislation, including the budget.

If *size* and the *partisan composition* of cabinets are combined, several distinct patterns emerge across the region. First, there has been the relative frequency of single-party minority governments in Norway and Sweden, the vast majority of them Social Democratic/Labour Party cabinets. In Sweden the Social Democrats were in office for all but nine of the thirty-six years since the move to a single-chamber Riksdag in 1971 to the time of writing (2007) and not once in that period did they enter government with other parties. Rather, they have at various times forged legislative coalitions with all the other parliamentary parties except the Conservatives and succeeded, on a 'divide and rule' basis, in keeping power to themselves. In Norway, the Labour Party governed as a minority cabinet for twenty-one years between 1971 and the 2005 general election, rejecting the formation of a coalition government so dogmatically that by the late 1990s many party veterans began to question the wisdom of such recalcitrance.

Second, there has been the ideologically or spatially connected character of both minority and majority coalitions in Denmark, Norway and Sweden. In Denmark, coalitions have been with only one exception either centre-left or centre-right in composition (Pedersen 2000: 372); in Norway and Sweden, they have been almost exclusively non-socialist. The only coalitions formed 'across the blocs' – that is, across the divide between socialist and non-socialist parties – were the Social Democratic–Agrarian cabinets in Sweden between 1951 and 1957, the short-lived Social Democrat–Liberal (Venstre) coalition in Denmark between 1978 and 1979, and the Stoltenberg Labour-led coalition in Norway in 2005, which included the Centre as well as the Socialist Left parties. In truth, as just noted, below the level of formal governmental co-operation, legislative coalitions 'across the blocs' have on occasions sustained minority Social Democratic governments in power in Sweden.

Third, ideologically diverse or spatially overarching majority or 'surplus majority' coalitions have been a feature of Icelandic and Finnish politics. None the less, 'bloc coalitions' have been formed; they have been non-socialist in composition. There was a series of centre-right Independence Party–Progressive Party coalitions in Iceland between 1995 and 2007, whilst in Finland the

Centre and Conservative parties governed together between 1991 and 1995 and have done so again after the 2007 general election. But the 'across the blocs' character of many Icelandic coalitions is illustrated in the fact that the Independence Party and Social Democrats have co-operated in government for over one-third of the period since independence and came together again after the May 2007 general election, under the premiership of Geir Haarde. Finnish coalitions had a socialist–non-socialist core of Social Democrats and Agrarian/Centre MPs from the late 1930s to the late 1980s, when the Social Democrats and Conservatives began a period of governmental co-operation. Indeed, the 'rainbow coalitions' under Lipponen, 1995–2003, may be regarded as the archetype of an 'ideologically diverse, surplus majority coalition'. It brought together, under Social Democratic leadership, the former communists in the Left Alliance, the Conservatives, the Swedish People's Party and the Greens (until their resignation in 2002).

Writing in the 1960s, Mogens N. Pedersen (1967: 154), borrowing from Robert Dahl on America, noted that, in Denmark, 'to say where the government leaves off and the opposition begins is an exercise in metaphysics'. Clearly, where minority government is routine, as in Denmark, the dividing line between executive and legislature will inevitably become somewhat blurred: some opposition parties will support the government some of the time, some opposition parties will support the government most of the time, whilst some opposition parties will support the government none of the time. In this connection, it may reasonably be speculated that a prerequisite of effective minority government – effective in the sense of having the capacity/resources to implement a legislative programme – is a power-sharing relationship between executive and legislature. How much power is shared and what forms the power-sharing arrangements take are, of course, a different matter.

The literature has suggested that in at least some of the Scandinavian states there has indeed been a power-sharing relationship between government and opposition. As noted in chapter 7, Leif Lewin, referring to Sweden, comments that 'by sharing power with the parties in opposition and including them in the rule of the country, the government is supposed to be regarded as representative of the people as a whole and consequently one that all can feel loyal to' (Lewin 1998: 203). The notion of a balanced relationship between executive and legislature is at the core of one of the three types of parliamentary democracy that Alan Siaroff (2003) has identified. There are those systems where there is 'executive dominance over the legislature', those polarised systems where there is 'a central role for a fragmented parliament' and those where there is 'fused parliamentarism' with 'co-operative policy-making diffusion'. Siaroff views Norway and (since 1948) Sweden as cases of executive–legislative balance systems. A power-sharing relationship between government and opposition is also at the heart of Arend Lijphart's characterisation of 'consensus democracy'. 'The contrast between executive dominance and executive–legislative balance is a very important aspect of the difference between majoritarian and consensus forms of democracy' (Lijphart 2003: 20) – and he views the Scandinavian states as exemplars of the latter. Wolfgang Müller and Kaare Strøm, however, have preferred the term *inclusionary democracy* to denote a polity in which policy influence may be gained without control of the executive branch (Müller and Strøm 1999: 288). Clearly, all things being equal, non-executive parties will gain greater policy influence when minority cabinets are in office – as routinely in Denmark, Norway and Sweden – than in situations of majority government, although the means or mode of influence may well vary from one country to the next.

The primary means by which opposition parties exert influence in situations of minority government is through participation in legislative coalitions. Legislative coalitions will vary in *size* (from 'minimal winning' to 'surplus majority'), *scope* (from issue-based to those covering a broad spectrum of policies), *duration* (shorter or longer life span) and the *degree of formalisation* (*ad hoc* or written agreements). Legislative coalitions will also display varying degrees of cohesion – greatest in all likelihood when the 'adjacency principle' is observed – that is, when they comprise a 'bloc majority' (for example a Social Democratic cabinet backed by centre-left parties or a Conservative cabinet supported by the other non-socialist parties) – and least when party system fragmentation means the bloc option is not available. Indeed, referring to Denmark, Christoffer Green-Pedersen and Lisbeth Hoffman Thomsen have argued that when the internal cohesion of the party blocs is low – as notably between 1973–81 and 1990–93 – and the use of bloc majorities is not a realistic option, weak minority government is likely to ensue, since opposition parties will possess veto powers and will be able to impose their policy preferences. The result will be ineffective government. If, on the other hand, the (minority) government can rely on a bloc majority, which in practice safeguards its position until the next election, broad-based legislative coalitions may be forged but any opposition party involved that is not part of the support bloc will lack the sanctions to impose its policy agenda (Green-Pedersen and Hoffman Thomsen 2005).

The characteristics of the legislative coalitions that have been integral to the majority-building process have varied somewhat across metropolitan Scandinavia. Norway, until recently, appears to have been marked by fluctuating legislative coalitions, negotiated on an essentially issue-by-issue basis, which have exhibited a low degree of formalism, have had variable majorities and have had a generally short duration. True, the radical rightist Progress Party put fifty questions to the prospective non-socialist coalition in 2001 and only on receiving satisfactory responses did it agree to back the Bondevik minority cabinet as a 'support party'. But the new government none the less stated publicly that it intended to build legislative majorities on a piecemeal basis. In truth, the Bondevik cabinet twice entered into (short) written agreements with the Progress Party on the budget between 2001 and 2005.

Nicholas Aylott and Torbjörn Bergman coined the term 'contract parliamentarism' to depict the situation in which the government is reliant for its legislative majority on a formalised pact with one or more opposition parties, which give it in practice a regular majority over a range of agreed policies (Aylott and Bergman 2004; Bale and Bergman 2006). Sweden and Denmark in recent years may be said to have displayed features of 'contract parliamentarism'. The legislative coalition between the ruling Social Democrats and their two 'support parties', the Left Party and Greens, between 2002 and 2006, contained 121 points, ran to over 4,200 words, covered the whole range of domestic policy, including the budget and the economy – the European Union (EU), defence and foreign policy were excluded – and was intended to last for the full four-year electoral term. In Denmark the 'contracts' have taken the form of 'package deal' agreements (*forlig*), often, though not always, negotiated at the pre-parliamentary stage, which are frequently written and then are binding on the participant parties. Flemming Juul Christiansen and Erik Damgaard (2008: 60) have noted how increasingly these package deals are committed to paper and have also become more detailed. The average length of the text of a 'package' between 1984 and 1987 was 550 words, whereas this rose to 2,650 words for the period 1998–2001. Importantly, parties to the package of measures are expected to abide by the agreement in public and they may not dissociate with it and adopt a modified stance without the unanimous consent of the other groups involved. This veto power may be regarded as one of the defining traits of package deals. The limited evidence would suggest that package deals have become more inclusive and at times they have incorporated parties at both ends of the political spectrum (albeit it rarely at the same time) and the *legislative coalition potential* of these parties – to adapt from Sartori – has consequently grown. Christiansen and Damgaard (2008: 58–61) have shown how, in the three decades since the 1973 'earthquake election' in Denmark, approximately two-thirds of the formal (written) package deals have been surplus majority legislative coalitions.

Summing up so far, then, the prevalence of minority governments in Denmark, Norway and Sweden over the last three decades and more has meant that policy-making has proceeded on the basis of legislative coalitions; these have varied in size, scope, duration and the extent to which they are formalised. Christiansen and Damgaard (2008) have discerned some move away from shifting majorities and *ad hoc*, issue-by-issue legislative coalitions towards more integrated relations between minority governments and their 'support parties'. Clearly, parties not involved in 'package deals' (I prefer this rendition of *forlig* to the ponderous term 'legislative accommodations' used by Scandinavian political scientists) will be marginalised in the decision-making process and, since legislative coalitions will normally hold firm in standing committees, these 'out-and-out opposition parties' may well concentrate on the chamber to profile their opposition. But if, *prima facie*, the metropolitan Scandinavian states appear cases of 'executive–legislative balance' rather than 'executive dominant' systems *à la* Lijphart, why have minority governments been so common?

Kaare Strøm argues that minority governments should be viewed in rational cost–benefit terms and that for some parties participation in government is not necessarily their best strategy. When there is a likely long-term electoral dividend from remaining in opposition – 'deferred gratification' he calls it – and significant policy influence can be exerted from opposition, minority governments are the likely outcome. In his words: 'Minority governments are likely to form when parties value voters and policy highly compared to office' (Strøm 1990: 242). Strøm coins the term *policy influence differential* to describe the difference in policy terms between the governing party (or parties) and the opposition parties. When this is low, minority governments will ensue. He adds that Norwegian political parties do not in comparative terms sacrifice a great deal of policy influence when they forego governmental participation (Strøm 1990: 211).

Strøm's argument is in many ways persuasive. His assertion that 'minority governments are promoted by institutions [notably standing committees] that enhance the power of the parliamentary opposition vis-à-vis the government' (Strøm 1990: 238) appears plausible. His focus is on why parties do not always choose to enter government, always presuming this to be an option. However, a common denominator in Sweden and Norway and, to a lesser degree, Denmark has been the presence of a dominant Social Democratic/Labour Party, falling short of an overall majority of seats but none the less able to call the shots. Minority governments in Scandinavia, in brief, have resulted in large part from the fact that the Social Democrats/Labour have wanted, and been able, to govern on a single-party basis. This is far from the banal conclusion it may seem, since it is questionable how far the perception of a small policy influence differential has persuaded prospective governing parties to remain in opposition. In Sweden, following the 2002 Riksdag election, for example, all six opposition parties (with the possible exception of the Conservatives) wanted to participate in government and the Left Party and Greens, the minority Social Democratic government's 'support parties' in the 1998–2002 parliamentary term, were particularly keen to do so. Yet the prime minister, Göran Persson, rebuffed both their advances, proceeding instead on the basis of 'contract parliamentarism' – a legislative deal with the Left and Greens, which in practice kept both at arm's length. This emphasis on the volitional aspects of the Social Democrats' approach to government-building – that is, on their strategic decision to monopolise cabinet posts – gains implicit reinforcement from Bjørn Erik Rasch. Referring to all three metropolitan Scandinavian states, Rasch notes that 'in a fragmented assembly without a majority party, if one party has a far larger share of the seats than any other party, it is likely to have a strong bargaining position' (Rasch 2004: 138–9). He adds that 'minority governments are more likely in systems with one centrally positioned, relatively large party' (Rasch 2004: 140).

The strong bargaining position deriving from the party's electoral strength is also one of the grounds Torbjörn Bergman suggests for the frequency of Social

Democratic minority cabinets in Sweden. He also emphasises the 'bloc nature' of politics, the traditional loyalty of the Left Communist Party as a support party and the way disagreements between the non-socialist parties have enabled the Social Democrats readily to form legislative coalitions with one or more of them (Bergman 2003: 225). In the Danish case, Mogens Pedersen (2000: 372) adduces four reasons for the frequency of minority coalitions. First, there is the fragmented party system, where the centre of politics has been occupied by a small number of parties. Second, the traditional political blocs and individual parties have rarely, if ever, been able to muster a majority on their own. Third, an incoming government has not been required to obtain a vote of confidence – 'not no confidence', or *non sfiducia* as in Italy, will suffice. Finally, in line with Strøm, Pedersen brings out the way opposition parties can profit from legislative coalitions.

Parliamentary executives and semi-presidential government

The contrast between Denmark, Norway and Sweden (routinely viewed as so-called 'executive–legislative balance' systems) and Finland and Iceland ('executive dominant' systems) extends beyond the size of cabinets to the structure of the political executive itself. The metropolitan Scandinavian states are constitutional monarchies with parliamentary governments. True, in Denmark and Norway the monarch still presides over the formal meetings of the Council of State (government). A ceremonial legacy of past times, these meetings are essentially rubber-stamping exercises. Indeed, the former Danish prime minister Anker Jørgensen has recorded amusingly how he particularly liked Council of State meetings because it was the only time he could be certain of getting half an hour's rest (Miller 1991: 54–5)! In Sweden, the 1974 constitution excluded the king from cabinet meetings and vested the Riksdag Speaker with the task of co-ordinating the formation of a new government. Moreover, the king is expected not to make political statements, still less to criticise the government of the day. He does not do so although, exceptionally, in an interview in the national daily *Dagens Nyheter* in January 2005, Karl Gustav XVI stated that, despite his best efforts, he had for two days been unable to glean any information about the *tsunami* catastrophe from either the foreign ministry or the prime minister's office. The Swedish constitution requires the prime minister to keep the monarch informed of current developments. Rare episodes of this type apart, the monarch in all three metropolitan Scandinavian states is a symbolic figurehead and, in line with the parliamentary principle, governments are accountable to the legislature. In all three, moreover, executive–legislative relations are predicated on the notion of so-called *negative parliamentarism* – that is, incoming governments do not need to obtain a vote of confidence. In other words, minority governments in Denmark, Norway and Sweden need only the tolerance of parliament. Indeed, minority governments have, in fact, been routinely defeated on legislative amendments and remained in office unless the prime minister has made the issue a matter of confidence. The cabinets led by Gro Harlem Brundtland (the first female Norwegian prime minister) in the 1990s incurred parliamentary defeats with increasing regularity while becoming more, not less ensconced (Narud and Strøm 2003: 167).

The 1919 Finnish constitution and 1944 Icelandic constitution created semi-presidential systems – that is, dual executives consisting of a popularly elected head of state vested with significant powers, working alongside a government responsible to parliament, in the manner of the metropolitan Scandinavian states. Constitutional change in Finland, culminating in the adoption of a new form of government in 2000, substantially reduced the role of the president (discussed shortly) and today the Icelandic head of state (curiously the minimum age for candidates is thirty-five years) possesses substantially greater *formal* powers – certainly in relation to the legislative process – than the Finnish counterpart. The Icelandic president has the authority: to appoint and dismiss ministers; to preside over the Council of State to discuss and underwrite 'laws and important government measures'; to convene the Alþingi after a general election and open its regular sessions every year; to dissolve the Alþingi; to convene extraordinary sessions of the Alþingi; to ratify laws; to submit bills and draft resolutions to the Alþingi; and to place before the people in a referendum a bill which, though having passed the Alþingi, becomes null and void if there is a popular majority against it. Finally, in the event of urgent need, the head of state is empowered to issue provisional laws between Alþingi sessions. In addition, the president exercises executive powers, although the constitution also states that he/she entrusts his/her authority to ministers, who assume responsibility for all executive actions. Legislation must also be countersigned by a minister in order to assume the force of law. Plainly, the intention was that presidential action should be constrained by the need for the consent of ministers.

Very occasionally the president has intervened decisively in events leading up to the formation of a new government. There have been five Icelandic presidents since independence (table 11.2) and the second head of state, Ásgeir Ásgeirsson (1952–68), was instrumental in building an historic Independence

Table 11.2 *Icelandic presidents since 1944*

	Term of office
Sveinn Björnsson	1944–52
Ásgeir Ásgeirsson	1952–68
Kristján Eldjárn	1968–80
Vigdís Finnbogadóttir	1980–96
Ólafur Ragnar Grímsson	1996–

Party–Social Democratic coalition which took office in 1959 and remained in power for twelve years. Until very recently, however, the Icelandic president has been a ceremonial figurehead who has remained steadfastly above the clash of day-to-day party politics. Vigdís Finnbogadóttir, Iceland's first and thus far only female president, would willingly be interviewed about the Icelandic sagas, French literature (her speciality), the arts or the latest in design, but never about politics! True, Vigdís once delayed appending her signature for nearly three hours as a symbolic protest against a particular piece of legislation. However, the responsible minister subsequently stated that he would have resigned had there been any further delay (Kristinsson 1999). Indeed, for the most part, Iceland has been 'semi-presidential' in name only and in practice considerably closer to the purely parliamentary government of Denmark, Norway and Sweden than to the other semi-presidential government in the region – Finland. For one thing, Icelandic presidential elections are not party-politicised. Gunnar Helgi Kristinsson (1999: 86) sums matters up nicely:

> The Icelandic republic was created to put an end to the relationship with Denmark rather than to create a new form of government. Political expediency rather than constitutional principles guided the constitution-makers at the initiation of the new regime in 1944. It seems beyond dispute that the intention of parliament at the time was to create a presidency with functions essentially similar to those of a monarch in a parliamentary democracy. This intention has shaped the tradition of the Icelandic presidency.

None the less, the constitutional powers of the president have on occasions allowed the incumbent to perform as a political actor and far to exceed the role of a constitutional monarch. We have noted Ásgeirsson's active involvement in building an historic coalition government 'across the blocs' in the late 1950s. More recently, Svanur Kristjánsson has referred to the *political presidency* of the current head of state, Ólafur Grímsson, who in 2004 refused controversially to ratify a new law designed to prevent media monopolies. This was the first time an Icelandic president had exercised the right not to ratify a law, which accordingly went to a popular referendum. Kristjánsson argues that 'by skilful leadership, Grímsson has returned to the political presidency as practised by Iceland's first two presidents. Grímsson has repeatedly emphasised the important and independent role of the president in the political system. It is clear that the political presidency is in principle supported by a sizeable majority of the people' (Kristjánsson 2004: 168). Grímsson was elected for a third consecutive term of office in June 2004 with 85 per cent of the votes cast for the three candidates. However, since 20 per cent of all ballot papers were blank and the turnout was the lowest since independence, it seems reasonable to believe that at least a section of the electorate was not happy with the president's proactive stance.

If the duality of the Icelandic executive during Grímsson's tenure as head of state has become somewhat more pronounced, there is no question that, over its first seven decades of independence, Finland had a semi-presidential system. The 1919 constitution empowered the president to appoint governments, present bills to parliament, ratify measures, appoint senior officials, open and close Eduskunta sessions, convene extraordinary sessions of parliament and head the armed forces. Crucially, too, article 33 stated that 'the relations of Finland with foreign powers shall be determined by the president'. When article 33 is taken in conjunction with article 2, which is in two parts – 'Legislative power shall be exercised by parliament in conjunction with the President of the Republic' and 'Supreme executive power shall be vested in the President of the Republic' – it can be seen that the president exercised legislative, executive and federative powers in John Locke's sense of the control of relations with other states. In addition, the second part of article 2 stipulated that 'for the general government of the state there shall be a Council of State comprising the prime minister and the requisite number of ministers' (Arter 1987: 79–117). The rationale for creating a (potentially) strong presidency was integrally bound up with the struggle for control of the newly independent Finnish state. Particularly on the political right, among the White victors in the 1918 civil war, there was deep mistrust of a purely parliamentary form of government. After all, in 1916 the Social Democrats had won the first and only absolute majority of parliamentary seats ever won in Finland – 103 out of 200 seats, with 47.3 per cent of the vote – and a strong president was viewed as a counterpoise to a leftist-controlled assembly.

The real power of the Finnish president grew at the expense of government and parliament after the Second World War, particularly during the long era of Urho Kekkonen's presidency (1956–81), when presidentialism was particularly evident in the federative sphere. The personalisation of foreign policy management and its concentration in presidential hands was already evident from the advent of the Winter War with the Soviet Union, beginning in late autumn 1939. The crisis management conditions of war from 1939 to 1944 led the head of state to take personal charge of the conduct of foreign policy and Risto Ryti (1940–44) became the first Finnish president to engage in bilateral discussions with the head of a foreign power when he met Hitler in 1942. That was during the so-called Continuation War against the Soviet Union (1941–44), when Finland fought as a 'co-belligerent' with Nazi Germany. However, after the Second World War, the supreme importance of foreign policy in the context of developing and maintaining amicable relations with the Kremlin considerably enhanced the status and powers of the head of state. Indeed, reference came to be made to the *official foreign policy* – the Paasikivi–Kekkonen line – named after two post-war presidents (see table 11.3).

Although in practice Paasikivi took all the important decisions himself, he did seek to conduct foreign policy through the government and with the assistance of his foreign minister. However, Kekkonen during his first year as president, 1956, took several decisions in a manner that diverged from Paasikivi's practice (Kalela 1993: 227–8). He personally took command of

Table 11.3   *Finnish presidents since 1919*

	Term of office
Kaarlo Juho Ståhlberg	1919–25
Lauri Kristian Relander	1925–31
Pehr Evind Svinhufvud	1931–37
Kyösti Kallio	1937–40
Risto Ryti	1940–44
Carl Gustav Mannerheim	1944–46
Juho Kusti Paasikivi	1946–56
Urho Kekkonen	1956–81
Mauno Koivisto	1982–94
Martti Ahtisaari	1994–00
Tarja Halonen	2000–

the top foreign ministry officials, bypassing the foreign secretary. His power, in short, extended to influencing the preparation of measures. He did all he could to prevent the foreign secretary being, or becoming, a strong politician and he deliberately set out to limit the role of the prime minister in foreign policy, particularly in *Ostpolitik*. Kekkonen's role in defusing two crises in Finno-Soviet relations – the so-called Night Frost Crisis in autumn 1958 and Note Crisis in autumn 1961 (discussed in chapter 12) – enabled him to keep foreign policy separate from other politics as an area specially reserved for the president and also to use the foreign ministry as his personal instrument. By the 1970s, under Kekkonen, it was possible to speak of the 'all-powerful Finnish presidency' – to adapt from Duverger referring to France – 'enlightened despotism' is a term I have used elsewhere – as the president's crisis-management style extended to the economy, for example railroading the leading economic interest groups into a broad incomes policy agreement in 1970 (Arter 1981).

In terms of the direction of foreign policy, there were few changes under Kekkonen's successor as president, Mauno Koivisto. When in the early 1980s a journalist requested him to describe the substance of Finland's foreign policy in three words, the president retorted *hyvät suhteet naapureihin* – good relations with our neighbours – and he remained faithful to this maxim until the final disintegration of the Soviet Union (Koivisto 1983: 19). However, a series of constitutional reforms during the second term of Koivisto's presidency (1988–94) strengthened the position of the government *vis-à-vis* the president. By 1994, the head of state was limited to a maximum of two consecutive terms of office – that is, twelve years – and in that year Martti Ahtisaari was elected on the basis of the two-stage popular ballot used in France. The process of constitutional change culminated in the enactment of a new constitution, which came into force on 1 March 2000, the day on which Finland's first female head of state, Tarja Halonen, began her first term of office.

Under the 2000 constitution, Finland has remained an 'executive dominant' system, but with the government and particularly prime minister assuming several of the functions previously performed by the president. Thus, the president has been divested of the legislative power earlier exercised conjointly with parliament, and this has passed to the government, although the latter is, of course, accountable to the Eduskunta (i.e. 'parliamentary government'). The president can now delay the ratification of bills for a maximum of only three months (previously this could be done until a newly constituted Eduskunta approved the measure). Moreover, the president is only formally involved in the formation of a new government, in so far as she or he rubber-stamps the Eduskunta's choice of prime minister and approves the slate of ministers proposed by the prime minister. Previously the composition of the cabinet was heavily influenced by the president, and the foreign secretary and defence secretary were effectively personal nominees. The president no longer has the exclusive right to dissolve parliament but can do so only at the instigation of the prime minister. Most significantly, the president no longer enjoys sole federative powers, but rather the direction of foreign policy is placed in the hands of the president working with the prime minister and government. Article 93 also states that the government bears responsibility for the national preparation of decisions to be taken in the EU and also for determining who represents Finland in European Council meetings. Although both president and prime minister may attend EU summits, the prime minister is in practice the leading actor in Union matters.

All this would (rightly) suggest the end of 'Finnish exceptionalism'. Yet the president is more than a ceremonial figurehead. The head of state retains the authority of a popular mandate and the presidency retains a high level of legitimacy among the population at large. Indeed, the status of the position allows the incumbent to act as an opinion leader and, in declarations to the nation on television, for example, to push a personal agenda. The president, moreover, retains the powers of certain appointments, including the members of the board of the Bank of Finland. She also chairs the cabinet committee on foreign and security policy, regularly leads foreign trade delegations and remains head of the armed forces. For the first time, under the second Matti Vanhanen government, formed after the 2007 general election, the foreign secretary is not from Halonen's former party, the Social Democrats, and an undercurrent of tension between the two has been evident. This has led to more vociferous calls for a clarification of the wording of article 93, to make it clear exactly how the co-operation between president and government in the direction of foreign policy should work or, more precisely, what should happen when it is not working. Conflict has arisen in recent years in relation to security matters, not least who takes the final decision in relation to the deployment in EU-led operations of Finland's rapid-reaction, crisis-management battalion. Whilst the constitutional powers of the Finnish presidency were much reduced in 2000, and the president is no longer involved in government-building or the legislative process, recent presidents (including Halonen), having previously been prominent party politicians, pronounce on political issues as and when the need or opportunity arises. To that extent, it would seem possible to speak of a 'political presidency' in Finland (as well as Iceland), although this is a far cry from the authoritarian presidency of Kekkonen in the 1960s and 1970s.

Towards prime ministerial government?

Outside Finland, the constitutional prerogatives of the Nordic prime ministers are few and the *de jure* specification of the role very limited. In Iceland, the only reference to the prime minister in the constitution is in article 73, which alludes to the 'prime minister's policy speech' at the start of each Alþingi session in October. Similarly in Denmark, virtually the only reference to the prime minister in the 1953 constitution is in paragraph 5 of article 38, which states that at the start of the new Folketing year the prime minister will present a 'review of the state of the realm' and the measures planned by the government. The 1814 Eidsvoll constitution in Norway is only marginally less parsimonious on the position of the prime minister. It stipulates the minimum size for a quorate cabinet meeting – the prime minister plus at least seven other ministers – and also that the counter-signature of the prime minister is required on cabinet decisions. The Norwegian prime minister also has an extra vote if the king is not in attendance at the Council of State and has the right to obtain any information required from government departments. The 1974 Swedish constitution has a section on the procedure for appointing a prime minister and stipulates that 'the prime minister shall summon other ministers to attend cabinet meetings and shall preside at such meetings'. But there is nothing on the real nature of the prime minister's task. Only in paragraph 66 of the 2000 constitution in Finland is the central role of the prime minister in the functioning of the political executive clearly recognised: 'The prime minister leads the work of the government and is responsible for the co-ordination of the preparation and deliberation of those matters falling within its remit.' It also states that the prime minister leads the debate – that is, chairs – the 'general sittings' of the cabinet (held on Thursdays).

While the constitutional prerogatives of the office are limited, the Nordic prime ministers combine two essential roles – they manage the work of the government and they head their party, which is usually, though not always, the largest party in the government. Managing the work of a coalition government, or a minority cabinet dependent on 'support parties', will clearly involve meeting challenges in the inter-party arena. Managing a ministerial team, not to mention the parliamentary party group (PPG), and beyond that the party membership, will entail intra-party skills. Obviously, each prime minister will have his/her own management style, dictated partly by the particular set of political circumstances and partly by the temperament and personality of the incumbent. Even the most forceful personality, however, will find the room for manoeuvre constrained in appointing a ministerial team, carrying the PPG and, in coalition cabinets, handling relations with the other governing parties. Against this backdrop, Johan P. Olsen noted almost thirty years ago that 'a Norwegian prime minister ... is unlikely to achieve a position as superstar' (Olsen 1980: 213). Richard Rose has put matters more prosaically:

> Since in most Scandinavian countries the government is almost invariably a coalition of parties, there is a tendency for the prime minister to represent the lowest common denominator of inter-party agreement. Instead of being a leader . ... instead of taking initiatives, the prime minister's job is to negotiate agreement when it can be found and to avoid issues appearing on the cabinet agenda that will split the coalition and cost him or her the top job. (Rose 1991: 16)

In contrast to Rose, the leadership role of the prime minister and the increased importance and power of the office have been emphasised in the recent Scandinavian literature. Olof Ruin has compared three Swedish Social Democratic prime ministers – Tage Erlander (1946–69), Olof Palme (1969–76, 1982–86) and Ingvar Carlsson (1986–91, 1994–96), all heads of single-party minority cabinets – and concludes that 'the office of the prime minister in Sweden has increased in importance over the decades since Tage Erlander first held it' (Ruin 1991: 80). In Iceland the Independence Party leader, Davið Oððsson, headed three coalitions between 1991 and 2004 – with the Social Democrats for the first four years and the Progressive Party thereafter – and, writing in the later part of this period, Svanur Kristjánsson comments that 'in Iceland in recent years, the prime minister has become more powerful than before' (Kristjánsson 2004: 160). In Finland the prime minister for long lived in the shadow of the president but, writing three years after the new constitution came into force, Max Jakobson noted that 'the prime minister is no longer chosen by the president and dependent on the president, but is the independent leader of the government' (Jakobson 2003). Heikki Paloheimo has put the point more expansively. 'As a result of the parliamentarisation of the Finnish political system ... the role of the prime minister has clearly strengthened. The prime minister is the effective executive head and a kind of managing director of the state' (Paloheimo 2003: 233).

There have been (to the time of writing) seventy-two prime ministers in the Nordic countries since the end of the Second World War – or, in the Icelandic case, the achievement of independence in 1944 (tables 11.4–11.8). The numbers have ranged from only nine in Sweden to twenty-two in Finland, where, until 1975, there were numerous stop-gap 'caretaker' cabinets. Longevity of tenure has been greatest in the case of Swedish Social Democratic prime ministers, since none in the post-war period served less than seven years in the job. Indeed, until Göran Persson in October 2006, no post-war Social Democratic prime minister in Sweden relinquished the post as a result of an

Table 11.4 *Swedish prime ministers since 1945*

Prime minister	Prime minister's party	Term in office	Cabinet parties
Per Albin Hansson	Social Democrat	1945–46	SD
Tage Erlander	Social Democrat	1946–69	SD (1951–57 with Agrarians)
Olof Palme	Social Democrat	1969–76, 1982–86	SD
Thorbjörn Fälldin	Centre	1976–78, 1979–82	C+L+Con[a]
Ola Ullsten	Liberal	1978–79	L
Ingvar Carlsson	Social Democrat	1986–91, 1994–96	SD
Carl Bildt	Conservative	1991–94	Con+L+C+CD
Göran Persson	Social Democrat	1996–06	SD
Fredrik Reinfeldt	Conservative	2006–	Con+L+C+CD

SD = Social Democrats; C = Centre; L = Liberals; Con = Conservatives; CD = Christian Democrats.
[a] In 1981 the Conservatives resigned from the Fälldin coalition over tax reform proposals.

election defeat. Tage Erlander retired voluntarily in 1969 after a momentous two decades in office, Ingvar Carlsson did likewise in 1996, while Olof Palme was assassinated on a Stockholm street in February 1986.

There have also been some notably long-serving prime ministers outside Sweden. In Norway the Labour leader Einar Gerhardsen held the post for seventeen years between the Second World War and the mid-1960s, whilst Gro Harlem Brundtland, also Labour, held the office for over eleven years in the 1980s and 1990s. In Finland the Social Democrat Kalevi Sorsa served as prime minister for ten years during the 1970s and 1980s but the prime minister with the longest record of continuous service is Paavo Lipponen, who headed two 'rainbow coalitions' between 1995 and 2003. Denmark has been distinctive in that, although the Social Democrats have been the largest party in all but three post-war elections (2001, 2005 and 2007), the longest-serving prime minister has been a Conservative, Poul Schlüter. He led a series of non-socialist minority cabinets between 1982 and 1993. In Iceland the most durable prime ministers have belonged to the largest grouping, the Independence Party. Ólafur Thors served as premier for nearly twelve years between independence from Denmark and 1963. However, the longest single stretch as prime minister was that of Davið Oððsson, between 1991 and 2004. At the other extreme, the first post-war, non-socialist government in Norway under John Lyng survived only three weeks in 1963.

In line with paragraph 66 of the new Finnish constitution, the task of the Nordic prime ministers, irrespective of partisanship and experience, is to lead the work of the government – that is, to direct the ministerial team that makes up the cabinet. Each prime minister will, of course, chair cabinet meetings in

Table 11.5 *Danish prime ministers since 1945*

Prime minister	Prime minister's party	Term of office	Cabinet parties
Knud Kristensen	Liberal	1945–47	L
Hans Hedtoft	Social Democrat	1947–50, 1953–55	SD
Erik Eriksen	Liberal	1950–53	L + Con
H. C. Hansen	Social Democrat	1955–57	SD
		1957–60	SD + SL + JP
Viggo Kampmann	Social Democrat	1960–62	SD + SL
Jens Otto Krag	Social Democrat	1962–68	1962–64 SD + SL; 1964–68 SD
		1971–72	SD
Hilmar Baunsgaard	Social Liberal	1968–71	SL + L + Con
Anker Jørgensen	Social Democrat	1972–73, 1975–82	SD (1978–79 with L)
Poul Hartling	Liberal	1973–75	L
Poul Schlüter	Conservative	1982–93	1982–88 Con + L + CPP + CD; 1988–90 Con + L + SL 1990–93 Con + L
Poul Nyrup Rasmussen	Social Democrat	1993–01	1993–94 SD + SL + CD + CPP 1994–96 SD + SL + CD 1996–01 SD + SL
Anders Fogh Rasmussen	Liberal	2001–	L + Con

SD = Social Democrats; Con = Conservatives; L = Liberals; SL = Social Liberals; CD = Centre Democrats; JP = Justice Party; CPP = Christian People's Party.

his/her own particular manner. The prime minister may also chair cabinet committee meetings, although in Sweden these have existed only during the non-socialist coalitions of 1976–82, 1991–94 (Bergman 2003: 213) and since 2006. There will also be extensive informal contacts with ministers. Most notably, there has been the celebrated Finnish 'evening class' (*iltakoulu*) or informal gathering of ministers (and increasingly officials and even interest group representatives) on Wednesday nights, prior to the full cabinet sitting on Thursdays. The institution of the 'evening class' declined, however, during the 1970s and effectively disappeared under Lipponen between 1995 and 2003. In Sweden, too, the previously daily cabinet lunches are now occasional and poorly attended.

Table 11.6 *Finnish prime ministers since 1946*

Prime minister	Prime minister's party	Term in office	Cabinet parties
Mauno Pekkala	FPDL	1946–48	FPDL + SD + A + SPP
K. A. Fagerholm	Social Democrat	1948–50	SD
		1956–57	SD + A + L + SPP
		1958–59	SD + Con + A + SPP + L
Urho Kekkonen	Agrarians	1950–53	A + L[a] + SPP + SD[b]
		1954–56	A + SPP[c] + SD
Sakari Tuomioja	Non-party	1953–54	Con + L + SPP
Ralf Törngren	Swedish People's	1954	A + SD + SPP
V. J. Sukselainen	Agrarians	1957	A
		1959–61	A + SPP
Rainer von Fieandt	Non-party	1957–58	
Reino Kuuskoski	Non-party	1958	
Martti Miettunen	Agrarian–Centre	1961–62	A
		1975–76	C + SD + FPDL + SPP + L
		1976–77	C + SPP + L
Ahti Karjalainen	Agrarian–Centre	1962–63	A + SD + Con + L + SPP
		1970–71	C + SD + FPDL
Reino Lehto	Non-party	1963–64	
Johannes Virolainen	Agrarian–Centre	1964–66	A–C + Con + L + SPP
Rafael Paasio	Social Democrat	1966–68	SD + FPDL + SDO + C
		1972	SD
Mauno Koivisto	Social Democrat	1968–70	SD + FPDL + SDO + C + SPP
		1979–82	SD + FPDL + C + SPP
Teuvo Aura	Non-party	1970, 1971–72	
Kalevi Sorsa	Social Democrat	1972–75	SD + C + L + SPP
		1977–79	SD + FPDL + C + L + SPP
		1982–83	SD + FPDL + C
		1983–87	SD + C + SPP + FRP
Keijo Liinamaa	Non-party	1975	
Harri Holkeri	Conservative	1987–91	Con + SD + SPP + FRP[d]
Esko Aho	Centre	1991–95	C + Con + SPP + CD
Paavo Lipponen	Social Democrat	1995–99	SD + Con + SPP + LA + Gr
		1999–03	SD + Con + SPP + LA + Gr[e]
Anneli Jäätteenmäki	Centre	2003	C + SD + SPP
Matti Vanhanen	Centre	2003–07	C + SD + SPP
		2007–	C + Con + SPP + Gr

SD = Social Democrats; FPDL = Finnish People's Democratic League; A = Agrarian Party (until 1965); C = Centre Party (formerly Agrarians); SPP = Swedish People's Party; SDO, Social Democratic Opposition; L = Liberals; FRP = Finnish Rural Party; CD = Christian Democrats (until 1999 Finnish Christian League); Con = Conservatives (National Coalition); Gr = Greens.
[a] The Liberals left the government in January 1951.
[b] The Social Democrats entered the coalition in January 1951.
[c] The Swedish People's Party left the cabinet in 1954.
[d] The Finnish Rural Party left the government in 1990.
[e] The Greens left the Lipponen II 'rainbow coalition' in 2002.

Table 11.7 *Norwegian prime ministers since 1945*

Prime minister	Prime minister's party	Term in office	Cabinet parties
Einar Gerhardsen	Labour	1945–51	Lab
		1955–63	Lab
		1963–65	Lab
Oscar Torp	Labour	1951–55	Lab
John Lyng	Conservative	1963	Con + C + L + CPP
Per Borten	Centre	1965–71	C + Con + L + CPP
Trygve Bratteli	Labour	1971–72	Lab
		1973–76	Lab
Lars Korvald	Christian People's Party	1972–73	CPP + C + L
Odvar Nordli	Labour	1976–81	Lab
Gro Harlem Brundtland	Labour	1981	Lab
		1986–89	Lab
		1990–97	Lab
Kåre Willoch	Conservative	1981–83	Con
		1983–86	Con + C + CPP
Jan P. Syse	Conservative	1989–90	Con + C + CPP
Thorbjørn Jagland	Labour	1996–97	Lab
Kjell Magne Bondevik	Christian People's Party	1997–00	CPP + C + L
		2001–05	CPP + Con + L
Jens Stoltenberg	Labour	2000–01	Lab
		2005–	Lab + C + SL

Lab = Labour; Con = Conservatives (Høyre); C = Centre Party (Agrarians until 1959); L = Liberals (Venstre); CPP = Christian People's Party; SL = Socialist Left.

In both minority and majority coalitions the prime minister must work to accommodate the 'partner parties' so as to achieve a satisfactory level of cabinet cohesion. This may be particularly challenging when the prime minister does not come from the largest coalition party. The Conservatives, not the prime minister's party, the Centre, were the largest party in the Fälldin coalition in Sweden between 1979 and 1981 and matters were further complicated by the fact that it had an overall majority of only one in the Riksdag. In only six of the nine post-war Norwegian coalitions (all but one non-socialist) has the prime minister come from the largest party. In the event of policy divisions within the coalition, the prime minister may well have to attend PPG meetings of the junior partners or, when it is a legislative coalition, forge good working relations with the party leaders of the support groupings.

There are intra-party as well as inter-party challenges for the Scandinavian prime ministers. The PPG of the prime minister's party normally constitutes the core support base of the government in parliament and, for that reason alone, cannot be taken for granted. Indeed, in some cases, though not all, the

Table 11.8　*Icelandic prime ministers since 1944*

Prime minister	Prime minister's party	Term in office	Cabinet parties
Ólafur Thors	Independence Party	1944–47	I + SD + USP
		1949–50	I
		1953–56	I + P
		1959–63	I + SD
Stefán Jóhann Stefánsson	Social Democrats	1947–49	SD + I + P
Steingrímur Steinhórsson	Progressive Party	1950–53	P + I
Hermann Jónasson	Progressive Party	1956–58	P + PA + SD
Emil Jónsson	Social Democrats	1958–59	SD
Bjarni Benediktsson	Independence Party	1963–70	I + SD
Jóhann Hafstein	Independence Party	1970–71	I + SD
Ólafur Jóhannesson	Progressive Party	1971–74	P + PA + ULL[a]
		1978–79	P + PA + SD
Geir Hallgrímsson	Independence Party	1974–78	I + P
Benedikt Gröndal	Social Democrats	1979–80	SD
Gunnar Thoroððsen	Independence Party	1980–83	I + P + PA
Steingrímur Hermannsson	Progressive Party	1983–87	P + I
		1988–91	P + SD + PA
Thorsteinn Pálsson	Independence Party	1987–88	I + P + SD
Davið Oððsson	Independence Party	1991–95	I + P + SD
		1995–04	I + P
Halldór Ásgrímsson	Progressive Party	2004–6	P + I
Geir Haarde	Independence Party	2006–7	I + P
		2007–	I + SDA[b]

I = Independence Party; SD = Social Democrats; USP = United Socialist Party; P = Progressive Party; PA, People's Alliance; ULL = Union of Liberals and Leftists; SDA = Social Democratic Alliance.
[a] The Union of Liberals and Leftists was founded by Hannibal Valdimarsson in 1969 and was strongly opposed to the Keflavík base.
[b] The Social Democratic Alliance (Samfylkingin) was formed in 1999.

prime minister does not have entirely free hands in appointing his/her party's slate of cabinet ministers. Frictions may be generated at the very outset if the norms guiding the recruitment of ministers are not fully observed. For Norway, Knut Heidar identifies three cardinal unwritten rules in selecting ministers from the prime minister's PPG. First, the prime minister's party's allocation of ministers must reflect the different parts of the country. 'A government without any minister "representing" North Norway would be crippled from the outset', irrespective of its base in parliament (Heidar 2001: 43). Second, there should be a fairly even gender balance and the presence of significant numbers of female ministers. Third, the government's relations with the Storting should be facilitated by the appointment of a number of experienced parliamentarians (Heidar 2001: 43–4).

In presenting her list of Centre ministers after the March 2003 general election, Anneli Jäätteenmäki, the Finnish prime minister designate, announced five selection criteria – ability, individual expertise, public performance capability, team player capacity and reliability. However, when regional factors were ignored, regional lobbies within the PPG were active in pressing the case for particular individuals to be appointed to ministerial office. Ultimately, there were formal votes on no less than four of the six Centre ministers (excluding the prime minister) (*Helsingin Sanomat*, 16 April 2003). When taken together with the fact that the PPG of the junior coalition party (or parties) will nominate its (or their) own ministers, there seems much in a former Norwegian prime minister's observation that 'if you cannot get the ones you want, you have to love the ones you get' (Olsen 1980: 218).

Plainly, then, executive leadership must be viewed in the context of the complex and dynamic power relationships that exist between the prime minister and his/her PPG, on the one hand, and his/her relationship with the party leaders and PPGs of the 'support parties' (whether members of an executive or legislative coalition), on the other. The prime minister will at various times be cast in the role of conciliator, co-ordinator, negotiator and bridge-builder. Some prime ministers will be better 'people managers' than others. In single-party governments, of course, the prime minister can always have recourse to a cabinet reshuffle to maintain momentum and direction. (This was the standard ploy of Göran Persson in Sweden between 1996 and 2006, when he appointed a significant number of ministers from outside the Riksdag.) The task of being a 'moderator within and between parties' – to cite Clay Clemens' summation of the primary role of the German chancellor (Clemens 1994: 47) – has also been a prerequisite for a successful Nordic prime minister. However, whilst the inter-personal duties associated with the job have changed relatively little over the years, it does not appear unreasonable to speak across the region of an expansion of the prime minister's role and of the existence of a 'prime ministerial agenda'.

On the first point, the growing internationalisation of politics, and the concomitant blurring of the demarcation line between domestic and 'European policy' in particular, has led the prime minister to assume primary responsibility for the management of EU affairs, in the process undermining to a degree the traditional role and authority of the foreign secretary. The prime minister's duties in the Nordic EU states do appear to have become significantly more demanding, not least because it is necessary to conduct important discussions without the aid of advisers and to create a network of effective working relations with the prime ministers of other EU member states. The prime minister will also be held to account by and need to work closely with the designated 'European committees' on the home front. Equally, involvement in European Council meetings has allowed the prime ministers of the Nordic EU states to appear international figures rather than simply heads of government. By fraternising with the leaders of the large EU countries, staging press conferences in Brussels and pronouncing on strategic EU issues, the prime ministers of Denmark, Finland and Sweden have been seen to rise above domestic politics and, with extensive media coverage, to become crucial opinion leaders on Union affairs.

On the second point, the enhanced personal standing accruing from the international and European duties of the office has probably facilitated and promoted the independent leadership aspects of the post and the articulation of a 'prime ministerial agenda'. A combination of experience in the post and security of tenure at the helm (the backing of a reliable parliamentary majority) will doubtless achieve the same end. Davið Oððsson well illustrates the point. Becoming prime minister immediately on entering the Alþingi in 1991, he became *the* dominant figure in Icelandic politics for the next thirteen years, his unwavering opposition to EU membership based principally on the costs of the loss of self-determination rights in Iceland's fishing waters.

Nothwithstanding appearances to the contrary under the forceful leadership of the likes of Oððsson, Persson or Lipponen, a seemingly dominant prime minister is not, of course, synonymous with the existence of 'prime ministerial government' – that is, the concentration of effective power in single hands. Rather, it is probably fair to assert that the tendency has been towards a decentralisation and sectoralisation of the work of the Nordic governments. Ministers are largely left to develop policy within their particular area of responsibility, ministers and the prime minister increasingly engage in bilateral discussions (the prime minister–finance minister axis is crucial) and the effective deliberation takes place within cabinet committees and informal working groups. Full cabinet meetings have become short, increasingly ritualistic and devoid of real debate. As Jørgen Grønnegard Christensen noted almost a quarter of a century ago, 'like the cabinets in Denmark's neighbouring countries, the cabinet [in Denmark] is neither a forum for policy discussions nor the real decision-making centre in central government' (Christensen 1985: 19).

Summary

1.   The chapter's point of departure was Lijphart's distinction between so-called 'executive–legislative balance' systems – as Denmark, Norway and Sweden have been routinely considered – and the 'executive dominant' systems of Finland and Iceland. The notion of 'executive–legislative balance' is by no means self-explanatory and has not been operationalised in the literature. There seems no reason why a numerically weak minority government could not, in the right circumstances, result in executive dominance.

2.   A notable feature of the political executive in the Nordic region has been the diversity of coalition types and the frequency of minority governments. Minority governments, both single-party and coalitions, have been routine in the metropolitan Scandinavian states, where policy-making has proceeded on the basis of various types of legislative coalitions. In contrast, majority

government has been the norm in Iceland, whilst 'ideologically diverse surplus majority coalitions' may be regarded as something of a Finnish 'speciality'.

3. Legislative coalitions vary in size, scope, duration and the degree of formalisation. Surplus majority legislative coalitions have been commonplace in Denmark, and minimal winning but detailed and written legislative agreements have been concluded in Sweden in recent years, whereas in Norway legislative coalitions have tended to be made on a flexible issue-by-issue basis.

4. The frequency of minority cabinets in metropolitan Scandinavia has resulted in large part from the fact that the Social Democratic/Labour parties have wanted, and been able, to govern on a single-party basis. These parties could readily have formed coalitions – witness Norway after the 2005 Storting election – but have preferred instead to monopolise the ministerial portfolios.

5. The achievement of statehood in Finland (1919) and Iceland (1944) spawned constitutions that prescribed semi-presidential systems and vested the head of state with potentially significant powers. Whereas for much of the post-war period Iceland has been to all intents and purposes a routine parliamentary democracy with a purely ceremonial presidency, it was possible in the 1970s under the long-serving Urho Kekkonen to speak with little exaggeration of an 'all-powerful Finnish presidency', to adapt from Duverger referring to France.

6. Constitutional change in Finland, however, has turned the conventional wisdom on its head. Under the 2000 constitution, Finland has remained an 'executive dominant' system, but with the government and particularly prime minister assuming several of the functions previously performed by the president. Today, the formal powers of the Icelandic presidency considerably exceed those of the Finnish institution and, in view of the 'political presidency' of the current Icelandic head of state, it appears that the real power of the office may well also do so.

7. Outside Finland, the Nordic constitutions say very little about the prerogatives and powers of the prime minister. In the recent literature, however, the increased importance and authority of the office have been emphasised. It seems reasonable to argue that the heightened status of the post consequent upon the performance of an ever increasing number of international/European duties has elevated the independent leadership aspects of the role and facilitated the articulation of a prime ministerial agenda. For much of the time, the prime minister has undoubtedly appeared the dominant figure in national politics. However, executive leadership should be viewed in the context of the complex and dynamic power relationships that exist between the prime minister and his/her PPG, on the one hand, and the party leader and PPGs of the 'support parties' (whether members of an executive or legislative coalition), on the other.

References

Arter, David (1981) 'Kekkonen's Finland: enlightened despotism or consensual democracy?', *West European Politics*, 4 (3), pp. 219–34.

Arter, David (1987) *Politics and Policy-Making in Finland*, Wheatsheaf: Brighton.

Arter, David (2006) *Democracy in Scandinavia*, Manchester University Press: Manchester.

Aylott, Nicholas and Torbjörn Bergman (2004) 'Almost in government, but not quite: the Swedish Greens, bargaining constraints and the rise of contract parliamentarism', paper presented at the Joint Sessions of Workshops, European Consortium of Political Research, Uppsala, April.

Bale, Tim and Torbjörn Bergman (2006) 'Captives no longer, but servants still? Contract parliamentarism and the new minority governance in Sweden and New Zealand', *Government and Opposition*, 41 (3), pp. 422–49.

Bergman, Torbjörn (2003) 'Sweden: when minority cabinets are the rule and majority coalitions the exception', in Wolfgang C. Müller and Kaare Strøm (eds), *Coalition Governments in Western Europe*, Oxford University Press: Oxford, pp. 192–230.

Christensen, Jørgen Grønnegard (1985) 'In search of unity: cabinet committees in Denmark', in Thomas T. Mackie and Brian W. Hogwood (eds), *Unlocking the Cabinet*, Sage: London, pp. 114–37.

Christiansen, Flemming Juul and Erik Damgaard (2008) 'Parliamentary opposition under minority parliamentarism: Scandinavia', *Journal of Legislative Studies*, 14 (1/2), 46–76.

Clemens, Clay (1994) 'The chancellor as manager: Helmut Kohl, the CDU and governance in Germany', *West European Politics*, 17 (4), pp. 28–51.

Damgaard, Erik (2000) 'Minority governments', in Lauri Karvonen and Krister Ståhlberg (eds), *Festschrift for Dag Anckar on his 60th Birthday on February 12, 2000*, Åbo Akademis Förlag: Åbo, pp. 353–69.

Duverger, Maurice (1980) 'A new political system model: semi-presidential government', *European Journal of Political Research*, 8, pp. 165–87.

Elgie, Robert (2004) 'Semi-presidentialism: concepts, consequences and contesting explanations', *Political Studies Review*, 2 (3), pp. 314–30.

Green-Pedersen, Christoffer and Lisbeth Hoffman Thomsen (2005) 'Bloc politics vs broad co-operation? The functioning of Danish minority parliamentarism', *Journal of Legislative Studies*, 11 (2), pp. 153–69.

Heidar, Knut (2001) *Norway. Elites on Trial*, Westview: Boulder, CO.

Jakobson, Max (2003) 'Pääninisterin uusi rooli', *Helsingin Sanomat*, 4 April.

Jungar, Ann-Cathrine (2002) 'A case of surplus majority government: the Finnish rainbow coalition', *Scandinavian Political Studies*, 25 (1), pp. 57–83.

Kalela, Jaakko (1993) 'Mauno Koivisto ja 90-luvun ulkopolitiikan puitteet', in Keijo Immonen (ed.), *Pitkä Linja*, Kirjayhtymä: Helsinki, pp. 221–53.

Koivisto, Mauno (1983) *Linjaviitat*, Kirjayhtymä: Helsinki.

Kristinsson, Gunnar Helgi (1999) 'Between form and content: semi-presidentialism in Iceland', in Robert Elgie (ed.), *Semi-presidentialism in Europe*, Cambridge University Press: Cambridge, pp. 86–103.

Kristjánsson, Svanur (2004) 'Iceland: searching for democracy along three dimensions of citizen control', *Scandinavian Political Studies*, 27 (2), pp. 153–74.

Lewin, Leif (1998) 'Majoritarian and consensus democracy: the Swedish experience', *Scandinavian Political Studies*, 21 (3), pp. 195–206.

Lijphart, Arend (1999) *Patterns of Democracy. Government Forms and Performance in Thirty-Six Countries*, Yale University Press: New Haven, CT.

Lijphart, Arend (2003) 'Measurement validity and institutional engineering – reflections on Rein Taagepera's meta-study', *Political Studies*, 51 (1), pp. 20–5.

Miller, Kenneth E. (1991) *Denmark. A Troubled Welfare State*, Westview Press: Boulder, CO.

Müller, Wolfgang C. and Kaare Strøm (1999) 'Conclusions: party behaviour and representative democracy', in Wolfgang C. Müller and Kaare Strøm (eds), *Policy, Office or Votes? How Political Parties in Western Europe Make Hard Decisions*, Cambridge University Press: Cambridge, pp. 279–309.

Narud, Hanne Marthe and Kaare Strøm (2003) 'Norway. A fragile constitutional order', in Wolfgang C. Müller and Kaare Strøm (eds), *Coalition Governments in Western Europe*, Oxford University Press: Oxford, pp. 158–91.

Nousiainen, Jaakko (2001) 'From semi-presidentialism to parliamentary government: political and constitutional developments in Finland', *Scandinavian Political Studies*, 24 (2), pp. 95–109.

Nyheim, Jan Erik (1967) 'Norway: the co-operation of four parties', *Scandinavian Political Studies*, 2, pp. 257–62.

Olsen, J. P. (1980) 'Governing Norway: segmentation, anticipation and consensus formation', in R. Rose and E. N. Suleiman (eds), *Presidents and Prime Ministers*, American Enterprise for Public Policy Research: Washington, DC, pp. 203–55.

Paloheimo, Heikki (2003) 'The rising power of the prime minister in Finland', *Scandinavian Political Studies*, 26 (3), pp. 219–43.

Pedersen, Mogens N. (1967) 'Consensus and conflict in the Danish Folketing, 1945–65', *Scandinavian Political Studies*, 2, pp. 143–66.

Pedersen, Mogens N. (2000) 'Coalition formation processes in Danish politics: reflections on norms, procedures and processes', in Lauri Karvonen and Krister Ståhlberg (eds), *Festschrift for Dag Anckar on his 60th Birthday on February 12, 2000*, Åbo Akademis Förlag: Åbo.

Rasch, Bjørn Erik (2004) 'Parliamentary government', in Knut Heidar (ed.), *Nordic Politics*, Universitetsforlaget: Oslo, pp. 127–41.

Rose, Richard (1991) 'Prime ministers in parliamentary democracies', *West European Politics*, 14 (2), pp. 9–24.

Ruin, Olof (1991) 'Three Swedish prime ministers: Tage Erlander, Olof Palme and Ingvar Carlsson', *West European Politics*, 14 (3), pp. 58–82.

Sannerstedt, Anders (1996) 'Negotiations in the Riksdag', in Lars-Göran Stenelo and Magnus Jerneck (eds), *The Bargaining Democracy*, Lund University Press: Lund, pp. 17–58.

Sannerstedt, Anders and Mats Sjölin (1992) 'Sweden: changing party relations in a more active parliament', in Erik Damgaard (ed.), *Parliamentary Change in the Nordic Countries*, Scandinavian University Press: Oslo, pp. 99–149.

Siaroff, A. (2003) 'Varieties of parliamentarism in the advanced industrial democracies', *International Political Science Review*, 24 (4), pp. 445–64.

Strøm, Kaare (1990) *Minority Government and Majority Rule*, Cambridge University Press: Cambridge.

Tsebelis, George (2004) 'Veto players and law production', in Herbert Döring and Mark Hallerberg (eds), *Patterns of Parliamentary Behaviour*, Ashgate: Aldershot, pp. 169–200.

Part VI

The strategic security environment

12

The changing security environment of the Nordic region: from Cold War 'security threats' to the 'security challenges' of today

> Given our geographical location, the three main security challenges for Finland today are Russia, Russia and Russia – and not only for Finland....
>
> (Häkämies 2007)

'All four [mainland Nordic] states, culturally Western and ideologically democratic, found themselves because of their geographical location on the strategic and cultural frontier between the superpowers and their nascent blocs as these were formed in the immediate post-war years', wrote Toivo Miljan in the late 1970s (Miljan 1977: 275). Norway and Finland were frontier states in a physical and doctrinal sense, sharing a common border with the Soviet Union as well as being situated at the ideological frontier between capitalism and communism. The division of Germany by 1948 also brought the Soviet Union, through its domination of East Germany, to within six miles of the Danish coast. Moreover, all four mainland Nordic states perceived the primary security threat as emanating from the Soviet Union. What were their responses to that threat? The first half of this chapter examines the nature of the post-war security system in northern Europe and the configuration known as the 'Nordic balance'. It asks: where was the 'balance' in the Nordic balance? The disintegration of the Soviet Union in 1991 spawned significant changes in the political geography of northern Europe. The last part of the chapter analyses the new security architecture in the region and the accentuated role of the North Atlantic Treaty Organisation (NATO) and the European Union (EU) as 'security providers'. Whilst the perception of a security threat is much diminished, the talk now is of 'security challenges' and 'security risks'.

The post-war security options for the Nordic states

In addition to their frontier station, the Nordic countries in the aftermath of the Second World War formed a region with two what might be described as

THE NORTH
CAPE

['top and tail' strategic security points.] At the top, there was the area north of the Arctic Circle known as the North Cape or *Nordkalotten*, which comprised the Norwegian province of Finnmark, Swedish and Finnish Lapland and the Kola Peninsula in the Soviet Union. There was a massive Soviet military and maritime concentration at Murmansk on the Kola Peninsula in the 1960s and 1970s, as the port remained ice-free in winter and provided access to the North Atlantic for the bulk of the Soviet nuclear submarine capability. Krister Wahlbäck has commented that (until the collapse of the Soviet Union in 1991) [the increased importance of the Soviet Kola base from the early 1960s represented the biggest change in the immediate security environment of the Nordic region in the twentieth century] (Wahlbäck 1982: 27). It shifted the lines of confrontation between the big powers to the northern extremities of the Nordic region in a way that was historically new and affected the entire region.

Soviet Kola
Base

BALTIC STRAIGHT At the tail, so to speak, the Baltic Straits, comprising the Sound (Öresund) between Denmark and Sweden, the Great Belt separating the Danish islands of Sjælland and Fyn, and the Little Belt separating Fyn and Jutland assumed increased strategic significance in linking the Baltic with the North Sea and North Atlantic. The secret protocol of the German–Soviet non-aggression [Ribbentrop–Molotov Pact of 23 August 1939 had assigned Finland, Latvia and Estonia to the Soviet sphere of influence – the two last-mentioned plus Lithuania were incorporated into the Soviet Union in 1940]– whilst by the mid-1950s the Soviet Baltic fleet was stationed in the Kaliningrad enclave (formerly Königsberg), wedged between Poland and Lithuania, which came to be known as the 'fourth Baltic republic'. If Franklin D. Roosevelt's sky-high blood pressure of 260/150 may have accounted for his concessionary approach to Stalin at the Yalta conference in February 1945, the bloodless coup in Czechoslovakia in February 1948 finalised the division of post-war Europe and by 1955 the bloc of Soviet satellite states had almost without exception been organised into the Warsaw Pact security alliance. In the light of such developments, what were the security policy options facing the Nordic states after the Second World War and which did they decide to pursue? In theory three security options were possible (Andrén 1977):

1939

YALTA 1945
CZECH COUP 48

ANDREN (1977)

1 to return to the [isolated national neutrality] of the inter-war period;
2 to create a [pan-Nordic regional security system;]
3 to conclude an alliance of one sort or another with the nascent super-powers.

Isolated national neutrality

The Danish case will illustrate the wider point that a return to the isolated national neutrality of the inter-war period was not a realistic scenario. In principle, the collapse of Germany and Russia as great powers after the First World War, and the reunification of North Slesvig with Denmark in 1920, offered the prospect of the neutral course Denmark had pursued since defeat by Prussia in 1864 proceeding without serious challenge. In a referendum on 6 September 1920, 96.9 per cent of Danes favoured the incorporation of Slesvig, albeit on a relatively low turnout of 50.1 per cent. The rise of Hitler completely changed the situation, however, and emphasised Denmark's exposed geo-political position as a state sharing a frontier with fascism. As John Fitzmaurice (1981) has noted, after 1933 a policy of neutrality and 'non-provocation', supporting the illusory collective security strategy of the League of Nations – albeit not to the point of decisive action – proved ineffectual. It may be, as Woodrow Wilson dolefully remarked, that the failure of the League of Nations demonstrated that 'justice is not the first fruit of the tree of knowledge, but the last', but Germany's withdrawal from the League (along with Japan) in 1933 marked the real end of the road for an organisation which the US Congress had refused to join and which, apart from its intermediation in the Finnish–Swedish dispute over the Åland islands, had achieved precious little. The resurgence of German power highlighted Denmark's dilemma as a small country bordering an expansionist big-power neighbour and seriously challenged the feasibility of neutrality as a security policy option. Not surprisingly, when in 1939 Germany offered the three Scandinavian states (Denmark, Norway and Sweden) a non-aggression pact, Denmark was the only one to accept. It may be, as Miljan (1977: 80) has observed, that the general foreign policy orientation of the Scandinavians in the immediate post-war years could be described as 'neutralism within the United Nations' – the League of Nations' successor. But the Second World War had conclusively demonstrated at least three things: the small-nation status of the Scandinavian states; the end of the possibility of isolationism (both Denmark and Norway were occupied by the Germans); and their subordination willy-nilly to the international security policy system. In short, they were involved whether they wanted to be or not.

A pan-Nordic regional security system

The creation of a pan-Nordic regional security system was attempted against the backdrop of the severely heightened East–West tension over the Berlin blockade of June 1948–May 1949. The blockade could well have led to a third world war; instead, it became a cameo of the wider Cold War confrontation developing between the capitalist and communist worlds and effectively sealed the East–West partition of Germany. In this inflamed international situation, Sweden initiated moves to create a Scandinavian Defence Alliance. The architect of the project was the Swedish foreign secretary Östen Undén, who, on 3 May 1948 in Oslo, proposed an exploration of possible military co-operation – 'in defence of Nordic neutrality' (Skodvin 1971: 132) – between Denmark, Norway and Sweden. In a government statement to the Riksdag in February 1949, Undén hinted at the basic rationale for a regional pact when reporting how, in discussion with his Norwegian counterpart, Halvard Lange, on 19

April 1948, he had detected a clear tendency for Norway to revise its previous foreign policy and assume a Western alignment or, in Magne Skodvin's phrase, an 'opening to the West'. The Scandinavian Defence Alliance was energetically canvassed by the new Swedish Social Democratic prime minister Tage Erlander, and supported by all political parties on condition that the proposed alliance remained independent of the superpower blocs. True, individuals such as Ture Neuman, editor of *Trots Allt*, Torgny Segerstedt, his counterpart at *Göteborgs Handels- och Sjöfartstidning*, and Johannes Wickman at the influential daily *Dagens Nyheter* favoured the emerging Western option. But Erlander believed that the Scandinavian states could isolate themselves from the orbit of great-power interests through a declaration of non-involvement, which would be reinforced with the resources to make intrusion into the area costly. He was concerned that Sweden should retain its traditional policy of neutrality and feared that the intrusion of superpower politics into Scandinavia would complicate that goal, as well as increasing tension in northern Europe. In sum, the Scandinavian Defence Alliance project was viewed as consonant with Sweden's traditional policy of neutrality.

The main opposition to the Scandinavian Defence Alliance came from Norway. Clearly, the German invasion on 9 April 1940 and subsequent occupation had been traumatic and highlighted the dangers of isolation. Equally, Norway (unlike Denmark) had had a government in exile in London, recognised by the Allies, and leading politicians, along with large sections of the citizenry, soon began to view close co-operation with Britain and the United States as an essential component of post-war foreign policy. According to Ib Faurby (1982), this was a significant factor in Norway's ultimate eschewal of the Scandinavian Defence Alliance. In Denmark, as in Norway, the German invasion and occupation, also beginning on 9 April 1940, had been a devastating experience. In June 1940 the four 'old parties' had come together in a crisis coalition led by Thorvald Stauning; Erik Scavenius, the foreign minister during the First World War, assumed his former duties and, unlike his predecessor, Peter Munch, Scavenius favoured greater accommodation with the Germans (Einhorn 1975). It was not really until the flight to London in May 1942 of the Conservative leader, Christmas Møller, forced out of the governing coalition because of his anti-German sentiments, that the credibility of the Danish opposition was established in Allied circles (Kirby 1995: 370). Perhaps most significantly for post-war developments, however, the German occupation prompted the Social Democrats to renounce their policy of unilateral disarmament. Yet as late as the beginning of 1948, the Social Democrat prime minister, H. C. Hedtoft, expressed a preference for neutrality, stating that 'We will not place our country inside any block' (Miljan 1977: 80). Thereafter he inclined towards the neutral Scandinavian Defence Alliance option and, when Norway jettisoned it, proposed a Danish–Swedish alliance as an alternative. Sweden, however, feared that in practice this would not be able to remain independent of the Atlantic alliance which was in the process of formation. Indeed, from a

Swedish standpoint, the Scandinavian Defence Alliance negotiations collapsed because of Norwegian demands for official military collaboration with the Western powers in the embryonic Atlantic pact.

Alliance with the nascent superpowers

Denmark, Norway and Iceland ultimately pursued this option and became (as we shall see) *conditional* members of NATO. However, it is important to emphasise the differences between Denmark and Norway regarding membership of the Atlantic alliance. Denmark may be said to have joined NATO as a last resort, only when faced with a lack of alternatives. Norwegian rejection of the Scandinavian Defence Alliance had scuppered a pan-regional security solution; memories of the German occupation were still fresh in Denmark and spawned a fear of future isolationism, whilst the communist coup in Czechoslovakia in February 1948 prompted real concern that the Soviets were going on the offensive. The Finno-Soviet Friendship, Co-operation and Mutual Assistance (FCMA) [FCMA (1948)] Treaty two months later and the start of the Berlin blockade in June 1948 all contributed to a general sense of unease. There had possibly been the feeling throughout the Scandinavian Defence Alliance negotiations, moreover, that it would be impossible to receive US arms deliveries if the three Scandinavian states combined to chart a common policy of neutrality between the nascent power blocs. Ultimately, therefore, NATO came to be viewed in Denmark as the only viable alternative. Yet there was not a cross-party consensus on the issue. The NATO treaty was ratified by the three 'NATO parties' – the Social Democrats, Conservatives and Liberals – but opposed by the Communists, Social Liberals (who proposed a referendum on the issue) and most of the Justice Party members. The Social Liberals did not moderate their position until 1957.

Norway *'Never again the 9th April' (HEIDAR, 2001)*

Though initially a contentious issue, there was in Norway, unlike in Denmark, a pro-NATO lobby from the outset among sections of the political elite. As Knut Heidar has put it: 'Never again the 9th of April was the political slogan denoting a pro-NATO membership stand, close US co-operation and a strong military' (Heidar 2001: 138). True, the aspiration to work through the United Nations (UN) and, in addition, to play a 'bridge-building' role between East and West dominated the first two or three post-war years. The Labour Party [Labour party esp. skeptical] in particular contained those sceptical of an Atlantic alignment, although it was significant that by early 1948 the party secretary, Haakon Lie, the chairman of the central blue-collar union federation, Konrad Nordahl, and the veteran Martin Tranmæl had come out in favour of a clearer West European orientation, in the spirit of the Bevin plan. The British foreign secretary, Ernest Bevin, worked, in the words of Roy Jenkins, 'to launch the Marshall [THE BEVIN PLAN] Plan, to create NATO, to connect the United States to Europe and to connect Britain to the United States' (Jenkins 1974: 64). But the Finno-Soviet FCMA prompted concern in Oslo that Norway might be invited to enter a similar type of agreement with the Soviet Union. The Berlin blockade, moreover, spelt the end of 'bridge-building' as a realistic policy and both the government and the opposition shifted towards a stronger West European orientation. For many Labour politicians Scandinavian co-operation was important, not least because there were Social Democratic governments in Denmark and Sweden, whilst for others a Western alliance with Britain would provide a 'third force' between the United States and the Soviet Union. However, by May 1948, when the Swedish foreign secretary, Östen Undén, visited Oslo to canvass the Scandinavian Defence Alliance idea, the Americans were signalling that they hoped Norway would join a broad Western defence pact and it was already clear that Britain was inclining towards it. Support for a 'Scandinavian solution' and opposition to involvement in a great-power alliance were strongest in the Labour Party, and a majority of the party's parliamentary group in the Storting and, indeed, most of the party press were opposed to entering the Atlantic alliance. This made the outcome of the Labour Party's annual conference on 17–19 February absolutely crucial. Addressing delegates in a powerful speech, Halvard Lange, the foreign secretary, noted:

> The government has come to the conclusion that the Soviet Union will not take any steps against us or any other state, which they think will be likely to lead to a new general war. Precisely because we evaluate the Soviet government's position in this way, we believe that a solidarity anchored in a treaty with the great democracies of the West will give us the greatest degree of security that is possible to reach in this imperfect world. (Miljan 1977: 33–4)

Following that, the conference voted by the unexpectedly large majority of 329 votes to 35 to support Norwegian membership of NATO, and this provided the basis for the affirmative vote in the Storting five weeks later. Incidentally, when Norway was invited to join the Atlantic alliance, there were those in Washington, including most prominently John Foster Dulles and George F. Kennan, who questioned the wisdom of incorporating parts of Scandinavia into the Western collective security system. As Mats Berdal has insisted, for them 'the strategic rationale for bringing Norway into the alliance was seen to lie almost exclusively in the *denial value* of its membership – that is, denying the Soviet Union control of any part of Norwegian territory' (Berdal 1997: 179, my italics).

Despite the overwhelming pro-NATO vote in the Labour conference and subsequent Norwegian membership of the Atlantic alliance, the proponents of a regional security policy solution condemned both the evidence and the methods used by advocates of NATO membership. Indeed, Berge Furre has described how, over the course of the Cold War, a series of myths relating to Norway's accession to NATO were propagated, involving suggestions of bias, intrigue and 'dirty tricks' (Furre 1993: 233). One propounded by NATO opponents in the 1950s and 1960s held that Norway was manipulated into supporting membership by government ministers such as Lange and the defence secretary, Jens Christian Hauge, the former in particular colluding with the Americans to sabotage the Scandinavian Defence Alliance. The evidence, it is said, can be found, among other things, in a document dating from September 1948 in which Lange urged the United States to make it clear that a neutral defence alliance could not count on US weapons supplies. Critics have interpreted this as a cynical attempt by Lange to torpedo the defence project. Others, especially the historian Knut Einar Eriksen, have insisted that Lange simply wanted to put his cards on the table and bring the reality of the situation home to the Storting as it began its autumn session (Furre 1993: 236). The Soviet Union, it was said, was planning an attack on the West and on Norway in the process and a 'new 9 April' was imminent. Events in Czechoslovakia seemed to give credence to this view. However, Magne Skodvin's work, based on archive material in the foreign ministry, makes it abundantly clear that the relevant Norwegian officials did not envisage a Soviet attack (Furre 1993: 233). The war had weakened the Soviet Union, which relied on conventional military forces, whereas the West had a monopoly of atomic weapons. According to Skodvin (1971), it was a concern that, in the event of superpower conflict, it would become exceedingly difficult for Norway not to become embroiled that was uppermost in foreign ministry thinking. As in the case of the Note Crisis in Finno-Soviet relations (discussed shortly), the truth, the whole truth and nothing but the truth regarding Norwegian accession to NATO may never be known.

In her detailed analysis of the failure of the Scandinavian Defence Alliance, viewed primarily from a Norwegian perspective, Barbara Haskel's thesis is that differences between the national leaders on three important and unavoidable questions prevented agreement on a joint pact and so opened the door to NATO. First, there was the likely response of the United States to the establishment of a regional defence alliance. The significance of the United States in the post-war security system of Western Europe was forcefully brought home to Lange in a confidential conversation with Ernest Bevin on 15 March 1948 in which the British foreign secretary made it clear that Britain alone did not feel able to protect Norway. Two other significant points emerged from the conversation: that Britain's energies were being devoted to enlisting a commitment from the United States to the defence of Western Europe; and that if such a commitment could be obtained, Britain would encourage the inclusion of Norway in any arrangement (Haskel 1976: 63). However, the Americans for their part were considerably more cautious in relation to Norway than towards Denmark (Haskel 1976: 63–4).

Second, a joint pact was likely to have little deterrent effect. In this context, Lange insisted at the Labour Party conference in February 1949 that not only Norway but also the whole of Norden was 'too small a unit ... to be a power factor strong enough to deter all [parties] from attacking' (Haskel 1976: 71). King Haakon, too, expressed little belief in the success of a regional defence pact and pressed his conviction that Norwegian security policy should be based on close co-operation with the Western democracies as the only source of help in an emergency. The US ambassador summed up the king's stance following a private dinner on 26 January 1949: 'In the event of an attack, only a push-button response from the US could save Norway' (Greve 1973: 182).

Finally, there was the likely impact of the domestic political environment not only on the first security preferences of the Scandinavian states, but also on their fall-back positions. In the Norwegian case the fact that the British Labour Party was in power in 1948 was important, partly because of Bevin's influence on Lange but also more generally because of the influence exerted by a large socialist party at the head of a close ally. According to Haskel (1976: 57), this helped to make the Atlantic alliance palatable to those within the Norwegian Labour Party who felt politically alienated from the United States. Equally, as Oscar Torp, the chairman of the Parliamentary Labour Party, argued to the prime minister, Einar Gerhardsen, if the Swedish Scandinavian defence plan were tried but failed to win US support, it could boomerang, that is, a hostile attitude would be created in Norway towards the Western powers, which would complicate the fall-back position of an Atlantic alliance. In short, it was too risky (Haskel 1976: 81).

As noted above, on 3 May 1948 the Swedish foreign secretary, Östen Undén, visited Oslo to sound the Norwegians out on the matter of a Scandinavian Defence Alliance. Nine months later, on 30 January 1949, the Norwegian government, together with the leaders of the opposition parties, came to the conclusion that 'for the moment it was not possible to achieve the necessary consensus with regard to either the conditions for, or the consequences of, a neutral defence alliance' (Bull 1982: 134). In Krister Wahlbäck's judgement, 'the discussions on a Scandinavian Defence Alliance were doomed from the outset to fail, since the Norwegian and Swedish standpoints were wholly irreconcilable' (Wahlbäck 1973: 89). Indeed, in his diary entry of 9 January 1949 even the Swedish prime minister, Tage Erlander, asked whether, deep down, he really hoped the proposed defence pact would materialise, noting that the Norwegians' 'Swedish complex' could well lead to constant tensions as and when Norway looked westward for support (Wahlbäck 1973: 91). In a longer perspective, in truth, NATO membership could be viewed, as Olav Riste has suggested, as merely the formalisation of an existing, but until then implicit, assurance that the control of Norwegian territory by a hostile great power would be intolerable to the West (Riste 1985: 20).

Sweden

The collapse of the Scandinavian Defence Alliance initiative left Sweden, alone in the region, to pursue its traditional course of neutrality, although from the Soviet standpoint this was viewed with the greatest suspicion. Swedish leaders were said to have 'bound the country to the enslaving Marshall Plan' and had joined the Council of Europe, which was regarded as an auxiliary implement

'The council of Europe... an auxilary implement to NATO'
— Allison, 1985

1945-1946
BALTIC
REFUGEE ISSU
5ᵗʰ OCT 1946
Russian Trade

of the North Atlantic Treaty (Allison 1985: 31). On the Swedish side, two events – the Baltic refugee issue of 1945–46 and the Russian trade deal of 5 October 1946 – sparked a vigorous debate on the Social Democrats' concessionary attitudes to the Soviet Union, which, it was argued, were incompatible with neutrality. The foreign secretary between 1945 and 1962, Östen Undén, in particular was frequently attacked for his reluctance to criticise Moscow. Certainly, the Soviet Union not only demanded but ultimately gained the extradition of 167 refugees who had been soldiers in the German army during the war. As to the trade deal, the Swedish government offered the Kremlin export credits worth up to 1 billion Swedish kronor, just over half of which was in fact used. Most notably, a former Social Democrat, Herbert Tingsten, now editor of the liberal broadsheet *Dagens Nyheter*, but also others in the media and private industry, were critical of this new market and there were rumours of the government pressing export firms to conclude agreements.

Although by the 1970s Swedish neutrality had achieved doctrinal status, that is, it had become tantamount to an official ideology which was deeply internalised among the population as a whole, it needs emphasis that it was not of the legal type, like Swiss neutrality, backed by international guarantees in the event of war. Moreover, until the later stages of the Second World War, Swedish neutrality was not even based on adequate national defences. Thus, whilst a conscious policy of neutrality had been promoted after the outbreak of the First World War, largely inspired by prime minister Hjalmar Hammarskjöld, Sweden succeeded in preserving its neutrality despite the fact that its military defences were in reality poor and inefficient. Things were little better during the Second World War, which, it seems, had not been expected, and defence had not been given the priority many citizens felt it deserved. Ironically, if its military defence was found wanting, Sweden approached the Second World War with a highly developed set of policies geared towards economic defence and the meeting of military and civilian needs during a war. In large part this was because the First World War had drawn attention to the depleted stock of food and other vital commodities, which was, in turn, the result of poor planning and organisation. In 1928 a commission on 'economic defence preparations' was set up, and it contained representatives of all the relevant sectors of the economy.

During the Second World War, commercial cross-pressures strained Swedish neutrality to the limit and beyond. At the start of hostilities, the German steel industry was based on annual imports of around 20 million tons of iron ore, almost half of it emanating from Sweden. Since steel was a crucial material for war production, the Allies exerted strong pressure on Sweden to terminate supplies to Hitler. For a short time Sweden successfully negotiated trade agreements with the Allies and with Germany, by balancing their respective economic interests. Soon, however, both sides brought economic pressure to bear and, as Ebba Dohlman has remarked, dependent on Germany for coal and on the Britain for metal goods, chemicals and oil, Sweden found itself in a precarious position (Dohlman 1989: 52). Indeed, in such circumstances, it was obliged to make concessions that, strictly speaking, were inconsistent with neutrality. Hence in June 1941 Sweden permitted the transit of a Nazi German division – the Engelbrecht division, comprising 14,712 armed troops – across Sweden to join Operation Barbarossa against the Soviet Union. The transport required 105 trains in all and lasted seventeen days. It has been claimed, though never verified, that King Gustav V threatened to abdicate if the German demand was not met. The exceptional four-party Social Democrat–Agrarian–Liberal–Conservative wartime coalition under the Social Democrat Per Albin Hansson was badly divided and many Riksdag members vigorously opposed the concessions to Hitler. Moreover, between June 1940 and August 1943 something in the order of 2,140,000 on-leave Nazi soldiers, travelling to and from Norway and Finland – the so-called *Permittenttrafiken* – were allowed to cross through Sweden. In his excellent analysis Hans Mouritzen (1988) argues persuasively that the exigencies of the Second World War prompted a shift in Swedish foreign policy from non-commitment to *semi-neutrality*, although, ultimately, the extent of Finlandisation, that is, 'adaptive acquiescence' (see below), remained relatively limited.

In the wake of the Second World War, Swedish neutrality entered a new phase. National defences were stepped up (only the Communist Party demurred) and, whilst Sweden accepted the obligation to back UN Security Council resolutions, it viewed the voting system as a guarantee that military sanctions would never in practice be required of it. Sweden also reformulated its security policy, and the new line was 'freedom from alliances in peacetime aiming at neutrality in war'. By the late 1960s economic defence had become an increasingly important element in Sweden's total defence policy and in 1979 a new organ, the Directorate for Economic Defence (Överstyrelse för ekonomisk försvar), was set up. In the same decade Nils Andrén (1977) noted: 'It is no overstatement to regard non-alignment as an extraordinarily fixed foreign policy direction – so fixed that even balanced bystanders sometimes regard it as a "sacred cow".'

The components of the Nordic balance

The security configuration that emerged in the Nordic region by the early 1950s came to be known as the 'Nordic balance'. It is a curious term in many ways and by no means self-explanatory. What were the constituent elements in the Nordic balance and, most importantly, where was the balance in the Nordic balance? The notion of the Nordic balance has, as we shall see, been used in three different senses – as a descriptive term, an explanatory tool and as a prescriptive concept. As a purely descriptive term, it contained three main components:

1 Danish and Norwegian membership of NATO on what might be described as 'minimum conditions';

2 the Swedish policy of non-alignment in peacetime and neutrality in war, backed by a relatively strong national defence;

3 Finland's ties with the Soviet Union through the 1948 FCMA Treaty.

Danish and Norwegian membership of NATO on 'minimum conditions'

John Fitzmaurice has referred to Denmark as a 'low profile' member of NATO, keeping its military and foreign policy commitments to a strict minimum (Fitzmaurice 1981: 147). Indeed, from the outset, both Norway and Denmark sought to reduce the provocative impact of their NATO engagement. Symptomatically, Mats Berdal (1997) has referred to Norway's *low tension* policy (*lavspenningspolitikk*). As early as 1 February 1949, in a note to the Soviet Union, Norway undertook not to permit the basing of foreign troops in peacetime on Norwegian soil, albeit reserving the right to do so if the danger of war increased. On 5 October 1953 Denmark followed suit. The self-imposed ban (self-denying ordinance) on the stationing of foreign armed forces on Norwegian territory in peacetime – the so-called 'bases policy' – was formalised a few weeks *before* the decision to join NATO and was primarily intended to reassure the Soviet Union about the defensive nature of the nascent Atlantic alliance. It came in response to a Soviet note on 29 January 1949 which asserted that Norway was planning to adhere to an aggressive alliance which sought bases in Norway adjacent to the Soviet border. Within three days Norway responded, acknowledging that it was considering membership of the Atlantic alliance, rejecting its aggressive intent and affirming that bases would not be permitted on Norwegian territory 'as long as Norway was not attacked or exposed to the threat of attack' (Haskel 1976: 48). On 5 February 1949, on the eve of the departure of the foreign secretary, Lange, for Washington to investigate the implications of the NATO option, a second Soviet note arrived, proposing a non-aggression pact between the two countries, and arguing that the 'bases policy' would allow Norway to claim that 'provocative rumours' of a threat of attack required it to permit the establishment of bases. On 3 March Norway replied to this second Soviet note, reiterating the commitment to no bases in peacetime and insisting that the Norwegian government would be the sole interpreter of the factual grounds of an attack or the threat of one (Haskel 1976: 48).

Incidentally, there were strong domestic reasons for the 'bases policy', since, as Lange stated during his visit to the United States in February 1949, it would be 'a political impossibility to get the Norwegian people to accept that Norwegian territory be put at the disposal of foreign troops in peacetime' (Riste 1985: 21). However, in a statement to the Storting on 21 February 1951, the defence minister, Jens Christian Hauge, made it clear that the base restrictions policy 'would not prevent Norway from participating in joint Allied exercises or being visited for short periods by the naval and air forces of our allies even in peacetime'. On 5 October 1953 Denmark made a similar decision.

The bases policies were extended in 1957, when a decision was made to arm NATO with tactical nuclear weapons. Neither Denmark nor Norway accepted the (essentially US) 'pre-stocking' of tactical atomic devices on its territory. In addition to the base and nuclear weapons restrictions, Norway effected the 'voluntary demilitarisation' of the area adjoining the Soviet naval base system on the Kola Peninsula. No military manoeuvres took place east of 24° longitude, that is, within a radius of about 125 miles from the Soviet border. The effect of this Norwegian policy of non-provocation, as Andrén (1977) has observed, was that on the Western side in peacetime there was no permanent counterpoise to Soviet capacity in the area.

Unlike in Denmark, there was little foreign policy debate in Norway for much of the 1950s and the NATO consensus went largely unchallenged. In part this was because of the (erroneous) popular belief that membership of the Atlantic alliance had been a _quid pro quo_ for the receipt of Marshall aid, whilst in addition the non-provocative nature of Norway's NATO commitment seemed well suited to the needs of the country's exposed geo-strategic position. It came as a considerable shock to ordinary Norwegians, therefore, when, following the Soviet shooting down of a U2 US spy plane over Sverdlowsk on 1 May 1960 – the aim had been to photograph intercontinental ballistic missile sites in the Soviet Union – their government came under attack. The aircraft had intended to land in Bodø on the north-west Norwegian coast after completing its mission and, accordingly, Nikita Khrushchev criticised the Norwegians, as well as the United States, for allowing their airfields to be used for hostile intelligence operations. According to the official Soviet note of protest, Norway was 'an accessory to provocative actions by the United States against Norway's neighbour, the Soviet Union' (Berdal 1997: 153). Although the Norwegian government vigorously denied all knowledge of the U2 exercise, it later transpired that several Norwegian intelligence officials knew exactly what was going on. Indeed, it is probably fair to conclude that, whilst the United States failed properly to inform the Norwegian authorities about the U2 operation, Vilhelm Evang, the head of the Norwegian Defence Intelligence Staff, certainly seems to have known more about US plans than he was prepared to admit at the time (Berdal 1997: 153).

In his detailed study, Carsten Holbraad insists that 'the relationship with NATO has revealed underlying tendencies towards neutrality in Danish foreign policy' (Holbraad 1991: 119). True, in 1951, the Danish Folketing approved the North Atlantic Council's (NATO's) decision to build an integrated European force under a US commander, and the Supreme Headquarters Allied Powers Europe (SHAPE) was established, with four subordinate commands, including the Northern European Command, covering Denmark and Norway and the approaches to the Baltic. Yet security policy was anything but a valence issue in Denmark in the 1950s and a strong pacifist and neutralist opposition continued, especially in the Social Liberal and Socialist People's parties. Holbraad has spoken of 'latent neutrality'. Thus, Denmark was less than fully enthusiastic about accepting West Germany as a full and equal member of NATO in 1955. The governing Social Democrats' nuclear restrictions policy, moreover, was at least in part dictated by domestic political tactics and the desire to form a coalition with the Social Liberals after the May 1957 general election. Ironically, in the 1980s, the Social Democratic Party in opposition turned hawkish on NATO and Poul Schlüter's 'four-leaf clover' non-socialist minority coalitions were defeated twenty-two times on foreign and national security issues during their tenure of office between 1982 and 1988. Denmark, incidentally, has had one of the lowest defence budgets in NATO.

Iceland, which, like Denmark and Norway, became a founder member of NATO in 1949, also insisted that no foreign military forces be stationed in the country in peacetime. Thus, in summer 1944, the Icelandic president, Sveinn Björnsson, and the foreign secretary, Vilhjalmus Thor, visited the United States at the invitation of Franklin D. Roosevelt and, at a press conference on 26 August, made it unequivocally clear that Iceland would not grant any nation military bases on its soil. As Thor put it: 'We are a nation of individualists and we did not establish our republic in order to become less independent.... We intend to own our country, all of it, and without any foreign interference' (Nuechterlein 1975: 39). Such a statement should be set in the context of the 'pre-emptive occupation' of Iceland by the British in 1940 – to prevent the use of its ports by German warships and seaplanes – and, when the British forces were required elsewhere, the arrival of the Americans in 1941.

On 10 May 1940, following the Nazi occupation of Denmark, the Alþingi announced that the Icelandic government would take over full powers from the Danish/Icelandic king. However, at four o'clock the following morning, an occupation force of 25,000 British troops landed in Iceland, put up notices of their intentions in garbled Icelandic and proceeded to arrest the German consul, who was 'burning some documents in his bathtub' (Karlsson 2000: 314). It was a pre-emptive occupation. Iceland had written neutrality into its 1920 constitution but there was no national army, navy or air force and thus no means of preventing the use of its ports by German warships. Hotel Borg, opposite the Alþingi building in the centre of Reykjavík, became the headquarters of the occupation force. When by July 1941 the Germans had reached the Channel Islands, about 60,000 American troops replaced the British forces in Iceland.

The economic consequences of the Allied occupation were enormous. The construction of roads, army camps and other installations required a vast workforce, full employment was created and the standard of living rose steeply. Moreover, after the war Iceland benefited from very generous Marshall aid. Gunnar Karlsson has estimated that between 1948 and 1952, 'every Icelander received on average 209 US dollars, while the war-harassed Dutch came a poor second with 109 dollars' (Karlsson 2000: 37). The United States was reluctant to leave Iceland. In 1946 Washington requested permission to maintain three military bases in Iceland for ninety-nine years, but this was unanimously refused by the Alþingi. Subsequently, however, the Icelandic government, albeit faced by vigorous opposition in parliament and vociferous condemnation in the country, agreed with the United States that Keflavík airport could be used as a transit post for US transport aircraft required for the occupation of Germany. As Sigurdur A. Magnússon has written: 'To many Icelanders this merely meant that the armed forces had changed into civilian clothes' (Magnússon 1977: 143). Indeed, it was against this background that a 'no bases' stipulation – that is, no military forces stationed in the country in peacetime – was written into the treaty between Iceland and the Atlantic alliance. The decision to seek conditional membership of NATO was facilitated by US sympathies and Norwegian practice.

Donald Nuechterlein has suggested, not altogether convincingly, that the anti-treaty violence initiated by the Icelandic Communists in March 1949 was a factor in the government's decision in 1951 to enter into a bilateral defence agreement with the United States (Nuechterlein 1975: 90). Under that agreement, the United States formally undertook responsibility for the defence of Iceland on behalf of NATO (Thorhallson and Vignisson 2004: 103). The US agreement became the cornerstone of Icelandic security policy throughout the Cold War, much as the 1948 FCMA Treaty had been for Finnish foreign policy. The Keflavík base was initially run by the US air force, its main purpose being to secure intermediate landings between America and Europe. In 1961 the US navy took over the base. The strategic importance of Keflavík, of course, needs little emphasis. It was ideally located for reconnaissance against Soviet naval movements from Murmansk using either the Danish straits between Greenland and Iceland and/or the waters between Iceland and the Faeroes. As for Iceland, it became totally dependent on the United States and, apart from a few patrol boats, visible during the Cod Wars with Britain in the 1970s, lacked a defence force.

The Swedish policy of non-alignment and neutrality, backed by strong national defence

Kjell Goldmann (1991) has identified two main elements in Sweden's security policy during the Cold War: neutrality based on a *credible* national defence against a superpower aggressor; and an internationalist programme for peace and security (the latter will be discussed in the final chapter). Precisely at what point a national defence capability becomes credible – that is, how much defence capacity is necessary to sustain a policy of neutrality – must, of course, remain an open question. However, Sweden's national defence strategy during the Cold War was predicated on the *marginality doctrine* or *rational deterrence theory*, both highly contested in the international relations literature. In essence the thesis was that since the main forces of a superpower would have to be deployed against its principal adversary, only 'marginal forces' would be available for use against a secondary object (like Sweden).

Goldmann explores various dimensions of neutrality but concludes that 'it is clear that the Swedish model of security policy included neither "ideological" nor "economic" neutrality' (Goldmann 1991: 125). Rather, the formula was military non-alignment in peacetime with a view to remaining neutral in the event of war – a policy often referred to as *armed neutrality*. Significantly, by the mid-1970s, partly under the influence of East–West *détente*, Swedish defence expenditure began to decline in relative terms. Indeed, between 1980 and 1988 Sweden's military expenditure decreased by almost 4 per cent, compared with an increase of 13 per cent for NATO countries excepting the United States. There was opposition to this downward trend, particularly from parties on the right of the political spectrum.

Goldmann (1991) notes that pressure for change in Sweden's security policy in the 1980s came principally from three sources: a series of submarine incidents; exponential European integration; and the collapse of the communist bloc in Eastern Europe. On the first, it was both dramatic and traumatic for Swedes when in 1981 a Soviet submarine, probably armed with nuclear weapons, went aground near the Karlskrona naval base in south-east Sweden; this episode was followed by another in September 1982, when a submarine was sighted in Hårsfjärden, close to a naval base in the Stockholm archipelago. The commission which reported (in spring 1983) on the second incident concluded that foreign submarine activity had been taking place for many years and was becoming increasingly frequent and provocative. The evidence, it concluded, clearly indicated a Warsaw Pact source, that is, essentially Soviet submarines, and this prompted an immediate and robustly worded protest from the Swedish government, followed in turn by a freezing of high-level relations for about eighteen months. In 1992 Boris Yeltsin, the Russian president, admitted that the Soviet Union had been responsible for the Karlskrona and Hårsfjärden episodes. The submarine incursions took place against the backdrop of the so-called 'new Cold War' and a superpower arms build-up in Sweden's neighbourhood, which appeared to reflect the increased strategic importance of the Baltic. Although the submarine violations challenged the underlying functional logic of a neutrality policy and the political parties agreed that Sweden had become more 'exposed', there were no fundamental demands for a revision in Sweden's neutrality in the mid-1980s.

However, a postscript on post-war Swedish security policy is in order since, although Sweden officially pursued a policy of unswerving non-alignment/ neutrality – which assumed 'sacred cow' status among the population at large – there is evidence that it undertook secret preparations for military co-operation with NATO in the event of, or possibly even in advance of, an attack on Sweden by the Soviet Union (Dahl 1999; Vaahtoranta and Forsberg 2000: 8; af Malmberg 2001). Recent reference has been made to Sweden as a 'pro-Western neutral' and the 'seventeenth NATO member'. Moreover, NATO, it seems, was willing to defend Sweden with nuclear weapons (if necessary), since it was considered to be strategically important for the defence of Norway and maintaining sea lines across the Atlantic. The full extent of Sweden's Cold War 'NATO connection' will doubtless emerge more fully from future research.

Finland's 1948 FCMA Treaty

Prior to the outbreak of the Winter War in late November 1939 – the 'white death', in Allen F. Chew's phrase – Finland was relatively unknown and the only event to raise the country to the attention of the world was the League of Nations' decision in 1921 to assign the Åland islands to it (Julkunen 1975: 14). G. A. Gripenberg, the Finnish ambassador in London, for example, commented at the time of the Winter War that there was certainly no clear conception of Finland among the British people. 'In forest industry circles, Finland was known as a trading partner; in the musical world Sibelius was revered; experts knew that Finnish architecture was of high standard; and various sportsmen were possibly known to the ordinary man in the street' (Julkunen 1975: 15). Yet Britain, because of its commercial contacts, was one of the nations better-informed about Finland. True, among its near neighbours, the Scandinavian and Baltic states, there was deeper knowledge, whilst Germany had traditional links with Finland, although they were becoming increasingly tenuous. But elsewhere in the world precious little was known about the country.

In the foreign policy sphere, Finland between the wars was dominated by fear of Soviet aggression and it therefore engaged in a search for allies. As David Kirby has noted, 'little or no attempt was made to come to terms with geographical reality by seeking better and more durable relations with the Soviet Union' and there was little comprehension of Moscow's security needs (Kirby 1979: 107). The Soviet Union had, after all, forfeited all the advanced bases of the old imperial fleet and was particularly concerned about the security of Leningrad. Finland entered the League of Nations in 1920, setting great store by the notion of collective security, and in the years up to 1926 there were (stillborn) proposals for security arrangements with the Baltic republics and Poland – the so-called 'border states' policy. By the end of that decade, however, the failure of the Finnish policy of co-operation was reflected in the characterisation by the foreign minister, Hjalmar Procopé, of the nation's foreign policy as one of 'splendid isolation' (Kirby 1979: 114).

The year 1935 marked a turning point in that, in the wake of the Anglo-German naval agreement of that year, Finnish foreign policy officially became one of neutrality in the context of alignment with the neutral Scandinavian states (Salmon 1997: 192), although the goal of neutrality later merged with the possibility of entering a regional defence pact with its Nordic neighbours. Against the backdrop of the Sudetenland crisis of spring 1938, the Soviet Union offered Finland a military and economic assistance pact, but it was rejected in Helsinki as yet another attempt by Moscow to drag Finland into its security system. Ultimately, the die was cast for Finland – and the balance of power in central and eastern Europe radically altered – by the secret protocol of the Ribbentrop–Molotov pact (see above). Stalin attacked Finland three months later, on 30 November, and set up a puppet government under the Finnish communist exile Otto Ville Kuusinen (who had long been resident in Moscow as general secretary of the Comintern), informing the Finns, via the Swedes, that Kuusinen's 'People's Front' cabinet was the real government of Finland.

By 12 March 1940 Finland, despite a brave show, was defeated. During the so-called 'phoney war' in Britain, Winston Churchill lauded the Finnish effort against the odds and described how 'the flame of freedom still burned brightly in the frozen North'. There were, moreover, early Finnish victories at Kemijärvi and Suomussalmi, where temperatures plunged to between –30°C and –40°C. At Suomussalmi, two Russian divisions, the 44th and 163rd, were almost completely wiped out by Finnish ski troops, who adapted far better to the forested terrain than the heavy tanks of the Red Army. In the end, however, 25,000 Finns died in the Winter War and the entire Karelian peninsula in south-east Finland was transferred to the Soviet Union. In order to regain its lost territory, Finland was, by late June 1941, at war with the Soviet Union again, this time as a co-belligerent of Nazi Germany, which had recently launched Operation Barbarossa (Jakobson 1999: 318–24). Ultimately, in backing Hitler, Finland backed the wrong horse and the 1944 Finno-Soviet armistice confirmed the borders of the Moscow Peace Treaty of 13 March 1940. The loss of the Karelian peninsula to the Soviet Union was confirmed; Finland lost its Arctic Sea outlet of Petsamo; the demilitarisation of the Åland islands was reaffirmed; Porkkala, at the narrowest point of the Gulf of Finland, was leased to the Soviet Union as a naval base for fifty years; and fascist organisations were proscribed whilst the Communist Party, banned in 1930, was re-legalised. There was also a substantial reparations sum, repayable largely in terms of heavy goods and machinery. The final peace treaty was signed in Paris on 10 February 1947 and came into force on 15 September 1947, when it was ratified by Britain and the Soviet Union. The United States had not declared war on Finland and was thus not a signatory. Article 13 imposed restrictions on the size of the Finnish defence forces: a maximum of 34,400 in the army; 4,500 in the navy and a maximum tonnage of 10,000; and 3,000 in the air force, together with sixty aircraft (these provisions had been revised by 1963). Paradoxically, British demands for restrictions on the size and scope of the Finnish defence forces were opposed by the Soviets. Britain, it seems, was concerned that Finland would ultimately augment the Soviet defence potential (Allison 1985: 16–17). There was a reiteration of the 1940 peace treaty commitment obliging all three parties to refrain from any attack upon one another and to form no alliance and to participate in no coalition directed against either of the other contracting parties.

The cornerstone of Finnish foreign and security policy between 1948 and 1991 was the FCMA Treaty with the Soviet Union, which was signed on 6 April 1948. The Finns themselves produced a draft text which served as the basis for the FCMA negotiations and, crucially, this draft led to a ten-year treaty (extended for twenty-year periods at intervals thereafter) which did not entail the type of military agreement incorporated into parallel Soviet friendship pacts with Hungary and Romania. The first two articles (set out below) placed Finland clearly within the Soviet sphere of influence, reflected the Kremlin's post-war concern about future German expansionism, but involved a defensive commitment rather than a military alliance:

> *Article 1.* In the eventuality of Finland or the Soviet Union through Finland becoming the object of an armed attack by Germany or any state allied with the latter, Finland, true to its obligations as an independent state, will fight to repel the attack. Finland will in such cases use all its available resources for defending its territorial integrity by land, sea and air and will do so within the frontiers of Finland in accordance with the obligations defined in the present treaty and, if necessary, with the assistance of, or jointly with, the Soviet Union. In the cases aforementioned, the Soviet Union will give Finland the help required, subject to mutual agreement between the Contracting Parties.
>
> *Article 2.* The High Contracting Parties shall confer with each other if it is established that the threat of an armed attack as described in Article 1 is present.

Two points on the FCMA are in order. First, mention was made in the preamble of Finland's desire to remain outside 'antagonistic great power interests'. It was a slender toehold but it became the basis of Finland's claims to post-war neutrality. Since the Soviet Union for long failed to recognise such claims – which were viewed elsewhere as in conflict with the defence obligations of the FCMA – Finnish foreign policy for at least the three post-war decades was a 'struggle for neutrality', in Juhani Suomi's words (Suomi 1996). To be more precise, it was a struggle to gain international acceptance and credibility for a policy described as neutrality, but which was not that either in a legal–constitutional sense or, as in Sweden, in an historical sense. Second, in article 6 of the FCMA Treaty both states pledged themselves to 'non-interference in the internal affairs of the other state'. In fact, the dividing line between domestic and foreign policy in post-war Finland was like a line drawn on water – it simply could not be maintained – and there was extensive evidence of Soviet interference in Finnish domestic politics. In turn, the style of the long-serving president, Urho Kekkonen, of 'preventative diplomacy' – consulting the Kremlin to avoid an adverse reaction – became part of the multi-faceted phenomenon of 'Finlandisation'.

As noted earlier, despite the reparations obligations and military restrictions imposed by the 1947 Paris Peace Treaty, along with the mutual defence provided for in the 1948 FCMA Treaty, Finland did not become a member of the Warsaw Pact, there was no requirement on Finland to engage in military consultations except when a demonstrable threat from Germany and/or one of its allies existed and in 1956 Finland re-acquired Porkkala, the leased naval base just outside Helsinki. This is not say that there were not crisis points in Finno-Soviet relations, and two – the Night Frost Crisis of autumn 1958 and the Note Crisis of autumn 1961 – can be sketched very briefly, since they bear materially on our later discussion of the Nordic balance as a security policy concept and the controversial and sensitive issue of Finlandisation in the 1970s.

In 1958 'night frosts' in Khrushchev's phrase – *yöpakkaset* in Finnish – came as early as August to Finland and throughout the autumn Finno-Soviet relations were frozen hard. Ironically, it was in the very depths of winter that the thaw set in. On 25 January 1959, Khrushchev delivered a luncheon speech in Leningrad in honour of President Kekkonen. It marked the normalisation of relations between the two countries and the end of a crisis which had engendered a psychosis of fear in the Finnish capital and prompted wild rumours of the impending severance of diplomatic ties by the Kremlin leadership (Arter 1987: 177–82). The root of the problem, it seems, lay in the inclusion of the Social Democrats, under their recently elected chairman, the fiercely patriotic and pro-Western veteran politician Väinö Tanner, along with the right-wing National Coalition Party (Conservatives), in the Fagerholm III coalition following the July 1958 general election. Tanner had been jailed as a war criminal until 1949 and was associated with the anti-Soviet patriotism of the war years. Indeed, as Max Jakobson observed: 'his election appeared a declaration of war on Kekkonen and a challenge to the authority of the Russians' (Jakobson 1981: 121). Tanner's assumption of the top job in the party in April 1957 split the Social Democrats – a faction leaving to form the Social Democratic Opposition (Työväen ja pienviljelijäin sosialidemokraattinen liitto, TPSL) – and although Tanner himself was not included in the Fagerholm coalition, two Tannerites were, Väinö Leskinen and Olavi Lindblom, both anathema to the Russians. The Kremlin was also almost certainly acting in part at the instigation of the communist-dominated Suomen kansan demokraattinen liitto (SKDL, Finnish People's Democratic League), which had been excluded from the post-election government despite equalling the Social Democratic Party as the largest single party. Certainly, in the Soviet embassy in Helsinki it was believed that a viable majority coalition could have been formed by the Agrarians, the SKDL and the TPSL. Viktor Lebedev, the Russian ambassador in Finland, left without so much as a word; trade negotiations between the two countries stalled; and difficulties were experienced in obtaining visas to the Soviet Union. The Kremlin's 'good friends', the Agrarians, whom Lebedev had counselled against participating in the Fagerholm coalition, ultimately resigned in December 1958 and in the following month the whole government collapsed. The appointment of a new Agrarian minority cabinet under V. J. Sukselainen in January 1959 was the prelude to an expeditious return to normal relations between the two countries.

At the lunch in Leningrad in January 1959 (see above) it was highly significant that Khrushchev concluded that 'It is Finland's own affair how it organises its society, but it is important for the Soviet Union that its neighbour observes the policy laid down in the 1947 Peace Treaty and the 1948 FCMA'.

Clearly, as Jukka Nevakivi has observed, for the Soviets, the aim of the Night Frost Crisis was to prevent the development of a situation in which a strong majority government – the Fagerholm cabinet had the backing of over two-thirds of the Eduskunta – acting independently of Kekkonen, could have led to his removal from power at the following presidential election, in 1962, and so to a more Western-oriented approach in foreign policy. After adverse reaction in Moscow had undermined the Fagerholm coalition, a strong presidential contender, Kekkonen was able to work with an unthreatening Agrarian minority cabinet under Sukselainen (Jussila *et al.* 1995: 253).

The other low point in Finno-Soviet relations, the Note Crisis, was precipitated by a communication handed to the Finnish ambassador in Moscow on 31 October 1961 whilst Kekkonen was in Hawaii preparing for a visit to the United States. It expressed Soviet concern at the prospect of renewed German militarism and proposed joint consultations under the terms of the 1948 FCMA Treaty. When the Finnish foreign minister later met his Russian counterpart, anxiety was also expressed about the unstable political situation in Finland, specific allusion being made to an alliance of 'Tannerite' Social Democrats and Conservatives, which was standing its own candidate, Olavi Honka, a former chancellor of justice, at the forthcoming presidential election. It took a top-level 'sauna summit' in Novosibirsk on 24 November 1961 to resolve the crisis. In the course of Kekkonen's *tête-à-tête* with the Kremlin leadership in Siberia, news came through from Finland that Honka had decided to renounce his presidential candidacy 'in the national interest'. Kekkonen was swept back into power in 1962 as the man trusted in Moscow and the status of the presidency was substantially elevated (Arter 1987: 182–6).

Probably the majority of Finnish historians *now* think that Moscow created the crisis in Finno-Soviet relations in large part to allow Kekkonen, in resolving it, to appear the hero of the hour and gain re-election. We can call this the *Nevakivi interpretation* of the Note Crisis. Nevakivi has written that 'after the creation of the Honka League, Moscow began to doubt Kekkonen's chances of re-election and for this reason used foreign policy as a weapon to demand military consultations as provided in the FCMA Treaty, citing the international tension as justification' (Jussila 1999: 279). Viktor Vladimirov, a senior KGB officer in the Russian embassy in Helsinki at the time, has reinforced this view, claiming that the Note Crisis was a Soviet initiative to ensure Kekkonen's re-election (Vladimirov 1993). Vladimirov, however, did not believe the Finnish president was implicated but, both at the time and later, several have argued that the initiative came from the Finnish side. We can call this the *Kare interpretation*. Thus, in the 1960s, the journalist Kauko Kare and Conservative MP Tuure Junnila, and later various Soviet writers (*inter alia* Arvid Pelshe and Juri Derjabin), have subscribed to a conspiracy theory, namely that the Note Crisis was 'ordered' to enhance Kekkonen's chances of re-election. They point to the timing of the delivery of the embassy note – that is, whilst Kekkonen and his entourage were in Hawaii prior to a state visit to the United States – which reduced the public perception of any presidential involvement in the intrigue. Hannu Rautkallio (1999), drawing on Soviet sources, has argued that the Note Crisis was indeed 'pre-arranged' and involved collusion between Kekkonen and various Soviet agents. For most Finns, however, the Soviet note came as a bolt from the blue and engendered a mood of real foreboding on the streets.

The note drew Finland's attention to West German military preparations in the area around the Baltic Sea, which were said to threaten Finnish and Soviet security. It stated that the Soviet Union/Warsaw Pact was in the process of adopting certain measures to reinforce its defensive preparations and those of its allies. It is probable that for much of the Cold War period the Finnish political class underestimated the genuine Soviet concern about a resurgence of (West) German military power. In any event, it is important in analysing the Note Crisis to view it from a Soviet perspective and, in particular, in relation to the conflict within the Communist Party of the Soviet Union (CPSU) over Russia's future security strategy. At the CPSU's twenty-second party congress, there was evidence of division between what might be described as the 'Easterners' – those wishing to align Soviet and Chinese communism – and the 'Westerners' – those seeking a *modus vivendi* between the Soviet Union and the Western security system. This forms the backdrop to a third line of interpretation of the Note Crisis, which we can refer to as the *Rusi line*. Alpo Rusi (2004) has argued that the note was a concession to Soviet military circles, whose interest in Finland was purely strategic. He contends that the note was not intended (primarily at least) to influence domestic Finnish politics but rather was a concession to the military–industrial complex in the Soviet Union. Indeed, recent Soviet sources suggest that the Soviet Union was genuinely concerned both about NATO encroachment into its 'near abroad' and about increased West German influence in NATO. In other words, the note reflected the Soviet concern to prevent NATO plans to assume control of the Baltic Straits by establishing the so-called Baltic Approaches Responsibility Area (BALTAP). From a Soviet standpoint, the situation was further inflamed by the recent visit to Oslo to discuss the BALTAP project of the bombastic West German foreign minister, Franz Josef Strauss.

Summing up, the *dénouement* of the Note Crisis was as rapid as the dispatch of the note was sudden and unexpected for the Finns. Khrushchev agreed to call off plans for joint military consultations and, in return, Finland agreed closely to monitor the developing situation in northern Europe and the Baltic area and to comment on it in Moscow if necessary. The Note Crisis considerably strengthened Kekkonen's power base, although it also served Moscow's purpose in discrediting Finnish neutrality in the eyes of the West. After all, Kekkonen had worked hard through recent state visits to Britain and (at the time of the note) the United States to promote an image of Finnish neutrality. In this connection, Max Jakobson concurs with the conclusion of the British ambassador to Finland at the time: 'The Note helped Kekkonen win the election, but it also reminded Finns of their dependency on the Soviet Union and undermined Finnish neutrality' (Jakobson 1999: 334). History is full of 'if's and 'but's and the definitive version of the Note Crisis may never be known. In terms of our analysis of the 'Nordic balance', however, Alpo Rusi's conclusion is arresting. He suggests that although unlikely, it is not imposs-ible that the Soviet Union would have sought to station nuclear weapons in Finland if, under pressure from NATO, Norway and Denmark had abandoned their nuclear restrictions policy (Rusi 2004). It will be recalled that in 1957 Denmark and Norway had both extended their bases policies when a decision was made to arm NATO with tactical nuclear weapons. Any relaxations of the restrictions policy under NATO pressure would clearly have upset the 'Nordic balance' in a way, Rusi speculates, that would have prompted a response from the Soviet Union on Finnish soil.

Where was the 'balance' in the 'Nordic balance'?

The term 'Nordic balance' may be said to have been used in three different ways in the literature. First, it has been deployed in a *descriptive* sense to depict the post-war security arrangements in the Nordic region, with the additional infer-ence that the security policies of one member state in the region were likely to affect those of the others, too. In other words, the Nordic balance signified a high level of mutual interdependence and awareness of the regional implica-tions of security policies, together with a high level of mutual understanding and consideration. Miljan (1977: 277) captures the point: 'The concept of the Nordic Balance may be regarded as the conceptual framework used by the Nordic countries to evaluate the possible effects of one country's actions on the others – and the feedback effects thereof on them – within the context of the bipolar system'. Increasingly, the term 'Nordic balance' acquired important normative elements and came to be used in a *prescriptive* sense; that is, the security configuration that emerged in the late 1940s was viewed as reflecting the best interests of the Nordic states. Conversely, initiatives such as Kekkonen's Nordic nuclear-free zone proposal in 1963 – initiated with at the very least the support of Moscow – which, if implemented, would have fundamentally altered security arrangements in the region, were opposed by reference to the deleterious implications for the Nordic balance. Finally, the term has also been used as an *explanatory* concept, that is, as a concept in explaining *why* the post-war security geometry in Norden emerged in the way it did and *how* it was preserved. In this last sense, it was essentially a theory about the presence and behaviour of the superpowers in northern Europe and the mutual relations of the Nordic states. Seen as part of the dynamics of superpower and small-power interactions in the region, the Nordic balance involved the operation of a type of law of anticipated reaction. Put another way, every attempt by a superpower to disturb the status quo of the Nordic balance would be followed by correspond-ing measures by the other superpower to restore the previous order. As Andrén (1977) has pointed out, this notion of *an automatic correction mechanism* was at the very heart of the theory of the Nordic balance. Notwithstanding Rusi's speculative conclusion about the Note Crisis, however, the evidence in support of such an adjustment mechanism is not readily available.

The term 'Nordic balance' is in many ways a curious one and begs the question 'where was the balance in the Nordic balance?' Three main points seem in order. First, the Nordic balance may be said to have involved a rough balance in superpower spheres of influence. Second, the Nordic balance involved balancing the particular needs and security interests of the individual Nordic countries and a cross-national commitment to maintain the balance. Finally, however, the term seems odd in view of the fact that there was a massive imbalance in military capacity in peacetime.

From a superpower perspective, there was a rough balance of power in northern Europe and the Nordic region was characterised by relatively low levels of tension. The United States had strategically situated allies and, in this respect, Denmark was crucial. It lay at the gateway to the Baltic, only four minutes fighter aircraft time away from East Germany and only a 'stone's throw' away from Kaliningrad, where the Soviet Baltic fleet was based. Indeed, because Denmark held Greenland and the Faeroes in the North Atlantic, vital defence areas for the United States, Canada and Britain, Denmark, it seems, was considered for NATO membership as early as May 1948 (Haskel 1976: 63–4). The United States also had a Defence Treaty (1951) with Iceland and a military base at Keflavík. By 1960, as Berdal (1997: 170) has noted, the United States had come to recognise 'the interdependence of security postures in Northern Europe'. The Soviet Union, in turn, had Finland in its sphere of influence through article 2 of the FCMA Treaty, had incorporated the southern Baltic states of Estonia, Latvia and Lithuania and had its fleet in the High North based at the ice-free port of Murmansk on the Kola Peninsula. This gave it maritime access to the North Sea and beyond.

From a Nordic perspective, Finland shared a 1,300-kilometre border with the Soviet Union and had conceded large tracts of Karelia, but article 6 of the FCMA Treaty pledged mutual non-interference and there was no obligation (in principle at least) in article 2 to hold military consultations, except when a threat from Germany or one of its allies existed. Denmark and Norway's security policy sought to be non-provocative in that it was based on low-profile and conditional membership of NATO through the 'base restrictions' and 'nuclear restrictions' policies. Sweden, the only 'non-frontier' state among the mainland Nordic states, pursued (officially at least) a neutral course, a policy of neutrality, which may, at the margins, have helped to reduce pressure on Finland.

All in all, the 'Nordic balance' formula could be stated thus: a balance of security interests + a recognition of differing security needs = regional stability. However, there is little or no evidence of the automatic correction mechanism associated with the concept in the literature and clear evidence of a huge imbalance in military capacity in peacetime. The Soviet Union's military power vastly exceeded that of NATO in northern Europe, creating an enormous dependency on a rapid US response in the event of conflict. Clearly cognisant of this, Nils Andrén commented in the late 1970s that: 'The Nordic balance ... is of a political rather than a purely military nature.... It is a result of the special forms characterising the affiliations of the Nordic countries to great-power blocs' (Andrén 1977: 10).

Kekkonen and Finlandisation

In international relations discourse, particularly in the late 1960s and early 1970s, the concept of 'Finlandisation' was used (pejoratively by the Germans and Americans) to denote the reduction in the independent decision-making powers of a West European state and its slide into the Soviet sphere of influence. George Maude, writing on Finland – and what he calls 'neutrality in the shadow of power' – referred to the phenomenon as 'Sovietisation the soft way' (Maude 1976: 45). The Finnish foreign policy leadership was understandably extremely concerned in the early 1970s to ensure that the slur of Finlandisation did not have a damaging effect on Western confidence in Finnish neutrality (based on the preamble to the FCMA Treaty) and was particularly worried, for example, that the official communiqué which followed the visit of Soviet president Nikolai Podgorny to Finland in 1969 no longer referred to neutrality but simply to Finland's 'aspirations to neutrality'. This was the time of the Strategic Arms Limitation Talks (SALT), held on a rotational basis in Helsinki and Vienna – in 1969, in the Finnish capital, the United States and the Soviets took a year to negotiate whether to negotiate! – the whole process culminating in the Conference on Security and Co-operation in Europe in Helsinki in the summer of 1975. Indeed, it was the growing likelihood of staging the European security conference which finally persuaded the Finns to recognise the two Germanies in 1972, a fact which was followed by a two-year dispute between the Finnish media and *Die Welt* over the latter's allegations of Finlandisation. Finally, on the eve of Kekkonen's visit to West Germany in 1979, *Die Welt* agreed to stop using the term (Salminen 1996: 240). However, shortly thereafter, in the so-called 'Midsummer Bomb' episode, the president reacted explosively to the allusion by the Centre Party chairman, Johannes Virolainen, to 'general reasons' (*yleiset syyt*) – shorthand for the 'Soviet factor' – when asked about the Conservatives' exclusion from government despite their best post-war election result. Virolainen's response was interpreted by sections of the German press as evidence of renewed Finlandisation and a livid Kekkonen commissioned television time publicly to denounce Virolainen and to deny the existence of 'general reasons' (Arter 1987: 189–91).

On the eve of the collapse of the Soviet Union, Timo Vihavainen (1991) produced a short history of Finlandisation entitled *Kansakunta rähmällään* (*A Nation on Its Stomach*), with its unmistakable grovelling metaphor. Since then, the opening up of the Moscow archives and, indeed, of the long-serving

President Kekkonen's archives, has spawned new books, new material and a renewed debate about Finlandisation. The basic facts can be enumerated in ten main points.

1. Finlandisation may well have begun on 7 September 1955, as Jukka Nevakivi has claimed – despite the return of Porkkala and Soviet acceptance of Finnish membership of the UN and Nordic Council – when the Soviet embassy in Helsinki, clearly acting on higher authority, proposed regular joint consultations on Finnish foreign policy (Nevakivi 1996).

2. Kekkonen's highly personalised management of Finno-Soviet relations and the confidence he enjoyed 'in high places' bestowed on the long-serving president, especially during his third term, from 1968 to 1974, unrivalled power as the sole arbiter and mediator of the national interest. Evidence of his autocratic style can be gained from the way in June 1968 Kekkonen (unsuccessfully) proposed to Leonid Brezhnev changes in the national frontier – the concession of part of Lapland in return for the re-acquisition of the Viipuri area in 'conceded Karelia' and Finnish recognition of the two Germanys – not in his capacity as head of state, but (albeit at the suggestion of A. J. Belakov, a Soviet foreign policy expert and subsequently Soviet ambassador to Finland) as a 'private citizen'. As Juhani Suomi has noted, it was not even mentioned in Kekkonen's detailed sixteen-page report on the trip and was certainly not known to the prime minister at that time, Mauno Koivisto (Suomi 1996: 55–66). Indeed, Koivisto (1997: 148) has admitted that, on subsequently reading of the whole episode in the Suomi biography, his gut reaction was to say that 'if I had ever said anything critical of Brezhnev I would never do so again, nor would I speak ill of the ill-fated [anti-Kekkonen] Honka-alliance' (in 1961)!

3. The corollary of Kekkonen's preventative diplomacy and unchallengeable power was his readiness to subordinate the entire parliamentary system, public word and even historical writing to the needs of a policy designed to maintain the confidence of the Soviet leadership and to avoid military consultations under article 2 of the FCMA Treaty. The most blatant victim of this Finlandised management style was the Conservative Party, which was excluded from government between 1966 and 1987 for 'general reasons'. In 1970 and 1979, in particular, the Conservatives were left empty-handed despite significant gains at the polls. The turning point for Kekkonen was almost certainly the Night Frost Crisis in 1958, since thereafter the president clearly believed that, in order to direct foreign policy, he had to control domestic policy.

4. The Soviet Union intervened routinely to influence Finnish domestic politics, initially in Kekkonen's favour, latterly in part at his behest. This was clearly in contravention of article 6 of the FCMA Treaty, which stated that: 'The High Contracting Parties pledge themselves to observe the principle of mutual respect of sovereignty and integrity and that of non-interference in the internal affairs of the other state'. Pertti Salminen (1995) has shown how, from 1954 onwards, Moscow sought *regularly* to bring the two armed forces together through joint military exercises. At the time of the 1961 Note

Crisis the aim was, by means of the organisation of joint manoeuvres, to apply pressure on Finland to purchase high-profile Soviet weapons so as to create the impression in the West that the two nations were engaged in a military alliance. Soviet military experts contended that Finland could not control its own air space and proposed both the acquisition of Soviet missiles and joint air defence plans. Although the note of 31 October 1961 is the best-known example, Soviet initiatives proposing military exercises involving the two countries continued until 1978, when one from the defence minister, Dimitri Ustinov, was politely rejected by President Kekkonen.

5. There was evidence of a 'decaying elite culture' – according to Jukka Nevakivi this was the only distinctively Finnish feature of Finlandisation – with favours sought from and bestowed by the Soviet Union (*Helsingin Sanomat*, 18 September 1996). In this respect, the senior KGB agent in Helsinki, Viktor Vladimirov, emerged as a godfather of the Finnish political elite. The Communists and Agrarians were the early beneficiaries of a 'special relationship' with the Soviet embassy in Tehtaankatu, but the invitation list widened steadily. From 1956 to 1986, Eino Uusitalo, an Agrarian–Centre parliamentarian and minister in several governments, took part in every annual celebration of the FCMA – known by the acronym YYA in Finnish – at the Soviet embassy in Helsinki and in 1975 proposed that 19 September, the date of the 1944 Finno-Soviet armistice, be adopted as Finland's second independence day (Hautamäki 2008)!

6. There was evidence of 'muted media' and, particularly in the 1970s, widespread self-censorship on radio and television and in the press. In part it was dictated by Soviet pressure to conform and the regulations governing the conduct of the media. The peace treaty in September 1947 expressly forbade anti-Soviet propaganda, whilst in April 1948 changes to section 14, paragraph 4A, of the criminal law made journalists liable to two years' imprisonment for writing slanderous material about a foreign state (in practice, of course, the Soviet Union) should the president wish to press charges (Salminen 1996: 33). Esko Salminen, however, has identified two forms of self-censorship. *Passive* self-censorship refers to the avoidance of criticism of Russia and the other socialist bloc countries out of genuine concern about the risks to Finland's *Ostpolitik*, the fear of Soviet threats and even Soviet intervention. *Active* self-censorship, in contrast, involved 'deliberate and tactical self-regulation emanating from considerations of power politics' (Salminen 1996: 21). This type of active self-censorship became endemic in the 1970s and involved competition between politicians and the political parties for the favours of Moscow and/or Kekkonen. The phenomenon was so insidious that Salminen (1996: 148) commented that 'democracy began seriously to decay in respect of a basic pillar of the state – the spoken word'. He noted, too, that, in contrast to the post-war 'danger years', 1944–48, the Finlandised value system of submissiveness and conformity had pervaded the young and the educated. There were, of course, the students – about 500 Finnish communists in total between

1954 and 1988 – trained in Moscow by the CPSU, who were offered not only full board but an allowance well in excess of the average Muscovite's wage (Krekola 1998). But it is also important to emphasise the enormous impact of 'new left', pro-Soviet ideas in Finland in the 1970s, ironically emanating from the campus unrest in the heartland of capitalism, the United States. Max Jakobson concludes that the 1970s constituted, in Aarne Saarinen's words, 'new danger years', not because of an outside threat, but from internal submission, compliance and surrender (*Helsingin Sanomat*, 31 October 1996).

7. All this amounts to evidence of a highly submissive or at best deferential attitude on the part of the intelligentsia towards the power-holders, that is, the absence of a critical and independent intellectual class. Partly this was related to Finland's small size and, as the writer Erno Paasilinna (1996) has noted in his *Tähän astiset elämän kirjaimet* (*The Alphabet of Life So Far*), the very limited supply of top jobs. In the 1970s, conformity to the official liturgy was a prerequisite in advancing a career. Doubtless, too, there was internalisation of the official value system/foreign policy line, although just how far this went must remain an open question.

8. Equally, as Heikki Mikkeli (*Helsingin Sanomat*, 18 September 1996) has observed, in contrast to Vihavainen's *A Nation on Its Stomach*, there is evidence that civil society was not Finlandised, at least totally – in other words, reduced to conformity – in, *inter alia*, support in the early 1970s for the protest populism of Veikko Vennamo's Rural Party. Vennamo was a known critic of Kekkonen and stood against him in the 1968 presidential election before polling over 10 per cent of the vote at the general election two years later. He had also been part of the ill-fated Honka alliance in 1961. Furthermore, to the question posed in a survey in autumn 1978 – 'Do the Finnish media in general give an appropriate picture of events and conditions in the socialist countries – the Soviet Union, for example?' – 26 per cent of respondents said the right picture was presented, 51 per cent claimed the picture was too favourable and 9 per cent thought it was too negative. In the same poll, over one-third of those interviewed believed that Finnish foreign policy had slipped 'too far to the east'. Whilst a single poll does not, of course, make a thesis, these results have been interpreted as indicating that the ordinary Finn in the street was not Finlandised, or at least was willing to speak his/her mind at a time widely viewed as the 'dark age' of Finlandisation.

9. Despite charges of Finlandisation, Kekkonen's *Westpolitik* was by no means unimpressive in commercial terms, and, as Jukka Seppinen (1997) has noted, particularly after Finland's associate membership of the European Free Trade Association in 1961, its foreign trade became overwhelmingly Western in its orientation. Membership of the Organisation for Economic Co-operation and Development in 1968 further cemented Finland's linkages with the West and in 1973 a free trade agreement with the European Economic Community was negotiated. There was also Finnish involvement from 1956 in the work of the Nordic Council. On this basis, Seppinen contends, the most negative side of

the Kekkonen era was in the domestic field and he emphasises how Kekkonen adapted history to his purposes and insisted that in the printed word there should be no criticism of the Soviet Union – something the media complied with, especially in the 1970s. He concludes that Kekkonen trampled over his opponents and gathered round him a group of ingratiators, who further stifled and polluted the atmosphere of public affairs, particularly in the 1970s.

10. Even so, Kekkonen's quarter of a century at the helm coincided with a sustained period of economic prosperity and welfare development, and it may well be that, for a section of the citizenry, the president's management style and its corollary, 'Finlandised politics', were regarded as legitimate means of delivering a prosperous society. This is the burden of the (highly simplistic) submission of Kaarlo Nordlund, writing in the 'Letters' section of *Helsingin Sanomat* (27 October 1997):

> For ordinary citizens, Kekkonen's term of office was the best period through which Finland has lived. People had work, hope for the future and never spoke of the national debt. If a presidential period is to be evaluated, the most important criteria, to my mind, are the welfare of the subjects and relations with foreign states. Both were in good order during Kekkonen's tenure of office. For the man and woman in the street, it does not matter if the president is in league with the devil himself as long as he can take care of his duties in the public interest ... Kekkonen bequeathed a prosperous state to his successor.

In much the same vein, Lauri Karelius (*Helsingin Sanomat*, 4 November 1997), writing to the same newspaper shortly afterwards, took issue with the facile hindsight deployed by modern critics of Kekkonen, insisting that the long-serving president was a man who grasped the stern realities of heading a small capitalist state situated on the border of Soviet communism. Underlining the popular authority enjoyed by Kekkonen, Karelius concluded that 'Kekkonen was truly the nation's father, and people sat up and paid attention when he spoke'.

Nordlund's letter, although painting an idealised picture, touches on an important point, since talk of Finlandisation, and the emphasis here on its domestic face, should not disguise the fact that Finland ultimately ended up on the 'winning side', in the sense that during Kekkonen's presidency the economy boomed – and was afforded a measure of counter-cyclical protection through its barter trade relationship with the Soviet Union – whilst the Soviet economy struggled and, by the advent of Mikhail Gorbachev in 1985, was in a state of near collapse. In this context, it is significant that, when interviewed on his sixtieth birthday in January 1997, Harri Holkeri, the leader of the very Conservative Party which was kept out of office by Kekkonen for 'general reasons', was solidly pro-Kekkonen and argued that the Eduskunta's extension of Kekkonen's term of office in 1974 (bypassing the popular vote required by the constitution) was justified in terms of protecting and promoting Finland's trade relations with the West. Holkeri went so far as to argue that Finland would not now be a member of the EU or, indeed, such a prosperous state had parliament not taken the decision to extend Kekkonen's presidency by four years. He did, however, concede that there was no democratic alternation of power under Kekkonen, that is, there was a domestic price to pay (*Helsingin Sanomat*, 6 November 1997).

The Kekkonen generation of politicians has either retired or is nearing retirement, whilst the younger generation who successfully pressed for constitutional change to prevent a possible recurrence of the excesses of the Kekkonen era is rapidly approaching middle age. The younger generation of historians and political scientists prefer in the main to look forward rather than back and generally skirt over Cold War politics in Finland, albeit not quite sanitising the Kekkonen years. Single-sentence references tend to suffice. The older generation of academics and former diplomats, however, continues publicly to wash the dirty linen of the past in new books and new revelations, although this seems to elicit much less of a reaction than a decade ago. In his study of Kekkonen, for example, Jukka Seppinen (2004) has referred to the 1970s in Finland as the 'revolutionary decade' and relates how twice, in 1970–71 and 1976–77, Finland was threatened with a communist revolution orchestrated from Moscow. Both attempts failed. Juhani Suomi's (2000) fourth volume of Kekkonen's diaries reveals just how much pressure the ageing Kekkonen came under from Moscow in respect of cabinet appointments, foreign policy statements, the internal affairs of the political parties and Finland's trade with the Soviet Union. Yet in Nokia-Finland, interest is limited. Finland is now very different to what it was in the Kekkonen period – confident, cosmopolitan and Internet-connected. Finland has moved on.

Post-Cold War security in northern Europe

Speaking of moving on, it is interesting that, in his essay on the changing security policies of the Nordic states after the Cold War, Tore Nyhamar (2004) makes no express reference to the notion of a 'Nordic balance'. It is, however, implicit in his assertion that 'although their choices of alignments differed, all the Nordics shared a desire to strike a balance between Soviet deterrence and reassurance' (Nyhamar 2004: 231). The demise of the Soviet Union, and the attendant collapse of the bipolar security system of the Cold War, of course, signalled the end of the Nordic balance era, although residual elements have remained – Norway's continuation of the 'base restrictions' policy, for example. Instead, the post-Cold War security system in northern Europe has involved a radically altered political geography and pluralistic security structures, together with an expansion of the notion of security itself.

The two main geo-political or geo-strategic changes can be summarised as follows. First, the disintegration of the Soviet Union meant that Finland and

Norway were no longer 'frontier states' in the ideological sense of marking the territorial border between capitalism and communism in northern Europe. The ideological demarcation line between the two superpower systems had been particularly clearly drawn in Norway, which, during the Cold War, had been the only NATO state to share a border with the Soviet Union. Equally, the mainland Nordic states, at least in the 1990s, were positioned at the economic frontier between the Europe of the rich and the Europe of the poor.

Second, the collapse of the Soviet superpower facilitated the renewed independence of Estonia, Latvia and Lithuania, which were confronted with the simultaneous internal challenges of democratisation, marketisation and social integration. The re-emergence of the three independent Baltic republics also meant that (if Poland is excluded) the post-Cold War Baltic comprised a region of essentially small states in the hinterland of the Russian Federation. Yet the extent of the changes to the geo-political map of northern Europe should not perhaps be exaggerated and, as the interminable boundary dispute between Russia and Estonia bears witness, the 'frontier state' concept retains salience in both a physical and strategic sense. Just how much, of course, depends on an assessment of the likely future security threat posed by Russia.

In this context, the Finnish defence minister, Jyri Häkämies, in a controversial speech in Washington in autumn 2007, pointed to the re-emergence of Russia as a global player and reasserted what he plainly saw to be the immutable lessons of history and geography: 'It would be foolish and mistaken to conclude that the new Russia will threaten Finland's security … but those who, at the end of the Cold War, were eager to proclaim that the era of geopolitics in Northern Europe was over were just plain wrong. Geopolitics is back and it is back with force…' (Häkämies 2007). Häkämies' view brought to mind Joseph Stalin's statement to a Finnish delegation in Moscow in October 1939 – a month before the Winter War – that 'we can do nothing about our geography. If you [Finns] were not our neighbours, we would not have all these difficulties' (Nykorp 1975: 56).

Aside from geo-political change, a more pluralistic security architecture emerged in northern Europe after the Cold War, based on an enhanced role for two main 'security providers' – NATO and the EU. Most striking, perhaps, has been the expansion of NATO to the Russian border. The Prague summit in November 2002 approved NATO membership for the three southern Baltic states and Latvia, Lithuania and Estonia joined the 'Atlantic alliance' in 2004, exactly ten years after the last Soviet troops stationed there withdrew. Moreover, despite defining their security position in the 1990s as one of 'military non-alignment and a credible national defence', both Finland and Sweden sought a close working relationship with NATO through membership of the Partnership for Peace programme and have undertaken to participate in the 25,000-strong NATO Response Force. NATO, in short, forms an integral part of the security landscape of northern Europe today, in a way that would have been inconceivable even in the later years of the Cold War.

The same could be said of the EU, although there is, of course, no equivalent to the collective defence commitment contained in article 5 of the NATO treaty. None the less, the EU's development of a 'northern dimension' has been a feature of the enlargement process since the mid-1990s. When, following its unilateral abandonment of the 1948 FCMA Treaty, Finland in 1995 became the first 'successor state' of the New Europe of 1919–23 to become an EU member (Sweden and Austria acceded at the same time) the eastern boundary of the Union adjoined the Russian Federation. Thereafter, the Nordic EU members (Denmark had already joined in 1973) worked energetically to promote Baltic membership of the Union and this was achieved in 2004. Annika Bergman has coined the term *adjacent internationalism* to refer to this distinct Nordic–Baltic co-operative project and claims that 'the Nordic states' collective efforts to support Baltic EU membership contributed to the emergence of a distinctive Nordic–Baltic sphere of community' (Bergman 2006: 86).

Clearly, a consequence of the disintegration of the Soviet Union, though not directly caused by it, has been an incipient bipolarity in the Western security system. On the one hand, NATO has evolved from an article 5-based collective defence organisation to become more of a collective security organisation and a cross-national forum for dialogue on security matters between full members and partner countries. On the other, the Treaty on European Union, agreed at the Maastricht summit in December 1991, contained a commitment to develop a common foreign and security policy (CFSP) leading to a common defence policy and possibly, too, a common defence capability. The need to adapt and respond to these twin institutional developments cast the two Cold War 'Nordic neutrals' in the role of security policy innovators in two senses. First, the process of intensified and highly public co-operation between Finland and Sweden on a range of concrete security- and defence-related issues – *inter alia* the publication of joint press articles by the respective foreign and defence ministers – was itself a novel development and laid the foundation for what was tantamount to a miniature Nordic CFSP (or at least a bilateral version of one). Second, the need to reconcile a policy of military non-alignment with a commitment to the EU's nascent CFSP prompted a degree of genuine policy origination. Thus, in an innovative joint proposal to the Amsterdam inter-governmental conference in 1996, Finland and Sweden made the case for strengthening the Union's crisis management capability by including in its terms of reference things such as humanitarian support, rescue operations and peace-keeping – the so-called 'Petersberg tasks'. In short, the two 'former neutrals' – they could no longer be regarded as 'politically neutral' having signed up to the CFSP – sought to be 'security producers' and, as new EU members, to be seen to be making a constructive contribution, without compromising their concern to remain militarily non-aligned. In many ways, the championing of the 'crisis management' concept represented something of a Nordic contribution both to the EU's CFSP and to the nature of security production itself, although, as mentioned, both Finland and Sweden drew a clear line between participation in crisis management operations and a commitment to collective defence.

In fact, all the mainland Nordic countries have participated extensively in international crisis management activity under both the EU and NATO flags, and this has involved the use of both military and non-military instruments. For example, Finland was represented in the first half of 2007 in one of the two fully operational, multinational, rapid-reaction EU *battle groups*. The troops came from Germany, Finland and the Netherlands. A 2,800-strong Nordic 'battle group', comprising Finnish, Swedish, Norwegian, Estonian and Irish troops was launched in January 2008. The remit of the battle groups involves the performance of the so-called 'enhanced Petersberg tasks' – that is, the provision of humanitarian support, search, rescue and evacuation duties plus, where necessary, the use of military force. In March 2008 the Finnish Eduskunta approved participation in the parallel NATO Response Force, created at the Prague summit in 2002, and Sweden followed suit the next month. Whilst Finland and Sweden have prioritised this type of 'trouble-shooting security', and involvement in crisis management activities has been largely a valence issue, it has been more controversial and politically divisive in Norway. Thus, Nyhamar (2004: 244) presents the official justification of Norway's policy of deploying troops in international operations – both peace-keeping and peace-enforcing – in rather paradoxical terms, namely its contribution to *national security*. This it can achieve by:

1 preventing terrorists entering Norwegian territory;
2 eliminating terrorists before they can do any harm;
3 disrupting the planning and training for terrorist attacks.

The common position of the former neutrals, Finland and Sweden, in the van of EU- and NATO-led crisis resolution projects has possibly disguised significant recent differences in the premises for their national security policy. Whereas Sweden is now concentrating on profiling itself on the global stage by developing a small, highly trained, highly skilled, rapid-reaction force for crisis management purposes, Finland still attaches primary importance to territorial defence. The minority Swedish Social Democratic government's 2004 Defence Act effectively marked the end of the manifest Cold War policy of *armed neutrality*. The bill stated that Sweden no longer perceived any serious threats to its national territory and, accordingly, placed the emphasis on the creation of an elite battalion for international duties. One-third of its thirty regiments were to be wound up, the number of submarines and fighter aircraft substantially reduced and the size of the defence staff cut by one-quarter. There were those who questioned whether Sweden would any longer have the capacity to defend itself, Leni Björklund, a former defence minister, claiming that in a crisis Sweden would withstand the first attack but thereafter the country would have to appeal to the UN for assistance!

In contrast to Sweden, where military service has in practice become optional – in 2007, 8,000 were called up out of an annual cohort of 55,000 males – Finland has continued to view with utmost importance the ability to defend its national territory and has consequently maintained general conscription. Häkämies noted in his Washington speech that if Finland mobilised in 2007 it would have an armed force of about 350,000 soldiers and he added that 'the PlayStation and Nokia generation of young men and women make excellent soldiers when given proper training and equipment' (Häkämies 2007). He also claimed that Russia viewed military force as a staple element in the conduct of international relations and that there was a concerted programme to bolster Russia's military capability. He concluded that Russia would reassert itself as a strong regional actor, especially in the High North, and saw evidence of the renewed strategic importance of the Kola Peninsula in the reappearance of Russian bombers in the seas around Iceland and northern Scotland. Russia, in short, constituted a security threat – or 'security challenge' to use the current euphemism – and, whilst the president and prime minister both distanced themselves from Häkämies' opinions, there is broad consensus at both the elite and the mass level about the importance of preserving a credible national defence.

Finland and Sweden remain the only Nordic–Baltic states that are not NATO members, although such external events as the Kosovo conflict have on occasions sparked an ephemeral debate about possible membership and, in turn, underlined the relevance of the question posed in respect of the two countries by Tapani Vaahtoranta and Tuomas Forsberg (2000) – namely, 'post-neutral or pre-allied?' In the Finnish case, the sharply contrasting views of two former presidents, in particular, stand out. Mauno Koivisto (1982–94) insisted that the NATO bombing of Serbia violated both international law and its own founding charter, and pointed up the way that NATO was dominated by the big powers. If Finland joined NATO, he argued, its chances of influencing the alliance's decision-making would be minimal. Elsewhere, Koivisto has maintained that Russia will reassert itself as a global player and continues to view Finland (along with the three Baltic republics) as part of the 'near abroad'. Finland should not join NATO, he concluded, because, among other things, it would damage relations with Russia.

Perhaps the most prominent pro-NATO figure has been Martti Ahtisaari, who was head of state between 1994 and 2000. In an arresting speech in November 2002, Ahtisaari insisted that:

1 Russia was no longer a threat to Finland;
2 NATO had changed character and remaining outside would not increase Finland's security;
3 there was a risk of marginalisation from influence, since EU and NATO membership was essentially overlapping and an increasing number of security questions were settled in NATO.

He subsequently held that, in order to lay to rest the bogey of Finlandisation, Finland should be a member of all those organisations to which Western democratic nations belong and that the domestic political parties should throw off their Cold War mentality.

Finnish opponents of NATO membership, including the former foreign secretary Erkki Tuomioja and the current president, Tarja Halonen, have used the adverse state of public opinion to their advantage (between two-thirds and four-fifths of Finns have consistently opposed NATO membership). In her 2003 New Year Address, Halonen stated that 'in a democracy, a basic pre-condition of a credible security policy is that it rests on the support of the people. The present policy [of non-alignment] does, and it should continue to do so in the future.' The official position was articulated in the government's security and defence policy statement to parliament in September 2004. Finland would continue its policy of military non-alignment up until 2012; the main task would be the defence of the national territory and over 95 per cent of the defence budget would be devoted to that end. The 2008 defence white paper, however, was due to include consideration of the pros and cons of NATO membership. A recent newspaper article by the former diplomat Max Jakobson was entitled 'Step by step towards NATO' (*Helsingin Sanomat*, 2 September 2007) but at present only small steps look likely.

In Sweden the Liberal Party has been vociferously pro-NATO, as have Conservative voices, including the former prime minister and foreign secretary from 2006, Carl Bildt. In February 2003, Bildt and the former Danish foreign minister, Uffe Ellemann-Jensen (Liberal – Venstre) wrote a joint article in the Scandinavian press (only one paragraph was in Danish, suggesting that Bildt was the driving force), which contained three main points. First, it was argued that Finland and Sweden should join NATO: 'Although there is no security deficit, which would demand NATO membership, we perceive there to be a growing threat of an "influence deficit" if Finland and Sweden are not fully involved in the discussion of European security'. Second, all the Nordic states should be EU members, something which could be achieved by 2009. The five Nordic states would have more votes in the Council of Ministers than Germany, France and Britain. Third, regional co-operation needs to be rethought, since in the future influence would be exerted by those who are EU members, members of the Economic and Monetary Union, and NATO members. Interestingly, the Swedish prime minister, Fredrik Reinfeldt, did not allude to non-alignment in the 2007 government declaration, although he subsequently played down the significance of this. Yet, as in Finland, a Swedish application for NATO membership does not appear imminent. The Left Party and Greens are steadfastly opposed and the Social Democratic Party leader, Mona Sahlin, who has criticised the non-socialist coalition for the breakdown in the tradition of government–opposition consultation on security matters, has also dismissed a NATO application (*Svenska Dagbladet*, 17 September 2007).

For opponents in Finland and Sweden, the 'added value' of full NATO membership – rather than the close working relationship with the organisation that already exists – has doubtless been less than obvious, given that the threat to national security from state actors appears to have receded. Their argument might be that the main concern should be with the security threats posed by sub-state groups and even individuals. Thus the Danish decision in March 2003 to support the US-led invasion of Iraq and the Muhammad cartoon episode – and its international ramifications – in the same country in 2006 heightened the need to step up intra-state security, as well as external measures, against a possible backlash from Islamist extremists. Indeed, in September 2007 Danish security police arrested eight militant Islamists in the Copenhagen area – said to have connections with the al-Qaeda network – on suspicion of preparing a terrorist attack. Equally, the cyber attacks on private and government Internet sites in Estonia – which rose sharply in May 2007 following the decision to relocate a Soviet-era Second World War memorial of a bronze soldier – pointed up the growing diversity of non-military security challenges. Cyber security is very much a twenty-first-century phenomenon. Indeed, it seems fair to point to a progression in international relations discourse from 'collective defence' to 'collective security' to the notion of *comprehensive security*, the latter incorporating, for example, the environmental risks posed by highly radioactive spent fuel – whether at the decommissioned nuclear power plants at Barsebäck in southern Sweden or the decaying nuclear submarines at Murmansk on the Kola Peninsula. Security, in short, is multi-faceted and whilst 'hard security' and territorial defence appear less paramount in the post-Cold War era – symptomatically the last US troops left Iceland in September 2006 – there is a varied 'soft security agenda', which has allowed the Nordic states to be active 'security producers' on the international stage.

Summary

1. The four mainland Nordic states occupied a frontier position during the Cold War and saw the Soviet Union as their primary security threat.

2. The security arrangements that were designed to accommodate this threat and create stability in northern Europe came to be known as the 'Nordic balance' and involved an armed but neutral Sweden, flanked to the east by Finland with its 'special relationship' with Moscow, and to the west by Denmark and Norway's 'low profile' membership of NATO.

3. The Nordic balance may be said to have reflected a rough balance in superpower spheres of influence, along with a balance between the particular needs and security interests of the individual Nordic countries – coupled with a commitment to maintain that balance. There was, however, a huge imbalance in military capability in peacetime and, in view of the Soviet Union's military

[handwritten margin notes: See: WWII relationship with Britain + British/US rel. → FCMA friendship cooperation mutual assura]

supremacy in the region, an enormous dependency on a rapid US response in the event of conflict.

4.   The disintegration of the Soviet Union and the collapse of the bipolar Cold War security system denoted the end of the Nordic balance. The EU and NATO have both expanded to the Russian border and the non-aligned Finland and Sweden have developed a close working relationship with the latter through the Partnership for Peace programme. (NATO)

5.   The mainland Nordic states have sought to be 'security providers' (in the NATO jargon) through participation in international crisis management projects and have served under both the EU and the NATO flags. They have also championed an agenda of 'soft security' issues.

security provider
↳ security risk

UNOBTRUSIVE

References

af Malmberg, Mikael (2001) *Neutrality and State-Building in Sweden*, Palgrave: Houndmills.

Allison, Roy (1985) *Finland's Relations with the Soviet Union, 1944–84*, Macmillan: London.

Andrén, Nils (1977) *The Future of the Nordic Balance*, Ministry of Defence: Stockholm.

Arter, David (1987) *Politics and Policy-Making in Finland*, Wheatsheaf: Brighton.

Berdal, Mats R. (1997) *The United States, Norway and the Cold War, 1954–60*, Macmillan: Basingstoke.

Bergman, Annika (2006) 'Adjacent internationalism: the concept of solidarity and post-Cold War Nordic–Baltic relations', *Co-operation and Conflict*, 41 (1), pp. 73–97.

Bull, Edvard (1982) *Norges Historien etter 1945*, Cappelens Forlag: Oslo.

Dahl, Ann-Sofie (1999) *Svenskarna och NATO*, Timbro: Stockholm.

Dohlman, Ebba (1989) *National Welfare and Economic Interdependence. The Case of Sweden's Foreign Trade Policy*, Clarendon Press: Oxford.

Einhorn, E. (1975) 'The reluctant ally: Danish security policy, 1945–49', *Journal of Contemporary History*, 10, pp. 493–512.

Faurby, Ib (1982) 'Decision structures and domestic sources of Nordic foreign policies', in Bengt Sundelius (ed.), *Foreign Policies of Northern Europe*, Westview: Boulder, CO, pp. 33–71.

Fitzmaurice, John (1981) *Politics in Denmark*, Hurst: London.

Furre, Berge (1993) *Norske historie, 1905–1990, Vårt hundreår*, Det Norske Samlaget: Oslo.

Goldmann, Kjell (1991) 'The Swedish model of security policy', *West European Politics*, 14 (3), pp. 122–43.

Greve, Tim (1973) *Haakon VII of Norway. Founder of a New Monarchy*, Hurst: London.

Häkämies, Jyri (2007) 'Similar yet different: a Finnish perspective on European security and transatlantic relations', speech at the Center for Strategic and International Studies, Washington, DC, 6 September.

Haskel, Barbara G. (1976) *The Scandinavian Option. Opportunities and Opportunity Costs in Post-war Scandinavian Foreign Policies*, Universitetsforlaget: Oslo.

Hautamäki, Jaakko (2008) 'Ystävien kesken', *Helsingin Sanomat*, 6 April.

Heidar, Knut (2001) *Norway Elites on Trial*, Westview: Boulder, CO.

Holbraad, Carsten (1991) *Danish Neutrality. A Study in the Foreign Policy of a Small State*, Clarendon Press: Oxford.

Jakobson, Max (1981) *Veteen piirretty viiva*, Otava: Helsinki.

Jakobson, Max (1999) *Väkivallan vuodet 20. Vuosisadan Tilinpäätös*, Otava: Helsinki.

Jenkins, Roy (1974) *Nine Men of Power*, Hamish Hamilton: London.

Julkunen, Martti (1975) *Talvisodan kuva. Ulkomaisten sotakirjeenvaihtajien kuvaukset suomesta, 1939–40*, Weilin & Göös: Helsinki.

Jussila, Osmo, Seppo Hentilä and Jukka Nevakivi (1995) *Suomen poliittinen historia, 1809–1995*, WSOY: Porvoo.

Jussila, Osmo, Seppo Hentilä and Jukka Nevakivi (1999) *From Grand Duchy to Modern State*, Hurst: London.

Karlsson, Gunnar (2000) *The History of Iceland*, University of Minnesota Press: Minneapolis, MN.

Kirby, David (1979) *Finland in the Twentieth Century*, Hurst: London.

Kirby, David (1995) *The Baltic World, 1772–1993*, Longman: London.

Koivisto, Mauno (1997) *Liikkeen suunta*, Kirjayhtymä: Helsinki.

Krekola, Jouni (1998) 'Oppia idästä – suomalaisten koomunistien koulutus Neuvostoliitossa', in Seppo Hentilä et al. (eds), *Vaikka voissa paistaisi, Venäjän rooli Suomessa*, WSOY: Helsinki.

Magnússon, Sigurdur A. (1977) *The Northern Sphinx*, Hurst: London.

Maude, George (1976) *The Finnish Dilemma. Neutrality in the Shadow of Power*, Oxford University Press: London.

Miljan, Toivo (1977) *The Reluctant Europeans?*, Hurst: London.

Mouritzen, Hans (1988) *Finlandisation. Towards a General Theory of Adaptive Politics*, Avebury: Aldershot.

Nevakivi, Jukka (1996) *Miten Kekkonen pääsi valtaan ja Suomi suomettui*, Otava: Helsinki.

Nuechterlein, Donald E. (1975) *Iceland: Reluctant Ally*, Greenwood Press: Westport, CT.

Nyhamar, Tore (2004) 'Security policies from constraints to choice', in Knut Heidar (ed.), *Nordic Politics*, Universitetsforlaget: Oslo, pp. 228–46.

Nykorp, Johan (1975) *Paasikiven mukana Moskovassa*, Kirjayhtymä: Helsinki.

Paasilinna, Erno (1996) *Tähän astiset elämän kirjaimet*, Otava: Helsinki.

Rautkallio, Hannu (1999) *Agenda Suomi, Kekkonen, Kekkonen, SDP, NKP 1956–66*, WSOY: Helsinki.

Riste, Olav (1985) 'The historical determinants of Norwegian foreign policy', in Johan Jørgen Holst (ed.), *Norwegian Foreign Policy in the 1980s*, Norwegian University Press: Oslo, pp. 12–25.

Rusi, Alpo (2004) 'Noottikriisi 1961: Neuvostoliitto haki tukikohtaa Suomesta', paper at http://kaares.ulapland.fi/home/hkunta/arusi/sk_noottikriisi.html.

Salminen, Esko (1996) *Vaikeneva valtiomahti? Neuvostoliitto/Venäjä Suomen lehdistössä*, Edita: Helsinki.

Salminen, Pertti (1995) *Puolueettomuuden nimeen. Sotilasjohto Kekkosen linjalla ja sen sivussa 1961–66*, Gummerus: Jyväskylä.

Salmon, Patrick (1997) *Scandinavia and the Great Powers, 1890–1940*, Cambridge University Press: Cambridge.

Seppinen, Jukka (1997) *Ahti Karjalainen. Poliittinen elämäkerta*, Otava: Helsinki.

Seppinen, Jukka (2004) *Urho Kekkonen – Suomen johtaja*, Ajatus kirjat: Helsinki.

Skodvin, Magne (1971) *Norden eller Nato? Utenriksdepartementet og alliansespørsmålet, 1947–49*, Universitetsforlaget: Oslo.

Suomi, Juhani (1996) *Taistelu puolueettomuudesta. Urho Kekkonen, 1968–72*, Otava: Helsinki.

Suomi, Juhani (2000) *Umpeutuva latu. Urho Kekkonen 1976–81*, Otava: Keuruu.

Thorhallsson, Baldur and Hjalti Thor Vignisson (2004) 'The special relationship between Iceland and the United States', in Baldur Thorhallsson (ed.), *Iceland and European Integration*, Routledge: London, pp. 103–27.

Vaahtoranta, Tapani and Tuomas Forsberg (2000) 'Post-neutral or pre-allied? Finnish and Swedish policies on the EU and NATO as security organisations', Upi Working Papers 29.

Vihavainen, Timo (1991) *Kansakunta rähmällään*, Suomettumisen lyhyt historia, Otava: Helsinki.

Vladimirov, Viktor (1993) *Näin se oli*, Otava: Helsinki.

Wahlbäck, Krister (1973) *Norden och Blockuppdelningen, 1948–49*, Utrikespoliticka Institutet: Stockholm.

Wahlbäck, Krister (1982) 'The Nordic region in twentieth-century European politics', in Bengt Sundelius (ed.), *Foreign Policies in Northern Europe*, Westview Press: Boulder, CO, pp. 9–32.

13

'Reluctant Nordics', 'reluctant Europeans', but 'moral superpowers'?

Scandinavia has emerged as a moral superpower by continuously and consistently advocating compliance with global standards of conduct and by working to develop, refine and maintain principles of mutual understanding in world politics.

(Ingebritsen 2006: 2)

Writing in the 1980s, Bengt Sundelius noted that 'history seems to indicate that the Nordic countries have failed dramatically when they have tried to undertake some major conspicuous co-operation projects' (Sundelius 1982: 181). The Sundelius citation provides the text, so to speak, for the first part of this chapter, which asks whether the Nordic states were 'reluctant Nordics' – 'reluctant to integrate with each other' in Miljan's terms – during the Cold War and, if so, whether the picture has changed over the last two decades (Miljan 1977: 282). In his analysis of the Danish rejection of the Maastricht Treaty (on European Union) at a referendum in June 1992, Hans Jørgen Nielsen claimed that 'the Danes are reluctant Europeans. They have never come to embrace the ideal of European institutional integration and are even among the most sceptical about binding co-operation' (Nielsen 1994). His compatriot Uffe Østergård has added that 'both sides [left and right] in matters European basically agree to do as little as possible, as late as possible, as cheaply as possible, and with as little enthusiasm as possible' (Østergård 1992: 168). The next part of our discussion considers whether the Nordic states have indeed been reluctant to integrate with Western Europe and, if so, how far this remains the case. During the Cold War the supposition was that small states played a predominantly reactive role on the world stage – that is, they reacted to events and developments spearheaded by the two superpowers. In this light, the final part of the chapter explores the basis for Christine Ingebritsen's claim that Scandinavia has emerged as a moral superpower and considers the ways in which the Nordic states have sought to influence the

agenda of international politics. Could it be, however, that the moral authority exercised by the Scandinavians – and by extension their reputation – have
been undermined of late?

Regional co-operation during the Cold War

Nordic regional co-operation long antedated the Cold War. The Norden
Associations (see chapter 1), multi-faceted cultural bodies which included
both organisations and individuals among their membership, were founded in
Denmark, Norway and Sweden in 1919 and extended to Iceland in 1922 and
Finland in 1924. In the inter-war period, moreover, the main societal interest
groups, the trade union movement, industrial federations, the employers and
farm producers all developed Nordic contacts. Regional co-operation, in short,
did not originate at the inter-governmental level. However, the early Cold War
decades witnessed a period of accelerated and institutionalised region-building
in northern Europe, which saw the creation of the consultative, inter-parliamentary organ, the Nordic Council, in 1952 and the inter-governmental Nordic
Council of Ministers in 1971 (see chapter 1). The formal structures of regional
co-operation were reinforced and legitimised by reference to the concept of
Norden – 'Nordicity' – which came to be propagated as an ideological 'super
glue'. Norden was essentially an elite construct grounded in, and facilitated by,
a nascent cross-national consensus around Scandinavian social democratic
values, and the concept was diffused and transmitted primarily through the
agency of political parties. The cross-national party groups in the Nordic
Council were in existence much before similar developments in the European
Parliament. At one level it seems reasonable to surmise that Nordic identity-
building represented an attempt to build a *security community*, in Karl Deutsch's
(1957) term, as a normative bulwark against the threat (internal and external)
from communism. The essence of Nordicity was thus security – not in a military sense, but security in terms of a community of values, beliefs and ideas.
At another level, regional co-operation proceeded on the basis of geographical
proximity and the search for solutions to common practical matters in relation
to such things as transport, labour migration, social services and environmental questions. It was pragmatic rather than ideology-driven co-operation
and achieved a good deal. Bengt Sundelius has noted that the 'Nordic countries
have a long and strong record of finding joint solutions to *neighbourhood issues*'
and, in this context, the early Cold War decades have been described as the
'golden age of Nordic co-operation' (Sundelius 1982: 181, my italics).

Thus, following the approval of a Passport Union in 1952, a Nordic Social
Security Convention was agreed in 1955, which entitled migrant Nordic
workers to social security and other benefits on the same basis as nationals.
The previous year a pioneering Common Labour Market Treaty (extended
to include Iceland in 1982) meant that no work permits were needed for

Table 13.1 *The main landmarks of Nordic regional co-operation during the Cold War*

Year	Initiative
1947	Scandinavian Airlines (SAS) founded
1952	Passport Union
1954	Common Labour Market Treaty
1955	Nordic Social Security Convention
1971	Nordic Cultural Agreement
1972	Nordic Transport Agreement
1973	Nordic Industrial Fund
1974	Environmental Protection Convention
1975	Nordic Investment Bank
1976	Nordic Cultural Fund
1978	Nordic Gene Bank
1985	West Nordic Council (Greenland, Iceland and the Faeroe islands)

nationals to work in another state in the region. Although Finland did not participate in the work of the Nordic Council until 1956 – and then only on condition that foreign and security matters were not on the agenda for discussion – it was a co-signatory of the Common Labour Market Treaty in July 1954, following which many Finns moved to Sweden in search of work. As George Maude cryptically observed, it may be said without exaggeration that for Finland, a small country with large-scale capital-intensive industry geared to exports, for many years the greatest importance of Nordic co-operation was the opportunity it created to export Finns (Maude 1976: 111)!

The main landmarks of Nordic regional co-operation during the Cold War are set out in table 13.1. During these years, moreover, informal inter-governmental contact between the civil servants in related policy fields of the central administration in the region's five states facilitated a constant exchange of detailed information, making the Nordic framework a cost-effective and pragmatic form of co-operation. Indeed, on the basis of the substantial inter-governmental co-operation between the Nordic states during the Cold War, the extent of the cross-national harmonisation of legislation in strategic areas that was achieved, the mosaic of sector-based policy communities that developed and the myriad of informal contacts between officials, it may not be wide of the mark to speak of a degree of *de facto micro-integration*. In sum, when the impressive record of joint responses to 'neighbourhood issues' is borne in mind, the label 'reluctant Nordics' seems a singularly inappropriate term with which to characterise Cold War regional co-operation. *Macro-integration projects*, on the scale, say, of the creation of a Nordic common market, however, conspicuously failed to reach fruition.

This was the fate of the intermittent discussions which took place between 1947 and 1959 on a Nordic customs union (the Finns were not involved until summer 1956). The prospect of Scandinavian economic co-operation was first raised by the Norwegians in July 1947, when Denmark, Norway and Sweden met to co-ordinate their positions for the forthcoming meetings of the Marshall Plan countries. When it became apparent that there was not a common stance, there was recognition of US interest in a European customs union and, at a Danish initiative, a committee of experts was set up – the Bramsnæs committee – to consider Nordic economic co-operation, including the removal of internal duties. The decision was announced to the Marshall Plan conference in Paris by the Danish delegation. However, early in 1950 the Norwegian members of the committee of experts held that a customs union would pose problems of such magnitude for Norway that 'only if special measures [loans] to balance the development within the customs union area were first taken' would membership of the union be in its interests (Haskel 1976: 89). Four years later, in fact, the Danes and Swedes conceded the need for 'capital transfers' to avoid disruptions in the Norwegian economy.

Critically, for much of the time, there were fundamental differences between the three metropolitan Scandinavian states over the nature of the proposed economic co-operation. Until the mid-1950s the Swedes and Danes were interested in a common market (a common external tariff and the elimination of internal trade barriers), whereas Norway sought capital investment to develop its water power into electricity. Sweden's aim was to expand the market opportunities for its thriving industries – by the 1950s Sweden was the most highly industrialised of the Nordic states and had a balance of payments surplus in its trading with each of the others. In contrast, Norway was the poor relation. Industrialisation there lagged behind Denmark and Sweden; with the exception of waterfalls, industrial resources were sparse; it had lost half its sizeable merchant marine – its primary source of foreign exchange – during the Second World War; and the far north (Finnmark and half of Tromsø) had been laid waste by the scorched earth policy of the retreating Nazi occupiers. In any event, the first proposal for a Nordic customs union was largely overtaken by events and by growing Danish impatience. Over the summer of 1957 the Organisation for European Economic Co-operation's intergovernmental Maudling committee was discussing a sixteen-nation West European Free Trade Area (WFTA – see below), whilst the move of Jens-Otto Krag from the post of minister for Nordic co-operation to become minister of foreign trade in the new Danish coalition of 1957 symbolised a shift in Danish interest away from Norden towards continental Europe. Ultimately, in sum, the first proposal for a Nordic customs union imploded because of the divergent economic interests and divergent levels of economic development of the participant states.

Nordek

The disintegration of a second macro-integration project – the Nordic economic union proposal or *Nordek* – in March 1970, when only the formalities needed completing, represented the last 'grand design' venture among the Nordic states and left a legacy of bitterness in its wake, especially between the Danes and Finns. Nordek was initiated by Denmark, which followed Britain in renewing its application for membership of the European Economic Community (EEC) in 1967. However, when French president Charles de Gaulle vetoed this second attempt to join, the Danish non-socialist coalition led by Hilmar Baunsgaard revived the Nordic customs union project at a Nordic Council meeting in February 1968. It was then that the Danish foreign secretary declared that the 'Nordic countries could try and make a constructive contribution during the stalemate in European market integration efforts which has occurred against Denmark's will and desire' (Miljan 1977: 102). Nordek was designed to be the Nordic equivalent of the European Community (EC) and was modelled in some measure on the 1957 Treaty of Rome setting up the Common Market. There were two main elements in a comprehensive blueprint: a plan for economic modernisation, which envisaged the transference of resources from non-competitive primary industries such as agriculture and fisheries to manufacturing industries; and the development of a common Nordic trade policy predicated on the creation of a customs union. A number of common institutions, including a central investment bank, were also to be created. The inter-governmental negotiations proceeded expeditiously over the course of 1969 and the Nordek treaty was ready for signature on 24 March 1970. The four states involved explicitly affirmed their continuing obligations as members of the European Free Trade Association (EFTA) and left the door open for Iceland – which was in the process of preparing an EFTA application – subsequently to join Nordek. It was further agreed: that regional integration should not prevent the parties later participating in an expanded EEC; that it should not constrain the aim of fostering Third World trade and global free trade; and that, crucially, an economic union should not jeopardise foreign and security policy arrangements in the region, that is, the 'Nordic balance' should not be upset (Arter 1993: 154–5). Yet, when senior diplomats gathered in Copenhagen to undersign the Nordek treaty, the Finnish prime minister sent dramatic countermanding instructions. He subsequently justified his action by reference to communist opposition in the cabinet and the confused post-election situation. Following the rise of the Finnish Rural Party and Conservative gains at the polls, the formation of a new government looked likely to prove a lengthy process and a 'caretaker cabinet', it was implied, did not have the authority to sign the Nordek treaty (Arter 1993: 157).

Unlike the first stillborn customs union proposal, which was sacrificed on the altar of divergent economic interests, Nordek failed for essentially political reasons bound up with EC enlargement, on the one hand, and the 'Soviet factor', on the other. Restated, although structural differences between the respective national economies persisted, accelerated industrialisation had dictated a growing measure of convergence and there was a significant growth in intra-Nordic trade between the early 1950s and late 1960s – greater, in fact, than the increase in transactions between the Nordic countries and their trading partners outside the Nordic region. In part, this was because EFTA membership had liberalised trade in manufacturing goods, but the main point is that the economic pre-conditions for a Nordic customs union were favourable in 1968 and, as the Dane Lasse Sonne (2006) has argued, the aim was to increase economic growth and welfare. In other words, the Nordek proposal may be said to have possessed a functional economic logic quite distinct from, and independent of possible enlargement of, the European Union (EU). This is not say it was not perceived as a stepping-stone to EC membership or a close working relationship with the EC – in neutral Sweden and particularly Denmark, this was precisely the case. But Nordek, unlike the first customs union proposal, had a sustainable economic rationale.

Inevitably, the motives for supporting Nordek varied among the participating countries, as, too, did their enthusiasm for the project. Sweden was probably its most effusive advocate, although not so much for the economic benefits it would confer as for the indirect political gain – that is, improved standing and a better bargaining position *vis-à-vis* the (possibly enlarged) Common Market. In 1961 Sweden had applied for no more than an 'association' with the Common Market, whilst curiously in 1967 the Erlander Social Democratic cabinet submitted an 'open' application which specified that adherence must be compatible with its foreign policy of neutrality but left the question of status open to negotiation. Significantly, however, when, early in 1968, the EC Commission reported on prospective members, it discussed only Norway, Denmark, Ireland and Britain, with not a mention of Sweden. It clearly took the view that the applicant state itself must decide what status it was applying for (Haskel 1976: 127–8). Against this backdrop of exclusion from the Common Market enlargement process, Sweden offered to make generous contributions to the Nordek project, particularly to the joint funds for transitional support measures for industry and structural reforms in agriculture. In 1969 Sweden offered to pay one-quarter of a joint bank's capital of $50 million and 46 per cent of three funds for agriculture, fishing and industry (Haskel 1976: 127). This enthusiastic pro-Nordek line, which was vigorously canvassed by big business and the Liberals and Conservatives, was based less on the anticipated economic benefits – by the late 1960s, for example, all the intra-Scandinavian industrial tariffs had been abolished in accordance with EFTA rules – than on the expected political advantages of reducing the isolationist burden of the nation's neutral foreign policy and of facilitating future links with the EEC. The Nordek project was thus seen as something of a back door into the EEC or at least a means of keeping Sweden on roughly the same footing as its Nordic neighbours, Denmark and Norway. Certainly, when in summer 1969 it appeared that the Nordek project had begun to stall – prior, *inter alia*, to the Norwegian general election in September – the advent of Olof Palme as Swedish prime minister in October revived the whole process and he in turn remained firmly of the view that its ultimate collapse represented a vital wasted opportunity in conducive circumstances to market Nordic co-operation (Koivisto 1997: 243).

For Denmark, too, political rather than economic motives were paramount in the Nordek negotiations – that is, factors relating to the politics of extra-regional economic integration. Put another way, Denmark tended to view Nordek, like EFTA, as little more than a temporary expedient and a pathway to the Common Market. Nordek could certainly not satisfy Denmark's aspirations to be a member of an organisation that encompassed both its main trading partners, Britain (in prospect) and West Germany. Although twice spurned by de Gaulle, Britain's overtures for Common Market membership forced the hand of several of its EFTA partners, and Denmark, which was concerned to protect its agricultural exports against a possible Anglo-French deal on farm products, decided to apply for membership in 1961. Six months after de Gaulle's first veto on British membership, in January 1963, in fact, the French president personally offered the Danish prime minister, Jens Otto Krag, EEC membership (full or associate) (Arter 1993: 153). Krag immediately consulted the British prime minister, Harold Macmillan, and the outcome was a strong declaration of solidarity with Britain and EFTA. Denmark followed Britain in renewing its EEC application in 1967 but, when de Gaulle vetoed this second attempt to join, Denmark looked around for regional alternatives. At the Nordic Council meeting in Stockholm in March 1969 – a month before de Gaulle's resignation – the Danish prime minister Hilmar Baunsgaard revealed his hand by telling his Finnish counterpart in confidence that what he was now seeking was a Nordic customs union that would proceed to secure a free-trade agreement with the EEC (Koivisto 1997: 216). Yet when Nordek foundered, Denmark maintained its public support for regional co-operation and Baunsgaard mooted a SCANDEK customs union – Nordek minus Finland – although it was countenanced neither by the Norwegian prime minister, Per Borten, nor by the Swedish premier, Olof Palme (Koivisto 1978: 58–9). However, for Denmark, Nordek had doubtless by then already served its purpose of strengthening bridges to the Nordic region before the magnetic pull of the EEC drew it inexorably further away from its regional neighbours. It was in this tactical context, Miljan (1977: 109) has argued, that Denmark 'made it clear that it did not matter much whether the formation of Nordek was successful or not, as long as the exercise was carried out'. Moreover, for the pro-EC government in Denmark, the failure of Nordek was by no means insignificant in domestic political terms, since it made it possible for Danish adherents of EC membership to stress the absence of viable alternatives (Pedersen 1996: 86).

Norway consistently adopted the most cautious attitude to regional economic integration projects. It was significant, for example, that during the 1950s the Norwegian Federation of Industry opposed the original proposal for a Nordic customs union on the grounds that a narrowly Scandinavian market would shut Norway out of the vital British market (Haskel 1976: 126). Norway was also the most guarded in its approach during the Nordek negotiations and fishery policy proved naturally a question of great concern. Norwegian hesitation was, however, overcome by an agreement to create a common fisheries policy to stabilise prices and to establish a special fishery fund. A certain amount of support was also earmarked from the general structural fund designed in this case to facilitate the modernisation of the fishing industry (Stålvant 1982: 117). None the less, the position of the prime minister, Per Borten, was never easy and a number of Labour delegates claimed vociferously that he viewed Nordek primarily as a means of preventing Norway joining the EEC (to which Borten's Centre Party was firmly opposed).

For the Finns, the Nordek initiative was less about the economics of regional integration – the advantages of a consolidated Nordic market – than about the politics of regional integration and the imperative of a *Westpolitik* that sought to extend contacts to another Western organisation following the nation's accession to the Organisation for Economic Co-operation and Development (OECD) in 1968. During the greater part of the Nordek negotiations, Finland clearly did not believe that the other participants would have an early opportunity of joining the EEC, at least on remotely acceptable terms (Koivisto 1978: 36). The *impasse* created by de Gaulle thus largely dictated Finnish tactics, since for security reasons it was imperative that, from a Soviet viewpoint, the nascent Nordek treaty should not be tarred with the Common Market brush. De Gaulle's resignation in April 1969, however, significantly increased the risk of Nordek being overtaken by events and at the Hague summit of the 'Six' on 1 December 1969 it was agreed to deal promptly with a third British application. At this stage the Finns were probably banking on a speedy outcome to the negotiations and the approval of a Nordek treaty before Denmark and Norway re-entered direct talks with the EC because, as mentioned, neither of the two last mentioned had disguised their view that Nordek was in large measure a stepping-stone to an accommodation – ideally a pan-Nordic accommodation – with the EEC.

By December 1969 the broad centre–left coalition was divided over the Nordek issue – the Centre and Communist parties now wishing to retard the whole process – and two days after the Hague summit the Finnish cabinet requested a postponement of an inter-governmental conference scheduled for the middle of the month. The foreign secretary, Ahti Karjalainen, in particular, was concerned about Soviet suspicion that the whole enterprise represented a 'back door into the EEC' at a time when Finno-Soviet relations were somewhat strained (Karjalainen and Tarkka 1989: 168). None the less, President Kekkonen felt able to proceed with Nordek, albeit with the caveats that, in the event of a proposed member state commencing negotiations on EEC membership, Finland should reserve the right to discontinue talks until such time as any outcome regarding the EEC was clear and that if the country in question proceeded to join the EEC the Nordek project should be shelved. Kekkonen held that it was crucial that blame for the possible collapse of Nordek should not subsequently be laid at Finland's door: 'Culpability must be made to rest with the nation that chose the EEC before Finland' (Kekkonen 1976: 58). In the event, the blame for the collapse of Nordek was indeed laid at Finland's door and the Danes in particular have seemed to have a long memory. When, following the bloody events in the Lithuanian capital, Vilnius, in January 1991, the Finnish president Mauno Koivisto declared that 'it was an internal Soviet matter', the Danes were so incensed they wanted to remove Finland from the Nordic Council and, as we shall see, there was initial Danish suspicion of the Finns' 'northern dimension initiative' in 1997.

Viewed from a Finnish standpoint, several remarks on the *dénouement* of the Nordek episode seem in order. First, it seems clear that the Soviet Union did not immediately rule out Finnish membership of Nordek and probably never *expressly* did so, even when negotiations had reached an advanced stage. In his account of events, Koivisto, the prime minister at the time, relates that when Kekkonen discussed the Nordek issue with the Soviet prime minister, Alexsei Kosygin, in Leningrad in May 1969 it appeared the Kremlin leadership wanted more time to consider the matter rather than ruling out Finnish involvement completely and, accordingly, Kekkonen felt able to authorise Finnish participation in the negotiations, albeit within strictly defined terms of reference (Koivisto 1997: 220).

Second, it seems probable that Kekkonen, who, incidentally, clearly saw that a longer-term connection between Nordek and the EEC would be to Finland's advantage, tried to the last to gain Soviet acquiescence in Finnish participation, but ultimately Nordek would have come at too high a price. Thus, in his discussions with Kekkonen in January 1970, according to Juhani Suomi's account (1996: 351–2), Leonid Brezhnev raised the possibility of linking Nordek and the 1948 Friendship, Co-operation and Mutual Assistance (FCMA) Treaty. If Finland joined Nordek, the FCMA Treaty could be 'improved' (Koivisto 1997: 236). This was something the Finns were not willing to entertain.

Third, whilst the Kremlin may not categorically have refused to countenance Finnish membership of Nordek, Soviet opposition was unmistakable. Symptomatically, Kekkonen was invited to pay an unofficial visit to Moscow in February 1970 and, at a meeting attended by the entire Kremlin leadership, was advised of the Soviet view that it would be better if Finland did not sign. Had Finland proceeded to do so, Suvi Kansikas has speculated that the Soviet Union might well have sought revisions in the FCMA Treaty and/or applied economic sanctions on Finland (Kansikas 2005, 2007).

Finally, whilst the Danish researcher Lasse Sonne (2007) may strictly be correct in asserting that Kekkonen was responsible for the collapse of Nordek – and the president's reference to the need to protect Finnish agriculture echoed real concern in his former party, the Centre, which was opposed to the project – the paramount factor was Soviet opposition. Sonne viewed as a secondary motive for Kekkonen's ultimate veto his readiness to discredit the prime minister, Koivisto, who had led the Finnish side in the Nordek negotiations and was emerging as the president's likely successor. This may have been the case, but it should not obscure the bigger picture – Nordek would have materialised had the Soviet Union not disapproved of both it and, more particularly, Finnish participation.

Nordic regional co-operation in the new millennium

Setting aside the dramatic collapse of Nordek, which would, after all, have been realised had Finland not pulled out at the last minute, and bearing in mind the considerable amount of co-operation on 'neighbourhood issues' (micro-integration), can it be said that the label 'reluctant Nordics' has become more appropriate *since* the Cold War than during it? In other words, has Nordic regional co-operation largely been overtaken by events – events such as the collapse of the Soviet Union and the demise of the 'Nordic balance', EU enlargement to include Finland and Sweden in 1995, and the emergence of a generation of politicians not steeped in Cold War thinking? Erkki Pennanen (*Helsingin Sanomat*, 1 October 1996) clearly believes so when writing that 'for Finland Nordic co-operation was from the outset a counterweight to the FCMA Treaty with the Soviet Union and a point of identification'. It was, in other words, a West-facing window. However, since 1999 Finland has been not only an EU member but the only Nordic EU member state to belong to the Economic and Monetary Union (EMU).

Plainly, Cold War Nordic regional co-operation performed different functions for different states in the region and, in this connection, the historian Matti Klinge put forward an even more unequivocal version of Pennanen's thesis the year after Finnish EU membership. Klinge argued that the case for Nordicity or a common regional identity was built on an artificial foundation and that the time for traditional Nordic regional co-operation was over. He held that in the Nordic Council/Council of Ministers Finland had suffered from a linguistic and political inferiority complex, whereas as an EU member Finland was a political and linguistic equal and, indeed, was ahead of Norway. He concluded, controversially, that learning Swedish (the second national language) was too high a price for Finns to pay for a bridge to Norden. Instead, Finland should be looking to Baltic co-operation and to Germany, Europe's real power centre.

Klinge's reference to Baltic co-operation prompts the point that the Nordic Council (Council of Ministers) is no longer the sole region-specific organ in northern Europe. Rather, it has representation on, and to a degree competes with, a plurality of other post-Cold War bodies focusing on the interests of particular 'sub-regions' – the Barents Sea, Arctic, Baltic Sea and so on. For example, the Nordic Council was granted permanent observer status on the Canada-initiated Arctic Council in October 2000, before formulating an Arctic Action Plan of its own in 2004. The individual Nordic countries have seats on the Barents Euro-Arctic Regional Council (BEAR) and the Council of Baltic Sea States (CBSS) and in 1986 the specific interests of the 'North

Atlantic Nordics' led to the creation of a West Nordic Council, with its (small) secretariat in Reykjavík. Significantly, too, the EU has a voice on both the BEAR and CBSS, as well as funding cross-border projects through the Inter-Reg programme (Baldersheim 2004: 204–5). Within the EU Nordic member states, individual counties, such as Finnish Lapland, increasingly promote their interests by lobbying directly in Brussels (Arter 2001), whilst the ethnic minority of Lapps (Saamis) have their own consultative bodies in Norway, Sweden and Finland. In view of the multiplicity of area-specific organs presently in existence in northern Europe, not to mention Nordic involvement in the wider European integration project – albeit in the case of Norway and Iceland through membership of the European Economic Area (EEA) – the earlier question can be restated. Is the tag 'reluctant Nordics' more appropriate in characterising the Nordic states' attitudes to regional co-operation today than it was during the Cold War?

When asked about the 'Nordic model' (*Helsingin Sanomat*, 11 June 2007), the Swedish foreign minister, Carl Bildt, responded mischievously that it was a combination of the Finnish education system, Swedish global business leadership, Norwegian oil, Danish labour markets and Icelandic fish! Bildt was, of course, tongue in cheek and, in any event, is a vigorous proponent of Nordic regional co-operation. However, there have been those who have publicly voiced concern that the formal structures of the Nordic model of regional co-operation – the Nordic Council and Nordic Council of Ministers (NCM) – which were developed during the Cold War – need to be replaced with something more modern, relevant and efficient. Thus, a number of parliamentary initiatives (*motioner*) submitted to the Riksdag by Conservatives and Liberals – notably, perhaps, one from Tomas Högström – proposing the abolition of the Nordic Council in its present form, prompted the Norden Association in Stockholm in April 2006 to call a meeting dubbed by the media 'The Battle of the Nordic Council' (*Norden – the Top of Europe*, email newsletter, May 2006). Högström claimed that the Nordic Council was too detached and inward-looking and did not reflect the legislative agenda of parliamentarians across the region. Moreover, when the national daily *Helsingin Sanomat* ran a series on regional co-operation over summer 2007, the deputy director of the Helsinki district chamber of commerce, Sampsa Saralehto, insisted that the structures of Nordic co-operation were overly bureaucratic and MPs lukewarm about them. He concluded that the Nordic Council and NCM could be abolished and replaced with an adequately resourced think-tank funded from the allocations that had previously supported the two Councils. Saralehto concluded that industry could support innovative projects and that, in order to ensure that the new institute was sufficiently international in its orientation, its working language should be English (*Helsingin Sanomat*, 12 June 2007).

In fact, there has been intermittent concern to modernise, streamline and focus the structures of regional co-operation. In the Nordic Council this has been evident in the reforms of its standing committee system over the years.

There are presently five specialist committees: Welfare; Culture, Education and Training; Citizens' and Consumer Rights; Environment and Natural Resources; and Business and Industry. The NCM has also been re-organised. In addition to the prime ministers and ministers for Nordic co-operation, the NCM has from January 2006 consisted of only ten specialist councils of ministers, compared with the previous eighteen, and there is greater co-operation between them. For example, within the NCM, the Council of Ministers for Gender Equality Legislation and Council of Ministers for Social Services and Health Policy co-operate and co-ordinate their activities on measures to combat human trafficking.

Formal structures aside, Nordic regional co-operation has been obliged to adapt to survive – that is, to respond to a rapidly changing external environment. During the Cold War, Nordic co-operation was primarily regional in focus. Today this is much less obviously so. Thus, reflecting on his time as secretary general of the NCM (between 2002 and 2006), Per Unckel claimed that Nordic co-operation had become more European – more integrated with what was going on in the rest of Europe – as well as being more international. Moreover, much of the contemporary agenda of intra-regional co-operation – namely common action within the Nordic region itself – can be viewed as a response to the challenges posed by globalisation. Nordic co-operation, in short, appears less region-specific, operates in arenas outside the region and has become increasingly concerned with promoting regional interests in the wider European community and beyond. In the sketch that follows, a distinction is drawn (in reality there is overlap) between Nordic co-operation in the EU, Nordic co-operation in the Baltic and north-west Russia, Nordic co-operation outside Europe and intra-Nordic co-operation.

It is probably fair to state that, subsequent to the EU's 1995 enlargement, *Nordic co-operation within the EU* – at least at the level of 'high politics issues' – was largely conspicuous by its absence. Divisions concerned the questions of the pace of further enlargement, membership of the EMU and the Finns' 'northern dimension initiative'. There was still some latent resentment in Finland about the way in October 1990 Ingvar Carlsson, the Swedish prime minister, had not directly informed the Finns of his country's decision to apply for EU membership. But disagreement between Finland and Sweden surfaced publicly in 1997 over the EU Commission's *Agenda 2000* enlargement programme, which proposed splitting the applicant states into two groups, with entry negotiations beginning immediately with the six best-performing nations. Not least because Estonia fell into the first group, Finland favoured the Commission model; Denmark and Sweden, however, preferred the so-called 'regatta model', in which negotiations would start with all the applicant states at the same time. When Göran Persson, the Swedish prime minister, publicly criticised Finland for supporting the Commission line at the EU summit in Luxembourg in December 1997 relations between the two countries deteriorated. There was undoubted irritation, too, in Sweden (where the Social Democratic government was opposed) and Denmark (which had an opt-out) over Finland's strongly pro-EMU stance and its unreserved and unashamed support for the unofficial 'Euro X club' of core EMU-member finance ministers within the Council of Ministers, which had been mooted by France and Germany. Indicative of the strains then in Finnish–Swedish relations was an incident described in the memoirs of the Swedish prime minister at the time, Göran Persson. Persson (2007) relates how, standing in front of him in the WC queue at the EU summit in Cardiff in June 1998, an irritable Finnish prime minister, Paavo Lipponen, turned round and warned his Swedish counterpart – who had clearly said something in plenary that Lipponen disapproved of – that he had better watch his step. A potentially inflammatory situation was dampened down when the South African president, Nelson Mandela, arrived and greeted both men!

In autumn 1997 the Finnish government launched its 'northern dimension initiative' in response to the request at the EU Dublin summit in December 1996 that the Commission should report on joint regional projects. It was viewed as a counterpoise to the EU's Mediterranean and central European programmes and was intended to be one of the primary objectives during Finland's EU presidency in the second half of 1999. The manifest rationale of the northern dimension initiative was the promotion of stability and socio-economic development in two sub-regions of the north – the Barents Sea and the Baltic Sea. As a lobby concept, the 'northern dimension' had at least two underlying goals. The first was to exploit the natural gas and oil resources of the Kola Peninsula and to put north-west Russia on the map in Brussels (Arter 2000). At a Barents Sea conference in Rovaniemi in Finnish Lapland in September 1997, at which the concept of the northern dimension was launched, Lipponen concentrated on the importance of utilising these vast energy resources. The second was to try to ensure that the revision of the EU structural funds did not deny to the northern peripheral areas of Finland and Sweden the type of support they were currently receiving through Objective Six funding for sparsely populated areas.

Yet it was symptomatic of the underlying tensions between the 'EU Nordics' that both Sweden and Denmark felt they had not been adequately consulted about the northern dimension initiative. Swedish officials at the launch conference in Lapland grumbled audibly in the corridors about the lack of prior dialogue, whilst the first version of a report on the initiative by the European Committee of the Nordic Council, prepared by the Dane Ole Stavad, could be construed as possible evidence of continuing resentment at the way the Finns had ditched Denmark's Nordek project. Stavad, a minister in the Social Democratic government at the time, wrote that 'the concept of the "northern dimension" is a reaction to the Finlandisation of the Cold War era.... Finland wishes to bind itself to the EU as tightly as possible so as to demonstrate that it is no longer chained hand and foot to the Soviet Union.' Small wonder that in late February 1998 the leaders of the Swedish Liberals, Danish Liberals (Venstre) and the Swedish People's Party in Finland published a joint newspaper article canvassing the need for strengthened Nordic co-operation within the EU!

All in all, one of the lessons of the first decade or so of Finnish and Swedish membership appears to be that differing national interests keep the Nordic states as much apart within the EU as they did when major Nordic co-operation initiatives were attempted in the period up to 1970. There was a powerful reminder of this in autumn 2007, when, it seems, the Swedes lobbied in Brussels against 'article 141 support', the national subsidy paid to those farmers in southern Finland who were experiencing 'serious difficulties' as a result of EU membership. Sweden, concerned to gain competitive access to the Finnish market for its own agricultural products, argued that 'article 141' represented a transitional support mechanism and should now be abolished, and the Swedes were supported in this by the Danes. (In the event, the Finns were permitted to continue to pay 'article 141 support', albeit only until 2012.) It may be that today there is a somewhat greater readiness to work together – for example, Sweden embraced the northern dimension initiative during its EU presidency in 2001. But the case for Nordic regional co-operation within the EU has none the less warranted restatement and in 2004 the Swedish foreign secretary, Laila Freivalds, remarked that 'the Nordic countries do not necessarily have a common standpoint, but in cases where they do agree it is of great importance to proceed with a common voice in the enlarged EU'. Yet, reflecting on the decade of Finnish and Swedish membership between 1995 and the 2004 enlargement, Paavo Lipponen insisted that the EU Nordics had not pulled their collective weight and, accordingly, had missed a golden opportunity that would not come again to influence the future course of the Union:

> We lack a common strategic line of thought. In our provincial way, we do not see that the EU is going well ahead of us. The Union is working with Russia and the adjacent areas. The Nordic countries have, because of their different points of view, sleepily watched their luck fly past them in many matters. When will the day come when we realise that having each other in the EU is a strength? (*Helsingin Sanomat*, 19 October 2005)

It was a searing indictment of the lack of Nordic regional co-operation within the EU.

If, as Lipponen claimed, the governments of the EU Nordics both severally (Finland presumably excepted) and collectively have lacked drive, direction and vision in Union matters – and such an assertion would need systematic empirical investigation – regional co-operation has also operated through the NCM, which, as one policy actor among many, has sought to bring influence to bear on EU policy. As a random example, in December 2005 the NCM set up a Nordic group for maritime policy to identify and implement activities where the Nordic countries could have an impact on the development of EU maritime policy. This was of particular interest to Norway and Iceland, non-EU members, for which the NCM and Nordic Council have assumed increased importance as a vehicle for consulting and influencing Denmark, Finland and Sweden on matters to be discussed in Brussels and hence for conducting a 'shadow EU policy'. For the most part, however, the NCM has sought to influence the EU through the machinery of the northern dimension 'action plans' and to do so in the second field we identified – that is, *Nordic co-operation in the Baltic and north-west Russia*.

In Annika Bergman's view, the concerted efforts of the Nordic states in the Baltic republics from the early 1990s onwards may well have rescued Nordic co-operation from the threat of irrelevance in the post-Cold War era. The Nordics quickly 'adopted' individual Baltic states – Finland championed Estonia, Sweden Latvia and Denmark Lithuania – and together promoted Baltic membership of the EU, although Finland and Sweden were lukewarm at best on Baltic membership of the North Atlantic Treaty Organisation (NATO). The NCM, in turn, set up an office in St Petersburg in 1995 and Kaliningrad in 2006, and has pioneered a number of projects, including a Nordic–Russian mobility programme, enabling Russian students to make study trips to Scandinavia. The NCM has also assumed an active role in developing a number of schemes through the EU's 'Second Action Plan for the Northern Dimension, 2004–2006'. One, for example, adopted in April 2006 and targeting the Baltic states and north-west Russia, is a three-year programme focusing on children and young persons (and their parents) with functional impairment. It sprang out of the October 2003 Oslo Declaration, which, underwritten by the NCM, eight international organisations and twelve individual countries, launched the 'EU's Northern Dimension Partnership in Public Health and Social Wellbeing'. Other cases include the various projects – dealing with water supplies, waste-water systems, district heating and nuclear waste management in Murmansk, Novgorod, St Petersburg and Kaliningrad – that form part of the EU's Northern Dimension Environmental Partnership. Mention might also be made of NORDunet – a high-capacity network for research programmes, created in 1995, which became a joint Nordic–Baltic venture in January 2008. There have been avuncular tensions – at one point Sweden appeared to try to cast itself in the 'lead role' of bridge-builder between the Nordic and Baltic states, but, familial strains and suspicions aside, the record of Nordic co-operation in the Baltic and north-west Russia has been far from exiguous.

More recently there has been concern to develop the potential for *Nordic co-operation outside Europe*. In this, opinion leaders have been important. For example, in 2008 exploratory work began on a proposal from the former Finnish prime minister Esko Aho that the Nordic governments open joint centres of excellence and innovation in India and China. The NCM is also investigating the potential demand for Nordic welfare – health care and care for the elderly, for example – in Asia. There is already co-operation between Finland and Japan in the field of care for the elderly. Regional co-operation outside Europe is likely to be intensified in the future.

It was argued earlier that the focus of Nordic co-operation is no longer exclusively or even primarily regional. This is not to suggest that regional problems are no longer of concern – far from it. At the 2007 annual Nordic Council session in Oslo, a special forum was created to work towards removing the routine difficulties experienced by citizens of one Nordic country when living, studying or working in another. A Finnish student, on a scholarship, for example, does not qualify for social security if he/she falls ill in Sweden, whilst an Icelandic passport is not accepted as proof of identification in a Stockholm bank. On a larger scale altogether, bureaucratic problems have arisen from the explosive growth of the Copenhagen–Malmö area, now connected by a road and rail bridge across the Sound. Denmark, for instance, differs from the other Nordic countries in that taxes are paid to the locality in which a person works, not where he/she lives. However, the *intra-regional Nordic co-operation* agenda could well be viewed as increasingly reflecting the wider challenges posed by globalisation. The recent practice has been for the annual Nordic Council session to be preceded by a summit of government and opposition leaders from the five states and three autonomous territories, and the theme to emerge from the Copenhagen 2006 summit was globalisation. Subsequently, at the summer 2007 meeting of Nordic prime ministers at Punkaharju in Finland, agreement was reached on founding a 'Globalisation Forum' – roughly modelled on the Danish Globalisation Council – which would bring together the Nordic prime ministers, representatives from industry, the world of research, interest groups and civic organisations. Three NCM policy objectives clearly mirror the impact of globalisation. First, there is climate change, which was the theme of the 2007 Oslo Nordic Council session. The aim is for the Nordic countries to be a pioneering bloc in the reduction of greenhouse gas emissions, so they might appear as exemplars to others at the 'climate summit' in Copenhagen in 2009. Second, in the field of research, innovation and education, an elite Nordic university with close links to the business community has been mooted but not yet agreed. Finally, there is the promotion of the international competitiveness of the Nordic bloc of countries – that is, the investigation of ways of jointly marketing the region internationally. Christopher Browning has referred to a decline of the *Nordic brand* compared with the Cold War years, when he claims the Nordic states 'were rather successful in marketing a Nordic brand on the international scene' (Browning 2007: 29). This, it seems, was implicitly accepted, as was the need to give remedial action a high priority.

Accordingly, the NCM Secretariat, together with the Danish think-tank Monday Morning, published a consultative document in October 2005 entitled *The Nordic Region as a Global Winner Region – Tracing the Nordic Competitiveness Model*. Twenty-seven Nordic opinion leaders drawn from industry, academia and the cultural world were asked to consider the prospects for the Nordic countries in the global economy, including an examination of whether any common Nordic values exist, whether Nordic business has profited from these and, if so, how the Nordic governments could promote and benefit from them.

All the opinion leaders pointed to the same four fundamental conditions and eight values that the Nordic countries share in the global economy. The fundamental conditions were:

1 the Nordic countries have the same social system;
2 the Nordic countries understand each other's languages (more or less);
3 the Nordic countries stand at the same level of 'self-realisation' (i.e. population lifestyle);
4 the Nordic countries have been using each other as primary frames of reference for many years.

The eight joint Nordic values identified were: equality, confidence, short power distance, all-inclusive opinions, flexibility, respect for nature, common work ethics and aesthetics. Although there was no direct empirical evidence, the opinion leaders found that a number of links existed between the above values and positions of strength, and they emphasised their belief that untapped competitive potential existed.

The Nordic states – (still) 'reluctant Europeans' or even more reluctant?

When applied to the Nordic states of the mid-1970s, the label 'reluctant Europeans' (Miljan 1977) has a *prima facie* appeal. Only Denmark was a member of the EEC and, even then, a majority in the Folketing was in favour of a new referendum had the so-called 'renegotiated terms' of Britain's membership been turned down by voters in the June 1975 British referendum. A majority of Norwegian voters, moreover, had rejected EEC membership in a referendum in 1972, Sweden's approach to Brussels for 'associate membership' had fallen on deaf ears and Finland was not even a full member of EFTA. True, the description 'reluctant European' lacked exclusivity. It had been applied to other states outside the west European integration project – Britain, for example. In addition, it also appeared to presuppose that states could be viewed as unitary actors and, for the Nordic countries, this was certainly not the case. Cabinets were at various times openly divided on European questions; 'pro-European' minority governments were obliged to engage in majority-building and were not always successful in doing so; the attitude of civil servants at times deviated in practice from the manifest government line; and European issues divided the political parties. Moreover, the approval of European treaties usually involved qualified majority support in the legislature – so vesting parliamentary opposition groups with veto potential – and/or approval in a popular referendum. None the less, for all the Nordic states the basic calculus during the Cold War years was the same – they had to weigh the economic benefits of accession to the Common Market (and later the EEC or EC) against the political costs of joining a project ultimately committed to building a federal union of states. In eschewing political integration, they could fairly be described as 'reluctant Europeans'.

Plainly, for Finland and Sweden the political costs of European integration during the Cold War were too high, for security reasons. For Finland, EEC membership would have severely compromised relations with Moscow, which had even blocked Finland's full membership of EFTA. For Sweden, EEC membership was viewed as compromising its policy of neutrality, although a relationship falling short of full membership was clearly envisaged. For their part, Norway and Denmark adopted an essentially instrumental and pragmatic approach to west European integration. All three metropolitan Scandinavian states stood apart from the 1951 European Coal and Steel Community (ECSC), which stated that 'the pooling of coal and steel production would immediately ensure the setting up of a common foundation of economic development, the first step in the *federation of Europe*' (Diebold 1959). However, it seems that Danish rejection of ECSC membership was mainly because the economic consequences for Denmark were unclear rather than out of any intrinsic ideological opposition – although in influential foreign ministry circles there was a fear that ECSC membership might in due course lead to the 'absorption of Denmark by Germany' (Pedersen 1996: 85). However, once Britain had applied to join the Common Market in 1961, the economic costs of remaining outside the 'European project' became too high for Denmark and Norway and they followed suit. In Carsten Holbraad's words, 'since the country would in any case be economically dependent on what went on in the EC, Denmark would be better off as a party to its decision-making than as an outsider' (Holbraad 1991: 116).

The collapse of the Cold War security system facilitated Finnish and Swedish applications in 1992 and three years later the EU acquired a 'Nordic dimension'. Yet the Maastricht summit in December 1991 and the subsequent Treaty on European Union, whilst making no reference to federalism, sought to advance the political integration inherent in the 'European project' and the treaty contained commitments, among other things, to Economic and Monetary Union, a common foreign and security policy and European citizenship. Against the backdrop of these developments, the notion of 'reluctant Europeans', when applied to the Nordic states, took on a rather different meaning and significance. Simplifying somewhat, the politico-economic elite (the Establishment) now accepted the political costs – in truth there were reservations, especially among the Social Democratic/Labour parties in Denmark, Norway and Sweden – whereas a majority of voters clung to such symbols of sovereignty as national citizenship and their own currency. The tone was set when the Danish referendum on ratifying the Treaty on European Union on 2 June 1992 demonstrated that popular attitudes towards European integration were considerably out of step with the overwhelming pro-Maastricht majority in parliament. In the Folketing, opposition to the treaty came only from the Progress Party, the Socialist People's Party and one Christian MP, but it was rejected by a narrow majority of 50.7 to 49.3 per cent of voters.

Since then, events have gone a long way to contradicting the Rokkan orthodoxy that 'votes count but resources decide' (Rokkan 1966: 197). Thus, Knut Heidar has written that 'the most demanding factor for Norwegian elites during the 1990s has been the mismatch between elite and voter opinion on the European Union issue – the dominant elite in favour, the dominant electorate against' (Heidar 2001: 175). Indeed, voters have rejected the Establishment line on European integration questions in all three metropolitan Scandinavian states since 1994. Norway rejected EU membership for the second time (previously in 1972) at a referendum in November 1994, Denmark rebuffed EMU and the euro at a referendum in September 2000 and the Swedes did likewise in a referendum in September 2003. Significantly, the Finns acceded to EMU on a majority parliamentary vote. The only exception to the preponderance of popular Euroscepticism in the Nordic region appears to be Iceland, which, ironically, is the only one of the Nordic countries never to have applied for EU membership. Baldur Thorhallsson comments that 'support for EU membership has been greater among Iceland's general population than among its political elite' – although, in fact, it has never comprised an absolute majority of voters (Thorhallsson 2004: 5). The following sections consider Denmark as a 'pragmatic European' and the first Nordic state to join the EC, how in 1995 the EU acquired a 'Nordic dimension', and the continuing strength of popular resistance to European political integration across much of the region.

Denmark – the first 'Nordic European'

The value Denmark and the other Scandinavian countries placed on the British market was reflected in their support for the Macmillan government's 'Plan G' or Grand Design in October 1956, which envisaged the creation of a WFTA comprising the 'Six' (ECSC and subsequently Common Market states), Britain and any other interested member state of the Organisation for European Economic Co-operation. When this was ultimately rejected by France, EFTA, a smaller free-trade area, was founded by the Stockholm Convention of 20 November 1959. It provided a ten-year period of trade liberalisation for industrial goods among its seven members – Britain, the metropolitan Scandinavians, Austria, Portugal and Switzerland – leading to the complete abolition of tariffs by 1970. There were, however, special concessions to Portuguese and Norwegian fishing interests and Danish bacon exporters. EFTA was conceived in large measure as a negotiating instrument *vis-à-vis* the Common Market and also as an interim arrangement from which, according to article 42, any member could withdraw at twelve months' notice.

None the less, EFTA proved a success for all its Nordic members – intra-Nordic trade increased by over 200 per cent between 1959 and 1967, and in 1961 it nearly matched the value of the region's trade with the EEC – but when, in the last-mentioned year, Britain submitted its first application for Common

Market membership, Denmark readily followed suit. Throughout, Denmark had been the most restless EFTA state and the Liberals (Venstre) had in fact opposed the ratification of the Stockholm Convention, citing as the reason EFTA's inability satisfactorily to accommodate Danish farming interests. The incipient bifurcation of western Europe following the plans to form a Common Market (including agricultural products) laid by 'the Six' at the Messina conference in 1955 threatened to create an 'economic iron curtain' between Denmark's two main markets for agricultural exports, Britain and West Germany. Accordingly, Denmark's optimal scenario was all-encompassing: the creation of a British-style WFTA, combined with the Nordic customs union (the first version was still being negotiated) and Danish inclusion in, or association with, the agricultural co-operation being developed by the Six. Indeed, early in 1957, with the Maudling talks faltering, Denmark considered applying for Common Market membership, and the foreign minister visited the EC to inquire about the conditions for an association agreement or possibly even membership (Pedersen 1996: 85). The eventual decision not to apply reflected the fact that the realisation of the WFTA was still not completely out of the question, whilst there was a strong pro-Nordic inclination on the part of the new centre-left government and there was increasingly vociferous opposition to Danish EC membership from the peak industry and blue-collar union federations (Pedersen 1996: 86).

None the less, when Britain applied to join the Common Market, Denmark promptly did likewise, sparking a serious crisis in relations with Sweden, which had sought to get the EFTA states to negotiate a joint association agreement with the EEC. In a curious episode, moreover, it seems that de Gaulle offered the Danish prime minister, Jens Otto Krag, Common Market membership in 1963, in spite of his (first) veto on Britain's application. This was declined following hurried consultations with Macmillan. However, throughout the 1960s, Denmark consistently perceived EFTA's primary role as building bridges to the Common Market rather than promoting measures of retaliation against it (Miljan 1977: 163–4). Following rejection of its second application in 1967, Denmark turned to the Nordek option as a stop-gap measure. In submitting a third application in tandem with Britain, the Danish minister of economics rejected the need for a transitional period and underlined the way Denmark had been 'restructuring' – that is, modernising its economy – since the late 1950s in readiness for membership. Playing up the economic benefits and playing down the supranational costs, the pro-membership lobby obtained a comfortable majority of 63.4 per cent to 36.6 per cent at the EC referendum in October 1972 (see table 13.2, pp. 318–19).

During the period 1973–89 Denmark appeared less than a fully committed EC member. As mentioned, in 1975 there seems to have been a Folketing majority ready to stage a referendum on Denmark's continuing membership had British voters rejected the Labour government's renegotiated terms. A combination of non-socialist minority governments and the largest party, the Social Democrats, in opposition, moreover, led to the 'foot-dragging' of the 'footnote politics' era between 1982 and 1988 – so-called because footnotes had to be appended to agreements in Brussels to accommodate the beleaguered minority Danish government. Typically, in 1984 Poul Schlüter's Conservative-led coalition, under pressure from the predominantly Eurosceptic Social Democrats in opposition, rejected the recommendations of the Dooge committee (set up by the European Commission) for a major institutional reform of the EC. When, further, on 14 January 1986 the Social Democrats declared that they intended to vote against acceptance of the Single European Act – the Social Liberals (Radikale Venstre) were also opposed – Schlüter called their bluff and called a referendum (rather than general election) on the issue, for 27 February. As Torben Worre (1988: 387) has commented, the 1986 referendum, like the one in 1972, was at heart a question of Denmark's membership of the EC and the majority of 56.2 per cent in favour of signing the Single European Act was largely the result of deep division among the Social Democratic electorate – as well as a low turnout on the 'no' side among the supporters of the governing parties.

A fundamental shift in Danish attitudes to the EU took place in October 1990, when seven of the Folketing parties, including, significantly, the Social Democrats, agreed on a memorandum of changes in the Treaty of Rome. Whereas earlier the EC had been viewed as performing principally an economic function, the political role of the EU was now commended. Indeed, the Maastricht Treaty on European Union was backed overwhelmingly in the Folketing, by 125 votes to 30. In militating towards this basic re-orientation in Denmark's policy on Europe, three external factors appear to have been highly important. First, there was the unification of East and West Germany and the need to contain the 'new Germany' within a supranationalist framework. Second, there were the autumn revolutions of 1989 and the EU Commission's active profile in relation to post-communist central and eastern Europe. The Commission's sympathetic stance towards the former Warsaw Pact states appears to have had a particularly positive effect on the EU's image in Denmark, especially in moulding a more favourable attitude on the part of the radical leftist Socialist People's Party. Finally, there was the prospect of a significantly widened EU, reflected in applications from the EFTA states of Austria (in 1989) and, above all, Sweden (in 1991). There were domestic factors at work, too, and in particular the emergence of a pro-EU consensus in the Social Democratic Party. The debacle suffered at the referendum on the Single European Act in 1986 was the turning point for the Social Democrats, but in seeking to unite the (long-divided) party the readiness of the leadership to argue the link between widening (EU enlargement) and support for deepening (major structural reform) was particularly important.

The first Danish referendum on ratifying the Treaty on European Union, on 2 June 1992, however, demonstrated that Social Democratic unity had been by no means achieved and, equally important, that popular attitudes towards

Table 13.2 *Scandinavia and European integration 1945–2007: a chronology of events*

Year	Event
1947	Formation of UniScan, a consultative forum for Britain and the Scandinavian countries
	July. Scandinavian states meet to co-ordinate their policies for the forthcoming meetings of the Marshall Plan countries
1949	*June*. Foundation of the Council of Europe
1950	*January*. Bramsnæs Committee recommends a Nordic customs union
1951	*March*. Agreement between the 'Six' on the ECSC
1955	*February*. British House of Commons approves an association agreement with the ECSC
	June. Messina conference of 'Six'. Britain declines invitation
1956	*October*. Britain launches 'Plan G' or the Grand Design for a West European Free Trade Area including the Six, Britain and any other OECD country
1957	*March*. Treaty of Rome sets up a European Economic Community. Scandinavians inquire (unsuccessfully) about the possibility of a British–Scandinavian free-trade area
1959	Collapse of the protracted talks on a Nordic customs union
	November. European Free Trade Association created by the Stockholm Convention
1960	*May*. Agreement between Finland and EFTA states (Finefta) reached, but Finns warned in a Soviet note
1961	*June*. EFTA comes into operation
	August. Danish application to join Common Market
	August. Swedish prime minister Tage Erlander's 'Metal Speech' rules out a full application to join the Common Market
1962	*May*. Norwegian application to join the Common Market
1963	*June*. De Gaulle veto, but the general offers the Danish prime minister, Jens Otto Krag, Common Market membership. Following hurried consultations with Britain, this is turned down
1967	Norway and Denmark re-apply, along with Britain, for EEC membership
	July. Sweden submits an 'open application' to Brussels
1968	*February*. Denmark launches Nordek project at the Nordic Council
1969	*January*. Iceland applies for EFTA membership
1970	*March*. At the eleventh hour Finland declines to sign the completed Nordek Treaty
	March. Iceland joins EFTA
1972	*July*. Britain, Ireland, Denmark and Norway sign accession treaties with the EEC
	July. Swedish industrial free-trade agreement with the EEC; Icelandic industrial free-trade agreement too

Table continues opposite

	September. In Norwegian EEC referendum 53.5 per cent to 46.5 per cent against membership. Turnout 77.6 per cent
	October. In the Danish EEC referendum 63.4 per cent to 36.6 per cent for membership. Turnout 90.1 per cent
1973	*October.* Finnish industrial free-trade agreement with the EEC
	July. Norwegian free-trade agreement with the EEC
1977	By this year the industrial tariffs between EEC and EFTA had been abolished
1984	*April.* On a Swedish initiative, the first EEC–EFTA ministerial meeting is held, in Luxembourg
1986	*27 February.* Danish referendum on the Single European Act, 56.2 per cent to 43.8 per cent in favour
1987	*May.* Norwegian government's policy paper underlines the need to adapt to the EC's single market
1990	*June.* Formal negotiations on the European Economic Area begin
1991	*July.* Sweden applies to join the EC
1992	*March.* Finland applies to join the EC
	May. European Economic Area agreement signed in Oporto
	2 June. Danish referendum on Maastricht treaty, 50.7 per cent to 49.3 per cent against ratification
	November. By a majority of 104 to 55, the Storting approves a Norwegain EU application on condition that negotiations are conducted in tandem with Sweden and Finland
1993	The EU opens negotiations with Austria, Sweden, Finland and Norway
	18 May. Second Danish referendum on Maastricht (the Edinburgh exemptions), 56.8 per cent to 43.2 per cent in favour of ratification
1994	*March.* Conclusion of EU membership negotiations
	European Economic Area agreement comes into force
	16 October. EU accession referendum in Finland, 57 per cent to 43 per cent in favour of joining
	13 November. Swedish EU referendum, 52 per cent to 47 per cent in favour of membership
	28 November. Second Norwegian EU referendum, 52.2 per cent to 47.8 per cent against membership
1995	*1 January.* Austria, Sweden, and Finland become EU members
1997	Finland launches its 'northern dimension initiative'
1999	Finland's EU presidency gives priority to the 'northern dimension initiative'
2000	*28 September.* Danes reject EMU membership by 53.1 per cent to 46.9 per cent
	The Finns become the only Nordic state (along with ten fellow EU members) to adopt the euro
2001	Sweden's EU presidency agenda includes greater transparency and higher environmental standards
2002	Danish EU presidency gives pride of place to EU enlargement
2003	*14 September.* The Swedes reject EMU membership by 55.9 per cent to 44.1 per cent
2007	Nordic EU members agree to the new EU Constitutional Treaty

European integration in Denmark – now with an expressly political as well as economic content – were considerably out of step with the overwhelming pro-Maastricht majority in parliament. A narrow majority of voters rejected Maastricht; less than 60 per cent of Social Democrats favoured it, whilst, according to survey data, 54 per cent of women voted 'no' compared with 47 per cent of men (Bertone 1998: 20). Two factors appear to have tilted the scales narrowly against Maastricht. First, the Social Democrats were engaged in an internal power struggle when the referendum was announced – only when Poul Nyrup Rasmussen was elected as their new chair following an extraordinary party conference could the Social Democrats turn their sights to the campaign – and, in any event, their voters remained badly divided on the issue, as they had been for two decades. Second, a series of scandals (arising, among other things, from charges levelled against a former minister of justice, Erik Ninn-Hansen, regarding the deportation of Tamil refugees) served to discredit the non-socialist coalition and, in particular, to increase the distance between politicians and the people. This contributed to a diffuse protest against Maastricht, which, in addition, variously embraced anxieties concerning future defence arrangements, objections to the standardising of immigration policy and, not least, opposition to the idea of European citizenship.

Subsequently, a seven-party 'National Compromise' was foisted on the Schlüter bourgeois minority government by the opposition-based Social Democrats, Social Liberals and, crucially, the (previously anti-Maastricht) Socialist People's Party, and this provided Denmark with a new negotiating stance. Accordingly, at the EU summit in Edinburgh in December 1992, the Danish government gained confirmation of four opt-outs – the so-called 'Edinburgh exemptions' – on a single currency, common defence, EU citizenship and co-operation in aspects of justice and home affairs – and these were comfortably approved at a second Maastricht referendum, on 18 May 1993 (Dinan 1994: 191). One of the stipulations of the National Compromise was that Denmark's EU decision-making procedures should be reformed so as to involve members of parliament and the general public to a greater extent. Indeed, the rechristening of the Folketing's Market Relations Committee, which became the European Affairs Committee in October 1994, stemmed indirectly from the anti-Maastricht referendum outcome on 2 June two years earlier and the concern expressed both during and after the campaign about the so-called 'democratic deficit' and the need for greater transparency (openness) in EU decision-making (Arter 1995b: 112).

'Reluctant Europeans' no longer?
The EU acquires a Nordic dimension

Sweden's and Finland's 'European policy' prior to the sudden disintegration of the Soviet Union was based on the search for an accommodation between the economic imperative of access to crucial Western export markets and the political imperative of preserving the credibility of neutrality and, in the Finnish case, the special relationship with the Kremlin (Rehn 1993). The economic side of this special relationship was attenuated in the late 1980s, when the concern of the Soviet reformists to attract foreign currency reserves by diversifying oil exports to the West led to a substantial decline in Finno-Soviet trade. In the nature of the barter trading arrangements between the two countries, the less oil was piped to Finland the lower was the value of Finnish export goods to the Soviet Union. From a figure of 25 per cent in the 1970s to 20 per cent in the early 1980s, Finnish exports to the Soviet Union then plummeted, to under 5 per cent of its overall trade in 1990 – the year Moscow unilaterally announced a shift from barter arrangements to hard currency transactions. It took effect from 1 January 1991 and hence, although the collapse of the Soviet Union plainly complicated matters for Finland, it did not cause them. The pressure to 'Westernise' Soviet trade mounted throughout Mikhail Gorbachev's fruitless pursuit of *perestroika*. In this light, the final collapse of the Cold War security system provided rationalisation, rather than a fundamental rationale, for Finland's EU application.

For the overwhelmingly pro-EU elite in Finland, including the president, Mauno Koivisto, there was recognition of the 'security dividend' of EC membership. Indeed, it seems the notoriously cautious Koivisto decided on the need for a Finnish EU application following the abortive hard-line coup in Moscow in August 1991 – that is, three months before the formal disintegration of the Soviet Union (*Helsingin Sanomat*, 1 May 2005). However, for obvious strategic reasons (as well as the depth of the popular commitment to neutrality) the security card could not be displayed in public at the time. Rather, economic arguments were emphasised, and these, it was hoped, would be sufficiently appealing at a time of deep recession and mass unemployment. Yet for many Finnish voters membership was viewed in essentially expressive rather than self-interested instrumental terms. It was seen as a way of anchoring Finland to the West European mainstream and of institutionalising its position as a member of the bloc of West European states, to which it had belonged by dint of its politico-economic system, if not geography, from the earliest years of independence (Arter 1995a). It was a question of identity and the importance of the outside perception of Finland as a West European state (Arter 1995a: 378). Accordingly, on 16 October, at the first of the three accession referenda in the Nordic states in autumn 1994, the Finns voted by a comfortable margin of 57 per cent to 43 per cent to enter the EU on the basis of the negotiated terms. On 1 January 1995 Finland became the first successor state of the inter-war period to become a full member of the EU.

When the Swedish prime minister, Ingvar Carlsson, stated Sweden's intention to apply for EC membership in autumn 1990, neither the Finns nor the Norwegians were consulted. They were, in fact, taken aback by the move. President Koivisto (1995: 547) has even noted that he felt Sweden, in order to gain a head start on its eastern neighbour, would have preferred Finland not to apply. Sweden's formal application to join the EC in July 1991 was the first from one of the remaining Nordic EFTA states. It pre-dated the formal disintegration of the Soviet Union and, significantly, represented a sharp reversal of earlier Social Democratic government policy. Ironically, unlike Finland, however, for Sweden EU membership was no 'big deal': it did not hold out the prospect of the same 'security bonus', nor was there the need to compensate for the collapse of its 'Eastern' trade. The Swedish economy was already closely integrated into that of Western Europe (Aylott 1997). True, in challenging the continued salience of Swedish neutrality, the collapse of the Cold War order facilitated a Swedish application. It removed the traditional security policy constraint stressed by the prime minister, Tage Erlander, in his 'Metal Speech' on 21 August 1961 – delivered at the annual conference of the Steel and Metal Workers' Union, in which he stated that EC membership was incompatible with Sweden's policy of non-alignment – and it was this fundamental change in the nation's security environment which Carlsson employed as his manifest justification for the approach to Brussels. But it did not *ipso facto* provide a sufficient case for proceeding to apply. Rather, the sudden *volte face* of the Social Democratic leadership related to a number of essentially domestic factors. First, there was the incipient recession, the austerity programme of early 1990 and the concomitant pressure to appease the money markets. The prospect of a flight of capital out of Sweden was a potent factor in concentrating the mind of the government. Second, there was the risk of being outflanked by the opposition-based Liberals and Conservatives, who came out expressly in favour of EU membership in summer 1990. Above all, there was concern to avoid the potentially calamitous electoral costs of an enforced devaluation of the Swedish krona. Importantly, however, Carlsson consistently explained and defended his government's abruptly changed stance on European integration in contextual terms, averring to the irresistible logic of the radically altered security environment in which Sweden now found itself. He never openly admitted to the Swedish public that the EU application was primarily dictated by the exigencies of a deepening economic recession. The opinion polls indicated a close result, but on 13 November 1994, two weeks after the Finns had voted for the EU (and possibly influenced in small measure by that vote – the pro-membership politicians had certainly hoped for a 'domino effect'), the Swedes voted by 52 per cent to 47 per cent to join too.

Norway was the last of the Nordic EFTA states to apply for EU membership – for the fourth time! – in autumn 1992. The trauma of the abortive referendum in September 1972, when a narrow majority of Norwegians voted 'no', weighed heavily and the 'European issue' was effectively removed from the political agenda until the late 1980s. Unlike its neutral neighbours, Norway's security was provided through NATO, whilst North Sea oil and gas boosted the economy from the early 1970s onwards. Access to the single internal market, moreover, was provided by membership of the EEA – largely a

Norwegian initiative, which, desirably from its viewpoint, excluded agriculture and certain elements of environmental and regional policy (Gstöhl 1996) – the treaty being ratified by the handsome margin of 130 votes to 35 on 16 October 1992. None the less, shortly after the Finnish moves to seek EU membership, the Labour Party mandated its own government under Gro Harlem Brundtland to commence negotiations for an application for full membership. The only condition stipulated by Labour was that freedom of opinion and expression should be respected in relation to party members, trade unionists and ordinary rank-and-file voters. Ultimately, on 19 November 1992 the Storting approved an EU application by 104 votes to 55, subject to the negotiations being conducted in tandem with those of the other Nordic applicants and the terms being submitted to the people at a popular referendum.

The referendum was held on 28 November 1994, two weeks after the Swedes had approved membership. The prime minister, Brundtland, made much of the argument that, whilst going into the EEC in 1972 would have separated Norwegians from most of their fellow Nordics (only Denmark was joining), staying out in 1994 really would leave Norway out in the cold. None the less, the result was 47.8 per cent for membership and 52.2 per cent against. The turnout was exceptionally high, at 88.9 per cent. As Martin Sæter (1996) has observed, the EU issue was effectively decided at the September 1993 general election – which largely focused on the membership question – since the 'no' side gained an enormous lead, which the 'yes' lobby was simply unable to pull back.

'Votes count' – the strength of popular Euroscepticism in the Nordic region

Since a majority of Norwegians declined EU membership in 1994, two more Euro-referenda in Scandinavia have been 'lost'. In September 2000 the Danes rejected the euro, whilst three years later the Swedes followed suit and refused to adopt the single currency canvassed by the government and backed by industry, business, the trade union movement and a large majority in parliament. All three results represented defeats for the Establishment and can be interpreted in part as anti-Establishment votes. Put another way, the strength of popular Euroscepticism – the term is used loosely to characterise those opposed to the government's stance at the three aforementioned referenda – whilst containing a number of common strands, cannot be understood without reference to the particular national context. More often than not, Eurosceptics opposed not only the idea of European integration itself, but also the politico-economic elite that appeared to be conspiring to drive it forward.

What is striking in the case of the 1994 Norwegian referendum was both the exceptionally high level of civic mobilisation – turnout was nearly 12 percentage points higher than in 1972 – and the similarity between the political ecology of opposition to EU membership and EC membership more than two decades earlier. Nearly every Norwegian voted in 1994 and, as in 1972, the further from Oslo one went, the greater the anti-Market/Union sentiment became. In September 1972, Oslo and its three hinterland counties voted to accede to the EC, whilst the remaining fifteen (largely rural) counties were opposed to joining. In November 1994, 67 per cent of Oslo voters favoured EU membership compared with only 29 per cent in northern Norway. In the most northerly county of Finnmark, the negative majority of 74.5 per cent was higher than in 1972. In the latter year, the campaign was an emotive and highly charged affair. There was exaggerated talk of trawler owners having to fill in VAT forms in French, bonfires were lit on the mountain tops above fjords and families split down the middle into the pro- and anti-membership camps. The political mood of the time was radicalised: decentralisation and regional balance were 'in the air', and students and a younger generation challenged authority, as well as the 'capitalist Establishment'.

In 1972 the 'anti-Marketeers' comprised a heterogeneous band which exhibited a diversity of motives – economic self-interest, intuitive nationalism, anti-bourgeois idealism – as well as plain historic prejudice. A contemporary (Derry 1973: 445) summed it up thus:

> The farmers feared competition in an industry where Norway is naturally weak, the fishermen in an industry where its natural resources are the richest in Europe. Many of the older generation dreaded the loss of sovereign independence through accepting the Treaty of Rome, while the youth organisations of every political party except the Conservatives agitated against the prospective surrender to monopoly capitalism.

Along the rural west coast in particular, moreover, there was undoubtedly residual anti-German sentiment emanating from the wartime occupation, since the Luftwaffe had bombed much of the route to Tromsø taken by the fleeing king and government. Yet if the outlying areas were solidly against the EEC, Hilary Allen (1979: 163) has insisted that:

> It is a myth that the Norwegian establishment was overwhelmed by the periphery in September 1972 if the establishment is understood as extending beyond the narrow bounds of parliament and the central administration. The referendum was won by an alliance of the economic and cultural 'periphery' – the primary sector and the rural conservatives – and important sections of the country's intellectual and political elite.

It was in essence the same alliance which, in an entirely different political setting, had under the Venstre standard contributed decisively to the achievement of parliamentarism in Norway in 1884.

The same type of centre–periphery alliance in opposition to European integration was in evidence in 1994 and, whilst the constituent elements were not identical, they were remarkably similar. As in 1972, Euroscepticism at the second Norwegian referendum on EU membership was a broad admixture of economic self-interest (farmers and public sector employees), nationalist sentiment (especially the older generation) and an intellectual critique of the 'growth–quantity of life' philosophy perceived as underpinning the Union (particularly among the younger cohorts). The farmers were in the van of opposition to EU membership, fearing that under the Common Agricultural Policy they would receive less than their existing level of national subsidisation. Unlike Finland and Sweden, where the former Agrarian (now Centre) parties, although divided, were formally in favour of EU membership, the Norwegian Centre was against both the EU and the EEA, and had in its leader, Anne Inger Lahnstein, the so-called 'No Queen', a highly effective populist figurehead, who, at the 1993 general election, made opposition to the EU the party's main campaign plank and gained it a record poll of nearly 16 per cent. In the referendum the Centre combined elements of nationalism, environmental chauvinism and an appeal for democratic (Oslo) rather than bureaucratic (Brussels) decision-making. Its three main campaign slogans were 'Democracy or the Union', 'Solidarity or the Union' and 'The Environment or the Union'.

In their study of the EU accession referenda in Finland, Sweden and Norway in autumn 1994, Pesonen et al. (1998) posit a number of hypotheses, one of which they call the 'sovereignty hypothesis'. According to this, 'the citizens of nation-states are very reluctant to transfer any aspects of their country's sovereignty to a supra-national level' (Pesonen et al. 1998: 29). In the case of Norway, an old nation but a comparatively young state (when Norway seceded from the Union with Sweden in 1905 it became the first 'successor state' of the twentieth century), the desire to maintain independence and national sovereignty was a major component of popular Euroscepticism in both the EC and EU referenda. The first signs of a new 'Nei' movement were evident in the late 1980s, when the EEA was being negotiated. Although agricultural and regional questions were excluded – and the economic advantages apparently secured without incurring the political costs – access to the single market came at a price, since EEA members were required to adopt the acquis communitaire in its entirety and implement directives from Brussels, without being able to exercise direct influence over them. In the months leading up to the 1994 referendum, the Nei til EU organisation boasted a mass membership of about 140,000 persons and on 7 June that year it organised a demonstration linking the anniversary of Norwegian independence to the fear of loss of sovereignty within the EU.

Incidentally, nationalism appealed to the head as well as the heart of ordinary Norwegians, who had an understandable concern about the implications of EU membership for their jobs and livelihood. In other words, nationalism and economic self-interest were at times two sides of the same coin. Pesonen et al. (1998: 31) have suggested that 'voters with a personal interest in upholding the welfare state model will be opposed to EU membership' and this was true of public sector employees, particularly female personnel.

Pesonen *et al.* (1998: 30) also propose an 'economic growth and recovery hypothesis', according to which the more pressing a country's current economic problems are, the greater will be the willingness of citizens to enter into 'permanently organized cross-national economic co-operation'. It is not clear that there is evidence to validate this hypothesis in Finland and Sweden, despite those countries suffering their worst-ever economic recessions in the early 1990s. But, in any event, in Norway the challenge was very different, namely how to spend its considerable wealth without overheating the economy. It was against the backdrop of a rags-to-riches Norway and the comfortable material-ism of its *nouveau riche* middle classes that a type of post-materialist critique of the 'growth and growth' philosophy of the European project developed and appealed to a younger generation of voters. Hence, in sharp contrast to Finland, where young persons were overwhelmingly pro-European, 55 per cent of Norwegians aged under thirty voted 'no', students in particular espous-ing an intellectual critique of the EU as an organisation concerned only with getting economically fatter and all too little with the endemic global problems of famine, drought and abject poverty.

At the November 1994 EU referendum in Norway the Establishment lost and (anti-membership) votes, to paraphrase Rokkan, were ultimately decisive. On 19 November 1992 the Storting had approved an EU application by 104 to 55 votes (subject to negotiations being conducted in tandem with the other Nordic applicants), the minority Labour government under Brundtland was strongly in favour of EU membership and in June 1994 the Labour Party conference supported membership by 197 to 93. However, the parliamentary party component of the Establishment, so to speak, was less solidary than in Finland and Sweden, and tactical considerations played their part in mobilis-ing a 'no' vote. The leading role of the anti-EU Centre Party has already been mentioned, but four other opposition parties were in the anti-membership camp – the Socialist Left (red–green 'eco-socialist' opposition), the Christian People's Party (post-materialist objections), the Liberals (which had split in two over the EC question in 1973) and the radical rightist Progress Party (which favoured the EEA but not EU membership). With five of the eight Storting parties against Norwegian accession, it is small wonder, perhaps, that Nick Sitter has argued that 'Euroscepticism is the politics of opposition' (Sitter 2001: 37). It was bound up with the dynamics of inter-party tactics and competition. However, the main chink in the Establishment's armoury was division in the governing Labour Party. In October 1993 the 'Social Democrats against the EU' was founded; at its congress in spring 1994 the central labour federation, Landsorganisation, came out against membership and the Labour Party Youth Organisation also indicated opposition. When opinion polls showed that only 45 per cent of Labour supporters would follow Brundtland's recommendation of membership, the die was well and truly cast.

Table 13.3 *Danish referenda on Europe*

Year	Proposal	Percentage vote for	Percentage vote against	Percentage turnout
1972	Joining the EEC	63.4	36.6	90.1
1986	Approving the Single European Act	56.2	43.8	75.4
1992	Ratifying the Treaty on European Union	49.3	50.7	83.1
1993	Approving the 'Edinburgh exemptions'	56.8	43.2	86.5
1998	Approving the Amsterdam Treaty	55.1	44.9	76.2
2000	Adopting the single currency	46.9	53.1	87.5

On 28 September 2000 Denmark became the first EU state to stage a referendum on the euro. Article 20 of the 1953 Danish constitution requires a five-sixths Folketing majority or, failing that, a referendum when the matter at hand involves surrendering a measure of national sovereignty and, in this case, the question was whether to reverse one of the 'Edinburgh exemptions' and adopt a single currency. The result was the highest negative majority of all six Danish 'European referenda' since 1972: 53.1 per cent of voters rejected the euro, on an extremely high turnout of 87.5 per cent (see table 13.3). The referendum also marked a significant change in the geographic and socio-economic profile of Euroscepticism.

Before 2000, Danish attitudes to the 'European project' had followed centre–periphery lines, albeit in the opposite direction to Norway. The geographical centre, the greater Copenhagen area, voted 'no', whilst the rest of Denmark, especially the peripheral areas of Jutland, where agriculture and fishing were strong, voted 'yes'. This distinctive centre–periphery or urban–rural pattern of EU support was replicated across the electoral constituencies, the large towns demonstrating a greater degree of Euroscepticism than country areas. By 2000, however, as Roger Buch and Kasper M. Hansen have shown, the regional contours of EU opinion were less clearly delineated (Buch and Hansen 2002: 13). In their words, 'developments have moved the frontline from an east versus west, countryside versus city or farmer/fisher versus industrial/public sector conflict to a conflict within the east and the west, the countryside and the city' (Buch and Hansen 2002: 23). They conclude that the significant change in the 1990s was a shift away from occupation-based voting to voting on the basis of general attitudes to the EU. In other words, at the 2000 referendum on the single currency, there appears to have been a 'nationalisation' of Euroscepticism, which was no longer narrowly anchored in particular groups such as the less wealthy and less educated in society.

This change in general attitudes must have occurred in part during the campaign, since at the outset pro-euro voters had a generous lead in the polls. Most of the political and economic elites also favoured the adoption of the single currency. The two Rasmussens – Poul Nyrup Rasmussen, the Social Democratic prime minister, and Anders Fogh Rasmussen, the leader of the largest opposition party, the Liberals (Venstre) – both championed the euro. The prime minister focused on the economic benefits – growth, increased employment, the containment of interest rates and so on – although it did not help his cause that the euro had lost 25 per cent of its value against the US dollar over the previous twenty months. Still, Poul Nyrup remained on the offensive, arguing, among other things, that staying outside the eurozone would mean the loss of more than 6,000 jobs (Downs 2001: 223). Anders Fogh concentrated more on the essentially political 'core of Europe' argument, namely that Denmark, as a small country, would gain influence by having a seat at the 'high table' (with large, 'core' member states such as France and Germany), around which *the* important decisions would be taken (this was precisely the public reasoning of the Finnish prime minister, Paavo Lipponen, although there was no euro referendum in Finland). In addition to the two Rasmussens, the main political parties, business and the trade unions all came out in favour of the euro. Outside the eurozone there would be problems of attracting inward investment and a possible exodus of capital. The fear was also expressed that Denmark would miss the 'high-tech boat' and slip behind its competitors in an increasingly globalised marketplace.

The disparate anti-euro camp juxtaposed nationalism and federalism in its campaigning and played on the threat to Danish democracy posed by the loss of control over monetary policy. The Socialist People's Party stressed that the adoption of a single currency would erode Danish sovereignty, individuality and identity; the 'People's Movement Against the EU' insisted that the euro represented another step on the road to federalism, whilst Jens Peter Bonde, the veteran of the 'June Movement' – the Eurosceptic organisation formed after the June 1992 Maastricht referendum – put the same point in readily digestible form: 'If you have a single currency, you need a single government and a single parliament. If you are not prepared to have those, you shouldn't have a single currency.' The leader of the radical rightist Danish People's Party, Pia Kjærsgaard, linked opposition to the euro to the defence of Danish identity and exploited the popular prejudices concerning an increase in immigration and the threat from multiculturalism. These small and polarised opposition groups both reflected and reinforced a mood of diffuse Euroscepticism which was less easily defined by its social structural characteristics than earlier. Surveys indicated that when respondents agreed that the euro would reduce Danish independence there was only a one in ten chance of their backing the single currency. Similarly, those concurring with the statements that the adoption of the euro represented a step towards a United States of Europe, that the 'European project' posed a threat to democracy and the welfare state, and that Danish national identity was strong were all likely to vote 'no' (Buch and Hansen 2002: 20–1).

At a referendum in Sweden on 14 September 2003 the single currency was rejected by a decisive majority of 55.9 per cent of voters on a high turnout of 81 per cent. According to the leading psephologist Sören Holmberg, the Swedish 'euro referendum was an election where the [economically] weak beat the strong, the periphery defeated the centre and both the "insecure sex" [women] and younger voters got what they wanted' (*Dagens Nyheter*, 15 September 2003). In the richest communes about four out of five voters backed the euro, whereas in the poorest the proportions were reversed. About 60 per cent of entrepreneurs and those in leading positions in the labour market favoured the single currency, but 65 per cent of the unemployed, those who had taken early retirement and those on retraining schemes voted against. Women were significantly more negative than men; the younger age groups were notably more euro-hostile than the older; the countryside registered an unequivocal 'no', whilst the three largest cities were narrowly in favour; and the political left opposed the euro and the right backed it. A British journalist, writing just before the Swedish referendum, held that, in Sweden, 'opposition to the euro is a mixture of economics, nostalgia and nationalism, the same brew familiar from EU referendums in Ireland and Denmark' (*Guardian*, 5 September 2003). Was this really why a majority of Swedes turned their backs on the euro?

Clearly, each election and referendum has a character and 'mood' of its own and this provides the lens through which voters perceive events. Depicting that mood and estimating its influence on the outcome of the ballot is, of course, a hazardous task. However, it seems fair to speculate that there was a degree of popular resistance to the way the Establishment seemed to be 'steamrollering' Sweden into adopting the single currency. Citizens witnessed: the wheeling and dealing between the ruling Social Democrats and blue-collar trade union federation Landsorganisation; the joint declaration from the Landsorganisation leader and her counterpart in the central employers' organisation; the common initiatives from politicians 'across the blocs' – the Social Democrats and Liberals, for example, shared a campaign platform; and the curious (to some macabre) sight of the Social Democrat foreign secretary joining forces with the leadership of the telecommunications' giant Ericsson in seeking to frighten voters with the damage to the economy that would ensue if the euro was rejected. Ericsson, incidentally, put significant resources into the 'yes' campaign. All this may have created the impression at the grassroots of an elite plot to bundle Sweden into the single currency and, to the extent that this was the case, there may well have been a reaction against it.

Equally, the economic case for the euro was plainly not sufficiently convincing. The pro-euro lobby argued that economic growth would follow the adoption of the single currency and the Social Democrat prime minister, Göran Persson, claimed that it would create 108,000 new public sector jobs. The case for rejecting the euro rested on three principal arguments. First, the Swedish economy was said to be in better shape than many in the eurozone and it made no sense to swap a good recipe for a bad one. Second, full immersion in EMU would deprive Sweden of control of its monetary (interest rate) policy. Finally, it was argued that EMU was basically an experiment that was not guaranteed success. If Swedes adopted the euro there would be no turning back, whereas it would always be possible to adopt the single currency later. This 'wait and see' line proved a winner. The 'no' campaign skilfully played this card and conveyed the message that it was quite possible to reject the euro without it being an anti-European act. Indeed, Persson himself stated two weeks before polling that Sweden did not necessarily have to conform to the original timetable of the beginning of 2006 for the change of currency. Extra time could be taken if the stabilisation programme agreed between the eurozone countries was seen not to be working. This so-called 'soft yes' strategy (Widfeldt 2004: 510) was viewed by opponents as a 'have your cake and eat it' approach, which was exploited to good effect.

As in general elections, the extensive media coverage of referendum campaigns has contributed to the increased personalisation of politics. Party leaders and individual opinion leaders matter more than ever and it was important from an anti-euro perspective, therefore, that the high-profile Eurosceptics appearing in television interviews and debates gave the 'no' campaign as eclectic an appeal as possible. This was achieved to a great extent when the backing of the Centre Party and various prominent persons – among them Nils Lundgren (a former chief economist at the Nordea financial services group and subsequently co-founder of the 'June List') and Margit Gennser (a former Conservative MP and chair of the 'Citizens against EMU' organisation) – ensured that the Eurosceptics could not be stigmatised and dismissed as comprising leftists, G(g)reens and sundry 'bearded loonies' (Widfeldt 2004: 510). It was important to prevent the anti-EMU side acquiring the sort of left–green complexion that would discourage non-socialist voters from supporting it. After all, unlike the EU membership referendum in 1994, significant minorities of Conservatives and Liberals opposed the euro and there was a 'non-socialist no' campaign (*Ett borgerligt nej*). However, pivotal to the outcome was the top-to-bottom division in the ranks of the governing Social Democratic Party. At its extraordinary party conference in March 2000 there was a two to one majority in favour of the single currency, but divisions on the issue among senior party figures were reflected in the composition of the cabinet following the 2002 general election, when five of the twenty-two cabinet ministers, including the deputy prime minister, Margareta Winberg, and economics minister, Leif Pagrotsky, were opposed to the euro. By the end of April 2003 these divisions came out into the open with a vengeance, prompting the press to refer to a 'fully-blown euro-war in the government' (*Dagens Nyheter*, 24 July 2003). Persson, moreover, scarcely endeared himself to his own voters by seeking to gag the anti-euro ministers (*Aftonbladet*, 29 April 2003). When one of the party's most prominent euro-advocates, the foreign minister, Anna Lindh, was murdered only a few days before polling, the backlash of revulsion might have been expected to favour the pro-euro forces. In the event, probably less than half of Social Democrat voters backed the single currency.

The strength of popular Euroscepticism in Iceland has not been tested through the ballot boxes simply because Iceland has never applied for EC/EU membership. Moreover, in contrast to the other Nordic states, where the centre-right parties have generally been keenly pro-European, the only Icelandic party to favour an EU application has been the Social Democrats and its successor the (Social Democratic) Alliance, which in 2002 argued that Iceland should seek EU membership and submit the terms of entry to a referendum. The Independence Party, consistently the largest group in the Alþingi, has equally consistently opposed EU membership, whilst the tendency of Icelandic political discourse to polarise around nationalist themes has made it difficult for politicians to advocate membership of a supranational body. Thus, Gunnar Helgi Kristinsson (1996) has described Iceland's failure to participate in EC membership negotiations (along with Finland, Norway and Sweden) between 1992 and 1994 as a 'non-decision', which was not based on a systematic study of the issues or a general political debate of the advantages and disadvantages of EU membership. True, an EEA agreement was reached in 1994, albeit after stormy parliamentary debate and much popular opposition, but EU membership was not an issue at the 2007 general election.

Probably the principal stumbling block to an Icelandic EU application has been fish and the strength of the fisheries lobby. The export of fish and marine products represents about two-fifths of total Icelandic exports of goods and services and the fisheries sector accounts for approximately 10 per cent of gross domestic product (GDP). EU membership would mean that decisions on the size of permissible catches would be transferred to Brussels and foreigners would be granted the right to invest in Icelandic fisheries. As a major competitor in European fish markets, the course Norway took was carefully monitored and the spectre of isolation avoided when Norwegian voters rejected EU membership for the second time.

Whilst 'elite Euroscepticism' could also be viewed as a function of Iceland's peripheral geographical location in relation to the European 'centre', Baldur Thorhallsson (2004) has suggested that the distinctively small size of Iceland's national administration may have reduced Iceland's capacity to participate in the European integration process. In the absence of sizeable government departments, ministers have tended to be reliant on the views of interest groups, most of which are opposed to EU membership. Equally, Iceland's foreign service (150 persons in 2001) is very small when compared with those of Norway (1,150) and Denmark (1,163) and, as a consequence, its diplomatic corps has not been so involved in the 'corridor dialogue' about the future 'European agenda' with officials and politicians in the core EU member states.

If, at the elite level, Iceland appears to be the 'reluctant European' among the Nordic states, opinion polls suggest that the level of grassroots Euroscepticism has differed relatively little from (and has probably been somewhat lower than) that in metropolitan Scandinavia. Thorhallsson (2004: 5) has noted that, in the last decade or so, between one-third and over half the Icelandic population has *supported* EU membership – a greater proportion than among the political class. Recent surveys emphasise the point. A Gallup poll in March 2005 indicated that 45 per cent of Icelanders favoured EU membership, 34 per cent were opposed and 21 per cent were undecided. By September 2007 the figures were 48 per cent of respondents in favour, 34 per cent against and 18 per cent undecided. A clear majority of Icelanders support EU membership, although there has been little public debate on the matter and an application is not presently on the horizon.

Moral superpowers?

It is probably fair to assert as a broad generalisation that during the Cold War the Nordic states were reluctant to engage in macro-economic regional integration projects and have been reluctant since to participate in moves to promote the political integration of the member states of the EU. Only when seeking to capture these twin points do the terms 'reluctant Nordics' and 'reluctant Europeans' have a certain utility. In contrast, the Nordic states have been far from 'reluctant internationalists'; rather, they have sought proactively to influence the agenda of world politics. During the Cold War, neutral Sweden, in particular, pursued an internationalist programme designed to influence developments in the direction of peace and security. In Kjell Goldmann's words, it became 'a deliberate objective of Swedish foreign policy to give Sweden a special and visible profile in world affairs' (Goldmann 1991: 122). International opinion formation was seen as a tool of statecraft. As the prime minister, Olof Palme, put it, 'not even great powers can disregard world opinion. We who believe in democracy also believe that opinion – the commitment, morals and convictions of people – can change the world' (Goldmann 1991: 129).

The outspoken Palme, however, took Sweden's role of 'world conscience' too far for the United States and when his fierce criticism of US involvement in Vietnam included comparing the Hanoi bombings in 1972 to the fall of Guernica during the Spanish civil war, Washington froze diplomatic relations with Sweden between January 1973 and spring 1974. This temporary hiatus notwithstanding, Christine Ingebritsen (2006) has argued that not just Sweden but 'Scandinavia has emerged as a moral superpower'. It acts as 'the conscience of the international community' and, she adds, Scandinavians are 'norm entrepreneurs in world politics' and cultivate the role of 'global good citizen'. Evidence can be presented to suggest that the last-mentioned role has been developed and projected in at least four ways, although two important caveats need noting:

1 other small states could and probably would claim similar 'track records' of 'enterprise' and influence on the world stage;
2 there is often a significant discrepancy between aspiration – a desired solution, target figure or whatever – and its achievement.

None the less, a persuasive catalogue could be compiled in support of Ingebritsen's claims.

First, the Nordic states have provided *conflict resolution agents*, whether individual negotiators or combat troops, and *conflict resolution sites*, often their national capital cities, as part of international initiatives designed to produce peace and security. Prominent Scandinavians have been assigned sensitive and high-profile roles by the global community in recent years. The Swede Hans Blix served as the UN weapons inspector in Saddam Hussein's Iraq and found no evidence of weapons of mass destruction. The former Finnish prime minister Harri Holkeri was one of the 'peace envoys' in Northern Ireland and a leading architect of the Good Friday Agreement. The former Swedish prime minister Carl Bildt served as the high representative for Bosnia and Herzogovina between December 1995 and June 1997 and then from 1999 to 2001 he was the UN secretary-general's special envoy for the Balkans. The former Finnish president Martti Ahtisaari has had several roles as international mediator and peacemaker. For example, having decided not to run for a second term as Finnish head of state in 2000, the British government appointed Ahtisaari to the team overseeing the IRA's weapons decommissioning in Northern Ireland, whilst in 2005 the UN secretary-general, Kofi Annan, nominated him as special envoy to Kosovo, which ultimately led to his proposal to the UN Security Council for supervised independence for Kosovo. Scandinavian forces have undertaken international peacekeeping duties under the UN, EU and NATO flags and the Finns and Swedes, in particular, as new EU members, pressed the importance of 'crisis management' (the 'Peterberg tasks'). During the Cold War, the Scandinavian capitals staged talks between the superpowers, aimed at achieving lasting *détente*. In 1969 in Helsinki the United States and Soviet Union negotiated whether to negotiate on strategic arms reductions – the so-called SALT talks – and six years later the Finnish capital was the venue for the inaugural Conference on Security and Co-operation in Europe (CSCE). The 1986 Reagan–Gorbachev summit was held in Reykjavík, whilst, symbolically, when in 1993 Nelson Mandela was awarded the Nobel Peace Prize his first speech after his long imprisonment was delivered in Stockholm.

Second, the Nordic states' search for moral authority on the world stage has been reflected, and possibly reinforced, in the importance they have attached to the reduction of global poverty. For example, during the later decades of the Cold War, the Scandinavians promoted the concept of a 'New International Economic Order', which involved equalising – or at least significantly reducing the gap in – living standards between the First and Third Worlds. The existence of Christian Democratic parties in the Nordic parliaments – and on occasion governments – has contributed to an acceptance of the norm that a minimum of 0.7 per cent of GDP is budgeted for development aid. Scandinavian (non-military) personnel have participated in a range of humanitarian (civilian crisis management) activity; a random example would be Danish engagement in water purification projects in Sri Lanka.

Third, the Nordic states have posed as custodians of human rights and vociferous critics of human rights violations. In the 1960s Sweden was vocal in its opposition to the Smith regime in Rhodesia, the Soviet (Warsaw Pact) invasion of Czechoslovakia and, in the early 1970s, continuing US involvement in Vietnam. All the Nordic states except Finland boycotted the Moscow Olympic Games in 1980 in protest against the Soviet intervention in Afghanistan, whilst the tenth anniversary gathering of the CSCE in 1985 spawned the celebrated Helsinki Declaration of Human Rights.

Finally, the Nordic states have been in the van of international initiatives on the environment and today seek to portray themselves as the 'environmental conscience' of the world. In 1972 Stockholm staged a UN Conference on the Environment and, five years later, a UN Commission on the Environment, headed by the former Norwegian prime minister Gro Harlem Brundtland, in its report *Our Common Future*, coined the term 'sustainable development'. The Finns have been active in promoting an Arctic Environmental Protection Strategy. In recent years, moreover, the Scandinavians have trumpeted the importance of striving to meet the Kyoto targets for the reduction of greenhouse gas emissions, worked through various international arenas to prioritise the need to deal with Baltic Sea pollution and emphasised a range of environmental security issues, including the safe storage of nuclear waste. Significantly, Copenhagen will host an international UN 'climate summit' in 2009.

Christine Ingebritsen has a point in asserting that 'for small states, it is strategic to be virtuous in world politics' (Ingebritsen 2006: 15). It is not a new point. Elder *et al.* (1982: 208), in the 1980s, noted that 'with an evangelical zeal well grounded in *realpolitik*, the Nordic countries have been engaged in a search for moral power and hence the force with which to influence post-war events in the direction of peace'. But have events and circumstances conspired to challenge and undermine the standing of the Scandinavians as 'norm entrepreneurs'? Are they still 'moral superpowers', if ever they were so? A number of brief points are in order.

First, the collapse of the bipolar security system of the Cold War era has meant that the Scandinavian states can no longer perform their coveted role as bridge-builders between the superpowers and cannot in the same way contribute as 'honest brokers' to the cause of international *détente*. Rather, that mediation role has devolved from the state level to prominent individual Scandinavians, who have been mandated by the international community with the task of brokering peace arrangements and/or territorial solutions in 'trouble spots' around the world.

Second, in the case of Sweden, the most polemical of the Scandinavian states during the Cold War, EU membership and the consequent 'slaughter' of the sacred cow of neutrality has largely removed the 'halo effect' it enjoyed in the eyes of the international community. Sweden can no longer occupy, still less monopolise, the moral 'high ground' and rail against imperialism, whether of the US or Soviet variety, as it did during the Cold War. Instead, their turns in the EU presidency have allowed the Nordic EU member states to orchestrate a collective voice behind their preferred agenda in international affairs.

Third, on the domestic front, gone are the days when delegations of British trade unionists made the pilgrimage to Sweden in search of the holy grail of harmonious industrial relations, whilst the celebrated Scandinavian welfare state has been obliged to adapt to the dictates of lower growth, an ageing population and the increased mobility of capital. Since the days of Huntford's 'new totalitarians' in the early 1970s, the 'welfare consensus' has been challenged externally by the Thatcher–Reagan class of neo-liberals and internally by radical rightist parties arguing either that the welfare state has spawned an army of dictatorial 'paper popes' (Glistrup) or that it no longer provides the welfare the most needy sections of society (the elderly, young parent families, etc.) deserve (Hagen) (see chapter 8).

Next, in recent years, the progressive image of the Scandinavians on the world stage has been tarnished – their reputation as liberal societies blemished – by the difficulties experienced in adapting to the transition to multicultural societies. True, reflecting on the Muhammad cartoon episode, the Danish prime minister, Anders Fogh Rasmussen, declared that 'across the world, there is respect that we didn't give in to the pressures of fanatical Muslim groups. In many places the story has put Denmark on the map and, except for a few countries, we have seen almost exclusively positive reactions.' But before the Muhammad cartoon crisis, EU and UN reports had been critical of Danish immigration policy. Anti-immigrant parties have drawn support from the 'old parties', including the Social Democrats, and in early autumn 2005 a poll indicated that 45 per cent of Danes thought it 'highly unlikely' that they would make contact with persons with foreign roots. At the 13 November 2007 Folketing general election, the radical right Danish People's Party managed an improved 13.9 per cent of the poll, the third best-supported party.

When applied to the Scandinavian states, the term 'moral superpower' contains much poetic licence. Before their involvement in the European project through EU and EEA membership, respectively, Finland and Iceland worked hand in glove with one of the two superpowers. Finnish neutrality was a 'designer neutrality', designed to meet the exigencies of the Cold War security system and it was not a neutrality taken too seriously by the West, still less by the Soviet Union. Iceland had a bilateral defence agreement with the United States and only really during the rounds of 'Cod Wars' with Britain did it appear on the pages of the international press. Norway's 'niche in world politics' (Ingebritsen 2006: 57), if not entirely fanciful, seems open to question.

True, Norwegian involvement in the Middle East peace process may have led in 1993 to the so-called Oslo Accord, but, as a conditional NATO member, Norway did not have 'free hands' as an international actor during the Cold War and it must be doubted how far playing the role of 'global good citizen' through the provision of generous amounts of Third World aid has conferred on it 'moral superpower' status. The same would broadly apply to Denmark. Sweden presented itself to an extent as a 'holier than thou' state during the Cold War, but its ability to use its 'moral authority' to influence the course of events was limited and does not justify the conferral of superpower status. Indeed, it may suffice to note that, although small states, the Nordic countries during the Cold War sought to be active and not simply reactive players on the world stage and that Denmark, Finland and Norway have continued that tradition within the EU, albeit not always working in unison. The onus now is on working together with non-Nordic states to set collective norms and propose collective solutions to common problems – terrorist threats, environmental security risks and so on – and to seek from within to influence the agendas of supranational bodies in desired directions. Long gone are the days of unilateral Palme-style pontification.

Summary

1.   When the impressive record of joint responses to 'neighbourhood issues' is borne in mind, the label 'reluctant Nordics' would seem an extremely inappropriate term with which to characterise Cold War regional co-operation. Rather, it seems feasible to speak of a significant degree of *de facto* micro-integration.

2.   During the Cold War Nordic co-operation was primarily regional in focus; today it is much less obviously so. Instead, it has become integrated with European developments, as well as being more international in nature. It seems legitimate to identify four analytically distinct dimensions of Nordic co-operation – Nordic co-operation within the EU, Nordic co-operation in the Baltic and north-west Russia, Nordic co-operation outside Europe, and intra-regional Nordic co-operation. One of the lessons of the first years of Finnish and Swedish membership of the EU after 1995 appears to have been that differing national interests kept the Nordic states as much apart within the EU as they did when major Nordic co-operation initiatives were attempted in the period up to 1970.

3.   During the Cold War the Nordic states tended to view macro-economic regional projects as second-choice options and/or temporary expedients, whilst in recent years they have been reluctant at the grassroots level to participate in moves to promote the *political* integration of the EU member states. Since a majority of Norwegians declined EU membership in 1994, two more European referenda in Scandinavia have been 'lost'. All three results represented defeats for the Establishment and can be interpreted, in part, as anti-Establishment votes.

↗moral superpower?

4. The Nordic states have been far from 'reluctant internationalists' and have sought proactively to influence the agenda of world politics. However, to call them 'moral superpowers' would involve a generous measure of poetic licence, although, especially during the Cold War, they sought to be active rather than simply reactive players on the global stage. Today, the EU presidency periods in particular have allowed the 'EU Nordics' to prioritise a set of issues and orchestrate collective support for them.

References

Allen, Hilary (1979) *Norway and Europe in the 1970s*, Universitetsforlaget: Oslo.

Arter, David (1993) *The Politics of European Integration in the Twentieth Century*, Dartmouth: Aldershot.

Arter, David (1995a) 'The EU referendum in Finland on 16 October 1994: vote for the West, not for Maastricht', *Journal of Common Market Studies*, 33 (3), pp. 361–87.

Arter, David (1995b) 'The Folketing and Denmark's "European policy": the case of an "authorising assembly"', *Journal of Legislative Studies*, 1 (3), pp. 110–23.

Arter, David (2000) 'Small state influence within the EU: the case of Finland's "Northern Dimension Initiative"', *Journal of Common Market Studies*, 38 (5), pp. 677–97.

Arter, David (2001) 'Regionalization in the European peripheries: the cases of northern Norway and Finnish Lapland', *Regional and Federal Studies*, 11 (2), pp. 94–114.

Aylott, Nicholas (1997) 'Between Europe and unity: the case of the Swedish Social Democrats', *West European Politics*, 20 (2), pp. 119–36.

Baldersheim, Harald (2004) 'Nordic regions in a European perspective', in Knut Heidar (ed.), *Nordic Politics*, Universitetsforlaget: Oslo, pp. 183–206.

Bergman, Annika (2006) 'Adjacent internationalism: the concept of solidarity and post-Cold War Nordic–Baltic relations', *Co-operation and Conflict*, 41 (1), pp. 73–97.

Bertone, Chiara (1998) *Bringing Gender into the Debate on the EC/EU. The Construction of a 'Women's Perspective' in the Danish Referendum Campaign*, University of Århus: Århus.

Browning, Christopher S. (2007) 'Branding Nordicity: models, identity and the decline of exceptionalism', *Co-operation and Conflict*, 42 (1), pp. 27–51.

Buch, Roger and Kasper M. Hansen (2002) 'The Danes and Europe: from EC 1972 to euro 2000 – elections, referendums and attitudes', *Scandinavian Political Studies*, 25 (1), pp. 1–26.

Derry, T. K. (1973) *A History of Modern Norway, 1814–1972*, Clarendon Press: Oxford.

Deutsch, Karl W. (1957) *Political Community and the North Atlantic Area: International Organization in the Light of Historical Experience*, Greenwood Press: New York.

Diebold, William, Jr (1959) *The Schuman Plan. A Study in Economic Co-operation, 1950–59*, Praeger: New York.

Dinan, Desmond (1994) *Ever Closer Union?*, Macmillan: London.

Downs, William M. (2001) 'Denmark's referendum on the euro: the mouse that roared ... again', *West European Politics*, 24 (1), pp. 222–6.

Elder, Neil, Alastair H. Thomas and David Arter (1982) *The Consensual Democracies?*, Martin Robertson: Oxford.

Goldmann, Kjell (1991) 'The Swedish model of security policy', West European Politics, 14 (3), pp. 122–43.

Gstöhl, Sieglinde (1996) 'The Nordic countries and the European Economic Area (EEA)', in Lee Miles (ed.), The European Union and the Nordic Countries, Routledge: London, pp. 47–62.

Haskel, Barbara G. (1976) The Scandinavian Option. Opportunities and Opportunity Costs in Post-war Scandinavian Foreign Policies, Universitetsforlaget: Oslo.

Heidar, Knut (2001) Norway Elites on Trial, Westview: Boulder, CO.

Holbraad, Carsten (1991) Danish Neutrality. A Study in the Foreign Policy of a Small State, Clarendon Press: Oxford.

Ingebritsen, Christine (2006) Scandinavia in World Politics, Rowman and Littlefield: Lanham, MD.

Kansikas, Suvi (2005) 'Kreml päätti vai Tamminiemi? Nordek-hankkeen kohtalo Suomen ja Neuvostoliiton suhteiden kuvastajana', in Klaus Lindgren (ed.), Ajankohta, Poliittisen historian vuosikirja: Helsinki, pp. 194–215.

Kansikas, Suvi (2007) 'Nordek is an Anti-Soviet Group. Soviet attitudes to Finnish membership of the Nordek plan', in Jan Hecker-Stampehl (ed.), Between Nordic Ideology, Economic Interests and Political Reality: New Perspectives on Nordek, Kirchhof and Franke: Berlin.

Karjalainen, Ahti and Jukka Tarkka (1989) Presidentin ministeri Ahti Karjalaisen ura Urho Kekkosen suomessa, Otava: Helsinki.

Kekkonen, Urho (1976) Kirjeitä myllystäni 2, 1968–75, Otava: Keuruu.

Koivisto, Mauno (1978) Väärää Politiikka, Kirjayhtymä: Helsinki.

Koivisto, Mauno (1995) Historian tekijät, Kirjayhtymä: Helsinki.

Koivisto, Mauno (1997) Liikkeen suunta, Kirjayhtymä: Helsinki.

Kristinsson, Gunnar Helgi (1996) 'Iceland and the European Union', in Lee Miles (ed.), The European Union and the Nordic Countries, Routledge: London, pp. 150–65.

Maude, George (1976) The Finnish Dilemma. Neutrality in the Shadow of Power, Oxford University Press: London.

Miljan, Toivo (1977) The Reluctant Europeans, Hurst: London.

Nielsen, Hans Jørgen (1994) 'The Danish voters and the referendum in June 1992 on the Treaty of Maastricht', in Morten Kelstrup (ed.), European Integration and Denmark's Participation, Political Studies Press: Copenhagen.

Østergård, Uffe (1992) 'Danish identity: European, Nordic or peasant?', in Lise Lyck (ed.), Denmark and EU Membership Evaluated, Pinter: London, pp. 167–77.

Pedersen, Thomas (1996) 'Denmark and the European Union', in Lee Miles (ed.), The European Union and the Nordic Countries, Routledge: London, pp. 81–100.

Persson, Göran (2007) Min väg, min val, Albert Bonniers Förlag: Stockholm.

Pesonen, Pertti, et al. (1998) 'To join or not to join?', in Anders Jenssen, Pertti Pesonen and Mikael Gilljam (eds), To Join or Not To Join. Three Nordic Referenda on Membershiop of the European Union, Universitetsforlag: Oslo.

Rehn, Olli (1993) 'Odottavasta ennakoivaan integraatiopolitiikkaan?', in Tuomas Forsberg and Tapani Vaahtorants (eds), Johdatus Suomen ulkopolitiikkaan, Gaudeamus: Tampere, pp. 166–231.

Rokkan, Stein (1966) 'Norway: numerical democracy and corporate pluralism', in Robert A. Jahl (ed.), Political Opposition in Western Democracies, Yale University Press: New Haven, CT.

Sæter, Martin (1996) 'Norway and the European Union', in Lee Miles (ed.), *The European Union and the Nordic Countries*, Routledge: London, pp. 133–49.

Sitter, Nick (2001) 'The politics of opposition and European integration in Scandinavia: is Euro-scepticism a government–opposition dynamic?', *West European Politics*, 24 (4), pp. 22–39.

Sonne, Lasse (2006) 'The response of Nordic economic co-operation to the question of EEC/EC enlargement 1961–73 with special reference to the Nordek negotiations 1968–70', paper presented at the XIV International History Congress, Helsinki, 21–25 August.

Sonne, Lasse (2007) *Nordek – A Plan for Increased Nordic Economic Co-operation and Integration 1968–1970*, Finnish Society of Sciences and Letters: Helsinki.

Stålvant, Carl-Einar (1982) 'Nordic politics: towards international economic co-operation', in Bengt Sundelius (ed.), *Foreign Policies in Northern Europe*, Westview: Boulder, CO, pp. 107–42.

Sundelius, Bengt (ed.) (1982) *Foreign Policies in Northern Europe*, Westview: Boulder, CO.

Suomi, Juhani (1996) *Taistelu puolueettomuudesta*, Otava: Helsinki.

Thorhallsson, Baldur (2004) 'Approaching the question', in Baldur Thorhallsson (ed.), *Iceland and European Integration*, Routledge: London, pp. 1–18.

Widfeldt, Anders (2004) 'Elite collusion and public defiance: Sweden's euro referendum in 2003', *West European Politics*, 27 (3), pp. 503–17.

Worre, Torben (1988) 'Denmark at the crossroads: the Danish referendum of 28 February 1986 on the EC reform package', *Journal of Common Market Studies*, 26 (4), pp. 361–88.

Epilogue

If it is probably fair to characterise the style of the Scandinavian political elite as predominantly pragmatic rather than pugilistic, primarily consensual rather than adversarial, it is none the less important to avoid perpetuating stereotyped images of Scandinavia as a block of depoliticised political systems. Scandinavian politics is not generally of the 'yah boo' Westminster variety, nor is it like Australian politics, which, according to Patrick Weller, 'is played like Australian sport, up front, down to earth and with a blatant desire to win at any cost' (Weller 2004: 633). Yet if 'zero-sum politics' is not intrinsic to the Scandinavian political style, the rhetoric of elite political discourse may well have become more strident in recent years – particularly with the advent of radical rightist parties as significant political players – whilst the mass political culture is certainly neither deferential nor quietist. Interest in politics remains generally high, although patterns of civic political participation appear to be changing and taking on new forms. Moreover, whilst the focus of this book has been on Scandinavian politics today – the general features and common denominators – the politics and political mood of the individual Scandinavian states today – that is, in May 2008 – reflect differing national concerns and challenges.

A reminder of the challenges posed by the transition to multicultural societies across Norden – although a seemingly trivial instance – was the animated debate in Oslo about whether the children in the traditional procession to the royal palace on Norway's national day, 17 May, should be able to wave flags other than those of Norway, Sámi Lapland or the United Nations. The city mayor, Fabian Stang, took a permissive view, whilst expressing the hope that the immigrant children in the parade would want to wave the Norwegian flag. In contrast, an opinion poll in the newspaper *Verdens Gang* revealed that two-thirds of respondents would allow only Norwegian flags and four-fifths did not want to hear anything other than Norwegian songs sung in the procession.

In Denmark and Sweden mass strike action pointed up the dilemma of financing an efficient welfare state. In late April 2008 about 100,000 Danish public service workers in the FOA trade union (mostly nurses, midwives and those providing care for the elderly) resorted to industrial action in pursuit of their demand for a wage increase of 15 per cent over a three-year period. The critically low levels of staffing meant that 8,000 nurses from 448 hospital wards were obliged to work during the strike. Significantly, according to a survey in *Berlingske Tidende*, over half of Danish voters supported the industrial action. At the same time, public service workers in Sweden went on strike, several averring to the success of the Finnish nurses, who, in November 2007, achieved notable wage increases by threatening mass resignations. It was noted in the non-socialist press in particular that the opposition Social Democratic Party leader, Mona Sahlin, made no mention of the strike in her May Day speech in Gothenburg. In Reykjavík, too, nurses and X-ray technicians at the National Hospital of Iceland threatened to resign and walk out on May Day, although an agreement was reached at the eleventh hour.

In Finland, Christine Ingebritsen's portrayal of the Scandinavian states as 'norm entrepreneurs' (see chapter 13) – that is, the purveyors of such fundamental values as justice, equality and human rights – was implicitly questioned by the decision of prime minister Matti Vanhanen to attend the opening ceremony of the 2008 Olympic Games in Beijing. Vanhanen was criticised for not following the example of the German chancellor and British prime minister, who are boycotting the Games in protest over alleged human rights abuses in Tibet. In fact, all the Nordic prime ministers were planning to attend. Of much deeper concern to most Finns, however, was the report of the investigation into the campus massacre in the small town of Jokela on 7 November 2007, in which six senior pupils, the health care officer and head teacher were indiscriminately gunned down by an eighteen-year-old schoolboy, an extreme rightist sympathiser, who also sought (unsuccessfully) to burn the school down before turning the gun on himself. It transpired from the report that he had planned the killings at least seven months in advance and modelled his action on similar 'school shootings' in the United States. There was much agonising in the media over why this 'loner' had not been identified by 'the system', as well as concern about the possible impact of extremist networks built up through the Internet on the behaviour of individuals with known feelings of social exclusion. There was a broad political consensus that the traumatic events at Jokela were a reminder of the need to build an ever-more tolerant, caring and attentive society, in which the extremism of alienation would be minimised.

As in the human person, the mood swings of the body politic will reflect the ever-changing issues of the day. However, when one or other of the essential 'body parts' of the democratic process appears no longer to be functioning properly, there is cause for deeper and lasting concern. Thus, in a recent edited collection entitled *The Crisis of Political Parties*, the director of the Institute of Philosophy at Helsinki University, Thomas Wallgren, argued that 'parties make bad policy because they have lost their active membership and there is no longer an internal policy debate. The remedy for this crisis is to stimulate the political imagination and participation of citizens' (see *Helsingin Sanomat*, 1 May 2008). Citizens, he concluded, should reclaim parties from the political leaders and elite of special advisers and political secretaries who run them.

Wallgren's critique of political parties pointed to a democratic paradox in the Nordic region as a whole. On the one hand, the traditional agencies of collective mobilisation – the basic linkage structures between state and society – have eroded in recent years. There has, in short, been a decline in both membership of, and identification with, political parties and a diminished engagement in historic popular movements such as trade unions. A 'democratic audit' in Sweden has even predicted that, if the decline in party membership continues at the same rate as in the 1990s, the parties will have no members at all by 2013! On the other hand, there has been no decline in civic interest in politics or general trust in politicians, and political participation has assumed new issue-based forms and what the Norwegian Power and Democracy Commission in its report in 2003 called 'here-and-now organisations' – the likes of self-help groups, neighbourhood action groups, bereavement groups, next-of-kin groups and so on (Christensen 2005). Equally, across the region, there does appear to be evidence of a connection between social and political exclusion, and immigrants, members of ethnic communities and, indeed, young working-class males have tended to remain outside the political decision-making system.

In the conclusion to their 2003 general election study, Lauri Karvonen and Heikki Paloheimo (2005: 293) noted that 'party-based representative democracy is clearly to a degree on trial in Finland'. Yet if there has been an attenuation of the linkage function of political parties, the digitalisation of politics has spawned new modes of communication between leaders and led. Thus, there has been a transformation in the mode of electioneering. Most parliamentary candidates across the region have personal websites; many, sometimes including the prime minister and leading cabinet ministers, produce daily blogs; and a minority even use YouTube videos. In Finland, candidate selection machines were first used in the elections to the European Parliament in 1996 (see chapter 9) in the hope that they would increase the voters' interest in and knowledge of candidates and so have a positive impact on turnout. Candidate selection machines provide a cheap way of communicating their views and of reaching or at least targeting younger voters in particular.

On the subject of the age cohorts making up the electorate, perhaps the greatest challenge facing Scandinavian social democracy in the new millennium is *generational renewal*. Once the dominant force, the social democratic parties boast increasingly senescent memberships and risk a decomposition of their traditional vote base. In mid-2008, social democratic parties were in governing coalitions only in Norway and Iceland, had lost all three general elections in Denmark since 2000, and in Finland in 2007 sank to the position of third largest party for the first time in the party's history. On the other hand, the increased 'greying' of the citizenry – that is, the growth in the proportion of retired persons among the electorate – has dictated the need to put up older as well as younger candidates. Indeed, for all the parties, not just the social democrats, the commitment to getting the right gender balance in the selection of candidates has been superseded by the need to strike a suitable *age balance* in the nomination process. This reflects the stark fact that the older age groups are often the most active part of the electorate. It is the younger generation that is increasingly turning its back on the traditional political parties. That is the reality of Scandinavian politics today. Indeed, regaining a basic legitimacy in the eyes of younger voters will be the foremost challenge for the political parties in the Scandinavian politics of tomorrow.

References

Christensen, Tom (2005) 'The Norwegian state transformed?', *West European Politics*, 28 (4), pp. 721–39.

Karvonen, L. and H. Paloheimo (2005) 'Demokratian näkymiä Suomessa', in H. Paloheimo (ed.), *Vaalit ja demokratia Suomessa*, WSOY: Helsinki, pp. 290–304.

Weller, Patrick (2004) 'Parliamentary democracy in Australia', *Parliamentary Affairs*, 57 (3), pp. 630–45.

Index

Table A1.1

Membership Trends: 1950–1990

	1950	1955	1960	1965	1970	1975	1980	1985	1990
Liberal Protestant									
Episcopal Church	2,417,464	2,805,455	3,269,325	3,419,905	3,285,826	2,857,513	2,786,004	2,739,422	2,446,050
Presbyterian Church (U.S.A.)	3,210,635	3,701,635	4,161,860	4,254,460	4,045,408	3,535,825	3,362,086	3,048,235	2,847,437
United Church of Christ	1,977,418	2,116,322	2,241,134	2,070,413	1,960,608	1,818,762	1,736,244	1,683,777	1,599,212
TOTAL	7,605,517	8,623,412	9,672,319	9,744,778	9,291,842	8,212,100	7,884,334	7,471,434	6,892,699
% of 1950 Membership	100	113	127	128	122	108	104	98	91
% of U.S. Population	5.0	5.2	5.4	5.0	4.5	3.8	3.5	3.1	2.8
Moderate Protestant									
Christian Church (Disciples of Christ)	1,767,964	1,897,736	1,801,821	1,918,471	1,424,479	1,302,164	1,177,984	1,116,326	1,039,692
Church of the Brethren	186,201	195,609	199,947	194,815	182,614	173,336	170,839	159,184	148,253
Evangelical Lutheran Church in America	3,982,508	4,672,083	5,295,502	5,684,298	5,650,137	5,401,765	5,384,271	5,341,452	5,240,739
Reformed Church in America	284,504	319,593	354,621	385,754	367,606	355,052	345,532	342,375	326,850
United Methodist Church	9,653,178	10,029,535	10,641,310	11,067,497	10,509,198	9,861,028	9,519,407	9,192,172	8,904,824
TOTAL	15,874,355	17,114,556	18,293,201	19,250,835	18,134,034	17,099,345	16,598,033	16,151,509	15,660,358
% of 1950 Membership	100	108	115	121	114	108	105	102	99
% of U.S. Population	10.4	10.3	10.1	9.9	8.8	7.9	7.3	6.8	6.3
Roman Catholic	28,634,878	33,396,647	42,104,900	46,246,175	48,214,729	48,881,872	50,449,842	52,654,908	58,568,015
% of 1950 Membership	100	117	147	162	168	171	176	184	205
% of U.S. Population	18.8	20.1	23.3	23.8	23.5	22.6	22.2	22.1	23.4
Latter-Day Saints									
Church of	1,111,314	1,230,021	1,486,887	1,789,175	2,073,146	2,336,715	2,811,000	3,860,000	4,267,000
Reorganized Church of	124,925	137,856	155,291	168,355	152,670	157,762	190,087	192,082	189,524
TOTAL	1,236,239	1,367,877	1,642,178	1,957,530	2,225,816	2,494,477	3,001,087	4,052,082	4,456,524

	1950	1955	1960	1965	1970	1975	1980	1985	1990
% of 1950 Membership	100	111	133	158	180	202	243	328	360
% of U.S. Population	0.8	0.8	0.9	1.0	1.1	1.2	1.3	1.7	1.8
Conservative Protestant									
Baptist General Conference	45,413	54,000	72,056	86,719	103,955	115,340	133,385	132,546	134,717
Christian and Missionary Alliance	58,347	57,386	59,657	64,586	112,519	145,833	189,710	227,846	279,207
Cumberland Presbyterian Church	81,806	84,990	88,452	78,917	92,095	94,050	96,553	98,037	91,857
Evangelical Covenant Church	51,850	55,311	60,090	65,780	67,441	71,808	77,737	84,150	89,735
Lutheran Church,-Missouri Synod	1,674,901	2,004,110	2,391,195	2,692,889	2,788,536	2,763,545	2,625,650	2,628,164	2,602,849
North American Baptist Conference	41,560	47,319	50,646	53,711	55,080	42,629	43,041	42,863	44,493
Seventh-day Adventist Church	237,168	277,162	317,852	364,666	420,419	495,699	571,141	651,954	717,446
Southern Baptist Convention	7,079,889	8,467,439	9,731,591	10,770,573	11,628,032	12,733,124	13,600,126	14,477,364	15,038,409
Wisconsin Evangelical Lutheran Synod	307,216	328,969	348,184	358,466	381,321	395,440	407,043	415,389	420,039
TOTAL	9,578,150	11,376,686	13,119,723	14,536,307	15,649,398	16,857,468	17,744,386	18,758,313	19,418,752
% of 1950 Membership	100	119	137	152	163	176	185	196	203
% of U.S. Population	6.3	6.9	7.3	7.5	7.6	7.8	7.8	7.9	7.8
Pentecostal/Holiness Protestant									
Assemblies of God	318,478	400,047	508,602	572,123	625,027	785,348	1,064,490	1,235,403	1,298,121
Church of God (Anderson, Ind.)	107,094	123,523	142,796	143,231	150,198	166,257	176,429	185,593	205,884
Church of God (Cleveland, Tenn.)	117,025	142,668	170,261	205,465	272,278	343,249	435,012	523,477	620,393
Church of the Nazarene	226,684	270,576	307,629	343,380	383,284	441,093	484,276	522,082	572,153

	1950	1955	1960	1965	1970	1975	1980	1985	1990
Free Methodist Church of North America	48,574	51,437	55,338	59,415	64,901	67,043	68,477	72,223	74,313
Salvation Army	209,341	249,641	254,141	287,991	326,934	384,817	417,359	427,825	445,991
TOTAL	1,027,196	1,237,892	1,438,767	1,611,605	1,822,622	2,187,807	2,646,043	2,966,603	3,216,855
% of 1950 Membership	100	121	140	157	177	213	258	289	313
% of U.S. Population	0.7	0.7	0.8	0.8	0.9	1.0	1.2	1.2	1.3
Total Membership **All Families** % of 1950	63,956,335	73,117,070	86,271,088	93,347,230	95,338,441	95,733,069	98,323,725	102,054,849	108,213,203
Total Membership	100	114	135	146	149	150	154	160	169
% of U.S. Population	42.0	44.1	47.8	48.0	46.5	44.3	43.2	42.8	43.3
U.S. Population	152,271,000	165,931,000	180,671,000	194,303,000	205,052,000	215,973,000	227,719,000	238,466,000	249,975,000
% of 1950 U.S. Population	100	109	119	128	135	142	150	157	164

Source: *Yearbook of American and Canadian Churches* (various annual editions)

Table A1.2
Five-Year Membership Growth Rates: 1950–1990

	1950–1955	1955–1960	1960–1965	1965–1970	1970–1975	1975–1980	1980–1985	1985–1990
Liberal Protestant								
Episcopal Church	16.0	16.5	4.6	−3.9	−13.0	−2.5	−1.7	−10.7
Presbyterian Church								
(U.S.A.)	15.3	12.4	2.2	−4.9	−12.6	−4.9	−9.3	−6.6
United Church of Christ	7.0	5.9	−7.6	−5.3	−7.2	−4.5	−3.0	−5.0
TOTAL	13.4	12.2	0.7	−4.6	−11.6	−4.0	−5.2	−7.7
Moderate Protestant								
Christian Church								
(Disciples of Christ)	7.3	−5.1	6.5	−25.7	−8.6	−9.5	−5.2	−6.9
Church of the Brethren	5.1	2.2	−2.6	−6.3	−1.8	−4.7	−6.8	−6.9
Evangelical Lutheran								
Church in America	17.3	13.3	7.3	−0.6	−4.4	−0.3	−0.8	−1.9
Reformed Church in								
America	12.3	11.0	8.8	−4.7	−3.4	−2.7	−0.9	−4.5
United Methodist Church	3.9	6.1	4.0	−5.0	−6.2	−3.5	−3.4	−3.1
TOTAL	7.8	6.9	5.2	−5.8	−5.7	−2.9	−2.7	−3.0
Roman Catholic	16.6	26.1	9.8	4.3	1.4	3.2	4.4	11.2
Latter-Day Saints								
Church of	10.7	20.9	20.3	15.9	12.7	20.3	37.3	10.5
Reorganized Church of	10.4	12.6	8.4	−9.3	3.3	20.5	1.0	−1.3
TOTAL	10.6	20.1	19.2	13.7	12.1	20.3	35.0	10.0
Conservative Protestant								
Baptist General Conference	18.9	33.4	20.3	19.9	11.0	15.6	−0.6	1.6
Christian and Missionary								
Alliance	−1.6	4.0	8.3	74.2	29.6	30.1	20.1	22.5
Cumberland Presbyterian								
Church	3.9	4.1	−10.8	16.7	2.1	2.7	1.5	−6.3
Evangelical Covenant								
Church	6.7	8.6	9.5	2.5	6.5	8.3	8.2	6.6
Lutheran Church, Missouri								
Synod	19.7	19.3	12.6	3.6	−0.9	−5.0	0.1	−1.0
North American Baptist								
Conference	13.9	7.0	6.1	2.5	−22.6	1.0	−0.4	3.8
Seventh-day Adventist								
Church	16.9	14.7	14.7	15.3	17.9	15.2	14.1	10.0
Southern Baptist								
Convention	19.6	14.9	10.7	8.0	9.5	6.8	6.5	3.9
Wisconsin Evangelical								
Lutheran Synod	7.1	5.8	3.0	6.4	3.7	2.9	2.1	1.1
TOTAL	18.8	15.3	10.8	7.7	7.7	5.3	5.7	3.5
Pentecostal/Holiness								
Protestant								
Assemblies of God	25.6	27.1	12.5	9.2	25.7	35.5	16.1	5.1
Church of God								
(Anderson, Ind.)	15.3	15.6	0.3	4.9	10.7	6.1	5.2	10.9
Church of God								
(Cleveland, Tenn.)	21.9	19.3	20.7	32.5	26.1	26.7	20.3	18.5

	1950–1955	1955–1960	1960–1965	1965–1970	1970–1975	1975–1980	1980–1985	1985–1990
Church of the Nazarene	19.4	13.7	11.6	11.6	15.1	9.8	7.8	9.6
Free Methodist Church of North America	5.9	7.6	7.4	9.2	3.3	2.1	5.5	2.9
Salvation Army	19.3	1.8	13.3	13.5	17.7	8.5	2.5	4.2
TOTAL	20.5	16.2	12.0	13.1	20.0	20.9	12.1	8.4
Total Membership All Denominational Families	14.3	18.0	8.2	2.1	0.4	2.7	3.8	6.0
U.S. POPULATION	9.0	8.9	7.5	5.5	5.3	5.4	4.7	4.8

Source: Appendix Table A1.1

Table A12.1
All-Respondent Regressions

Step (N):	With MEMBER Dependent				With ATTENDANCE Dependent			
	1978 (1306)		1988 (1991)		1978 (1306)		1988 (1991)	
	r	Part r	r	Part r	r	Part r	r	Part r
I. Church Member					.580	.275	.619	.332
II. Church Voluntarism	−.221	−.120	−.223	−.132	−.233	−.106	−.349	−.191
Church Personalism	.238	.062	.230	.105	.245		.264	.094
Church Org.	−.266		−.189	−.051	−.334	−.098	−.275	−.096
III. Commitment to Christ	.397	.120	.435	.176	.442	.007	.420	.051
Frequency of Prayer	.422	.158	.402	.112	.504	.164	.458	.128
Belief	.332	.094	.351	.071	.356	.037	.355	
Religious Experience	.153		.154		.223		.198	
IV. Traditional Values	.141		.159		.152		.163	
New Morality	−.282	−.054	−.212		−.294		−.233	
V. Religious Socialization	.299	.133	.292	.116	.291	.062	.252	
Sex (Male)	−.101		−.105		−.158		−.106	
Age	−.176	−.067	−.135	−.051	−.139		−.114	
Education							−.090°	−.069
Region:								
S & MW & Mt	.077°		.115		.095°		.088°	
W	−.120	−.112	−.158	−.076			−.113	
Family Cycle								
Married & Kids 4-17			.078°	.041			.088°	.050
Married, No Kids					−.126		.085°	.062
Never Married	.077°		−.143		−.165		−.150	

Step Summary	1978		1988		1978		1988	
	R² Ch	Cum R²	R² Ch	Cum R²	R² Ch	Cum R²	R² Ch	CumR²
Step 1					.336	.336	.383	.383
Step 2	.116	.116	.114	.114	.055	.392	.079	.463
Step 3	.165	.282	.168	.283	.082	.474	.041	.504
Step 4	.008	.290	.002°	.285	.000°	.474	.000°	.505
Step 5	.043	.334	.036	.321	.007°	.482	.012	.517

° Only coefficients significant at less than .05 entered, unless marked with an asterisk.

°° Independent variables entered stepwise in blocks.

°°° r = zero-order r.

°°°° Part r = part correlation with all other independent variables controlled.

°°°°° Region and Family Cycle entered as dummy variables coded (0,1). "NE & MA" and "Divorced & Widowed" are the respective omitted dummy variables.

Table A12.2
Conservative Protestant Regressions

(N)	With MEMBER Dependent 1978 (244)		With MEMBER Dependent 1988 (396)		With ATTENDANCE Dependent 1978 (244)		With ATTENDANCE Dependent 1988 (396)	
	r	Part r	r	Part r	r	Part r	r	Part r
I. Church Member					.478	.227	.559	.340
II. Church Voluntarism	−.263	−.152	−.296	−.176	−.304		−.410	−.210
Church Personalism	.190				.160		.173	.140
Church Org.	−.218		−.130		−.252		−.258	−.104
III. Commitment to Christ	.308	.112	.389	.177	.340		.295	
Frequency of Prayer	.320	.172	.299		.433	.170	.357	.154
Belief	.194		.279	.117	.248		.233	
Religious Experience	.217		.180		.411	.143	.176	
IV. Traditional Values								
New Morality	−.202				−.196		−.126	
V. Religious Socialization	.131		.231	.114	.244		.108	
Sex (Male)	−.214				−.240			
Age	−.103							
Education			−.117	−.082	−.121		−.188	−.116
Region:								
S & MW & Mt	.202		.126		.102			
W	−.153							
Family Cycle:								
Married & Kids 4-17							.145	.097
Married, No Kids					.108			
Never Married		−.169		−.109		−.211		−.131

Step Summary	1978		1988		1978		1988	
	R² Ch	Cum R²	R² Ch	Cum R²	R² Ch	Cum R²	R² Ch	CumR²
Step 1					.228	.228	.313	.313
Step 2	.104	.104	.096	.096	.051	.280	.106	.420
Step 3	.108	.213	.138	.235	.131	.412	.021	.441
Step 4	.008*	.221	.004*	.234	.002*	.414	.000*	.442
Step 5	.032*	.254	.041*	.281	.028*	.443	.040	.482

°   Only coefficients significant at less than .05 entered, unless marked with an asterisk.

°°   Independent variables entered stepwise in blocks.

°°° r = zero-order r.

°°°° Part r = part correlation with all other independent variables controlled.

°°°°° Region and Family Cycle entered as dummy variables coded (0,1). "NE & MA" and "Divorced & Widowed" are the respective omitted dummy variables.

TABLE A12.3
Liberal Protestant Regressions

(N)	With MEMBER Dependent				With ATTENDANCE Dependent			
	1978 (249)		1988 (354)		1978 (249)		1988 (354)	
	r	Part r	r	Part r	r	Part r	r	Part r
I. Church Member					.481	.255	.427	.186
II. Church Voluntarism	−.209	−.112	−.215	−.148	−.349	−.195	−.377	−.243
Church Personalism	.200		.225		.142		.275	.138
Church Org.	−.229		−.157		−.247	−.091	−.241	−.120
III. Commitment to Christ	.391	.153	.371	.237	.402		.350	.101
Frequency of Prayer	.272		.240		.444	.180	.341	.160
Belief	.332	.125	.182		.326		.253	
Religious Experience	.190		.123		.322		.226	
IV. Traditional Values					.179			
New Morality	−.224				−.216			
V. Religious Socialization	.169		.115		.125		.113	
Sex (Male)					−.167			
Age	−.189	−.163	−.107					
Education	−.139	−.100					−.054°	−.115
Region:								
S & MW & Mt			.170					
W		−.79	−.136	−.270	−.128			−.141
Family Cycle:								
Married & Kids 4-17							.098°	.071
Married, No Kids	.110				−.115			
Never Married	.032°	.158			−.101			

Step Summary	1978		1988		1978		1988	
	R² Ch	Cum R²	R² Ch	Cum R²	R² Ch	Cum R²	R² Ch	CumR²
Step 1					.232	.232	.182	.182
Step 2	.089	.089	.101	.101	.081	.313	.138	.318
Step 3	.122	.211	.107	.209	.098	.411	.041	.385
Step 4	.014°	.225	.001°	.210	.006°	.418	.000°	.386
Step 5	.087	.313	.046	.257	.019°	.437	.029	.416

° Only coefficients significant at less than .05 entered, unless marked with an asterisk.

°° Independent variables entered stepwise in blocks.

°°° r = zero-order r.

°°°° Part r = part correlation with all other independent variables controlled.

°°°°° Region and Family Cycle entered as dummy variables coded (0,1). "NE & MA" and "Divorced & Widowed" are the respective omitted dummy variables.